If the King Only Knew

If the King Only Knew

Seditious Speech in the
Reign of Louis XV

· ❦ ·

Lisa Jane Graham

University Press
of Virginia
Charlottesville
& London

The University Press of Virginia
© 2000 by the Rector and Visitors
of the University of Virginia
All rights reserved
Printed in the United States of America
First published in 2000

Frontispiece: Actions de grâces de la France
pour la préservation de la vie du Roi.
*(Courtesy of the Bibliothèque Nationale,
Collection Histoire de France)*

⊗ The paper used in this publication meets the minimum
requirements of the American National Standard
for Information Sciences—Permanence of Paper
for Printed Library Materials,
ANSI Z39.48-1984.

Library of Congress Cataloging-in-Publication Data

Graham, Lisa Jane, 1963–
    If the king only knew : seditious speech in the reign of
Louis XV / Lisa Jane Graham.
        p.   cm.
    Includes bibliographical references and index.
    ISBN 0-8139-1927-4 (cloth : alk. paper)
    1. Louis XV, King of France, 1710–1774—Public opinion.
2. France—Politics and government—18th century—Histori-
ography. 3. Sedition—France—History—18th century—
Archival resources. 4. Public opinion—France—History.
I. Title.

DC133.4.G73 2000
944'.034'092—dc21   99-046302

For my parents

Pouvez-vous laisser ignorer que le monarque est le miroir dans lequel se regardent tous les sujets, qu'il est le modèle par lequel se forme ces citoyens.

JEAN-LOUIS LANGLOIS (painter and hack writer), 1765

CONTENTS

· ❁ ·

ILLUSTRATIONS

· ❧ ·

ACKNOWLEDGMENTS

· ❀ ·

THIS BOOK BEGAN as a dissertation and has received generous support from institutions and individuals from start to finish. Fellowships from the Johns Hopkins University covered my tuition and living expenses at various stages of my graduate career. A Bourse Chateaubriand from the French government and a Dissertation Research Fellowship from the Social Science Research Council allowed me to spend two years in Paris completing my research. Archival work was facilitated by the cooperation and expertise of the staffs of the Bibliothèque Nationale, the Bibliothèque de l'Arsenal, the Bibliothèque Historique de la Ville de Paris, the Archives Nationales, the Archives de la Prefecture de Police, and the Musée Carnavalet. I thank Oakland University, Haverford College, and the Society for French Historical Studies for subsequent grants that allowed me to return to Paris and supplement my original research. In the final stages, a subvention from Haverford College arranged by the provost, Elaine Hansen, ensured the successful publication of this book.

Gratitude expands in proportion to the time spent working on a project. My graduate adviser, Robert Forster, provided guidance, encouragement, and prodding, all in due proportion, from the project's inception. I will never forget his enthusiasm and the care he devoted to each of my lengthy chapters. It was a privilege to be his last graduate student. All French historians at Hopkins had, in effect, two advisers, whether this was officially recognized or not. From the day I met him, Orest Ranum has been a kindred soul who was always willing to listen to my ideas in their most unpolished stages. Orest never once doubted the feasibility of this book, and I can never repay him for that confidence. The book could not have materialized without the assistance and friendship of Dale Van Kley, who has been generous with his advice and knowledge. The manuscript has benefited immeasurably from his suggestions. My undergraduate adviser, Steven L. Kaplan, has been a source of unwavering *fidelité* ever since I wandered into his course on the French Revolution during my sophomore year at Cornell. His class literally changed my life, and his passion and commitment have been a continual source of inspiration. He has shared his expertise in the archives and French academic culture with me and has never been too busy to heed my call for help.

In France, many individuals opened their doors and their seminars to this expatriate scholar. I am especially grateful to Roger Chartier, Robert Descimon, Arlette Farge, Alain Guery, Ran Halevi, Christian Jouhaud, and Jacques Revel for their advice and support. Roger Chartier read and commented on the entire dissertation, and his seminar forced me to think more critically and creatively about the discipline of history. My other French mentor, Jacques Revel, kindly invited me to present a portion of my research to his seminar in the spring of 1991. His friendship and encouragement have been invaluable. The years spent researching in Paris are among the highlights of my life, largely due to the generosity and enthusiasm of my friends. I have never felt like an outsider in Paris thanks to Marie and Franck Accart, Quentin and Emmanuelle Bajac, Valérie Dubois, Hervé and Bohdana Huyghes, Claudine Hanau, Françoise Mark, and Christopher and Lilliane Stead.

This book is the product of different institutions and places, each marked by the presence of colleagues, friends, and students. My colleagues in the history departments at Oakland and Haverford have listened patiently to my obsessions with the police, the monarchy, and the Old Regime, and they are therefore excused from reading the book. Special thanks to Linda Benson, Linda Gerstein, Leo Gerulaitis, James Krippner-Martinez, Roger Lane, Paul Smith, and Susan Stuard for their moral support. Students are often unaware of how much they contribute to my sanity and good humor. I thank Caitlin Barnes, Christopher Coulston, Adam Freed, Ian Greenspan, Scott Heacock, James Head, Brian Murphy, Nicholas Popper, Marlayna Schoen, Adam Schran, Flora Tyll, Brent Wible, and Joseph Younger. Over the years the following individuals have bolstered my spirits with their encouragement and friendship: Chris Adams, Richard Blond, Phil Bruder, Richard Buckley, Israel Burshatin, Chris and Margo Cairns, Jack Censor, Thomas Christensen, Seth Fein, Graeme Fife, Elborg Forster, Eric Furstenberg, Billy Galperin, Niels Herold, David Herrman, Phil Hicks, Brad High, Will Hitchcock, Al Kuhn, Anna McCarthy, Christine Meyer, Jim Moorhead, Stefan Nolke, Ulrich Schoenherr, Scott Spector, Gus Stadler, Emma Varley, Geoff Wawro, Judy Young, and Tina Zwarg.

In the last stages of manuscript preparation my research assistant, Benjamin Reeves, provided impeccable editorial assistance and honest criticism. My friend Richard Albright was a gracious and enlightened patron who supplied a splendid apartment in Paris as needed. The patience and support of my editor at the University Press of Virginia, Richard Holway, has guided this project and brought it to fruition. I thank him, Ellen Satrom, and their assistants at the press, as well as the members of the Cowen Prize committee and Mme Claudine Cowen for their generous assistance and recognition. I am grateful to my copyeditor, Joanne Allen, whose polishing skills made the final text sparkle. In addition, two individuals deserve special mention. Gonzalo Sanchez, my fellow historian, Francophile and bon vivant, has sustained me with his wit, wisdom, and compassion ever since we met in the Archives Nationales in 1990. Paris is never the same without him. From the day I arrived in Baltimore, William M. Kuhn has been a friend in the truest sense of the word, believing in me when I did not believe in myself. This book could not have been written without his kindness, intelligence, and coaxing every step of the way. Finally, this list must acknowledge my parents, Barbara and George Graham, and my brother and sister-in-law, Peter and Rachel. Their love and humor have kept despair at bay, and I would never have stayed the course without them. It goes without saying that I alone am responsible for any errors or omissions.

A NOTE ON TRANSLATIONS

ALL TRANSLATIONS of archival material are my own. I have done my best to capture the flavor of the evidence as well as the literal meaning. The sources are not readily translatable given that they are often written transcriptions of verbal testimony, and the language itself is eighteenth-century spoken French. Moreover, both the interrogating official and the defendant are referred to in the third person, which makes for a certain awkwardness. I have inserted minimal punctuation, such as commas, where necessary to assist the reader in following the sentence flow. I have not bracketed off these insertions because such intrusions would interrupt the text and reduce their readability. When a word or idiomatic expression seemed to lose its meaning in translation, I include the original to make the point clear. Given the centrality of language to this study, I have aimed to be faithful to the original documents both in style and in content.

If the King Only Knew

Loyalty, Sedition, and Royal Authority

· 🐾 ·

IN MAY 1758 several witnesses reported to the police that a bailiff named Jean Moriceau de La Motte had uttered *mauvais discours* against King Louis XV in their presence. Such charges prompted an investigation, and La Motte was taken to the Bastille, where he was questioned over a period of several months. At the time of his arrest La Motte was carrying *libelles* and seditious flyers that he apparently intended to sell and distribute. The written evidence contained comments similar to those already on the record and reinforced the official case against him. When Lieutenant of Police Gabriel de Sartine interrogated him about his attitudes toward the king, La Motte was unequivocal and "said that he would always recognize the king as his sovereign master and obey his laws, that the true quality of a Frenchman, in his opinion, was to be attached heart and soul to the Sovereign who governs us, to respect the laws it pleases him to give us, that if he [the king] had found a thousand people who shared these same convictions, the king would have found a thousand loyal subjects."[1] This impassioned language of loyalty could be read as a defendant's desperate efforts to save his skin in the presence of the police. Yet this interpretation would be flawed for two reasons. First, it overlooks the fact that La Motte would have been more likely to garner sympathy, even leniency, if he had admitted his guilt outright rather than justified it within a language of loyalty. Second, if his declarations of fidelity are simply dismissed as forced testimony, the historian loses an essential piece of the conceptual vocabulary that shaped and defined La Mottes's understanding of royal authority and his relationship to it.

Like many of his contemporaries arrested for similar infractions, known as *mauvais discours,* or seditious speech, La Motte failed to convince the police of his fidelity to the king. The memory of Robert François Damiens's attempt to stab Louis XV a year earlier was still too fresh for La Motte's case to be overlooked. On the contrary, one senses that it had to be exemplary. Thus, on 6 September 1758 the Parlement of Paris found him guilty of "seditious utterances and attacks against royal authority."[2] He was sentenced to be hanged in the Place de Grève after making his amends on the steps of Notre Dame. The Parisian lawyer Edmond-Jean François Barbier noted in his journal that La Motte's punishment struck contemporaries as excessively severe. There was a consensus "that the crown should not sentence individuals to death for words or simple writings; others hoped that he would be pardoned."[3] Barbier's terse summary reveals a gap between the official view of La Motte's case and what might be called the judgment of public opinion. La Motte's punishment appeared severe, if not unwarranted, in light of the intellectual and cultural changes wrought by the Enlightenment. Although an official censorship mechanism remained in place, it could no longer be sustained either theoretically or practically in the eyes of the increasingly literate and informed Parisian populace. The crown found its monopoly on the word, whether written or spoken, under siege by the middle of the century.

This brief summary of La Motte's case offers a glimpse of the essential points of the analysis that follows. To begin with, it reveals that definitions of loyalty were intrinsically bound up with expressions of resistance in mideighteenth-century France. Individuals such as La Motte, arrested for crimes of *mauvais discours*, often failed to see the subversive implications of their written words or verbal utterances. Finding themselves in front of the crown's judicial officers, the majority of these French men and women insisted on protesting their personal allegiance to the king. The powerful emotions and convictions that underlay these declarations of loyalty should not be underestimated, if only because they played such a crucial role in shaping assumptions about royal authority. To understand why Louis XV's subjects were disappointed with their king and felt moved to criticize him, it is necessary to identify more precisely what they expected. Embedded in expressions of loyalty were the hopes and aspirations that, if left unfulfilled or explicitly violated, would manifest themselves as grievances if not as crimes. The task of elucidating perceptions of kingship is therefore twofold, requiring an inquiry into both fidelity and sedition.

It is unfashionable to speak of loyalty in the context of the eighteenth century, especially outside of the nobility, for it flies in the face of some deeply rooted assumptions about the Enlightenment and its links to modernity. Loyalty, as Henry Louis Gates Jr. has argued, is a premodern virtue that corresponded to a society structured in chains of mutual dependencies and grounded in a principle of partiality, a criterion that necessarily fell short of the Enlightenment creed of purely rational choice. Gates suggests that the triumph of the Enlightenment, with its rationalist, universalistic, and abstract outlook, undermined and eventually killed the value and virtue of loyalty.[4] Since 1789, loyalty in its traditional sense has been viewed as a quaint historical curiosity that should be tolerated but not encouraged. More importantly, it has been redefined to conform to the utilitarian morality of the Enlightenment: one is loyal to the nation, not to a grandmother. Gates harnesses history to serve his analysis of contemporary American politics, yet his argument is relevant to this study because it identifies the eighteenth century as the critical historical moment when new ideas and vocabularies about the individual and government emerged that challenged and eventually displaced the familiar language of loyalty. The police files of individuals arrested for seditious speech during Louis XV's reign attest to the powerful emotional and ideological conflicts this difficult transition unleashed.

Political Culture, Popular Culture, and Public Opinion

This book reflects an important shift in French historiography in the past decade and attests to the renewed interest in the politics and culture of the Old Regime. It should be recalled that for much of the twentieth century scholars were dissuaded from pursuing topics in political and institutional history. This bias reflected the methods and concerns of the two prevailing interpretative models: Marxism and the Annales. Both models emphasized economic and social history and inclined toward local studies and quantitative data. Scholarly attention focused on reconstructing demographic trends, price indexes, and the organization of labor.[5] The Annalistes were less dogmatic than their Marxist colleagues, and their methodological contribution has proved more enduring. From its inception the Annales encouraged an interdisciplinary approach to the study of historical change. This cross-fertilization initially turned to anthropology and sociology; in recent years the number of fields has expanded to include art history, literary criticism, and linguistic theory. In many ways the Annales paved the way for the current interest in cultural history.

The decline of communism, both in France and abroad, liberated scholars to pursue topics in political history that had previously been taboo. The publication of François Furet's *Penser la Révolution Française* in 1978 marked a turning point in French historiography. A former member of the French Communist Party who had gravitated to the right by the 1980s, Furet insisted that the domination of a Marxist interpretation of the Revolution had prevented historians from grasping the political dimensions of the crisis. Furet argued that the collapse of the monarchy created a vacuum of power at the center of government. He suggested that when "power lost its moorings," language itself provided the only tool for claiming and legitimating power in the unstable situation in France.[6] Furet's argument, although focused primarily on the Revolution and what followed, established a new agenda for historians of the Old Regime. Scholars turned their attention to the evolution of political life and discourse under the absolute monarchy to illuminate the intellectual and ideological habits that had prepared the French for the rupture of 1789. While this research marked the return of politics, it was no longer based in the traditional study of institutions and their officials. Rather, the political was expanded to encompass cultural practices, social configurations, forms of representation and communication, as well as theoretical forays into gender studies and cultural criticism; hence the term *political culture*.

This emphasis has had two significant consequences for scholars of eighteenth-century France. First, it has weakened the teleological pull of 1789 by focusing on the historical significance of the Old Regime as a worthy object of inquiry in its own right. Following Furet's initial gesture, subsequent work has tended to adopt a Tocquevillian line emphasizing the interdependencies and continuities that span the century and link the two periods. Second, it has generated considerable research on the monarchy as the preeminent political institution of the Old Regime. The construction of French absolutism in the seventeenth century and its conceptual dismantling in the eighteenth century has received enormous attention in the past decades. Pursuing the implications of Kantorowicz's study *The King's Two Bodies*, Ralph Giesey and Sarah Hanley have analyzed royal ceremonies in order to illuminate the theories and assumptions that shaped the growth of absolutism in France.[7] Other scholars, such as Keith Baker, Jeffrey Merrick, and Dale Van Kley, have examined the monarchy's attempts to sustain itself politically and ideologically in the face of the onslaught of ecclesiastical and constitutional efforts to limit its authority.[8] Concurrently with this interest in high politics, historians began casting their gaze further afield—into taverns, print shops, and prison cells—where they sought to tap into a deeper strata of attitudes and opinions. The most significant contributions here are Robert Darnton's seminal work on the literary underground of the Enlightenment and Arlette Farge's inquiry into popular political opinion. Bridging the gap between high and low are Roger Chartier, Lynn Hunt, and Sarah Maza, who have explored the interaction between print culture and public opinion in an effort to chart the changing political attitudes of French men and women over the course of the eighteenth century.[9]

Much of this debate concerning the political culture of the Old Regime is framed by the theoretical terms proposed by the German sociologist Jürgen Habermas in his model of the public sphere.[10] Originally published in German in 1962, *The Structural Transformation of the Public Sphere* had an enormous impact on Anglo-American historiography when the English translation appeared in 1989. The English edition coincided with the revival of interest in politics as well as the emergence of new fields in cultural history, such as gender and private life. Habermas's model not only defined the terms of an ongoing discussion among scholars but also established an agenda for future research that has been followed almost programmatically. Building on his argument that the key change in eighteenth-century France was the emergence of an autonomous public sphere, freed from both absolutist and corporatist constraints, historians have pursued the sites identified by Habermas, such as Masonic lodges, scientific academies, salons, and museums, to test the validity of the thesis. Habermas suggests that in these spaces, constructed on principles of voluntarism and equality, royal subjects acquired an apprenticeship in democratic civil society. According to this schema, individuals first learned to formulate opinions in the aesthetic realm, and these critical skills were later transferred to the political arena.

The success of Habermas's model's derives in part from the appeal of a linear narrative linking the Enlightenment, understood more as a set of cultural practices than as canonical texts, to the outbreak of revolution in France in 1789. This reading has inspired creative research on unfamiliar topics such as musical appreciation, art criticism, and letter writing.[11] Moreover, Habermas's emphasis on the aesthetic realm and the conjugal family as important sites for the cultivation of subjectivity has opened lines of communication between eighteenth-century scholars in different disciplines. Nonetheless, the model has overshadowed the field to such an extent that it is easy to ignore its blind spots. Although it is heuristically useful, the majority of the research it has inspired has been limited in sociological terms to individuals who met the criteria of literacy, leisure, and material comfort. Yet, if one seeks to demonstrate a connection between Enlightenment practices and political revolution, a broader social sampling is certainly required. Is there evidence, for example, of growing critical detachment or heightened subjectivity among individuals who fell outside the bourgeois public sphere of the salons and the academies? And if so, how was it articulated and manifested?

Arlette Farge's book *Subversive Words* is an important effort to address these issues by examining police files as well as the clandestinely published Jansenist newspaper *Les Nouvelles Ecclesiastiques.* Farge convincingly demonstrates, especially in her analysis of the impact of *Les Nouvelles Ecclesiastiques,* that the eighteenth century provided the material and philosophical tools that enabled royal subjects to claim the right to formulate their own opinions. Later in the century the demands would escalate to an insistence that these opinions be heeded and recognized as legitimate. As Farge correctly insists, however, the right to an opinion was a radical claim in the context of Old Regime France, in which the crown sought to control all aspects of the opinion-making process. The notion of opinion both challenged the crown's monopoly on political discussion and subverted the corporatist social structure of the Old Regime by emphasizing the individual as a unique, rational, and reflective creature. Farge's book, which covers almost the entire century, is important, even though it resists definitive conclusion because of her stated desire to avoid generating a linear narrative. Although she and I have read many of the same archives, we have adopted different approaches to the material, reflecting our different interests and arguments. Whereas Farge was influenced by the work of Michel Foucault, with whom she collaborated on a study of *lettres de cachet*, and its emphasis on rupture and epistemological inquiry, my own thinking has been shaped by the work of cultural historians in the early modern field, ranging from the Annaliste notion of *mentalité* to microhistory and new historicism.

With the exception of Farge, therefore, the majority of this recent scholarship has clarified the attitudes of ministers, magistrates, and clergymen during the tumultuous mid-century decades. Yet, even if one recognizes their indisputable influence, these privileged groups constituted a minority of the French populace. By contrast, the political concerns of Louis XV's other subjects, members of the sprawling Third Estate, which encompassed peasants, artisans, domestic servants, and wealthy bourgeois, remain sketchy. This imbalance in part reflects the limitations of the source materials. Members of the Third Estate rarely left diaries or voluminous correspondences, let alone publications, before the nineteenth century. When such individuals surface in archives, it is usually because of an infraction they have committed, and their words come to us filtered through the minds of the policing authorities. This last point raises a methodological dilemma that has prompted different responses. Marxists and some Annalistes rejected the tainted data in favor of demographic and quantitative studies of topics such as criminality or material existence, where the evidence was, they insisted, more neutral. Other historians used the official records but focused on reconstructing the behavior and motivation of the crowd, whether it was riotous or carnivalesque. Thus, outside of the political elites, the individual existed as a statistic or as a member of an anonymous crowd. In the past decade, however, a handful of determined scholars have broken through this historiographical impasse.

The scarcity of qualitative information perpetuated the misconception that the mental world of the less educated and unprivileged was so limited as to be of little interest. Yet, the cumulative work of a handful of historians concentrating in the early modern field strongly suggests that such assumptions are unfounded. In the skilled hands of Natalie Zemon Davis, Carlo Ginzburg, Giovanni Levi, and David Sabean otherwise taciturn evidence has yielded qualitative richness and texture. Their microscopic lens reveals a complexity and subtlety of thought processes heretofore unsuspected among members of the laboring populace.[12] Periodically, through luck or perseverance, an extraordinary source is unearthed, such as the journal of the eighteenth-century Parisian glazier Jacques Louis Ménétra, discovered by Daniel Roche.[13] In such cases, whether Ginzburg's Friulian miller Menocchio or Roche's glazier Ménétra, the reader is struck by the resilience and cunning of individuals who were determined to speak their mind or seek their fortune in the face of considerable economic, social, and political constraints.

This book is a product of the conjunction of these two historiographical trends and borrows methods and arguments from both. On the one hand, it testifies to the renewed interest among historians of France in the political institutions, especially the monarchy, of the Old Regime. Through the window opened by a police dossier, it tests larger historical arguments about the desacralization of the monarchy and the importance of public opinion in undermining royal authority and introducing new social and political practices.[14] On the other, it seeks to move outside of the privileged estates without sacrificing the dense analysis that accrues to more eminent historical figures. It offers a series of case studies designed to explicate the concerns and attitudes of individuals who by the hazards of birth or the force of circumstance were excluded from membership in the narrow category that constituted the political nation of eighteenth-century France. Only a handful of men from the upper echelons of the first two estates had a recognized right to offer the king advice and hence to have an opinion. Moreover, even these men had to exercise caution when proffering advice if they hoped to retain their consultative capacities. By contrast, nobody else could claim the right to have such thoughts, let alone to express them or expect them to be given serious consideration. The evidence from the police archives suggests, however, that by the middle of the eighteenth century this official understanding of what constituted the legitimate political nation was increasingly at odds with the convictions and expectations of Louis XV's urban and literate subjects. Either the conceptual category would have to be modified and expanded to reflect the altered cultural terrain or it would become the source of bitter, ultimately violent contestation. The story of this challenge and the responses it engendered lies in the crown's efforts to police its subjects for crimes of seditious speech.

Police Archives:
Mode d'Emploi

To discern what French men and women thought about their sovereign, it was necessary to observe closely the ways they addressed him in speech and writing. The search for such information quickly led me to the police archives of eighteenth-century Paris. These collections contain the records of the officials who made up the Parisian police force; their responsibilities and concerns are analyzed in chapter 1. Suffice it to say that police files provide a wealth of detailed information about topics other than crime and are therefore invaluable sources for French historians, as the work of Richard Cobb, Robert Darnton, Arlette Farge, and Steven Kaplan has demonstrated.[15] The files provide the documentary core of this book.

This book is based on an analysis of police archives spanning the years 1744–74, the years when Louis XV chose to rule without a first minister. This period proved ideal for a study of attitudes toward the king since Louis XV was perceived as being personally responsible for his government and its decisions. Moreover, recent research by Keith Baker, Jeffrey Merrick, and Dale Van Kley has emphasized the significance of the 1750s as a crucial turning point in the history of the French monarchy.[16] According to these scholars, a protracted series of ecclesiastical and constitutional struggles seriously undermined the crown's authority to rule and established precedents for a more participatory form of politics than France had ever known. Bearing these arguments in mind, I begin each chapter by surveying the political and cultural terrain to alert the reader to salient grievances and concerns that will reappear, albeit somewhat altered, in the police archives.

Within this chronological framework, the book examines the police dossiers of individuals arrested for crimes of *mauvais discours*. The term *mauvais discours* was a rubric that included various criminal offenses ranging from seditious speech and subversive literature to conspiracy plots against the crown. It cannot be overemphasized that such infractions were considered very serious crimes. The perpetrators were severely punished; some were sentenced to death, as the example of Jean Moriceau de La Motte illustrates. These cases provoked acute anxiety and were subjected to rigorous investigation. They constituted a challenge to the crown's authority by calling into question both popular affection for the monarchy and the ability of its officials to enforce the laws of the realm. Although most of these cases were intentionally kept out of the law courts in order to minimize potentially damaging publicity, the few cases that went to trial can usually be traced in the appropriate records of the Parlement. The approximately five hundred cases examined for this book are drawn from three different archival collections. In several instances the evidence for a case is scattered in two or three libraries.

The Bibliothèque Nationale's Joly de Fleury Collection contains eleven volumes of criminal records and official correspondence concerning individuals denounced or arrested in the aftermath of the Damiens affair. They testify primarily to the crown's campaign to purge the kingdom of all *mauvais sujets* and their *mauvais propos*. Yet, official zeal had unintended consequences: by encouraging denunciations, it unleashed spiteful tongues. The majority of the cases investigated between 1757 and 1759 involved slander or lies. The police were visibly exasperated by this development but unable to do much besides pursue the false leads if only to invalidate them. The cases varied in length; some received extensive documentation, whereas others faded from view in less than five pages. The years surrounding the Damiens affair offered an ideal entry point because political events crystallized otherwise inchoate grumblings and grievances. My survey of the Joly de Fleury volumes *en bloc* suggested that my analysis would need to account for the omnipresence of the term *fidelité,* as well as the element of popular manipulation of police officials, if it were to reflect the sources. These two preliminary conclusions were confirmed by subsequent research and proved central to the final argument.

The second and most extensive phase of research concentrated on the Archives de la Bastille, located at the Bibliothèque de l'Arsenal.[17] These dense files concerning individuals detained in the Bastille were exceptionally rewarding (see fig. 1). In addition to the usual transcriptions of official proceedings, the cartons of the Bastille contain troves of personal memorabilia. Since incarceration periods could be long, many prisoners kept journals or wrote letters, to the king or the lieutenant general of police, to stave off boredom and fight for their release. The cartons for cases in which an individual was arrested for a clandestinely published text often contain a manuscript copy of the work in question. The wealth of qualitative information enables the historian to reconstruct in detail both the motives for these crimes and the concerns they provoked.

To complete this project, it was necessary to work in the X and Y series of the Archives Nationales. This book draws foremost on the papers of the Paris police commissioners, as well as on records of trials and decrees of the highest court in the land, the Parlement of Paris. Since neither series is indexed by subject heading, I had to devise strategies for locating relevant information efficiently. One tactic involved following up cases begun in other collections, using dates or the names of specific commissioners to orient the search. I supplemented this research with selective sampling, concentrating on the five moments of heightened political tension that correspond to the chronology of the five case studies.

Figure 1.
La Bastille. Vue du coin du Boulevard, 1789.
(Courtesy of the Bibliothèque Nationale
de France, Collection Hennin)

Many scholars are skeptical about using information filtered through the records of officials as a guide to anything other than the attitudes of the authorities themselves. These methodological reservations stem from the conviction that individuals who appeared before representatives of authority were unable to speak freely.[18] In its most extreme form this view establishes a rigid dichotomy between a uniform official culture and the unsuspecting and essentially passive populace upon which it was supposedly arbitrarily imposed. This question will be addressed more fully in chapter 1; however, a few preliminary comments are in order here to justify my endeavor.

In 1984 Roger Chartier published an article entitled "Culture As Appropriation," in which he introduced an important conceptual tool, the notion of appropriation, which he has built upon and expanded throughout his prolific scholarly career.[19] The essay was written for a conference held at Cornell University on the then relatively new subject of popular culture. Chartier took the category "popular culture" and problematized it, arguing that historians overemphasize content at the expense of other significant issues, such as material forms, social practices, and cultural constraints, all of which contribute to the task of constructing meaning. Thus, Chartier insisted that "popular" should not be a label attached to an inventory of book titles read by members of the laboring populace but should be used to qualify a set of relationships between individuals and cultural artifacts. In effect, popularness resided less in what one read than in how one read it, and the historian should pay as much attention to consumption as to production. The emphasis here is on interaction and the view that the construction of meaning is a highly individual and complex operation. As Chartier noted in a recent collection of essays, "Reception always invents, shifts things about, and distorts."[20] Not only does Chartier dismiss rigid cultural categories such as high and low as essentially misleading but he undermines arguments based on social control that deprive individuals, whatever their origins, of agency in the important process of making sense of their lives and their world.

Chartier's methodological insights have been gleaned through many years spent researching the history of the book and print culture, in particular the connections between texts and practices, ideas and revolution. His conclusions, however, capture the essence of much of the recent work in early modern cultural history. He summarizes his view in the following words: "The fundamental object of a history that aims at recognizing the way social actors make sense of their practices and their discourse seems to me to reside in the tensions between the inventive capacities of individuals or communities and the constraints, norms, and conventions that limit (more or less strongly according to their position within relations of domination) what it is possible for them to think, say and do."[21] Chartier's assessment of the historian's task captures the guiding imperative in early modern cultural history as exemplified by scholars such as Natalie Zemon Davis, Carlo Ginzburg, and David Sabean. Their work demonstrates the exploratory possibilities opened by Chartier's proposed agenda. All three scholars examine judicial archives recording the encounter between an individual or a group and a representative of royal or ecclesiastical authority. Through close textual readings, they reconstruct the material and cultural resources available to these individuals and trace the process of mental *bricolage* that enabled them to confront their world and maneuver within its constraints. Confirming Chartier's early conclusions, this research suggests that the boundaries between official and popular culture were porous and that relations of power were continually being tested and negotiated.

This last point is eloquently asserted by Natalie Zemon Davis in the introduction to her study of sixteenth-century requests for royal pardons, where she describes the encounter between supplicants and judicial officials as "a cultural exchange conducted under the king's rules."[22] This interpretation applies equally well to the police files examined in this book. Although the stakes for the defendant, the witnesses, and the officials differed, all were engaged in a dialogue concerning the strengths and limitations of royal authority. Moreover, as the analysis demonstrates, the balance of power between the police and the people was constantly shifting. The documents attest primarily to the ingenuity and resourcefulness of the defendants, who devised ways to manipulate royal officials in the service of ambition, vengeance, or profit. Careful analysis of these cases reveals both the obstacles and the strategies that were devised to surmount them. This information exposes specific sources of disappointment with Louis XV's performance as king by indicating what contemporaries would have considered plausible charges or criticisms. These grievances can then be used to reconstruct the ideal standard for evaluating kingship that was in place in eighteenth-century France. It is important to identify these expectations in order to grasp the sense of disappointment and betrayal that erupted when the crown failed to fulfill them.

History through Case Studies

Following an introductory chapter on the police, this book is divided into five chronologically arranged chapters. Chapters 2–6 each focus on a single case selected for its ability to illustrate themes that characterized discussions about kingship at a particular moment in the reign of Louis XV. The dates correspond to periods of heightened political tension when debate crystallized around the monarchy. Although the cases highlight prevailing concerns about royal authority, they do not make claims for typicality. Such claims, in order to be substantiated, would have required a statistical study and produced an altogether different book. If anything, the chapters hew closer to the spirit of Richard Cobb, who observed in his autobiographical essay: "In all that I have written, I have tried to use individuals in order to illustrate the attitudes and assumptions of a society at a given period."[23] Like Cobb, I eschew squeezing individuals into monolithic social theories. Instead, like the microhistorical scholarship described in the preceding section, the chapters emphasize strategic choices, manipulation, and temporary reversals of power. Although each case is unique in terms of structural details, logistics, and denouement, one can identify a series of recurring images, grievances, fears, and expectations that together constituted a repertory and a vocabulary for discussing royal authority in the second half of the eighteenth century.

The book necessarily opens with a discussion of the police, who were responsible for generating and compiling the documents being studied. It seeks to evaluate the evidence as the product of a specific set of official concerns that blended absolutist imperatives with Enlightenment methods and goals. By examining official definitions of *fidelité* and *mauvais discours,* it prepares the reader for the debates concerning these terms in the chapters that follow. The analysis then unfolds in a series of five case studies. The dossier of Marie-Magdeleine Bonafon, a chambermaid at Versailles, serves as the point of departure. Bonafon was arrested in 1745 for writing an allegorical novel, *Tanastès*, that satirized the king's extramarital affair with Mme de Châteauroux. Close examination of Bonafon's text introduces two significant concerns that traverse the three decades: the unpopularity of the royal mistress and the fear of despotism. More importantly, it suggests that the two themes overlapped and combined to form a language for denouncing arbitrary authority.

The figure of the royal consort provides a link between Bonafon and the next chapter, which focuses on the dossier of Antoine Allègre, a schoolmaster from Marseilles. Allègre was arrested in 1751 for sending anonymous letters to the king warning him of a plot to poison his much resented *maîtresse en titre*, Mme de Pompadour. When the police proved that Allègre had forged the letters in the hopes of securing financial reward, he was severely punished. The strain of extended incarceration took its toll on Allègre and arguably transformed him from an essentially loyal petty crook into a truly *mauvais sujet*. Despite his suffering and resentment, Allègre refused to hold Louis XV responsible for his plight. Like Bonafon, Allègre deflected his attacks off the person of the king and onto his mistresses and ministers through a language of despotism designed to sustain the principle of monarchy while criticizing its shortcomings.

From Allègre, the book moves to the case of Auguste Claude Tavernier, a former munitions officer, and illustrates how individuals used calumnious accusations to manipulate the police and secure personal advantages. Tavernier's unruly behavior as a young man had prompted his parents to request a royal *lettre de cachet* to have him detained. Finding himself locked up in a fortress on the Ile Sainte-Marguerite, Tavernier schemed for his release. He denounced a plot to murder Louis XV, promising to reveal the details if he were granted a hearing before the Parlement of Paris. Timed to coincide with the residual concern provoked by Damiens's attempted assassination of Louis XV, Tavernier's allegations were given serious consideration. His case revealed growing intolerance for paternalism as the basis for any authority, including that of the king. His proposals for reform offer an image of restrained kingship very different from that found in classical absolutist theory.

In chapter 4, the soldier Paul René du Truch de La Chaux carries Tavernier's fictitious conspiracy one step further. On 6 January 1762 La Chaux was found injured in a corridor of Versailles and claimed that he had been attacked by two strangers whose primary target was Louis XV. Within three days, however, La Chaux confessed that he had invented the story. He had stabbed himself in the hopes of receiving a financial reward for his heroic efforts to defend the king. The notion of fidelity was central to La Chaux's efforts to justify his crime and plea for mercy. His palpable sense of horror and chagrin when he found himself accused of *lèse-majesté* reveals growing confusion over the meaning of fidelity. It also suggests that the traditional language of fidelity could not be sustained in the face of the Enlightenment emphasis on the individual as a source of unique needs and inviolable rights.

This Enlightenment language of rights and law is central to the final chapter, which explores the case of the retired barrister Pierre Denis de La Rivoire. La Rivoire was arrested in 1771, in the wake of the Maupeou coup, for having sent a dozen offensive letters to Louis XV. As in the preceding cases, La Rivoire's dossier was permeated by an obsessive fear of despotism, which he, in a radical move, equated with divine-right kingship. Although a staunch supporter of the monarchy, La Rivoire offered a distinctly secular vision of kingship. His case provides an appropriate conclusion to a reign marked by its failure to resolve an unending series of conflicts between representatives of sacred and secular authority. It attests to the considerable influence of legal discourse in formulating the more rational and utilitarian view of politics that would triumph with the collapse of the monarchy at the end of the century.

Print, Politics, and Criticism

This overview of the five cases permits a preliminary effort to delineate structural patterns and continuities central to the analysis that follows. As a group, individuals arrested for crimes of opinion spanned the social spectrum of eighteenth-century France, excluding the extremes of wealth and poverty. Although most were caught in Paris or its environs, few were native Parisians. Some had been living there for several years, whereas others had come with the specific purpose of contacting the king or his ministers. In addition to this geographic diversity, the men and women arrested practiced various professions. The five individuals considered in this book include a domestic servant, a schoolmaster, a former munitions officer, a soldier, and a retired lawyer. From the juridical perspective of the Old Regime, all but La Chaux, the soldier, were members of the unprivileged Third Estate. Although La Chaux could claim minor noble ancestry, he was materially worse off than any of the others. Bonafon, Tavernier, and La Chaux all had experienced direct or indirect exposure to the life of the court and the *haute société* through occupation or family connections. This exposure had familiarized them with the manners and mores of the Old Regime's elites. It also had provided them indirect access to books and newspapers, as well as to information gleaned through conversations and gossip. By consequence, they were less culturally isolated and more politically informed than their station might convey. Furthermore, like the denizens of Darnton's Grub Street, they may have experienced acute frustration at finding themselves so close to a world that was desirable but inaccessible, suggesting a possible connection between the accumulation of resentment and the motivation for crime.[24]

While the educational backgrounds of the defendants varied, all were literate and referred to literary activities as fulfilling diverse personal needs. Prisoners complained of literary deprivation as much as they did of physical hardships. Michel Mitre Touche spoke for many of his fellow prisoners when he insisted that "my greatest fear is to have no books to prevent me from regretting the loss of my liberty."[25] Most of those detained were allowed to receive books from friends and family or to borrow them from the Bastille's library. Many were furnished with pen and paper for writing letters or justificatory *mémoires*. In certain cases the police encouraged writing in the hopes that it would yield information that they suspected had been withheld during questioning. Yet these privileges were quickly revoked as punishment for bad behavior.

Reading was repeatedly referred to as a source of diversion and information. The police dossiers are filled with book requests by prisoners desperate to stave off boredom and mental collapse. The books requested covered the gamut of Enlightenment literature, ranging from scientific and mechanical treatises to works by the most renowned contemporary authors, such as Voltaire. This desire for texts revealed the extent to which the Enlightenment, the spirit of inquiry, had penetrated deeply into French society by the second half of the century. Individuals, especially those who lacked the educational advantages conferred by a noble birthright, turned to books as tools for increasing knowledge and improving skills. They relied on pamphlets and newspapers for information on current affairs and looked to scientific treatises and manuals to sate their appetite for invention. The category *mauvais discours* was by definition linked to the act of writing since a verbal utterance was more difficult to substantiate unless it could be corroborated by other evidence. Moreover, print was more durable, and therefore more threatening, than speech from a police perspective. Many of the individuals arrested were authors of clandestinely published novels, pamphlets, or plays, which suggests that authorship itself was no longer viewed as the reserve of privilege and power. In addition to these forays into print, some individuals drafted anonymous letters to substantiate their calumnious accusations and fictive plots. The literary element of these crimes can be seen on another level as well. The cases often read like scenarios from plays or novels, elaborately contrived and unabashedly theatrical. The perpetrators made a conscious effort to build suspense through cryptic allusions to furtive plans and sinister assassins. In each instance the emphasis was on staging a crime that attained the highest possible level of *vraisemblance*, a point vividly illustrated by La Chaux in chapter 5. Yet the scripts shared a tragic flaw: all relied on the figure of the king as a stock character. The disrespect manifested in such a decision was not to be lightly dismissed.

It is difficult to pinpoint the ideas and convictions that gave birth to these lies and false alarms. A combination of unprivileged status, thwarted ambition, acute need, and limited resources nurtured growing critical detachment from prevailing norms and authorities. These men and women, often gifted and determined despite modest social origins or impoverished circumstances, resented their continued exclusion from the decision-making process, especially when the crown's decisions affected their personal interests directly, as in the case of La Rivoire. Possessing no legitimate sphere of political activity, they were expected to serve and obey the crown, not to advise or judge it. Yet the police archives testify to the unwillingness of Louis XV's subjects to accept this passive role. With more printed matter in circulation, in more accessible formats, French men and women were better placed to inform themselves and formulate opinions. Under Louis XV, the crown was increasingly and aggressively summoned to account for its policies by all segments of the populace.[26] Yet, and this point must be emphasized, the perpetrators of these crimes did not see their yearning to participate in political decision making as a challenge to the monarchy. For this reason, the archives abound with declarations of fidelity to the king. The goal was reform, not revolution, and it was to be achieved by reaffirming the primordial ties binding French subjects to their king even if this entailed criticizing his mistakes.

From a survey of the police files a distinct vision of kingship emerges that suggests a conscious effort to reconcile traditional customs and practices with the ideological innovations of the Enlightenment. This point is illustrated by defendants' trying to justify their actions by arguing that it was the duty of a loyal subject to provide counsel when the king was being deceived. Criticism, according to this argument, was a more honest mark of personal attachment to the king than indifference or flattery.

This pervasive desire to advise the king affirmed a popular ideal of kingship and reflected entrenched hostility toward absolutism and its goal of an administrative monarchy. Louis XV's intensely private nature led him to withdraw from the public eye more than any of his predecessors, and this aggravated the perception that the king was being controlled by evil advisers at the expense of his loyal subjects. By the eighteenth century the crown was most familiar to its subjects in the guise of its myriad officials. In ceremonial terms, as Michèle Fogel has demonstrated, this shift manifested itself in the decline of rituals requiring the king's presence, such as the royal touch, in favor of those that did not, such as the singing of Te Deums.[27] Yet the populace resisted the administrative monarchy, constantly evoking the myth of a sovereign who was accessible to his most humble subjects. These efforts assumed different forms, such as pleas for pardon or requests for an audience with Louis XV. Whatever the ploy, the desire for a direct channel of communication with the king was omnipresent and deeply embedded. It is evident throughout this book and has to be recognized as a structural characteristic of French political life. Not even the presidents of the Fifth Republic have been able to ignore this need to maintain the illusion of direct lines of communication between the government and the governed.[28]

This clinging to a traditional, paternalistic, and personalized definition of kingship was also reflected in the obsessive fear of despotism that permeated the police dossiers. The power of the word *despotism* within the political lexicon of eighteenth-century France cannot be overemphasized, and it provides a thematic and linguistic undercurrent linking the separate cases. For example, certain words, such as *caprice* and *volonté*, were relied on as rhetorical cues to indicate that the monarchy had degenerated into despotism. The language of despotism provided one of the most universal and compelling critiques of royal authority in the second half of the eighteenth century. It was indebted, whether explicitly acknowledged or not, to Montesquieu's tripartite division of government on the basis of motivating principles and his definition of monarchy. In his erotic satire *Persian Letters* and in his more famous study *The Spirit of the Laws*, Montesquieu warned his readers that monarchy was constantly in danger of degenerating into despotism unless power was restrained through legally constituted intermediary bodies. Echoing Montesquieu's concerns, the defendants in these cases sought not to deny the king his full power but rather to prevent him from, or reprimand him for, abusing it. This distinction is significant because in condemning despotism none of these individuals was calling for the overthrow of the monarchy. On the contrary, most sought to restore luster to a tarnished crown before it was too late.

In one respect, however, these suggestions for reform reflect the impact of the Enlightenment and its emphasis on reason at the expense of the sacred. Although the individuals who appeared before the police continued to refer to their sovereign as a sacred person, these terms of address sounded increasingly formulaic. Too many of their ideas openly contradicted or undermined the sacred basis of royal authority. Thus, in keeping with the spirit of a skeptical and profane age, these five individuals mark stages in the process of redefining kingship to fit the criteria of secular logic. Their very actions and utterances denied the divine-right basis of the monarchy by insisting that the king was accountable to more than God alone. My analysis suggests that if the monarchy had been willing to accommodate a more secular definition of itself, it might have found a way to survive the challenges that confronted it later in the century.

Fidelity and Kingship

This book proposes an alternative reading of the police files that is guided by two fundamental principles. First, it shifts the focus of analysis away from content and onto the element of manipulation embedded in each case. Complaints about the monarchy were as old as the monarchy itself and numbingly repetitive. What changed in the eighteenth century was less the content of the critique than the forms and means selected for expressing it. Second, it suggests that notions of fidelity were intimately linked both to subversive acts and to perceptions of the king. Moreover, fidelity sheds light on definitions of crime and treason if only by highlighting areas of disagreement between the crown and its subjects.

Most historians have used the police archives to chronicle the rising tide of popular discontent in prerevolutionary France. This interpretation, based on records of *mauvais discours* as evidence of growing hostility to the crown, is problematic in light of the fact that most of the allegations were false. Thus, the documents cannot be read as records of actual thoughts and utterances. By contrast, they can be used to indicate prevailing attitudes about the king by subjecting their manipulative stratagems to close scrutiny. Each ruse provides a guide into the realm of the plausible or credible of the eighteenth-century French political imagery since the lies were designed to be convincing in order to attain specific ends. Herein lies the originality of this book.

The decision to center each chapter on a single case reflects these methodological concerns. The pervasive element of manipulation is as historically significant as the alleged utterances in evaluating arguments about the growing critical detachment or politicization of members of the Third Estate. To support this contention, it was necessary to narrow the focus in order to deconstruct these intricately crafted crimes. This analysis consciously looks for links between the planning of these crimes and the political and cultural backdrop against which they unfolded. Rhetorical strategies only make sense if the assumptions and attitudes that guided them can be identified and uncovered. The decision to emphasize the manipulative aspect of these crimes does not minimize their subversive implications but displaces them by suggesting that the element of subversion lies elsewhere than in the content. A parallel can be drawn to Natalie Zemon Davis's method in her analysis of sixteenth-century pardon requests. Although Davis relies on literary theory to undergird her analysis and I do not, we both focus on the criteria individuals used to select arguments to construct criminal plots and defend themselves when their schemes unraveled.[29]

There was unquestionably an offensive element in this decision to deploy a false threat against the king in the service of personal interest. To begin with, it undermined the absolutist language of love and reciprocity by calling into question French subjects' affection for their sovereign. Moreover, the incorporation of the king as a prop in a scheme to secure money, honor, or revenge was disrespectful of his sacred person. Much like blasphemy, bantering the king's name about rendered it banal, dispelling the mystical aura that distinguished the king from ordinary mortals. Lacking the social distinctions that were the prerequisites for making claims, the individuals arrested for *mauvais discours* had opted to include the king in order to guarantee that they would draw official attention. Unfortunately, although most were essentially loyal, minor offenders, they drastically underestimated the gravity of their offense. They were horrified to find themselves treated with rigor and charged with crimes of treason.

This last point leads us back to the notion of fidelity and the critical role it played in each case. It may seem curious that a study of *mauvais discours* should devote space to a discussion of ideas about loyalty. Yet, the term *fidelité* was omnipresent in the police files and an integral part of the manipulative strategies about to be examined. Moreover, defendants continued to protest their loyalty long after they had acknowledged their misdemeanors. In effect, they relied on the currency of loyalty even if their delinquent actions had devalued it. The police, however, understood the consequences and worked diligently to restore loyalty to its original face value. The confusion surrounding loyalty and what it entailed cannot be ignored. It reflected growing ambiguity about the relationship between the king and his subjects, as well as a desire to embrace change and tradition simultaneously, an impulse that would destabilize French political activity from the end of the Old Regime right through the Revolution and beyond.

The refrain "if the king only knew" provides a leitmotif for this book. It attested to an instinctive desire to shield the king from direct attack. French subjects longed to believe that their sovereign was infinitely good, merciful, and just. Anything that threatened to dispel or contradict this illusion had to be dismissed on the basis of the king's ignorance or evil advisers. The king's subjects clung to this reassuring paternalistic image even as they became more politically engaged and demanding. Louis XV's subjects did not see any inherent contradictions between their desire for political participation and the continuing existence of the monarchy. It is important to recognize that these two principles seem mutually exclusive only with the benefit of hindsight. To the men and women in the streets of Paris in 1789 it was neither ignorance nor confusion that allowed them to think that they could support the king while embracing the principles of the Revolution.

To recover the full spectrum of emotions and aspirations the monarchy inspired in its subjects, it is necessary to examine notions of fidelity in conjunction with expressions of resistance. The same tensions detected in the encounters between Old Regime police officials and defendants would resurface during the Revolution when successive leaders confronted the task of erecting a new social and political order. The volatile and divisive debates concerning the king's fate during the Revolution, as well as the instability that plagued French government throughout the nineteenth century, testify to the enduring appeal of the absolutist myth. The construction of this myth, the basis of its appeal, and the sources of its exhaustion are revealed by the gaps in the police files between what defendants said and what they did, between discursive forms and social practices. It follows that this book is as concerned with the words and perceptions that legitimated and delegitimated authority as it is with the strengths and weaknesses of the monarchy in eighteenth-century France. Moreover, the analysis suggests that by probing deeply the historian can retrieve the information needed to make an undistinguished individual whom contemporaries had consigned to silence into a worthy object of inquiry.

Chapter 1

Police, Crime, and Public Order in Enlightenment Paris

· ❧ ·

THE FIVE INDIVIDUALS whose stories follow owe their existence in the historical record to the diligent efforts of a specific set of Old Regime officials: the police of Paris. It is therefore appropriate to begin by familiarizing ourselves with the organization and concerns of the men whose documents can now be used for very different purposes than those originally intended by the Bourbon monarchy. The policing of the kingdom was linked to the growth of absolutism in France, a historical process whose defining characteristics were centralization and bureaucratization. According to Tocqueville, the consolidation of royal authority entailed "keeping a watchful eye on everything that was happening in the country and . . . issuing orders from Paris on every conceivable subject." As the crown extended its authority, it became more systematic and efficient in its administrative technique.[1] This evolution was most evident in the monarchy's relationship to the city of Paris, which possessed the most developed and most extensive police force in the realm by the eighteenth century. Paris was also the seat of the highest court in the land, the Parlement of Paris, whose jurisdiction extended over one-third of the realm. This concentration of policing and judicial agents in the capital was linked to the presence of the court, which was both the primary royal residence and the center of government. It is no surprise that crimes of opinion, including *mauvais discours* and conspiracy plots against the king, the court, and royal ministers, were concentrated in the metropolis and its environs. Moreover, capital crimes such as treason and *lèse-majesté*, regardless of where they originated, were always transferred to Parisian authorities for investigation and judgment.

In order to clarify these criminal categories and their implications, this chapter examines the criteria and assumptions that guided police officers in the task of maintaining public order. The analysis suggests that the police are best understood as hybrids of enlightenment and repression, men whose techniques, ideals, and files reflected the fundamental tensions of their age. Although their approach to the problem of crime can be qualified as enlightened in methodological terms, their conception of human nature, crime, and society was firmly anchored in a traditional Christian outlook. It is precisely this rich blend of systematic detail, intellectual curiosity, and moral purpose that makes their archives invaluable for the reconstruction of otherwise irretrievable attitudes, aspirations, and grievances.

The Task of Observation

Louis XIV's establishment of a royal police force in Paris displayed his concern with tightening control over the historically unruly city.[2] The crown's policy provoked considerable resistance from municipal officials, who found their ancient jurisdictions and responsibilities abruptly subordinated to the commands of the newly minted police authorities. Like most administrative bodies of the Old Regime, the police of Paris were specialized officials arranged in a tight hierarchy of rank and duty. These men were dedicated to the collection, classification, and processing of information concerning every aspect of daily life in the metropolis. A strict system of daily reporting ensured the steady flow of information from the base to the summit of this official pyramid, presided over by the lieutenant general of police, who transmitted the information directly to the king.

The position of lieutenant general was created by Jean-Baptiste Colbert in 1667 to supervise policing activities in the capital; the lieutenant general was both a magistrate and a royal administrator.[3] By the eighteenth century, administrative requirements outweighed judicial functions, and the lieutenant general was effectively the king's intendant of Paris. Selected personally by the king from among the *maîtres des requêtes,* an elite corps that supplied the crown with its most important administrators, the lieutenant general was a royal commissioner whose charge, although purchased, was always revocable. Like a provincial intendant, he received a mandate from the crown and was accountable directly to the king.[4] There was no aspect of urban life that did not fall under the lieutenancy's purview. Consequently, the lieutenant general was an important liaison between Versailles and Paris, keeping the king informed of developments in the city, whose history of unrest still haunted the crown in the eighteenth century. Both Louis XV and Louis XVI maintained an extensive private correspondence with their various lieutenant generals. Supplying the king with a daily gauge of popular sentiment, the lieutenant general was an essential and unique resource.

The lieutenant general supervised the activities of approximately three thousand men who were responsible for policing a city of six hundred thousand inhabitants by the mid-eighteenth century.[5] That there were twenty types of officials is not surprising given the staggering array of activities that fell under the lieutenancy's purview. It is important to recall that the word *police* had much broader connotations under the Old Regime than it does today. The narrow semantic association between *police* and repression is a distinctly modern phenomenon. Two centuries ago the term referred to various activities involved in the governance and regulation of a city. The possession of a police force was a source of pride and praise in the age of Enlightenment, when it was understood as a mark of civilization. By contrast, societies that lacked policing forces were seen as primitive and barbaric.[6] Combining judicial and administrative functions, the police of Paris provided a host of services for a society that had acute need and limited resources. In addition to the more familiar task of confronting crime, police responsibilities included municipal lighting and sanitation, market supervision, and regulation of the grain trade. Within the broad category "crime" one finds subdivisions such as publishing and censorship of the book trade, prostitution, and *délits d'opinion* (crimes of opinion). The files on crimes of opinion form the basis of this book.

An individual who was arrested immediately became the subject of a police dossier. The investigative process produced a bundle of paper whose thickness depended on the seriousness of the case. The police dossiers contain official transcriptions of interrogations, depositions of the defendant and witnesses, and reports on the prisoner's condition by prison officials, doctors, and priests. In addition, the files contain reports of spies and informers, where relevant, along with any evidence seized at the time of the arrest. Most dossiers include official correspondence between the lieutenant general, his officers, and royal ministers, as well as copies of the relevant royal decrees. The few cases that went to trial can be followed in parlementary records of proceedings and sentences. The majority of these cases, however, were decided outside of the courts due to a combination of insufficient evidence, the ambiguous legal status of the offenses, and the crown's desire for secrecy in cases where publicity was unwelcome and potentially damaging. Some suspicious individuals were detained indefinitely because the police were afraid to set them free in the streets of Paris. Their dossiers grew thick with the years of incarceration, containing five hundred pages and more, because the police kept copies of everything the prisoner wrote, including letters, book requests, justificatory *mémoires,* and appeals for pardon. Some dossiers offer a neat narrative, allowing one to trace a case from start to finish. Many, however, end abruptly, thwarting efforts to discover the conclusion of the case. Such vagaries, while frustrating, must be accepted as part of the terrain.

The figure of the lieutenant general looms large in these dossiers since he oversaw each segment of the investigation and conferred with the king about protocol, strategy, and punishment. His authority was also reflected in the eyes of the accused, who identified the lieutenant general as the arbiter of their fate and addressed their pleas and letters accordingly. The lieutenant general relied primarily on commissioners and inspectors, who were responsible for making arrests, collecting information, conducting interrogations, and evaluating the culpability of the accused. Two commissioners whose names reappear in the dossiers, Miché de Rochebrune and Lenoir, a future lieutenant general himself, were relied on as skilled and shrewd interrogators in these affairs involving sensitive political issues and seditious utterances. It was not uncommon to find specialists within the larger field of policing, such as, for example, Inspector d'Hémery, who monitored the book trade and kept files on five hundred Parisian authors, from struggling hacks to established luminaries.[7]

The post of commissioners was created in the fourteenth century to provide administrative assistants to the provost of the Châtelet, whose officials were responsible for administering justice in the jurisdiction of Paris. Commissioners were career officials who, like the magistrates, had purchased their expensive offices from the crown. Most of them had a legal education and experience as barristers or solicitors. By the eighteenth century forty-eight commissioners covered the city's twenty *quartiers*. Since the commissioners lived in their assigned *quartier*, they were accessible and familiar figures to the local populace. Like the lieutenant general, who was responsible for the entire metropolis, commissioners combined judicial, administrative, and investigative duties within their *quartiers*. They could arrest, interrogate, and jail anyone caught committing a crime, and they were responsible for transmitting information about suspicious persons or activities to the lieutenant general. Serving as ready-made judges, a role emphasized by the black robes they wore, commissioners helped contain local disputes, resolving them as they erupted.[8] Scholars familiar with police archives recognize that the relationship between the commissioner and the urban populace was ambivalent. At times the commissioner was an ally, called upon to settle arguments between friends and neighbors; in other instances, such as when he closed the taverns at night or arrested debtors, he was a symbol of royal repression.[9] In this book, commissioners appear primarily in their judicial capacity, making arrests, confiscating clandestine literature, and interrogating prisoners. The information they compiled constituted the basis of the police dossier.

The commissioners were assisted by the inspectors, who were charged with specifically investigative duties. When the position was created in 1708 there were forty-eight inspectors, but Lieutenant of Police Feydeau de Marville reduced this number to twenty in 1740, when he introduced reforms to improve the efficiency and reputation of the corps.[10] Unlike the commissioners, who owed their allegiances to the Châtelet, the inspectors had purchased their offices directly from the lieutenant general. They were his personal *valets d'armes*, roaming the city, fastidiously recording all they observed, executing search and arrest warrants, confiscating illegal printed matter, and closing down printing shops. They specialized in information gathering, and their daily reports allowed the lieutenant general to monitor suspicious persons, places, and activities. The distinctions between the commissioners and the inspectors were blurry, at times fostering unproductive competition. Their conflicts reflected the longstanding struggle between the provost of the Châtelet and the lieutenant general for supreme authority in the administration of Paris.[11] Unlike the commissioners, the inspectors were

not permanently attached to a particular *quartier.* Consequently, the populace perceived their presence as primarily a repressive one. More mobile
than the commissioners, inspectors distinguished themselves through their
expertise in specific categories of crime, such as prostitution or clandestine
literature. They were aided in their tasks by a network of informal spies
known as *mouches. Mouches* ranged from regularly paid informers such as
tavern keepers and brothel madams to convicted felons or former criminals;
men whose desperate situation, combined with their knowledge of the urban underworld, made them useful guides and eager observers. Thus, the
inspectors tried to supplement their own manpower with local underlings to
keep order and monitor the mobile populace of the capital. Both commissioners and inspectors were familiar figures, sometimes welcome and sometimes resisted, grudgingly tolerated as indigenous features of the urban
landscape.[12]

Whatever the title of the official, observation was the distinguishing activity of policing in Old Regime France. Tocqueville suggests that the
"habit of surveillance became almost an obsession with the central government" as administrative technique evolved and grew more efficient.[13] Observation assumed greater weight during the eighteenth century because it
was integral to the Enlightenment's fundamental project of comprehending
society and improving pubic order. The two goals were intertwined on the
Enlightenment agenda, where society had to be described in order for it to
be understood and effectively governed. The police and their files can be
seen as fitting into what Jacques Revel identifies as a larger administrative
effort to comprehend society through systematic written descriptions. In an
article exploring the relationship between learned and popular culture in
France between 1650 and 1800 Revel discerns an intellectual shift beginning
in 1750 marked by writings that adopted a "pre-ethnographic" attitude toward their object of study. Previous interest in popular culture had been restricted to a handful of experts whose research was inspired by the desire to
discredit popular beliefs as contrary to the laws of truth and reason.[14] By
contrast, the pre-ethnographic writings that began appearing in the second
half of the eighteenth century were distinguished by a new sense of discov-
ery and curiosity. These later efforts reflected a different objective on the
part of royal administrators: the desire to understand an element of their

own society that remained elusive and unfamiliar. Neither dismissive nor condescending, these officials, doctors, and economists were searching for data to establish links between themselves and the objects of their research. They were motivated by the desire to construct a collective cultural genealogy of humankind over time. These underlying concerns help explain why police dossiers include information seemingly extraneous to the investigation of a crime, such as reading and drinking habits. From an official perspective, crime was an area of research and experimentation, a database of information relevant to these other intellectual and social agendas.

If careful observation embodied the inquisitive spirit of the age and its accompanying desire for understanding, it was also instrumental to the task of maintaining public order in a busy metropolis. In a recent analysis of the language and concerns found in police reports, David Garrioch suggests that these officials should be viewed as "enlightened social reformers" as much as agents of repression. Garrioch argues that the police were motivated by humanitarian concerns, including universally applicable notions of justice and public utility. Like Revel, who identifies a shift in learned attitudes at mid-century, Garrioch demonstrates that enlightened vocabulary gradually replaced notions of Christian duty and God-given responsibility in the police reports of the second half of the eighteenth century. He rightly insists that the concept of public order, which today entails the prevention of crime, encompassed, in a much wider sense, the smooth running of society.[15] Both Revel and Garrioch are interested in how Old Regime officials understood themselves and how these perceptions shaped their responsibilities and their methods. They provide a useful framework for assessing the information contained in police files if only because they force us to reconfigure the categories of policing and enlightenment by demonstrating that the two are neither diametrically opposed nor mutually exclusive.

This last point brings me to the work of Michel Foucault, who reminds us in *Discipline and Punish* that "the 'Enlightenment,' which discovered the liberties, also invented the disciplines."[16] In his analysis of the evolution of the disciplinary apparatus in the eighteenth century Foucault problematizes the categories crime, policing, and punishment by exposing their epistemological grounding in scientific, legal, and political discourses they both produce and sustain. The subtleties in Foucault's analysis often get lost in the rush to harness his argument to a narrative linking the rise of repressive mechanisms to the growing power of the state, an interpretation Foucault explicitly denies.[17] Unfortunately, this skewed reading of Foucault has obscured the liminality of the eighteenth-century police, figures who operated as insiders and outsiders, friends and foes, agents of enlightenment and repression. The police were as much products of the society they sought to regulate as they were opponents of it. It was these tensions and the evidence they generated, more than a desire to uncover the mysteries of statecraft, that preoccupied Foucault.

Turning to Foucault after two years of reading through police archives, I found several of my preliminary conclusions implicated in the logic of the arguments set forth in *Discipline and Punish*. Foucault suggests that concepts such as discipline and order can only be historically understood as mechanisms for generating, collecting, and classifying information. Echoing Tocqueville, Foucault insists that there was a direct and ineluctable relationship between the power of the crown and its ability to gather knowledge about the realm and its inhabitants. In the late seventeenth century, according to Foucault, this knowledge was linked to the technique of the examination, a procedure that "situates individuals within a network of writing; it engages them in a whole mass of documents that capture and fix them." Police files documenting utterances, opinions, gestures, and actions were arguably techniques for assigning attributes to an individual in a process that defined him or her *qua* individual in the midst of a society that was conceived of in exclusively corporatist terms. A necessary corollary to this development was the concurrent emergence of a power of writing: writing not only manifested authority but also conferred it. In the process of disciplining delinquent individuals the police produced case files that constituted them as autonomous subjects if only with the goal of containing them. Otherwise undistinguished royal subjects discovered their own significance through their ability to pose a threat to a police official, whose repressive activities thus contributed, albeit unintentionally, to the experience of subjectivity under the absolute monarchy.[18]

This last point implies that a police dossier offers a twofold object of inquiry, the police and the policed, and documents their dynamic and complex interplay. Each case captures a set of power relations continually in flux, a shifting set of alliances, confrontations, and temporary inversions, that reveal the dynamics of "micro-powers" operating within and against a larger field of social and political tensions. As the ensuing chapters demonstrate, there was never a definitive shift in the balance of power in these encounters but rather an ongoing set of interactions and exchanges between the police and the accused.

The arguments of Revel, Garrioch, and Foucault provide insights into the *mentalité* of the police and the documents they produced. Despite their distinct approaches and purposes, all three scholars suggest that the notion of the police as mere agents of repression is too reductive. By expanding our analytical lens, we acquire a picture with greater breadth and depth. The wealth of detailed, frequently extraneous information contained in the criminal dossiers suggests that the police were as much the products of the Enlightenment as they were impediments to it. Although law enforcement was an undeniable feature of police activity, it was not the only one. The police demonstrated an enlightenment penchant for understanding the social world through direct observation and empirical knowledge. These concerns contributed as much to their self-perception as the more familiar and less progressive aspect of their repressive activities, to be discussed shortly.

The crown relied on its police officers for information concerning the populace. Moreover, with the waning of religious practice, the monarchy needed agents of law enforcement to instruct its subjects concerning their duties, morals, and conduct. The eighteenth century produced a welter of articulate opponents to the monarchy's longstanding monopoly on public discourse and authority. The prevailing message that emerged from this cacophony of philosophes, Jansenists, and magistrates was that obedience was no longer unconditional and even resistance was justified in certain circumstances. This challenge demanded a response on the part of the monarchy, whose first reflex was to turn to the church. Yet, the role of the church as a moral guide and corrective was seriously undermined by the internecine struggles and doctrinal debates generated by the Jansenists. Unable to depend on the church as an ally, the crown enlisted a secular task force, the police, to instill moral values and enforce social norms among its subjects. The police, like their spiritual predecessors, sought to deter through example and inspire through mutually reinforcing codes of speech and conduct. The discourse of policing therefore combined pedagogy, morality, and discipline in the pursuit of public order under the enlightened banner of reason.

The Topography of Crime

The police were determined to approach their project empirically, gathering evidence, verifying its accuracy, and using it to make informed decisions. Nonetheless, the task of observation did not proceed unobstructed. On the one hand, the police were hindered by their own assumptions about crime and society, creating blind spots in their collection and assessment of information. On the other, the populace demonstrated a keen awareness of official assumptions and sought to manipulate them in their favor. Both sets of concerns need to be identified so that we may recognize and evaluate them when they appear in the case analyses.

To begin with, police officers were intrigued by the study of human nature, especially in relation to criminal behavior. They were cautious and astute judges of character, drawing fine distinctions within the range of delinquent activity confronting them. This critical process is revealed, for instance, in official responses to the case of Gaspard Ferlin and Toussaint Courtin. Courtin, a carter for timber merchants, had accused Ferlin, who served in the mounted constabulary of Rouen, of uttering *mauvais discours* against the king in his presence. The police, convinced that Courtin had ulterior motives and was counting on Ferlin's checkered past to weigh in favor of his accusation, suspected calumny. Yet they were cautious in pursuing allegations and avoided hasty conclusions, as the following assessment of Courtin's charge indicates: "Ferlin may be capable of shady dealings, for which he is currently being pursued by the Provost of Lille, but a rogue need not be a monster of nature capable of conceiving of such a horrible crime as assassinating his King and his Master."[19] This quotation reveals that official understanding of criminal activity was arranged in distinct categories that reflected the Old Regime's deeply embedded sense of hierarchy. A petty crook was not necessarily a regicide.

Encompassing a broad spectrum of delinquent activity, crime was a field in which assumptions about human nature, the appropriate use of knowledge, and the display of power collided to produce an infinite set of subtle, gradated criteria that shaped police assessments and responses. The distinctions in the criminal underworld mirrored those that riddled the social world of eighteenth-century France. For the police, crimes reflected the qualities and capacities of their perpetrators, including income, education, literacy, and occupation. These parameters were established at birth and combined to define one's station in life. The notion of *état* conferred a sense of permanence or stasis since one was expected to conform to its constraints. Resistance was undesirable if not dangerous. Evaluations of individuals and evidence by criminal officials proceeded on the assumption that crime and *état* were inherently and irrevocably linked. There were different types of offenses, some requiring more cunning and ingenuity than others. Thus, official investigation of criminal activity reinforced a hierarchical social vision based on assumptions about the connections between *état*, knowledge, and authority.

This conflation of criminal, epistemological, and social categories provided the police with an interpretative grid that was brought to bear on the evidence and the accused. We can detect this grid in the following case studies, explicitly shaping official lines of questioning and implicitly prompting defensive stances that both reproduced and resisted it. Such suppositions were most evident in the assumption that members of the working populace were the hired instruments of their social superiors, paid to carry out the nasty work and take the blame if caught. Thus, when the police were confronted by a domestic servant like Bonafon or Damiens, their instinctive response was to unmask the aristocrat responsible for masterminding the plot.

Many cases involving *mauvais discours* were presented as one person's word against another's. The police approached this problem empirically by collecting evidence for the purpose of determining an individual's proclivity for crime. Of particular interest were incidents of prior misconduct since crime was explained in moral and ontological rather than structural terms. The police looked to character more than circumstance, convinced that crime was a symptom of personal defect, not social ills. It was customary "in accusations involving His Majesty and which are supported by only one witness, to inform oneself about the accuser, his morals [*moeurs*], his reputation, his fortune, . . . as well as to learn about the life and morals of the accused, his *état*, his fortune, . . . to discover whether he has ever voiced any bitter complaints about the government or anything contrary to the respect and submission he owes the sovereign."[20] The dilemma confronting the police in most instances was that protestations of loyalty were being manipulated and deployed in the service of personal ambition or vengeance, making it impossible to distinguish the *mauvais sujet* from the *fidèle sujet*.

Official responses to cases involving crimes of opinion reflected deeply rooted convictions about the nature and the meaning of the term *fidelité*. The word was omnipresent in the police files and played a crucial role in official decisions regarding guilt and punishment. During interrogations and depositions the police and the people exchanged views concerning what the demonstration of fidelity entailed. These dialogues allow us to identify areas of continuity and rupture between the two understandings of loyalty. The cases examined in the following chapters suggest that there were growing discrepancies between official and popular notions of fidelity. The official line was noticeably consistent during the three decades under study here, 1744–1774.[21] Police officers reiterated an almost formulaic expression of fidelity that provided the criteria for evaluating these crimes. Popular views of fidelity, on the other hand, apparently were expanding and migrating over the same period.

Commissioner Rochebrune was frequently assigned to cases of *mauvais discours*. Rochebrune was a shrewd questioner and routinely integrated a lucid summary of the crown's position regarding fidelity into his interrogations. An example of this tactic can be seen by returning to the case of Gaspard Ferlin, accused of uttering *mauvais discours* against Louis XV by the carter Toussaint Courtin. During his examination on 12 March 1758, Rochebrune reminded Ferlin

> that one owes the king both inner and outer forms of respect, that inner respect consists of the love one feels for his person, accompanied by the fear one has of his power and the belief in his benevolence, and that outer respect consists of words and actions because subjects must honor their sovereigns through their words, always speaking of them with respect and choosing words capable of inspiring others with this same respect, and that, in addition, they must honor them through their actions by obeying the laws, both divine and human, because Saint Paul teaches that all power comes from God, that rulers are established by God, and that those who resist are resisting the order of God.[22]

This citation reveals the fundamental assumptions that shaped official definitions of fidelity and the extent to which these corresponded to a specific conception of royal authority.

Rochebrune upheld a traditional vision of sacred kingship, in which the king derived his authority from God. This insistence on sacredness, as will be seen, was the most contentious element of the official stance, given the impact of the Enlightenment's hostility toward the sacred and its representatives. The sanctity of the king's name and person had to be vigorously defended in order to reinforce his sacred status. Like blasphemy, the utterance of offensive words or the contemplation of certain deeds in connection with his person was a crime of the highest order. This last point cannot be overemphasized. False alarms and derisory language were perceived as threats against a divinely ordained order. The potency of the word, whether spoken, written, or imagined, can only be grasped within the context of the king's sacredness. The word itself was understood as a royal prerogative derived from God and was carefully regulated in terms of its written and spoken expression. The subject's power to offend through speech or writing was linked to this conviction. In refusing to remain silent, especially on topics where the law imposed silence, the subject usurped the king's prerogative.[23]

The constraints on the word were built into the economy of power of the Old Regime and its accompanying culture of ceremonial display. The crown enacted its authority before spectators summoned to witness coronations, royal entries, and public executions. In each of these manifestations a carefully established code of rituals and gestures was accompanied by texts and speeches designed to clarify and instruct. Words implicated all those present, actors and spectators alike, in these scripts of power. Ideally, all public behavior should reinforce respect for the sovereign and submission to his will. This assumption guided Rochebrune's harangue on fidelity, in which he insisted that individuals be circumspect in their speech. As he reminded Jean-Louis Langlois, a hack pamphleteer arrested in 1765 for addressing offensive letters to the king and the court, "He should honor his king not only with inner respect through attachment and submission to him but also with outer respect, which consists in speaking of him with the greatest circumspection in terms that inspire in others the sentiments with which a loyal subject [*fidèle sujet*] should be intimately penetrated."[24] Nothing should be uttered that could be misconstrued by weak or evil minds. Rochebrune's statement demonstrates the official conviction that fidelity was mutually reinforcing: Proper words would inspire correct behavior and instill appropriate attitudes in others. They could strengthen weak resolve and check manifestation of disloyalty, thereby assisting the crown's officials in the policing of public opinion.

Rochebrune's emphasis on the twofold nature of respect, internal and external, is significant. In monitoring the Parisian populace the police were guided by the conviction that "we often indicate our feelings in our words and that our actions are the touchstones of our feelings."[25] Words and gestures were relied on as clues to character as the exterior world of observation helped map out the hidden recesses of subjectivity inside the individual. Although the two forms of respect, inner and outer, should theoretically coincide, the police were keenly aware that they often did not. This discrepancy cleared a space where private interest could accumulate and eventually override one's sense of loyalty and duty to the crown.

A Society of Policemen

In their study of the Old Regime practice of detaining family members by royal *lettres de cachet,* Arlette Farge and Michel Foucault suggested that "a science of policing was in place in the eighteenth century, that is certain, but not a true police force."[26] Their remark draws attention to the gap between a discourse of public order, be it absolutist or enlightened, and the available resources. In the eighteenth century the administration of Paris was no small feat. The city experienced many of the economic and demographic pressures that accompanied urban growth in preindustrial Europe, such as food shortages and overcrowding. Even though the Parisian police force was the most extensive in Europe, it fell far short of its task in terms of manpower and means. To compensate for these limitations, the police attempted to mobilize the populace in the struggle against disorder and crime.

Several historians have noted that eighteenth-century Paris operated as a collection of self-regulating communities, such as guilds and neighborhoods.[27] This arrangement relied on internal group mechanisms rather than external agents to enforce social cohesion and monitor behavior. It mobilized the populace to police itself by integrating the duties of police into the definition of a *fidèle sujet*. Thus, fidelity required that subjects report offensive or suspicious behavior to the appropriate authorities without delay. Failure to denounce incidents, particularly those involving *mauvais discours,* was interpreted as tacit support for the seditious views being expressed. The archives testify to the success of this project, since many individuals did rush to the police, often prefacing their denunciations with the following words: "as a loyal subject, he believed he was obliged to reveal what he knew about attacks on the state and religion."[28]

It was clear to many of Louis XV's subjects that their policing role was not a voluntary one. It was, in fact, one of their most fundamental obligations to the state and the sovereign. As the master weavers Joseph Clement and Louis Belleguele, of Amiens, asserted in their allegations against one of their fellow masters, François Routtier, "In denouncing, as guards of their guild, a public utterance which offended the royal Majesty, they had only done what the law required, failing which they risked being considered accomplices to the crime . . . it had been a patriotic act worthy of loyal subjects."[29] In legal terms, an individual who maintained silence in cases involving physical or verbal assaults on the king's person would be considered an accomplice to the crime. Yet the police were never entirely effective in elevating denunciation to a civic duty because the gesture was so easily misconstrued and adapted to undesirable ends. Some individuals delegitimated the endeavor by manipulating police officers with false information couched in a language of loyalty. Others simply refused to play the role of policeman.

Many men and women did not feel comfortable informing on their friends, family, and neighbors. Affective ties created allegiances that could, and often did, conflict with loyalty to the king. Others were unwilling to transform themselves into professional informants. As Jean Moriceau de La Motte, the outspoken bailiff arrested in 1757 for posting seditious flyers, explained to Lieutenant of Police Sartine, "The profession of denouncer had never been to his liking."[30] Yet, La Motte discovered that informing was not an optional but a compulsory activity when Sartine reminded him that "in such circumstances every good and loyal subject is obliged to inform the judicial authorities."[31]

Ultimately, however, the problem confronting the police resulted from excessive rather than insufficient zeal on the part of the populace. The police

were arguably too successful in communicating their message and its accompanying sense of vulnerability. They soon found themselves dupes of
the very populace they sought to control. From 1744 to 1774, particularly in
the aftermath of the Damiens affair, the majority of cases classified as *mauvais discours* involved slander or false information. Individuals, sensing official susceptibility to promises of secret information, consciously sought to
take advantage of the situation. Recognizing their heightened importance as
purveyors of a desired commodity, individuals produced the very rumors
and threats the crown was so eager to track and eradicate. The police were
not unaware of this development, as their response to Jean Philippe
Paquet's letters warning of a conspiracy against the monarchy in 1764 make
clear: "It must be concluded that Paquet, whose brain has certainly become
addled by misery, believed he could render himself necessary and important
by inventing these fables." The memorandum ends with the observation
that it would be too dangerous to release Paquet and recommends sending
him to "the islands so that he will be completely forgotten."[32] The police
were never truly alarmed about Paquet's alleged conspiracy, although they
did follow up his leads just to be sure. Nonetheless, he had to be punished
for pestering the court, generating a false alarm, and making a mockery of
royal justice. During the brief moments while the police worked to distinguish the *vrai* (true) from the *vraisemblable* (seemingly true), individuals
like Paquet enjoyed the upper hand. When, however, the false tales were
unraveled, the perpetrators were severely punished since their actions offended not only the king but also his appointed servants.

The police responded to the chaotic proliferation of lies and calumny by
enforcing stricter criteria for acceptable proof. Thus, individuals who found
themselves being interrogated frequently received a detailed list of instructions on how they *should* have reacted in a given situation. For example, in
late November 1757 Alexandre Louis Marchal, a journeyman hatter from
Paris, claimed to have met a stranger in a tavern who had boasted of a plot
to murder Louis XV. One month later, during an interrogation, Commissioner Rochebrune berated Marchal for his incompetent handling of an important situation and clarified what would have been appropriate if his story
were true:

[Marchal] was told that a stranger who shared such criminal plans displayed great confidence in the person to whom he confided them and that such revelations ought to have prompted the Defendant to ask the stranger to identify himself, . . . to find out where he lived and where he was coming from, as well as to discover the source of the stranger's grievances against the king . . . that the Defendant should never have allowed this opportunity for questions to escape because he would have been better able to support his allegations with some concrete evidence.[33]

This quotation illustrates two important points. First, it reveals the pedagogical aspect of police interrogations, whereby commissioners sought to improve the policing skills of the populace. Second, it demonstrates a keen sensitivity on the part of the police to narrative inconsistencies and unsubstantiated allegations.

If a subject were to be an effective policeman, he had to learn the rules and follow them. Unrestrained accusations produced chaos and derided royal officials. As Commissioner Rochebrune reminded Paquet in response to his vague information about a plot to overthrow the monarchy, "Such warnings should never be ventured, and once one makes such statements, one must be ready to support them with proof sufficient to secure a conviction . . . that what he advanced was more the effect of an overheated imagination than a mind enlightened and instructed on its subject."[34] Rochebrune's reprimand reflected his frustration at being confronted with an individual who had turned the very principles of policing against the police themselves. He, along with his colleagues, found their mission distorted by the proliferation of red herrings and wild-goose chases. He recognized that such abuses ultimately made a mockery of the entire judicial apparatus and for this reason alone had to be severely punished even if they could not be eliminated.

In most cases involving calumny the evidence did not survive official scrutiny, and the defendants either retracted their initial statements or admitted their lies. Even when the alarms proved false, the authorities had to determine appropriate punishment for such unconventional yet unquestionably delinquent behavior. These incidents were problematic because so much of French jurisprudence followed the dictate of precedent and it was difficult to classify cases that did not conform to traditional categories of criminal behavior. Although murmurings against the king had existed as long as the monarchy itself, they acquired greater potency in the eighteenth century with the rise in literacy and the increased availability of printed matter. Verbal utterances that had previously been ephemeral were more likely to be captured in ink, ensuring them both a longer life and a wider audience than before. These circumstances augmented the crown's sense of vulnerability with regard to the populace and explains its diminishing threshold of tolerance for irreverent remarks.

In general, the perpetrators of these crimes were severely punished. Many spent the rest of their lives in prison, others were sent to the galleys, and a few were sentenced to death. Some who worked assiduously to demonstrate remorse were rewarded with exile or placement in a religious order. The gravity of the official response reflected a consensus that the individuals who became involved in such crimes threatened the social order. Whether the king was in any real danger was beside the point. Individuals were condemned on the basis of their decision to invent such tales and its implications. These assumptions were factored into the calculation of threats and punishments in equations than can appear unbalanced if they are overlooked.

Disease and the Body Social

It is important to pause and consider the fears and assumptions that underlay the expressions *mauvais discours* and *mauvais sujet*. For the police, the *mauvais sujet* was the inversion of the *fidèle sujet*. Just as fidelity should ideally reinforce appropriate behavior and attitudes, seditious utterances would necessarily inspire delinquent acts. These convictions about the ineluctable connections between speech, thought, and action are important because they explain why the police classified vague threats and lies as serious offenses. To grasp them, we must examine the analogies between crime and disease that framed the Old Regime's approach to crime and criminality.

Police officials saw themselves as doctors of the body social and metaphorically linked crime and disease. *Mauvais discours* were the equivalent of infectious germs, threatening those exposed to them. Just as some individuals were at higher risk of disease than others, some minds were more susceptible to the lure of dangerous ideas. Most vulnerable were men and women whose low birth and lack of education guaranteed a lesser capacity for rational thought than their social superiors had. Although the Enlightenment view of human nature emphasized man's rationality, the police felt obliged to qualify this noble assertion. For them, reason was not distributed evenly across the social spectrum. On the contrary, it was mapped directly onto the hierarchy of the Old Regime, its strength dwindling as one descended the social ladder. If human beings were a mixture of reason and passion, then passion was the dominant attribute of the unprivileged masses. Thus, inflammatory rhetoric posed the greatest threat to the majority of the king's subjects, whose feeble reasoning powers offered little resistance to their volatile emotions. Given this logic, the police instinctively sought to remove the *mauvais sujet* from society as a preventive measure against a contagious disease.

Another distinguishing feature of the *mauvais sujet* was an unregulated or overexcited imagination. The word *imagination* recurs throughout police reports as a descriptive and analytical term directly associated with criminal behavior. Police commissioners described many of the individuals arrested as having "une imagination échauffée" or "une imagination déreglée." Imagination provided a central reference point in the dialogues between the police and the people, often relied on as an explanation for the origins of subversive ideas and texts. Unlike its other Enlightenment incarnations, imagination had exclusively pejorative connotations for the police, who saw it as the source of a host of undesirable activities.[35] Imagination in these cases was assigned to a distinct social milieu, that of the unprivileged, and to their engagement in literary activities, especially the reading of novels. Since printed matter stimulated imaginative faculties with unpredictable and often pernicious results, it was imperative that access to texts be limited to those who could indulge without risk. Reading was bound to lead untrained minds into situations where they did not belong and were likely to err. An excited imagination was frequently likened to a state of intoxication, in which rational inclinations were ignored in favor of impetuous decisions.

Taken together, these assumptions about what constituted a *mauvais sujet* linked social status, intellectual capacity, and proclivity for crime in an interlocking grid that the police relied on to guide them in their task of maintaining public order. Just as they worked to clear the Parisian streets of sewage and refuse, the police aimed to contain the dissemination of undesirable ideas. Both contributed to the state of public health, physical and ideological, and thus both fell within their purview. The official response to the case of Valerie de Brulz du Tilleul vividly illustrates this point. Arrested in 1761 for denouncing a plot to kill Louis XV, Mme du Tilleul failed to substantiate her allegations. Frustrated by her endless series of lies and fantasies, the police refused to release her even though they were soon convinced that the king's life was not at risk. Inspector d'Hémery's memorandum assessing Du Tilleul's situation captured official concerns about the threats such individuals posed to society at large: "Given that this woman is dangerous and garrulous, it is not advisable to leave her in France even should she be confined in an asylum because of her wicked tongue, which would make an impression on evil or weak minds."[36] Du Tilleul was relatively fortunate to be released with an exile from the realm. In other instances risky individuals were locked away indefinitely without legal redress, indicating the relative lack of control the police thought they had over outspoken subjects once they were free to roam the streets.

The procedure in cases involving crimes of opinion was always shaped by the imperatives of secrecy and minimizing exposure. Thus, the police worked to identify the culprit and make a speedy arrest to prevent the seditious germs from spreading. The goal was to remove the *mauvais sujet* as discreetly as possible since arrests could provoke a scene and provide an occasion for an offensive exchange detrimental to public opinion. It was preferable, for example, to make arrests or prison transfers under cover of night. Thus, in 1765, when Mme Renart, the wife of an innkeeper in Reims, was arrested for *mauvais discours*, the *procureur* in charge of the case emphasized in his report that all precautions had been taken to ensure that the arrest was made at night, "without creating any noise or scandal."[37]

Mauvais sujets and the views they expressed publicly embarrassed the crown. Like public executions, which became excuses for popular protest rather than displays of royal power, *mauvais sujets* were glaring symbols of the limits of royal authority. They threatened to dispel the absolutist myth of a good king and his loving subjects by calling attention to discontent and grievances. Moreover, the process of investigating accusations forced the police to question witnesses concerning the *mauvais propos*. Rather than focus so much attention on undesirable topics, officials often pursued investigations indirectly through informal spies. While evidence was being gathered, the suspect was detained until his or her innocence or guilt was established.[38] Royal officials recognized the delicate balance that had to be maintained between the investigation of such incidents and their repression. Chancellor Lamoignan summarized the crown's policy in these affairs when he wrote: "We must try to suppress them [*mauvais discours*] rather than pursue investigations that only serve to create a scandal."[39] Furthermore, rumors that the king's life was in danger were sure to provoke anxiety among the populace, hardly desirable from the standpoint of public order.

Although the tracking and repression of *mauvais discours* was quite intentionally shrouded in mystery, the veil was periodically lifted to reveal horrific spectacles of punishment and retribution. The maintenance and manipulation of this tension was a distinguishing feature of the crown's policing mechanism. Thus, the Old Regime's system of criminal justice operated within this curious dialectic between secrecy and publicity, the effectiveness of the one inherently dependent on the existence of the other. This logic can be detected, for instance, in the staging of Damiens's execution.[40] As Commissioner Rochebrune explained to Jerome Michel in April 1758, fear of similar punishment should have checked his rash tongue if fidelity to the king had not. Michel had been arrested for boasting of his intention to imitate Damiens. Rochebrune reminded him of Damiens's ordeal and asked, "How could he have wanted to execute the plan he had formulated of imitating the rascal Damiens, whose horrible sufferings should have dissuaded him from pursuing such a scheme even if the love, respect, and attachment he should feel for the king, so appropriately named the Well-Loved [*Bien-Aimé*] were incapable of deterring him?"[41] Rochebrune's reprimand clarifies the official understanding of the role of law and exemplary punishment in the discussion of crime. These were measures of last resort, taken when the individual's internal policing mechanisms of loyalty and respect broke down and failed to check his or her deviant behavior. The public execution was calibrated within the register of criminal proceedings to achieve its desired effect. It was not relied on as the primary deterrent but was reserved for spectacular moments of royal intervention in exceptional cases.

The rigorous response to *mauvais discours* cases arguably reflected royal weakness more than royal strength. Harsh punishments meted out for false alarms and fictitious plots attested to official frustration toward individuals who were consciously manipulating the desire for public order in the service of private interest. According to Richard Andrews, the spectacles of exemplary executions should be read as efforts to mask the crown's failings given all the criminals and accomplices who succeeded in slipping through its repressive grasp.[42] This last point should be kept in mind when confronting cases such as that of La Chaux, in chapter 5, whose final parlementary sentence struck contemporaries as excessively severe in proportion to the crime.

The police were notably exasperated by the proliferation of calumnious accusations in the aftermath of the Damiens affair. For example, the intendant of Moulins, in a report to the secretary of state, the comte de Saint Florentin, insisted on the need to act with severity in repressing calumny: "It is extremely important that we stop such calumnious accusations from spreading. We have already seen several examples inspired by vengeance and animosity alone . . . it is only by severely punishing the calumniators that we can put a stop to such calumnies."[43] Thus, many individuals saw their lies and false alarms classified as crimes of treason and punished as such. Their initial shock gave way to dismay when they discovered the heavy penalty to be paid for their miscalculation.

Official frustration grew over the course of the eighteenth century as more French subjects assumed the right not only of formulating political opinions but also of expressing them.[44] Since there were few channels available for articulating grievances, individuals resorted to lies and ruses as a means of communicating with their government. This pattern disrupted the normal flow of information between the king, his ministers, and his subjects. This point is illustrated by the case of Jean Baptiste Manem, who decided to go to the Prussian court in 1757 after his requests for an audience with Louis XV had been repeatedly ignored. Manem claimed that he had information concerning a conspiracy to topple the French monarchy and establish a republic in Marseilles. During the interrogation Commissioner Rochebrune reprimanded Manem for overstepping the confines of his *état* and reminded him of his duties: "In society each citizen should concern himself with his own affairs or with his work, and . . . if the accused had political views that could be of some service, he should have had his discoveries printed rather than resort to roundabout channels and anonymous letters to depict the talents he believed he possessed, and finally, . . . the ministers to whom he had addressed himself . . . had made clear by their silence that he was not as enlightened in such matters as he imagined himself to be."[45] Rochebrune's sarcasm could not hide his discomfort in the face of Manem's willful disobedience. One senses that he was implicitly addressing a much larger public, that Manem's case was symptomatic of a pattern of inappropriate behavior the police found increasingly difficult to contain.

Crime and the Language of Sin

If officials defined crime through a secular language of disease, their moral understanding of their mission was grounded in Christian teachings regarding sin. Thus, like the age in which they lived, the argument the police relied on to frame and legitimate their task was both sacred and secular. Crime not only threatened the health of the social body, it was viewed as an attack on the divine order that underlay and justified society. This connection was most evident in cases involving offenses to the king, whose person represented the fusion of sacred and secular authority on earth. Consequently, violation of the king's laws constituted an affront against God, who had appointed his minister to rule in his place. Such reasoning provided a second layer of motives for the police, who felt obliged to repress crime if only to avoid provoking divine wrath. The extended ritual of public execution for capital offenders aimed not only to display the king's authority and deter future offenders but also to realign the community with God through the criminal's public confession. It simultaneously purged the community of the offending member while affirming the rights of the sovereign and the judicial process over which he presided. It was, in Foucault's words, "a ceremonial in which a momentarily injured sovereignty is reconstituted" for all to see.[46]

A similar logic informed the more mundane rituals of police investigation on the microcosmic level, where the invincibility of the king had to meet the challenge raised by those who dared to violate his laws or utter his name in vain. Not only did judicial authorities borrow from the church's discourse on sin but they integrated elements of religious ritual into all stages of the judicial process, from the black robes worn by the judges to the ubiquitous confessor at the scaffold. The emphasis on confession, guilt, and absolution distinguished the legal procedure of the Old Regime from its modern counterparts; yet this did not mean that justice was either illusory or arbitrary.

Although judicial procedure was permeated by religious rites and references, legal culture was also resolutely scientific in the eighteenth century. The methods established in the 1670 ordinance on criminal procedure were essentially investigative rather than repressive. The code offered a system of rules for investigating evidence, ascertaining guilt, and determining the appropriate punishment. The process of subjecting the defendant and the crime to careful scrutiny was slow and onerous, especially for the innocent.[47] The methods relied on for evaluating evidence and assigning responsibility were analytical and empirical.

Police officials frequently consulted experts such as doctors and handwriting specialists to verify evidence and uncover lies. Whereas experts represented the penetration of scientific culture into judicial thinking, religious trappings imbued legal procedure with the mystery and power of otherworldly authority. The sacred borrowings helped establish the appropriate roles of judge and penitent and elicited the desired postures of equity, humility, and candor. This overlapping of scientific expertise and religious ritual represented the joint efforts of the monarchy and the church to maintain social harmony and public order in premodern Europe.

The combined authority of throne and altar carried considerable moral weight and powers of intimidation against offenders. Individuals who found themselves hauled into the Bastille or the Châtelet entered an unfamiliar terrain whose rules had to be quickly learned. It was difficult to communicate with friends and family. Once arrested, the accused was surrounded by a wall of silence interrupted by periodic visits of criminal officials and prison attendants. The defendant played a critical role in his or her own case since he or she was presumed to be the best source of information concerning the charges on record. Defendants were never formally informed of the incriminating accusations but had to infer them from the questions posed during the interrogations. The questions were designed to elicit information about the crime, to gather details and determine whether the evidence was sufficient to prosecute the accused. If the evidence was not sufficient, the defendant was released. Unlike modern liberal jurisprudence, Old Regime justice was not grounded in the principle of presumed innocence. Nonetheless, it should be stressed that the criteria for proof of guilt were strict, rational, and carefully documented.[48]

Most of the cases involving *mauvais discours* were resolved without a trial. After intensive questioning, the police determined the punishment based on their assessment of the accused and the evidence. Depending on their decision, individuals who were not released could be detained in prison indefinitely, transferred to less expensive hospital facilities, or exiled from Paris or the realm. Like Christian teachings on sin, issues of intentionality were central to official evaluations of criminal behavior. It is important to recall that Old Regime jurisprudence defined crime as a combination of intention and act. A crime was not simply an act prohibited and penalized by law. It also included the malicious disposition of the individual who knowingly and intentionally committed a wrong.[49] In the cases examined in this book the question of intent was the pivotal one, outweighing more tangible factors such as harm inflicted or retribution.

Since most of these incidents involved alleged or fictitious regicidal plots, the police had to focus their efforts on revealing malice aforethought and the desire to do harm rather than its actual execution. The legal culture of the Old Regime was arguably less concerned with the crime as an event than it was with evil volition. This principle is significant because it explains the efforts expended to investigate the five cases that follow. From the perspective of the twentieth-century observer, the time and energy seems unwarranted given the mendacious nature of the threats involved.

The determination of intent rested on a set of assumptions about the human personality rooted in Christian conceptions of morality and sin. For the police, human nature was the site of an ongoing struggle between conscience and rationality on the one hand and a proclivity for sin and crime on the other. Worldly temptations and impulsive passions continually threatened to overwhelm man's reasoning capacities. Thus, police officers and magistrates saw themselves as the secular counterparts of their ecclesiastical peers: both were engaged in a battle to teach, instill, and reinforce right thinking and moral conduct.[50] These authorities envisioned a society structured around an interlocking set of corrective mechanisms, from family and guild to confession and policing. Each worked to correct and contain a chronic offender, although some individuals managed to slip through the gaps. In their efforts to determine an individual's criminal capacity the police turned to these auxiliary units for evidence of prior misconduct to help them establish that the individual had a delinquent or malicious personality. The guiding principle was that evil did not spring out of a vacuum but reflected a pattern of behavior and thought.

In his study of confessional practices in early modern Europe, Jean Delumeau emphasized the role of intentionality in the debates concerning the distinctions between venial and mortal sins.[51] Ecclesiastical determination of guilt was based on the extent to which an individual had willingly consented to or planned an act he knew to be wrong. This definition echoes the legal notion of evil volition. In the course of the eighteenth century, according to Delumeau, a concerted movement arose within the church to enforce more rigorous confessional standards. This ecclesiastical reaction against laxism and probabilism may have influenced prevailing attitudes toward crime and guilt. Questions of premeditation and intention were central to the classification of crimes. It was important to consider the amount of time and effort devoted to plotting these acts given the rule that the more contrived the crime, the more serious the offense.

A few cases of *mauvais discours* were deemed sufficiently serious to merit a trial, as the example of La Chaux in chapter 5 demonstrates. Lies alluding to the king's death constituted capital offenses and were defined as crimes of *lèse-majesté*. A verdict of guilty normally led to an extended ritual of repentance and execution. It was customary for individuals condemned to death to be tortured before their execution in an effort to extract every ounce of information concerning accomplices. Torture, known as the *question préparatoire*, could be ordered only in cases of crimes subject to the death penalty and was strictly regulated. It aimed to elicit a full confession when evidence remained inconclusive or contradictory in order to complete the proof of guilt. Moreover, it was necessary for the criminal to purge his or her conscience in preparation for absolution. According to both theologians and jurists, an individual who confessed guilt earned salvation in the process of sacrificing his or her life to the law.[52]

The persistence of torture in Old Regime criminal justice makes a twentieth-century reader wince and seems jarringly inconsistent with the rationalist and humanitarian tendencies of the Enlightenment. It is important to remember, however, that torture was more a vestige of the inquisitorial techniques that had guided criminal justice since the sixteenth century than a foreshadowing of modern totalitarian regimes. Torture was never a systematic part of summary justice, nor was it integral to an ideology of elimination. Moreover, both torture and the death penalty were on the decline in the eighteenth century. Torture was a prominent target in the philosophes's campaign for criminal law reform, and historians have discerned changes in legal practices decades before the codes themselves were actually overhauled and rewritten to reflect new beliefs about criminal behavior, sovereignty, and punishment.[53]

The form and content of the police investigation remained the same whether or not a case went to court. Commissioners focused their energies on persuading the defendant to confess his or her crime.[54] In most cases the issue of proof was problematic. Evidence was often incomplete or tendentious, consisting of only the testimony of a single witness or a similarity of handwriting. Defendants frequently contradicted themselves from one interrogation to another, especially in cases involving calumnious accusations and false alarms. Confessions themselves were scrutinized on the basis of strict criteria. In order to be convincing proof a confession had to provide a coherent, sustained admission of guilt.[55] A full avowal by the prisoner was a triumph for the police since it provided incontestable support for their suspicions and affirmed the mechanism of criminal justice itself.

In their efforts to coax a prisoner into confessing, police officers played upon the analogies between crime and sin. Like their spiritual colleagues, commissioners worked to gain the confidence of the defendant in order to encourage him or her to relieve a guilty conscience. In exchange for an avowal the accused was promised peace of mind and spiritual salvation. Thus, in 1757, when Commissioner Rochebrune suspected that Toussaint Courtin had invented a story about a plot to assassinate Louis XV, he impressed upon Courtin that "it is better for his conscience that he confess the truth rather than commit perjury."[56] It was not easy to establish this bond of trust because, like the relationship between priests and penitents, this dialogue was grounded in fundamental inequalities.[57] Moreover, the efficacy of the threat of eternal damnation waned as the century progressed because of the philosophes' attack on the church and the spread of anticlerical sentiment.

Everyone summoned to give testimony before the police swore an oath of truth. The violation of this oath compounded an individual's guilt, constituting an additional offense against God. The police consciously relied on this oath to sanctify the criminal proceedings conducted, and its compelling force should not be underestimated, as the following exchange between Commissioner Rochebrune and Michel Mitré Touche makes explicit. Touche was arrested in February 1760 for writing a set of anonymous letters to Louis XV in which he vilified the king's mistress, Mme de Pompadour. Despite Rochebrune's persistence, Touche refused to admit that he had authored offensive letters. Rochebrune mustered divine wrath in his efforts to pressure Touche into a confession:

> ROCHEBRUNE: Asked if he were convinced that the oath he had just taken was a religious act.
>
> TOUCHE: Answered yes.
>
> ROCHEBRUNE: Asked if he were persuaded that there existed a God who knew the most secret thoughts and who punished lies and perjury.
>
> TOUCHE: Answered yes.
>
> ROCHEBRUNE: Asked if he knew that lying entailed speaking against one's conscience and contrary to the truth and that to perjure oneself was to confirm while under oath that a fact was false when one knew it to be true.
>
> TOUCHE: Said that he understood all the horror of perjury . . . that he was persuaded . . . of the truth of what we had just explained to him.
>
> ROCHEBRUNE: Pointed out to him . . . that if he were lying . . . he was submitting himself to divine vengeance.[58]

Touche may have been innocent. It is more likely, however, that like many of his contemporaries, Touche was less awed by ecclesiastical authority than he was by its secular counterparts. He opted to defend himself against the tangible forces of the crown even if this meant risking the ultimate salvation of his soul.

By borrowing language and arguments from the ritual of confession, the police recreated a context that would have been familiar to most of Louis XV's subjects. It was not unusual for prisoners who were detained for extended periods to accept these criminal officials as secular substitutes for spiritual advisers. Many transferred their anxieties onto the figure of the lieutenant of police, pleading with him for pardon while seeking atonement for their misdemeanors. They confessed to him in writing, drafting letters and *mémoires* into which they poured their hopes and fears.

Just as the priest mediated between divine grace and venial sin, the lieutenant of police provided a channel through which the crown's subjects could appeal for a royal pardon. Mercy, or pardon, was an attribute of the divinity embedded in the mystique of sacred kingship.[59] When the king chose to exercise this gift of forgiveness, he acted as God in redeeming a lost soul from eternal damnation. The king's intervention momentarily suspended the normal workings of justice while collapsing the chasm that separated the sovereign from his subjects. Pardons, like executions, were carefully choreographed spectacles, displaying royal authority through the miracle of grace rather than the force of punishment. Pardon was a necessary ideological underpinning of the Old Regime's logic of criminal justice, requiring that all supplicants first acknowledge their guilt, and hence the king's law, before applying for forgiveness. The belief in the king's mercy, however distant and illusory, was infinitely appealing and persuasive. It provided a glimmer of hope for absolution, and prisoners clung to it tenaciously. Clemency was one of the king's most enduring and endearing graces from the perspective of his most humble subjects.

Police officers were remarkably consistent in terms of the criteria they used to evaluate defendants' character and proclivity for crime. The police subjected most prisoners to a series of interrogations in order to discover contradictions in their claims. Individuals who elaborated on or retracted an initial account were immediately suspect. So, too, were those who seemed too forthcoming. The police were aware that there were individuals who made a career out of denunciation, seeking to profit from their voluntary services. It was important to distinguish integrity from ambition within the web of motives that prompted these allegations. In all instances the police made a concerted effort to gather detailed personal data to illuminate an individual's behavior prior to incarceration. In assessing an individual's potential for criminality, the police considered everything from familial relations to financial assets, drinking habits to religious practices.

Although most of those arrested denied any intention to offend or alarm the king, the police refused to accept these arguments. Clearly, defendants needed a different strategy to exculpate themselves. From an official perspective, any individual who felt comfortable manipulating the threat of the king's death was by definition dangerous. Intentionality involved more than a mere statement of motive. The police held individuals responsible for the implications of their actions no matter what their professed intentions may have been. Thinking certain thoughts was regarded as a crime whether or not one succeeded in executing them. A *fidèle sujet* was, by definition, incapable of contemplating the king's death without revulsion and horror. The absence of these intuitive restraining impulses was symptomatic of a pronounced lack of respect and affection for the king. This detachment, no matter what the accused might assert to the contrary, was the indelible mark of a *mauvais sujet*.

· ❧ ·

Official assumptions regarding fidelity, *mauvais sujets*, and crime shaped the investigation and interpretation of the incidents explored in the following chapters. They cannot be ignored for they underlay the types of questions posed and the information that was eventually recorded. While public opinion about the monarchy vacillated considerably in the course of Louis XV's reign, official definitions of fidelity and duty were noticeably unvarying. As captured in a police dossier, the confrontations between the crown's officials and its subjects are revealing. They highlight precise areas of consensus and disagreement concerning the nature and boundaries of royal authority.

It remains to be seen whether official concerns were misplaced or exaggerated with regard to the proliferation of false alarms and calumnious accusations. It is ironic that in their efforts to contain *mauvais discours* the police actually sustained them, temporarily through their solicited repetition, and permanently by committing them to paper. There is no doubt that the individuals involved in such schemes were taking enormous risks. Yet it is not so clear that their efforts were directed primarily against either the person of the king or the institution of the monarchy. Their grievances reflected disappointment as much as resentment, frustration more than anger. We need to listen more closely to what individual subjects have to tell us about Louis XV and kingship in order to ascertain the depth of popular disenchantment with the monarchy.

The police were unanimous in their conviction that these were very serious crimes, whether imaginary or not. What disturbed them most profoundly was the evidence of growing callousness toward and disdain for the principles of sacred kingship and its judicial institutions. Commissioner Rochebrune captured official concern in his interrogation of Jean Baptiste Manem on 18 May 1757. Manem had just admitted that he had lied about a conspiracy to kill Louis XV and the Dauphin. In his rebuke of Manem, Rochebrune inquired, "Is it permissible for a subject to play with his King and the presumptive heir to the throne in such a way?"[60] The most interesting word in this question is the verb *play* because it captures both the prankish quality of these crimes and the explicit mockery of revered officials and institutions that constituted a grave offense. It also reinforces the paternalistic bonds that structured relations between the king and his subjects, suggesting that mischievous subjects, like children, needed to be disciplined by their stern and prudent elders, the police. Yet, as the ensuing pages demonstrate, playing in these cases was not innocuous, for the stakes were high both for the crown and for its subjects. Playing easily escalated into a more serious challenge as mockery assumed a critical edge and jest turned into crime. The police were fully aware of these subversive implications even if those arrested were not. The right to "play with the king" was a more radical demand than it appears at first glance and could assume various guises, encompassing a range of claims and grievance. It inevitably constituted a challenge to royal authority on two levels, explicitly through an individual's imposing his or her views on the king personally and implicitly because such presumption broke the boundaries of silence the crown had established in the name of duty, loyalty, and public order.

Chapter 2

Fiction and Authority
in the *Tanastès* Affair

· ❧ ·

Louis XV est ressucité
c'est une pure vérité
avec son peuple il chantera
alléluya

Décampez vite Châteauroux
du peuple évitez le courroux
si non il vous lapidera
alléluya

Grande Reine consolez vous
votre sort va devenir doux
toujours Louis vous chérira
alléluya

Quand avec vous il couchera
Je suis sur qu'il vous fera
un beau garçon qui chantera
alléluya[1]

IN THE SUMMER OF 1745 Lieutenant General of Police Feydeau de Marville learned that a clandestinely printed novel entitled *Tanastès* was circulating at Versailles and in Paris. Published anonymously and designed as a roman à clef, *Tanastès* satirizes the king's recent illness at Metz as well as his adulterous relationships with his mistresses. Like the popular song quoted above, *Tanastès* addresses public concerns about Louis XV's sexual conduct with an unwelcome measure of candor and lubricious detail. Little could be done about the ribald song, but the text merited a police investigation. Marville ordered his officers to confiscate the offensive novel and arrest the individuals involved in its publication. The police rounded up twenty-one individuals, working their way back from booksellers in Paris and Versailles to Widow Ferrand's print shop in Rouen. The last person to be identified was the author, who, ironically, turned out to be a resident of the royal palace. On 29 August 1745 Marie-Magdeleine Bonafon, a chambermaid at Versailles, was arrested and taken to the Bastille for questioning.[2]

Marie Bonafon, who was twenty-eight years old at the time of her incarceration, was employed in the household of the princesse de Montauban. The police records indicated that Bonafon had written several plays and a novel before *Tanastès*. She had miscalculated, however, when she decided to publish *Tanastès* in the hope of earning some extra money. Although *Tanastès* was designed as a fairy tale, "it was easy to detect insulting allusions to the king, the queen, Mme de Châteauroux, the duc de Richelieu, the Cardinal de Fleury, and other great ladies of the court."[3] As the police correctly feared, the French reading public, including members of the court, among whom the novel was especially popular, had no trouble deciphering the thinly veiled allegory. The tale offered an explicit condemnation of the king's sexual philandering and a warning he could not afford to ignore.

Tanastès is an allegory set in the mythical land of Zarim/France in which a false king, Agamil, is substituted for the heir to the throne, Tanastès. This elaborate plot allowed Bonafon to address widespread concerns about Louis XV's behavior without holding the king personally responsible. The novel is brimming with allusions to sensitive issues, including adultery, and lingering concerns about Louis XV's integrity as a ruler. Despite their invented names, all of the characters in the novel correspond to actual members of the French court. Furthermore, Bonafon introduced a note of caution into discussions concerning the legitimacy of royal authority. She suggested that since power could be abused, it did not always merit unqualified obedience.

This is the first of two chapters dealing with cases during the period prior to Damiens's attempted assassination of Louis XV on 5 January 1757. In both instances, the primary target of criticism was the royal mistress and not the king. Two issues underlay this decision. First, it reflects a conscious decision to shield the king from direct attack. By displacing criticism from the king to his mistress, Bonafon was able to express dissatisfaction or disappointment without undermining the principle of royal authority itself. Second, the attack on the mistress reflected deeper changes in French attitudes toward the family, sexuality, and women. In place of the court and its aristocratic ethos of libertinage and largesse, the eighteenth century offered the model of the egalitarian public sphere, which rested on the bourgeois family and the cult of domesticity. This evolution in attitudes about conjugal relations, sexuality, and gender roles would certainly have altered expectations about the preeminent couple in the realm, the king and the queen. Furthermore, recent feminist scholarship has suggested that the emerging public sphere, which offered an institutional alternative to absolutism, was explicitly hostile to women's participation in politics. Therefore, the campaign against Louis XV's mistresses reflected hostility not only toward royal authority and the aristocratic society that sustained and was sustained by it but also toward women's place in the political sphere.[4] To recover the full impact of Bonafon's text, it must be read in the light of these ongoing social and political debates that were transforming French culture in the age of Enlightenment.

Royal mistresses played a pivotal role in shaping perceptions of the king in the history of the French monarchy. They enjoyed an officially recognized position at the court based purely on royal favor. Like all royal favorites, mistresses aroused misgivings about the king's independence. They were deeply embroiled in court politics because of the power they allegedly exercised over the king in the boudoir and frequently became the centers of factions, identified with specific policies and individuals whose careers they promoted. In the eighteenth century mistresses were consistently implicated in the most damaging charges leveled against the crown, namely, of instigating a famine plot to starve the people.[5] Evidence from police archives and other contemporary sources indicates that hostility toward the king's mistress traversed the Old Regime's social spectrum. Members of the Third Estate joined their social superiors in denouncing the king's female favorite and his lascivious conduct. The mistress owed her success to her ability to satisfy the king's basest needs. Her influence drew public attention to the weakness of his mortal body and helped subvert the juridical fiction of the king's two bodies. Although historically the king's mistress had been a symbol of regal potency and virility, eighteenth-century public opinion identified her with royal weakness and debauchery. Moreover, the mistress represented an older politics of secrecy in an age that demanded transparency and accountability from its rulers.

Because of her proximity to the king, the mistress's fate could not be separated from that of her royal lover. The police of eighteenth-century Paris were aware of these connections even if the perpetrators of *mauvais discours* claimed not to be. Consequently, commissioners and inspectors made a concerted effort to track down and arrest individuals who mocked or threatened Mme de Châteauroux and, later, the marquise de Pompadour and Mme du Barry. They correctly perceived that dangerous patterns of criticism were being established that could eventually be transferred onto the king himself. Such concerns were evident in their investigation of the *Tanastès* affair and account for the thick dossier the case produced, in addition to the confiscated copies of Bonafon's novel.

Bonafon's case raises the question of the role of criticism within a monarchical polity. Unlike the English monarchy, the French monarchy did not acknowledge the legitimacy of a loyal opposition. Public discussion or assembly was forbidden unless it was desired by the king and conducted under his auspices. Although Bonafon's ultimate goal may have been to instruct and restore, not destroy, her behavior was classified as criminal and punished accordingly. It should be recalled that the theory of sacred kingship required that a certain distance be maintained between the king and his subjects. The act of fictionalizing the king demonstrated a psychological familiarity that threatened to dissolve this distance. In Bonafon's novel Louis XV was stripped of his quasi-divine status and reduced to the status of one character among many. His fate depended not on divine providence but, like that of all the characters, on the strokes of the author's pen. In casting Louis XV as a character in her novel, Bonafon, no matter what her intentions, had subjected her sovereign to the leveling power of ink.

The Legacy of Metz

Tanastès is best understood as the product of a tense political moment in which mounting expectations, followed by crushing disappointment, shook the French people's faith in their divinely appointed king. The death of the Cardinal de Fleury, Louis XV's chief minister, on 29 January 1743 unleashed power struggles within the court to secure the vacant spot as trusted councilor to the king. Louis XV, however, surprised everyone by deciding that he would not replace Fleury but would rule without a chief minister. This decision signaled a victory for the secretaries of state, who would now meet individually with the king to determine policy. The king himself would coordinate and oversee his ministers, restoring an element of secrecy to the conduct of government that was personally appealing to Louis XV.

The death of Emperor Charles VI in 1740 had destabilized the Continental balance of power and paved the way for war by mobilizing a court faction of powerful nobles held together by their hostility to Austria. With Fleury on his deathbed, Louis XV yielded to the pressure of the anti-Austria interests and committed France to war. Originally a struggle to secure the imperial crown for Charles Albert, elector of Bavaria, against the claims of Maria Theresa, the war soon degenerated into a series of tactical diversions and inconclusive skirmishes. France originally entered the war as an auxiliary power but by the end of 1743 had become one of the principal belligerents. The conflict would not be resolved until 1748 with the Peace of Aix-la-Chapelle.[6]

The declaration of war against Queen Maria Theresa on 26 April 1744 prompted public speculation about the king's potential role in the military campaign. Rumors of incompetent leadership and undisciplined troops encouraged a demand for the king's presence to restore order at the front.[7] Nonetheless, there was lingering concern about Louis XV's capacity as a warrior. The king had a reputation for laziness and self-indulgence that was countered only by his passion for hunting, in which his zeal was often perceived as excessive to the point of cruelty.[8] Another king might have tried to dispel such unflattering images, but Louis XV was reticent by nature and studiously avoided the public eye. Uncertainty about the king's true character added to the already widespread anxiety associated with the war. Everyone assumed that the king would take command of his troops, but nobody, including ministers and members of the royal family, knew the king's precise intentions. As Lieutenant of Police Marville observed to Secretary of State Maurepas, "Paris is preoccupied with the king's departure. Some say he will leave tomorrow, others say he will delay until next Tuesday or

Wednesday, and I believe that in truth few people have been informed of the king's plan."[9] The king's refusal to make an official statement only exacerbated the situation.

In a clandestine set of maneuvers Louis XV departed for the battlefield at 3:00 A.M. on Sunday, 3 May 1744. As the Chevalier de Mouchy, a police informer and newsmonger, noted in his report, "The king kept the hour of his departure a mystery until the last moment." The king headed north to assume command of his troops. Along the route he was greeted with enthusiasm, and as Mouchy noted, "Everybody is extremely confident that his presence at the front will encourage his troops."[10] The king's burgeoning popularity was short-lived. In early June his two mistresses, the duchesse de Châteauroux and Mme de Lauraguais, joined him at Lille. The mistresses threatened the tenuous bond that had developed between the king and his people and revived concerns about his competence and intentions as a ruler. As Arlette Farge has observed, there was a firmly rooted belief in French political culture that love and war did not mix. They were incompatible spheres of activity that were best kept separate. A warrior had to conserve his energy for the battlefield; he could not afford to dissipate it in amorous pursuit. Moreover, the king lacked discretion. In each town where he stopped he had a special corridor built over the streets connecting his bedchamber to those of his mistresses.[11] Louis's decision to include his mistresses at the front was a serious miscalculation in terms of public opinion, and he would be judged harshly for it.

On 7 August, shortly after his arrival in Metz, Louis XV returned in the evening from inspecting his fortifications looking pale and weary. He awoke the next morning with a fever and a headache. In the ensuing days his health deteriorated rapidly, and on 11 August the attending physicians pronounced his condition to be serious. Fearing for his life, Louis XV summoned his first chaplain, M. de Fitzjames, the bishop of Soissons, and M. de Saint-Simon, bishop of Metz. Loosely associated with the Jansenist opposition to the crown, Fitzjames seized the opportunity to chastise the king publicly for his licentious conduct. When Louis XV requested the last rites, the bishop refused to dispense them unless the mistresses were banished. Convinced he was dying, Louis XV ordered the women and their entourage to leave.

They fled in a carriage with the blinds tightly drawn to shield them from a
jeering populace. Finally, after a public acknowledgment of his sins, Louis
XV received absolution.

The dire predictions of the king's doctors proved wrong: Louis XV did
not die at Metz. In fact, the day after his confession he began to recover, and
the queen arrived to find her husband out of danger. By early September
Louis XV had resumed control of government. The king's recovery produced an outpouring of popular affection and earned him the title Louis le
Bien-Aimé (the Well-Loved). Te Deums were sung throughout the realm to
thank God for preserving his life, and festive processions greeted him in
each city he entered (see fig. 2).

Figure 2.
Les hommages rendues à sa Majesté Louis XV le Bien Aimé
sur son heureuse arrivée à Paris, le 13 novembre 1744.
(Courtesy of the Carnavalet Museum)

Public opinion seized upon the incident at Metz as a parable of royal misconduct and divine intervention. This interpretation was encouraged by the
church and its supporters at court, known as the *parti dévot,* in sermons,
prayers, and pamphlets. A king appointed to rule by the grace of God was
no ordinary man.[12] Not only was he bound by oath to protect his land from
heretics but he was expected to set an example of Christian moral conduct
for his subjects. In a divine-right monarchy, in which all power theoretically
derived from a single source or body, the king's body was a highly charged
symbol for the state of the kingdom.[13] Thus, when Louis XV banished his
mistress at Metz, he was acknowledging that his adulterous conduct had offended his wife, his people, and above all, God. A sinful king risked exposing his kingdom to divine wrath. By restoring harmony within the royal
family, the king earned his kingdom God's grace.

Louis XV's recovery in 1744 marked the height of his popularity during
his long and turbulent reign. A flurry of panegyric literature, songs, allego-
ries, and odes celebrated the French people's love for their king. Although
the authors were often anonymous, the majority were clerics since the
church staged a series of commemorative ceremonies in cities throughout
the kingdom. The texts for these prayers and rituals reaffirmed the sacred
and paternalistic base of the French monarchy. Linked to this theme was an
emphasis on the role of the king's subjects, whose devotion had stayed the
hand of divine vengeance, as in the following ode:

> Enfin touché de nos prières
> et propice à nos voeux ardents,
> Le ciel rend le meilleur des Pères
> aux plus fidèles des enfants.[14]

Like dutiful children, the people loved their king, who, in turn, looked after
them like a benevolent and responsible father. Thus, a contract based on
love was forged between the sovereign and his subjects.[15] This euphoria surrounding the king's recovery was not destined to last. In less than six
months it gave way to disillusionment when Louis XV revealed that along
with the shadow of death, his contrite thoughts had dissipated.

On 14 November 1744 the marquis d'Argenson, minister of foreign affairs and incisive memorialist, noted in his journal, "The king arrived in

Paris yesterday, where he will stay for four days. Few people cried out 'Long live the king!' The people had cried for him, sung for him, during his illness and his convalescence. The rumor that he will take back the Château-roux is having a negative effect on public opinion."[16] Within a few months of his return to Versailles Louis XV had resumed his adulterous activities. Mme de Châteauroux died shortly thereafter, but she was replaced within the year by Mme de Pompadour. Pompadour would remain his constant companion until her death in 1764.

In taking mistresses Louis XV was conforming to a pattern of behavior established by his Bourbon ancestors. His amorous liaisons were no more scandalous or numerous than those of his predecessors on the French throne. Consequently, it is historically perplexing that public opinion judged him so severely on this account. On the one hand, it may have re-flected the changing tone of the century in which he reigned. The rise of a bourgeois sensibility extolling the virtues of family and domesticity stood in sharp contrast to a courtly culture of gallantry and libertinage.[17] In his vig-orous pursuit of erotic pleasure outside the conjugal bed, Louis XV was not in tune with the tenor of his time. He flaunted the behavior and codes of an older aristocratic order in an age increasingly hostile to it. Resentment of the king's mistresses, however, was not the reserve of the monarchy's oppo-nents. There was a powerful faction at the court, the *parti dévot,* led by the queen and the Dauphin, which mounted a persistent campaign against the mistresses and their influence over the king. The forlorn queen, Marie Leszczynska, stood as a symbol of the French people abandoned by their selfish king. Louis XV was charged with neglecting his responsibilities as husband and father in his own home and in his kingdom. Finally, the vehe-mence of the attacks on the mistress may have been a direct response to the declining visibility of the king himself. As Jean de Vignerie has emphasized, the king's ostensible accessibility was an ideological foundation of the French monarchy. Louis XV, reserved and uncomfortable in large gather-ings, had wrought subtle changes that effectively negated this fiction of ac-cessibility. Seeing less of their sovereign, an uninformed populace attrib-uted the king's disappearance to his overweening mistresses.[18] Thus, the issue of the king's sexual behavior was central to his public image since it mobilized at least three different sets of popular concerns.

The incident at Metz and its aftermath produced widespread disappointment with the royal figure. The king's atonement in 1744 was seen as a sham; the royal couple remained a parody of conjugal felicity. The queen's perceived estrangement from her husband both saddened and angered the French populace. This sense of disenchantment gave rise to murmurings in the streets, illicit pamphlets, and literary satires. Bonafon's novel captures these sentiments of fleeting joy and lingering unease. As a resident of the palace Bonafon was well situated to obtain inside knowledge about the individuals and events at the center of public attention. She also had direct exposure to the censure of the king's conduct by the *parti dévot* since her employer was a member of the queen's household. It is not surprising, therefore, that her novel evinces sympathy for the neglected queen. Bonafon's case allows us to trace the interplay between fiction and history on the one hand and fiction and criticism on the other through the eyes of an individual whose occupation and gender would normally have precluded her commenting.

Fiction and History

Marie Bonafon was born in the parish of Versailles on 20 October 1716 to Jean-Pierre de Bonafon, *écuyer* (squire) to Sieur d'Albert, and Marie Le Noir. The title *écuyer* was the lowest-ranking title within the nobility and was often usurped by individuals intent on gaining the threshold of the privileged order in name if nothing else.[19] It is unclear how Bonafon obtained her place in the service of the princesse de Montauban, although family connections may have played a role. As Sharon Kettering has argued, domestic service in a noble household offered one of the few dignified career alternatives to entering a convent for women lacking dowries or husbands.[20] Bonafon never referred to her childhood or her family except for an aunt and a cousin to whom she wrote from prison. This aunt resided in a convent at St. Rémy des Landes. She apparently knew the marquise de Pompadour because Bonafon repeatedly implored her aunt to write to the marquise on her behalf.

Bonafon fits the profile of a *femme de chambre* serving in a good house.[21] In 1740, when she was twenty-three years old, Marie Bonafon moved into the royal palace as a member of the princesse de Montauban's household.

The princess was a lady-in-waiting to the queen,[22] and it is not inconceivable that she played some role in the *Tanastès* affair, although there is no evidence to confirm this hypothesis. Bonafon was in charge of rearing Mme de Montauban's daughter, Mlle de Rohan, a girl of twelve or thirteen. When questioned by the police, Bonafon's employers testified that they had been completely satisfied with her service.

During the first interrogation Bonafon revealed that she had nourished literary ambitions for some time. *Tanastès* was not her first attempt to enter the world of print. She had written a comedy, *Le Destin,* which was being reviewed by the son of a M. Minet at the Comédie-Française.[23] In addition, the police discovered the manuscript for an unfinished historical novel entitled *Le Baron de XXX* when they searched her bedroom. In his initial questioning, Lieutenant of Police Marville pressed Bonafon to reveal the identity of the individuals who had helped her write *Tanastès*. He was convinced that someone of her station *(état)* was intellectually incapable of writing a novel unassisted, especially one that demonstrated such a firm command of current affairs and court politics. As in the case of Damiens, the domestic servant who attempted to stab Louis XV in 1757, the police were certain that the accused was merely covering for persons of superior rank.[24] Thus, Marville asked, "Had she not consulted with some person familiar with the composition of texts in order to learn the rules of style she had to respect in the texts she intended to write?"[25] Bonafon could not have been clearer in her response, insisting that "she never sought assistance from anyone, but since she reads a great deal she developed a taste for writing; furthermore, she expected to earn some money for herself by writing, that nobody taught her the rules of the theater, that she learned them by reading plays . . . that for *Tanastès* and the other novel she just mentioned, she worked on them on her own."[26] Bonafon confirmed what Marville suspected but tried to deny: the "taste for writing" was spreading to individuals outside the spheres of privilege and power. Throughout her incarceration Bonafon claimed full responsibility for what she had written. She was proud of her creative talents, which challenged official assumptions about the abilities of women and domestic servants.

Bonafon's interrogators refused to accept her response. They were convinced that someone had supplied her with literary models or at least explained the rules governing plot construction and character development. This bias hindered their ability to gather information because it prevented officials from asking relevant questions and hearing an accurate response. Although there was mounting evidence to the contrary, the police of Old Regime Paris continued to regard reading and writing as activities restricted to a privileged few. This attitude reflected, in part, the unacceptable and often offensive nature of material produced by and for a nonelite public. Nonetheless, by 1750 more printed matter was in circulation that was geared to a more socially diverse readership.[27]

If the police had been willing to listen, Marie Bonafon could have been a useful guide to the underground world of illicit authorship. Instead they confronted her with their conviction that "there are certain things in this work which her station would not normally permit her to know" and "summoned [her] to tell us by whom she had been instructed."[28] As a female domestic servant, albeit from a "good house," Bonafon was by definition precluded from participating in and enjoying literary activities.

The police were convinced that Bonafon was standing in for her employer, a plausible scenario since the princesse de Montauban was educated and personally involved with the persons and events described. She had a reputation for wit and intelligence and was directly associated with the queen's circle. There is, however, no tangible evidence to confirm this hypothesis, and it risks reproducing the interpretation of the police themselves. Thus, barring evidence to the contrary, I am inclined to believe Bonafon rather than her accusers if only because of her stubborn refusal to disclaim responsibility. Once they realized that Bonafon was not going to implicate her masters, the police redirected their questions to focus on her motives and intentions.

As a chambermaid attached to the royal palace, Bonafon was constantly moving back and forth between two distinct worlds. She belonged to an unprivileged milieu, but she catered to a privileged one. She would never be treated as an equal by the individuals with whom she lived on intimate terms.[29] Her familiarity with the world of the court enabled her to evoke it with skill and to cater to its literary tastes. Her masters and their friends were simultaneously the targets and the audience for her mocking pen. Bonafon claimed that financial hardship had incited her to write for publication. According to Françoise Weil, money was the primary motive for most authors writing novels in the first half of the eighteenth century. Moreover, the vogue for allegorical novels peaked in the 1740s, precisely when Bonafon was writing.[30] She knew that *Tanastès* would sell, and she was willing to risk provoking offense. Thus, she decided to apply her literary talents to profitable ends even if she had to incur considerable risk.

Yet economic distress, although a legitimate extenuating circumstance, could not justify the literary abuse of the king's person. Bonafon's desire for money had produced a satirical depiction of a sensitive political incident and could not be readily dismissed. The police were obliged to evaluate Bonafon's loyalty in order to determine her intentions. They found her case perplexing because she did not neatly fit the definition of a *mauvais sujet*. Even if Bonafon could clear herself of charges of malice, she was still guilty of some unnamed but grave offense. Her decision to use Louis XV as a character in her novel, which mocked his sexual misconduct, signified a reversal of the appropriate relations between a domestic servant and a sacred sovereign.[31]

Bonafon tried to convince Lieutenant of Police Marville that her novel was no more offensive than the public discussions on which it was based. When Marville asked her to clarify the actual composition process, Bonafon explained "that she composed her work unassisted, that she relied on her imagination; she admits nonetheless that having her head filled with the public discussions concerning all that had taken place during and since the king's illness, she sought to incorporate these discussions into her work, unaware of the consequences of her actions and without any evil intentions."[32] Her response highlighted the difficulties the police encountered in investigating these cases. It was difficult to assign blame when individuals' explanations included vague references to their imagination or to the public.[33] When royal authority was being contested, such explanations were profoundly unsatisfactory. Thus, the police pressed Bonafon to identify specific individuals who had encouraged or paid her. The term *imagination* was suspicious because it stood for everything the police as administrators were attempting to regulate or suppress—the irrational, the individual, the private, and the unregulated. These traits were traditionally associated with women more than men and were correspondingly linked to the novel, a literary genre that was gendered female in terms of authorship and readership. The novel stirred the imagination, encouraging highly subjective and impulsive responses on the part of the reader.[34] Royal authorities viewed the novel as a special problem within the larger task of censorship. When Henry-François d'Aguesseau became chancellor in 1737 he stepped up the campaign against the novel, making it clear to his officials that no novels were to be granted permission for publication. Ultimately, the chancellor's efforts failed to stifle the novel; instead, they drove it underground into the world of clandestine publishing. In the first half of the eighteenth century, according to Françoise Weil, the novel flourished in the form of fictional political satire such as Montesquieu's *Lettres persanes* or Diderot's *Les bijoux indiscrets*. After the 1740s, interest in the novel waned and it was supplanted by scientific and economic treatises.[35]

The verbal exchanges between Bonafon and Marville pitted disorderly female imagination against rational male administration. Bonafon frequently referred to her "imagination" when describing her writing process and described her crime as "une faute d'imagination" (an error of the imagination). These responses frightened the police because imagination could not be observed and controlled. Moreover, imagination was part of an aristocratic vocabulary of intellectual creation, labor of the mind as opposed to labor of the hands. It was not a quality to be claimed by those engaged in domestic service or manual tasks. Like the act of writing itself, imagination, to be properly exercised, had to be restricted to persons of rank and education. The majority of individuals could not be trusted to restrain their imagination, which, if left unchecked, would distract them from their duties and encourage delusions of grandeur likely to culminate in crime.

If Bonafon was indeed the sole author of *Tanastès*, she still had to clarify her intentions. Her success in this part of her defense would have a crucial impact on the severity of her sentence. When questioned about her motives, Bonafon replied "that she had no intention other than to tell a story, and if there were certain parts of the work that could be read as allusions to actual persons or events, it was by chance, her head being filled with all that was being discussed at that time; [she] does not deny having sensed that there were some applications that could be made, but . . . she deluded herself that the public would not pay them any attention."[36] Bonafon's last point about inferences that could be made from her allegory seemed disingenuous in light of the fact that she had supplied *Tanastès* with a key to aid the reader in identifying the main characters.[37] In Marville's eyes, an evaluation of Bonafon's intentions hinged on her ability to account for this key.

It took Bonafon three months to write *Tanastès*. During that time she shared her work in progress with her partner in crime, Nicolas Mazelin, *valet de chambre* to Mme de La Lande, the subgoverness for the royal children. Bonafon had known Mazelin for three years, and he proved to be a useful and enthusiastic ally. She conceded that his initial reaction to her manuscript had raised some misgivings, "that Mazelin had pointed out to her that the work was dangerous, that on hearing this she had been tempted to burn it, and that only her pressing need for money had prevented her from doing so."[38] That her instincts had advised caution attested to her integrity. Should Marville accept that the need for money had temporarily overwhelmed her sense of duty and respect for the king's person?

Mazelin had cautioned her about the inferences to be drawn from her novel, but he had also been quick to volunteer his services to help her get it published. He had offered his experience in the world of clandestine publication, and Bonafon had accepted, giving him the first volume of *Tanastès* once she had finished writing it. Mazelin took the manuscript to Nicolas Dubuisson, a bookseller at Versailles, and Dubuisson sent it to one of the three major print shops in Rouen, the one run by Marie-Madeleine Labulle, known as the Widow Ferrand.[39] *Tanastès* was written and printed in two parts, the first in late January and the second in May. The initial print run was a thousand copies, a large figure for an unknown author and indicative of the novel's anticipated success.[40] Dubuisson promised Mazelin two hundred free copies as recompense, which Mazelin in turn would share with Bonafon. After *Tanastès* was printed, it was sent back to the Dubuissons, who sold it at their shop in Versailles and forwarded it to booksellers and hawkers in Paris.[41]

Bonafon remarked that she had been surprised when she noticed that the text had been furnished with a Latin inscription, "Qui potest capere, capiat," on the title page, as well as a preface (see fig. 3). The preface offered a standard disclaimer found in clandestine publications, asserting that the author had merely transcribed an old manuscript discovered by chance, a gesture designed to minimize responsibility for any offensive material. That both had been added without Bonafon's knowledge is not implausible because a novel passed through numerous hands en route to publication. The police accepted Bonafon's explanation since they were not all that concerned with either of these items. They were, however, much more rigorous in their discussion of the key.

In her first interrogation Bonafon claimed that she had never been informed of the decision to include a key. The key in question was a handwritten list identifying the fictional names with their real-life counterparts

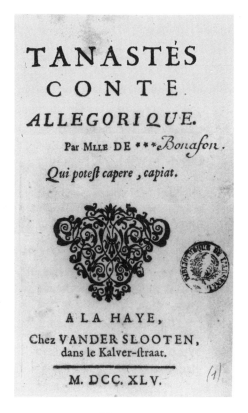

Figure 3.

Title page of Marie Bonafon's novel *Tanastès.*
(Courtesy of the Bibliothèque Nationale de
France, from the Bibliothèque
de l'Arsenal)

(see fig. 4). She said that she had discovered it attached to the copies of the manuscript being sold by Mme Dubuisson in a bookstore near Versailles, and that "when she had been instructed of the key she had been tempted to burn the book, . . . that she had only been restrained by her dire need for money at the time and the hope of being able to earn some with her book, . . . that she had nothing to do with the key and had not given any instructions to work on it."[42] Dissatisfied with this ambiguous response, the police returned to the issue six days later, when Bonafon changed her story and suggested that without her knowledge Mazelin had clarified the novel's allusions to the Dubuissons in order to help sell it. To substantiate her innocence, Bonafon insisted that "seeing Dubuisson's wife selling the work with the key, she reproached her for it."[43] The police were still unconvinced, and their suspicions were confirmed a month later in her third interrogation.

Bonafon altered her testimony once again. Perhaps she was aware that the police had arrested many of the individuals involved in the affair. Or perhaps she was getting tired of life in the Bastille and hoped that a confession might reduce her sentence. Whatever the case, she declared that one of the Parisian distributors, M. Maillend, concierge for M. and Mme de Prye, had "asked for the explanation of the book in order to be able to sell it, [that] she decided to make a key, that she wrote it herself, . . . that she gave it to Mazelin, who . . . forwarded it to the said Maillend, instructing him, as she had requested, that this key was for him only, to help him understand the text, [and] that he should make sure not to give it to anyone else."[44] Thus, she assumed responsibility for the key but emphasized her unwillingness to supply it. The key had never been intended for public scrutiny: it was a marketing device to be used in selling the novel.

The police were dubious about this confused line of reasoning. As Lieutenant of Police Marville remarked sardonically, "It was unlikely that in sending the key to Maillend, she instructed him not to share it with anyone else, this key having been made solely to facilitate the sale of the book and the book having been sent to Maillend in order for him to sell it." Bonafon insisted that "her intention was not for Maillend to distribute copies of this key and that she had sent it to him in order that by understanding the book he would be ready to explain it to those who might buy it." Lieutenant of Police Marville was quick to point out the inconsistencies in this answer, that

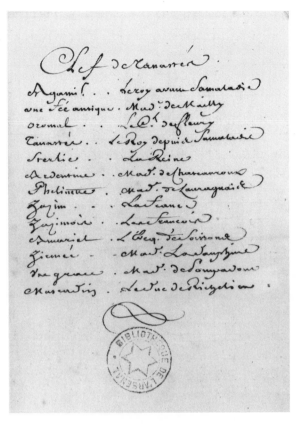

Figure 4.

Copy of the original key to characters in
Marie Bonafon's novel *Tanastès*.

*(Courtesy of the Bibliothèque Nationale de
France, from the Bibliothèque de l'Arsenal)*

"between giving the key in writing [and] providing a verbal explanation of
the book there is not a big difference."[45] This was a point Bonafon was
forced to concede.

Once the word had leaked that arrests were being made, everyone attempted to burn their remaining copies of *Tanastès*. Some, such as Dubuisson, panicked and dumped extra copies on an unsuspecting acquaintance
with assurances that there was nothing to worry about.[46] The police moved
swiftly, however, and some of the suspects, such as members of the Ferrand

family, were discovered with the evidence still in their possession. Most of the individuals arrested in connection with the affair were detained from six months to two years. Nicolas Mazelin was released but exiled to his native village, Vaucouleurs, and the Dubuissons were released in February 1747. Despite the numerous arrests and confiscations, *Tanastès* continued to circulate secretly among members of the court. In June 1746 Lieutenant of Police Marville was dismayed to learn that the king's own daughter, Mme Adelaide, had been discovered reading a copy more than a year after the novel was confiscated.[47]

Fiction and Criticism

A twentieth-century reader who locates a copy of *Tanastès* may initially be disappointed. The police investigation promised a salacious tale of sexual intrigue at the pinnacle of French society. Yet, *Tanastès* is tame in comparison with the pornographic *libelles* that would appear in France just two decades later.[48] This gap between the perspective of the twentieth-century reader and that of eighteenth-century French officialdom is revealing. The novel was not dismissed as a fairy tale, and its author was detained for fourteen years. To understand the severity of the crown's response, we must work to recover the novel's audacity, its ability to provoke offense. By framing the analysis in these terms, we can use the text and its repression to reveal the permissible and the plausible in contemporary discussions about kingship and royal authority.

Tanastès opens with the queen of Zarim/France giving birth to an heir to the throne and the festivities that greeted this joyous occasion. Perched on the clouds, Amaziel/Fitzjames observes the popular celebration with detached cynicism: "What an excess of folly! . . . What do you think of these mortals who give themselves over to outbursts of joy for the birth [of a master] whose good or bad inclinations remain unknown? Should they not rather be apprehensive that he whose arrival they celebrate might not give them cause to regret their premature cheerfulness if he were to become their tyrant and not their protector" (*Tanastès*, 1:4).[49] Enthusiasm tempered by caution would be a more appropriate response until the virtues of the successor had been tested and proved. Through the voice of Amaziel/ Fitzjames, Bonafon cautions against the blind devotion that could foster tyranny. Embedded in this statement is the assumption that not all rulers are inherently good and morally upright. Experience had shown them to be all too human, inconsistent in their policy and their conduct. Bonafon's statement implicitly questions the sacred premise that underlay the French king's claim to authority. By suggesting that rulers do not merit unqualified obedience, Bonafon offers a strategy for legitimate criticism. She is, in fact, holding the king accountable for his actions before his subjects rather than before God.

After these initial remarks, Amaziel/Fitzjames decides to conduct a political experiment. He sends one of the fairies, Célénit, to find an infant who physically resembles the newborn king, and Célénit returns with the son of a slave. This substitute child, Agamil/false king, will be reared in the court, while the true heir, Tanastès/true king, will be groomed for the throne by Amaziel/Fitzjames. Eventually, when Tanastès is deemed ready, the gods will reveal the genuine king and return him to his people, as Amaziel/Fitzjames explains. "In order that this people be not the dupe of their good faith, I have an idea. This Prince has many years before he will be able to govern alone; during this interval let us conceal him from his subjects: formed under our guidance, he will only be more worthy one day to assume the throne for which he is destined; but in order that nobody notices our theft, let us substitute in his place a child that looks enough like him to be able to deceive those closely attached to him" (1:5). The goal of this experiment is to teach the Zarimois/French a lesson in political caution as well as to form a wise and virtuous ruler removed from the corrupting influences of the court. Thus, the first volume of *Tanastès* sets up parallel but distinct destinies for the two monarchs, who represent contrasting facets of the reigning king, Louis XV. There is much in this plot that resonates with the inquisitive and experimental character of early Enlightenment thought. Bonafon traces the character development of the two men, emphasizing that environment plays as significant a role in shaping their inclinations as do their radically different birthrights.

By adopting this literary strategy of true king/false king, Bonafon could incorporate references to sensitive issues without holding Louis XV personally responsible. Moreover, the notion of duality was central to traditional discussions of French kingship. Most French men and women were accustomed to thinking of their sovereign in terms of two bodies, one mortal and one immortal. Bonafon's doubling of the figure of the king therefore fit into this familiar paradigm of duality while directing it toward a different end. In *Tanastès* Bonafon offers a pastiche of events surrounding the king's illness at Metz. Although her account is not strictly chronological, her readers would have had no trouble deciphering her allusions. The allegory, as the police correctly feared, was transparent.

The first part of the novel focuses on the childhood and education of the two boys. Tanastès is raised in isolation by Oromal/Fleury, an allusion to the first three decades of Louis XV's reign, when the orphan boy relied on Cardinal Fleury as father, mentor, and chief minister. A moody and diffident adolescent, Louis XV eschewed strong leadership until Fleury's death in 1743. Thus the connection between Tanastès and Louis XV is established in the first pages. By contrast, the less fortunate Agamil is surrounded by the corrupt influences of the court and evolves into a weak and selfish ruler. He is rapidly seduced by Ardentine/Mme de Châteauroux, an ambitious fairy who has assumed human form and recently joined the court. Agamil's wife, Sterlie/Marie Leszczynska, is dishonored by this infidelity, and the people of Zarim/France suffer under Ardentine's/Châteauroux's despotic hand.

Tanastès/true king longs to intervene and restore order to the kingdom, but he is forced to wait. Ardentine/Châteauroux is assured of her invincibility until one day Tanastès/true king replaces Agamil/false king and scorns the false king's consort. An enraged Ardentine/Châteauroux seeks vengeance for this disgrace and wreaks havoc on the kingdom. At this point Tanastès/true king is allowed to assume his rightful place on the throne. He banishes Ardentine/Châteauroux to an underworld of gnomes and dwarfs, restoring peace and harmony within his palace and his kingdom.

The second part of the novel opens with a lengthy description of the glorious reign of the good king, Tanastès. Contrasts are stressed between him and the former king, Agamil, and between the two kings' ways of organizing the court and conducting government. Amaziel/Fitzjames orchestrates spectacles to celebrate Tanastès' virtues and inspire awe among his devoted subjects. The land is united in its affection for the sovereign, in much the same spirit that accompanied Louis XV to the battlefield in 1743 and greeted the news of his recovery in 1744. Yet despite this effusion of popular support, all is not well in the kingdom: Ardentine/Châteauroux is busy plotting her revenge.

Having secured her release from the gnomes, Ardentine/Châteauroux devises a plan to sabotage the beloved Tanastès. Cloaked in invisibility, she steals into the palace and poisons Tanastès' food. The king falls dangerously ill, yet no one can explain the nature of the malady. The reference to Louis XV's illness at Metz in 1744 is fairly explicit. "Tanastès' melancholy increased nonetheless from day to day, the palace was filled with an air of sadness that could not fail to spread itself outside; the example of the master influences everything" (2:96–97). Ardentine, with the help of one of her *créatures*, Muscadin/duc de Richelieu, reveals herself and attempts to seduce Tanastès/true king. Bonafon's description suggests an allusion to Louis XV's attempt to recall Mme de Châteauroux to Versailles after banishing her at Metz: "Convinced of her success and impregnability, Ardentine committed a fatal error. On leaving the palace, she let herself be seen by the Zarimois with that assured air . . . it would be difficult to describe the terrible effect her sight produced in the people; the memory of the past, the fear of the future, and the horror of the present provoked a lugubrious confusion" (2:135). Once again, it is Amaziel/Fitzjames who intervenes in order to prevent the outbreak of chaos. He manages to eliminate Ardentine, this time permanently, and restore peace. Thus, his action recalls the bishop's refusal to administer the last sacrament to Louis XV unless he publicly renounced his mistress, Mme de Châteauroux. Her flight from Metz was an unequivocal triumph for the *parti dévot*, whose agenda was guided by the interests of the queen and the Dauphin.

This outline of the allegory and its allusions renders the police reaction to the case more understandable. In 1745 the incident at Metz was still fresh in the minds of both the king and his people. Louis XV had been humiliated, and he would never forget the blow. Neither he nor his officials were inclined to dismiss Bonafon's novel lightly.[50] It was inappropriate to criticize the king's behavior and to refer to his private life. No variations on these themes rendered them more palatable; they simply were not available for fictional adaptation or public amusement. If the king's person were subjected to close scrutiny, his mortality could not fail to be noticed and his authority diminished. The fictionalization of the king was, in effect, a banalization of his figure that collapsed the necessary distance between the sovereign and his subject.[51]

A close inspection of the novel's major themes suggests that Bonafon was making a conscious effort to distribute blame in order to salvage respect for the king. Her reluctance to confront the king's character more directly suggests lingering attachment to and respect for his person. Bonafon's first target was the world in which she lived and worked: the court. The image of the court as a corrupt and artificial environment had a long history by 1745. Criticism of the court had accompanied its establishment as an institution of state and conduct.[52] Moreover, the trope of a decadent court provided a convenient shield for the French king, who was by definition divinely appointed and incapable of wrongdoing. Nonetheless, the king, especially when he was young and inexperienced, was susceptible to the pernicious influences of the court. Even good kings could find themselves misled or distracted by idle flatterers. The corollary to this thesis stipulated that a loyal subject was duty-bound to warn the sovereign when he was being led astray.

Bonafon did more than reassert this old argument in defense of Louis XV's recent behavior: she contrived a story to demonstrate its validity. The newborn king, Tanastès, is immediately removed from the court to be raised by Oramil/Fleury. Agamil, the unwitting participant in this pedagogical experiment, is snatched from his mother and reared in the court. The results are not surprising:

> But age having developed their inclinations, the infinite difference between the two was soon visible. Tanastès, instructed by Oromal in all that was necessary to make an honest man and a great prince, was naturally inclined toward the good. It would have been easy to know that he had been made to give orders to others: the air of goodness that shone in him seemed a sure presage of the love his people would one day bestow upon him. Agamil, left to the courtiers, raised in indolence, respected even in his faults by those who should have corrected him, abandoned himself all the more willingly to his whims, [and] nobody dared to recall him to his duty: [since he was] incapable of any serious task, pleasure was the only thing that inspired him. (1:7–8)

The characters of the two men corresponded to two distinct forms of rule: benevolent monarchy and unrestrained despotism.

Tanastès/true king embodies royal virtues; his authority will be enhanced by the affection of his people. Agamil/false king, on the other hand,
is guided by caprice and obeyed through fear. Fear, as Alain Grosrichard reminds us, was the distinguishing feature of despotic government as it had
been defined by Montesquieu, who remained the principal authority on the
subject throughout the century. It held together the despotic regime because
it provided the common emotional bond between individuals and allowed
the despot to enforce his will without resistance.[53] As Bonafon emphasizes in
her description of Agamil/false king, nobody questions his decisions because they fear the loss of royal favor. While an absolute monarch was to be
respected, he was also expected to seek counsel on policy from the representatives of his kingdom. His ministers were qualified advisers, not syc-
ophants. A king ruled by law, whereas a despot ruled by force. According to
Bonafon, the success that Tanastès enjoys as king is linked to the fact that
"his empire, strengthened more by love than by supreme power, inspired his
subjects to do what fear and duty do everywhere else" (2:40). These boundaries between love and fear are important because they demonstrate very
precise ideas about the nature of royal authority. They were relied on in
eighteenth-century political discussion to distinguish between the subjects
of a monarch and the slaves of a despot. Bossuet had captured these sentiments at the beginning of the century when he insisted that people living
under a despot knew no law except the despot's will. Montesquieu had pursued this same topic in his satirical *Persian Letters,* showing that a political
system based on fear was bound to self-destruct.[54]

Bonafon makes a point, however, of indicating that the court is not an inherently corrupt environment. The court is the king's orchestra; his skills as
conductor determines the quality of its performance. Any strengths or
weaknesses in the king's character would be amplified in the court's response to his directions. Proof of Tanastès' wisdom and virtue as a ruler is
the transformation of court society under him, which offers a sharp contrast
to its form under his predecessor, Agamil/false king: "The reins of state
were entrusted to enlightened ministers, assiduous courtiers, gallant and of
good company, who knew how to combine their duty with their pleasure
with a skill heretofore unknown. Oh happy times! Oh reign of Tanastès!"
(2:3–4). By asserting that the king was responsible for the performance of

his courtiers and ministers, Bonafon leveled an implicit charge at Louis XV.
It was the king's duty to take control of his court and discipline his courtiers.
Bonafon used the story to encourage Louis XV to assume a stronger, more
engaged leadership role. She also cautioned him to choose his ministers with
care since "kings are the least capable of men when it comes to distinguishing the true from the false; Tanastès, on this count, was no different from
any other king" (2:126).

Theoretically absolutism was based on a reciprocal relationship: the king
used his authority to serve and protect his subjects, who in turn were grateful and obedient. The French king was loved because he successfully fulfilled a wide range of duties and expectations. Traditional images of a paternal and benevolent protector strengthened the bonds linking the French
king to his people. The notion of a contract based on love rendered the
monarch's absolute authority somewhat more palatable. Curiously, however, Bonafon introduces a note of caution in her text regarding popular affections for the ruler. The novel opens with Amaziel/Fitzjames commenting on the foolishness of the Zarimois/French: their reckless rejoicing at the
birth of an heir to the throne should be tempered until the ruler has shown
himself worthy of their praise.

Bonafon's observations about the Zarimois are, of course, actually words
of advice to her compatriots. Her description of the Zarimois is not a flat-
tering one. She depicts them as a gullible and undisciplined mass incapable
of making informed political decisions:

> This people, the most frivolous and lively that nature had ever produced,
> changed its manner of thinking as often as objects appeared capable of occu-
> pying them; completely opposing sentiments rapidly succeeded one another
> in their hearts . . . novelty above all had invincible charms for them; they sac-
> rificed to it goods, repose, health, it was their idol and the motor that made
> them act: an event of eight days was already old, it was no longer spoken of,
> they languished waiting for a new one to draw them out of the lethargy into
> which they had fallen. (2:5)

Bonafon's attitudes toward the *peuple* belied a deeply held conviction that
monarchy was the only form of government suitable for France. A fickle
and unstable populace was incapable, in her mind, of providing an effective

ruling body. These were the perennial fears of adopting an English-style parliamentary government described as "stormy and bizarre."[55] The point of substituting Agamil for Tanastès had been to teach the Zarimois/French a lesson. They should not grant their love unconditionally to an untested ruler because they might find themselves the slaves of a tyrant. It was their responsibility to hold their rulers to a standard of legal and moral conduct. The institution of kingship was not being challenged so much as transplanted onto secular soil, where sovereignty was rooted in popular consent as opposed to divine sanction.

So far we have examined three subjects that contributed to the maintenance of order in the kingdom: the court, the king, and the people. Yet in Bonafon's allegory each is assigned an indirect role, a role contingent upon other factors. The source of the problem in Zarim/France is the royal mistress, who assumes excessive and illegitimate power over the king and hence the government. Once she secures Agamil/false king's favor and insinuates herself at the court, her authority is unlimited. The character of Ardentine/Châteauroux plays upon a spectrum of fears in mid-eighteenth-century France, ranging from the role of women in the public sphere to despotism. These concerns would eventually be conflated, as Sarah Maza has demonstrated, in the legal briefs of the causes célèbres in the 1770s and 1780s.[56] An exploration of Bonafon's construction of the evil mistress reveals the ways in which these various concerns intersected with traditional expressions of loyalty for the king to produce an ambivalent message about royal authority.

While Tanastès/true king is raised in seclusion, Agamil/false king is surrounded by the decadence of court society. He quickly succumbs to the charms of an ambitious young fairy, Ardentine/Châteauroux. Her name, derived from the adjective *ardent*, corresponds to her character. Ardentine/Châteauroux is a creature of passion, driven by ambition and instinct and ruthless with her enemies. Her goal is to conquer the throne by seducing Agamil/false king and turning him into her puppet king. Since authority is vested in his person, no one can legitimately intervene once she has secured his affections: "Ardentine was soon at the height of her power and her grandeur: she commanded despotically; everything followed her whim and everything went wrong. Agamil obeyed her like a slave, his title of king only served to highlight his vices" (1:14). Here Bonafon was sending a warning: kings had to be more circumspect in their actions than ordinary men because their regal status set them apart as role models. Since a king lived in the public eye, he could not hide his failings, and he risked undermining his own authority by setting a bad example.

To facilitate her conquests, Ardentine/Châteauroux is endowed with supernatural powers. These were commonly attributed to women in early modern Europe who were perceived to be overstepping the prescribed gender boundaries.[57] Ardentine is not mortal; she is a fairy who has decided to abuse her extraordinary gifts. She is described as cunning and deceitful, using magical potions and casting spells. Thus, to explain the reversal of the traditional balance of power between the sexes at the political center of Zarim/France, Bonafon invented a superhuman woman with exceptional strength.

The character traits attributed to Ardentine/Châteauroux are the same as those traditionally associated with despotism in French political discourse. Monarchy was based on rationality, restraint, honor, and respect for the laws of the realm, traits typically attributed to men. Despotism, on the other hand, corresponded to the rule of passion, the lack of restraint, arbitrary and selfish authority, stereotypically female characteristics.[58] In *Persian Letters* Montesquieu too had provided a repertoire for the eroticization and feminization of authority that was characteristic of despotic rule.

According to the terms established by Montesquieu, despotism was defined as distinctly non-French. It corresponded to Oriental regimes, in which it had established historical precedents and patterns. Yet the popularity of Montesquieu's novel reflected the growing conviction among French readers in the 1720s that what they observed in fictitious Persia was actually happening in contemporary France. The regency had produced an evil minister in the form of the abbé Dubois; a young and vulnerable child king, Louis XV, who needed protection; and a debauched ruler in the duc d'Orléans. Like Bonafon's, Montesquieu's critique of despotism was not limited to the political realm. The power of *Persian Letters* lay in its revelation that despotism also corrupted the sphere of intimate human relations, replacing love with fear, reciprocity with coercion. Neither a state nor a marriage could long survive the rule of a selfish despot. Thus, it was not unusual that fears of despotism in France would surface in response to Louis XV's adulterous affairs and his neglect of his young queen. The king's treatment of his wife was directly linked to, if not modeled on, the way he ruled his kingdom.

In Bonafon's allegory despotism is embodied in a woman. Thus, a political regime that was alien to French traditions was linked to the unnatural situation of a man's being dominated by a woman. The distortion of conventional gender roles, strong women and emasculated men, was symptomatic of a corrupt polity because only a corrupt polity could allow such imbalances to occur in the first place.[59] The imposition of a foreign form of government, despotism, corresponded to the invasion of the sacred sphere of kingship by a woman. The expulsion of the mistress would simultaneously solve both problems by removing the despotic principle and restoring patriarchal authority. Bonafon's novel thus spoke to prevailing concerns about despotism as well as the role of women in the public sphere and suggests an implicit connection between the two themes by 1745.

It should be recalled that the story of *Tanastès* is based on the initial premise of a doubling of the king's body. Bonafon relied on this device in order to shield the real king, Tanastès, or Louis XV, from her attack. Agamil represents the weaker, or mortal, side of Louis XV, the monarch who flaunted his mistress and provoked divine wrath. Fortunately, Agamil is a temporary phenomenon, a testing ground. It was also assumed in 1745 that Louis XV had sincerely repented for and renounced his prior misconduct. The literary device of the two kings emerges even more powerfully in the depiction of the queen. For if Ardentine/Châteauroux provides the paradigm for female malice, the forlorn queen represents female virtue.

The custom of the land requires that a wife be chosen for Agamil/false king when he reaches a certain age. He marries Sterlie/Marie Leszczynska, the daughter of a neighboring monarch. Sterlie is kind and beautiful, innocent and virtuous. At this point Bonafon constructed an elaborate scheme that prevented Sterlie from being unfaithful to her real husband. Each night Tanastès/true king replaces Agamil/false king in Sterlie's/Leszczynska's bed, while Agamil is supplied with a replacement whom he cannot distinguish from his wife. Recall, moreover, that Ardentine is Agamil's, not Tanastès', mistress. Thus the reputations of Tanastès/true king and Sterlie/Leszczynska remain untarnished. Neither the true king nor the legitimate queen ever commits an adulterous act. The intricate disguises and confusion of roles read like a scene from one of Marivaux's plays and reflect, perhaps, Bonafon's interest in contemporary theater and her own efforts as a playwright.

Bonafon's sensitive depiction of Sterlie's position evoked popular sympathy for Louis XV's wife, Marie Leszczynska. This attitude is not surprising when we recall that Bonafon's employer, the princesse de Montauban, was a lady-in-waiting to the queen and allied with the *parti dévot*. Bonafon would have been exposed to the queen's plight firsthand, and she may have been encouraged to address it in her novel. Furthermore, in supporting the queen Bonafon was implicitly criticizing the king, who was responsible for her isolated position.[60] Bonafon dramatizes the queen's suffering even further: In the middle of the night Sterlie/Marie Leszczynska is treated with tenderness and affection by Tanastès/good Louis XV. To her confusion and dismay, however, she awakes to find a completely different person beside her. By morning Agamil/bad Louis XV has returned and treated her with scorn as he rushed off to Ardentine/Châteauroux: "What! not a word of tenderness! nothing which approached those charming raptures which had rendered him so sensitive a few hours earlier! What a difference between the husband of the night and that of the morning!" (1:39). Thus, the two kings correspond not only to two different forms of rule, monarchy versus despotism, but also to two different models of husbands, affectionate and faithful versus indifferent and unfaithful. In the 1740s the queen became a rallying point for those who, while loyal to the crown, were uneasy about their king. French men and women, especially women, could identify with the chagrin and dishonor imposed upon Marie Leszczynska as a result of her husband's infidelity.[61] The queen symbolized the people of France abandoned by a negligent spouse. Bonafon's novel established clear connections between the kingdom and the household, the polity and the family. The good ruler was likewise a sensitive and loyal husband, just as the tyrant was selfish and indifferent toward his wife.

What emerges most powerfully from Bonafon's depiction of the king, the queen, and his mistress is the complexity of the issues and emotions involved. Bonafon's text is riddled with ambiguities and contradictions in which images of unbridled female sexuality and enfeebled male authority become central paradigms for an unsatisfactory political situation in need of reform. These were significant themes because they would become, as Sarah Maza has demonstrated, central parables in the legal narratives of the *mémoires* of the 1770s and 1780s for criticizing the monarchy and calling for reform.[62] Bonafon confirms Maza's assertion about the universality and impact of such concerns by revealing their presence and centrality in a text written three decades earlier. These same images simultaneously provide the underpinnings for a language of loyalty by helping to displace responsibility from the figure of the king. The reliance on the figure of the evil mistress as a foil for the king provided an effective remedy for the kingdom's ills. Health could be restored by removing the infected part, be it Mme de Châteauroux or the marquise de Pompadour. Although the solution was neat, how effective was it in shielding Louis XV?

The presentation of conflicting images of kingship, despite the attempt to distinguish the good monarch from the evil despot, arguably undermined the royal mystique. The power of the absolutist myth lay in its structural unity. Although the king assumed a variety of roles, they were necessarily interrelated and mutually supportive. Since the king was no ordinary mortal, he had to be held up to different standards. He could not be considered wise and virtuous if he were prone to repeated lapses in his personal conduct. The depiction of the royal figure as weak and servile in one instance, prudent and restrained in another, fractured this unified vision. A king who had been metaphorically emasculated could not be reendowed with virile strength without losing something of his sacred mystique in the process. Once accustomed to viewing their king as a mere mortal with human weaknesses, Bonafon's readers would have trouble restoring him to his sacred status.

It can be argued, moreover, that the distinctions between Agamil and Tanastès are insufficiently sharp to prevent confusion in the reader's mind. Throughout the text their identities are interchanged, to the bewilderment of everyone in the novel. At times it is difficult for the reader to distinguish one from the other. In effect, Louis XV is neither one nor the other fictional king but both since the two embody the character of the real king, whose virtues and vices were still vivid in popular memory. Bonafon is able to draw her fictionalized account to a happy ending because the pejorative aspects of royal authority are identified with an impostor on the throne in the thrall of a domineering mistress. When the true king/Tanastès assumes the throne of Zarim/France, harmony reigns.

Yet once the connections had been drawn between Zarim and France, no such literary device could satisfactorily resolve the problem of Louis XV's character and conduct. There was no guarantee that the French king might not succumb to temptation in the future. Thus, Bonafon's text succeeded in focusing attention on weaknesses in the royal character without providing a solution to the problem of his personal inconsistencies. She had given offense because it was not her role to comment on such matters. In rebuking the king's sexual behavior, she was also implicitly questioning his political conduct. As a consequence of Louis XIV's decisions to live his life in the public eye all aspects of daily activity, including the intimate and the mundane, were endowed with political significance. As a result, there were no distinctions between the public and the private, and the king's private life was charged with political concerns. Although this conflation of the personal and the institutional initially strengthened royal authority in the late seventeenth century, it became a liability in the eighteenth century, when the practice of scrutinizing the king's behavior helped legitimate bold claims for governmental accountability on the part of an enlightened public. Moreover, the entire endeavor of commenting on and attempting to salvage Louis XV's reputation involved a satirical fictionalization of his person. Arguably, the political effects of fiction were the most subversive aspects of Bonafon's case.

This last point offers two interpretative possibilities by way of conclusion. On the one hand, it could be argued that the police were interested in Bonafon's novel less because it mocked real events than because the act of fictionalizing the king was disturbing.[63] The novel as a genre dissolved the social distinctions and hierarchy that underlay the Old Regime through the narrative process of fiction. All characters, whether high or low, regal or ordinary, were presumed to be equally engaging or interesting. Not only did the novel have a leveling effect in terms of subject matter but it was a relatively accessible literary genre that disseminated information in a less easily controlled fashion. *Tanastès* could be read and enjoyed by anybody familiar with current affairs. It did not presuppose formal education or training beyond basic literacy. Thus, the process of fictionalizing kingship was incompatible with the fundamental tenets of the Old Regime because it ignored the traditional criteria for social distinctions and it threatened the crown's ability to monitor the flow of information and define its own public image.

At the same time, Bonafon's text may have raised alarm because it failed to fictionalize the king sufficiently. As the police remarked early in their investigation, the allegory was transparent: it was easy, despite the invented names, to identify the persons and events discussed. Bonafon had not established enough distance between fiction and reality; the text was too close to the world she was mocking. Louis XV was readily identifiable, replete with all his foibles and follies, to a reading public more inclined to demand accountability from its leaders than to acquiesce docilely. Ultimately what was at stake in the issue of fiction, no matter how it was read, was the right to represent the king to the public, a contest the crown could not afford to lose in the middle of the eighteenth century.

Repentance and Retribution

With her incarceration at the Bastille, Marie Bonafon bid farewell to her nascent literary career. Her conduct over the next fourteen years confirmed the sincerity of her repentance. The act of writing had appealed to her intellectually and aesthetically and had promised her a degree of financial independence. Nonetheless, it had been a dangerous diversion because the pleasures of the pen had led her to offend her sovereign. Extended confinement forced her to reflect upon and define the dimensions of her loyalty to Louis XV.

After several months in the Bastille and a series of protracted interrogations, Bonafon understood the gravity of her crime. She worked to repair the offense she had inadvertently provoked. She could not bear to live with the burden of these "sins" forever on her shoulders. Writing to Lieutenant of Police Marville, she described her predicament in the following terms: "I feel that it is impossible for me to continue living much longer a prisoner and hated by those persons of the world whom I respect most sincerely. Allow me . . . to work to repair my fault, permit me to demand help from Mme de Pompadour. She can soften the temper of the king by portraying all my suffering."[64] She asked for permission to write to her aunt, who had an indirect connection to Louis XV's new *maîtresse en titre*, the marquise de Pompadour, and ask her to intervene on her behalf.

The historian is struck by the irony of Bonafon's strategy. She had been arrested for an allegory that revolved around the character of an evil mistress. Suddenly she found herself turning to that same figure as a way of gaining access to the king. The symbolic complexity of the royal favorite reemerged. Her proximity to the king could mean different things at different times for the same people. On the one hand, she could be a symptom of royal weakness and corruptibility, of the vulnerability of the king's mortal body. In this role, she was an easy scapegoat for political and social problems. On the other hand, her intimacy with the sovereign could be interpreted as an extension of royal grace and power, an enhancement of her own virtue rather than a loss of his. Her physical proximity implied a transference of the sacred aura that surrounded the king and inhered to his person.[65] Individuals in mid-eighteenth-century France did not hesitate to play on both of these registers, depending on their needs, in particular circumstances.

Conditions in the Bastille could be harsh; only the strongest constitutions managed to survive. In December 1746 concerns about Bonafon's health were raised since "if she were detained much longer, she ran the risk of dying, being of a weak constitution and poor health."[66] These observations were brought to the attention of the comte de Maurepas, secretary of the king's household. Maurepas transferred Bonafon to a convent of Bernadine nuns near Moulins. Mme Bourdier, the mother superior, was given strict instructions regarding her new ward. She was asked to observe Bonafon closely and send regular reports back to the new lieutenant of police, Nicolas-René Berryer. Maurepas's instructions read, in part:

> There is nothing to fear from her except the desire to write and the company of people from the outside world. I beg of you that she not be allowed, under any pretext, to go to the parlor, and if she needs to go in order to have a word with a servant, please make sure that she does so only in your presence. . . . For the rest you can leave her at liberty inside the house. . . . Notify her also not to write to anyone and not to try passing any letters except by your hands, even those that she may write to me, and you will send to me all those that she does write.[67]

The primary concern was to prevent Bonafon's pen from committing an "error of the imagination" similar to the one that had produced her first crime.

In the ensuing decade the mother superior reported that Bonafon's conduct was above reproach. She appeared to be sincerely repentant, shunning human contact and conversation. Bonafon was not permitted to write despite her repeated appeals to Berryer for permission. Not, she hastened to explain, to exercise her creative imagination but rather for "copying, or for arranging my own ideas in writing on the condition that none of these would leave the convent, not to communicate them to anyone except, perhaps, my confessor, to burn them afterwards or to hand them over to the Mother Superior."[68] In this passage Bonafon affirms the private and intimate purpose writing fulfilled for her. It helped her to remember and stimulated reflection; it also provided an outlet for expressing problems that troubled her. In this instance her desire to write was altogether different from the financial motives that had produced *Tanastès*. She was not an author seeking publication and renown but an individual yearning for self-knowledge in a peculiarly eighteenth-century fashion of self-reflexive writing.[69]

Although it was not clear that Bonafon ever understood the nature of her crime, her many years in prison convinced her that she had been at fault. She believed, however, that she had acquired knowledge in the process of recognizing and repairing her mistake. In a letter to her only cousin in 1754 she wrote, "I am pleased that you occupy your free time with efforts to know yourself, this is the most solid form of study; be careful, however, that this is not a vain speculation, the real knowledge of ourselves is the one that helps us to correct our defects."[70] This focus on the self and the attempt to improve one's character was in keeping with various strands of Enlightenment thought. Bonafon's attitude supports those historians who argue that a connection existed between the development of a critical attitude and a familiarity, scant or profound, with written culture. The power of this critical faculty was its flexibility, for although it may have begun in private or small circles, it was transferable to a broader public sphere. In the Enlightenment reading, writing, and discussion became implicitly linked to a growing sense of autonomy or personal freedom.[71]

In this same letter to her cousin, Bonafon revealed that her literary inclinations had not been completely stifled. It was apparent that she continued to ponder questions of style and grammar and longed for access to literature, as evidenced by the words with which she closed this missive: "You ask for my advice on your style, and I will give it to you in two words. You try a bit too hard to demonstrate cleverness in your letters, this is a novice's flaw. Don't contort your thoughts. . . . One does not write well unless one writes clearly . . . to avoid all these problems write as often as you can to persons who are capable of correcting you. Pursue good readings and cultivate, above all, the company of honest men."[72] Bonafon continued to esteem two of the cultural attributes of privilege, reading and writing, as avenues to self-improvement and self-knowledge. Clearly, her repentance had not led her to renounce her claim to the written word.

In 1759, when she received the news that the king had pardoned her, that she was to be released from the convent, Bonafon was emotionally overcome with joy: "The multitude of sentiments that fills my soul renders me incapable of expressing myself . . . a circumstance so desirable and yet so unexpected, the king pardons me, he gives me back my liberty, he grants me a pension, what prodigious mercy! I am dying of confusion for having ever been able to offend such a good master!"[73] Thus, she saw her liberty as a manifestation of the most endearing of the royal virtues: pardon. The majority of the population continued to view clemency as one of the most powerful attributes of the French king, and one of the clearest examples of his divine sanction. As a result of the monarch's mercy, Bonafon would be able to resume her life as a loyal subject. Her freedom was a token of the sincerity of her repentance because Louis XV had recognized the purity of her intentions. In the light of this magnanimous royal gesture, Bonafon was genuinely contrite about her previous actions.

Even before her release, however, Bonafon had clarified her loyalty to her sovereign. The text of *Tanastès* distinguishes between the fear associated with despotism and the love that defines monarchy; both qualities also guided her own defense. In one of her many letters to M. Duval, secretary to the new lieutenant of police, Bertin de Bellisle, Bonafon expounded on the nature of her sentiments: "I am detained by the king's order, and yet far from complaining about his severity, I have only been treated with enormous mercy . . . it was not fear that inspired so much submission to his orders on my part but rather my repentance, my love, and my gratitude for the best prince in the world. If the sacrifice of my life could prove to him the truth of my sentiments, I would regard the last of my days as the most beautiful one of my life."[74] Bonafon recognized that submission in response to coercion, whether to God or to his viceroy on earth, was superficial because love, not fear, was the source of true repentance. It also confirmed her loyalty since it supported her assertion that her intentions in writing *Tanastès* had not been malicious. Force was required for truly *mauvais sujets*, those who were not imbued with proper respect for their sovereign. For Bonafon, on the other hand, fidelity had always shaped her attitudes toward Louis XV. Consequently, she said, it continued to inspire her during her long detainment.

Bonafon offered her life as proof of her supplication. This gesture, as will be seen, was a central feature of fidelity in these decades. It affirmed the gulf separating humble subjects from their mighty sovereign. Bereft of material possessions, individuals of modest origins had nothing but their lives to offer as evidence of their loyalty. Individuals who lacked physical proximity to the royal figure relied on expressions of self-sacrifice to affirm a personal tie to Louis XV. The image of laying down one's life for that of the king was a recurring one. It was the most powerful means of conveying loyalty for those who were unlikely to enjoy the privilege of a royal audience in the course of their lifetime. It confirmed the absolute nature of fidelity, a value that allowed for no compromise. A truly *fidèle sujet* could not bear to live knowing that he or she had offended the sovereign. If death was the only option left for clearing one's name, it was deemed preferable to a life of perpetual dishonor.

The case of Marie Bonafon raises an issue that we will encounter repeatedly. Like so many other individuals arrested, Bonafon seems to have been mistakenly classified as a *mauvais sujet*. In her own mind, although she was guilty of a "faute d'imagination," she believed in her loyalty to Louis XV. Part of the problem was that the police, acting under the crown's auspices, allowed no room for slippage. By adhering to brittle definitions of fidelity and criminality, the police eliminated any possibility for actions to fall somewhere between loyalty and treason. Fidelity was a raft afloat troubled seas. If one fell overboard, even accidentally, there was little hope of ever regaining the vessel. One was immediately sucked down into a whirlpool of delinquent activities and attitudes.

By adhering to such rigid categories, the criminal authorities gradually lost their ability to distinguish between real and imaginary threats. The variety of crimes that qualified individuals as *mauvais sujets* was astounding. This situation was not unique to the system of penal classification. It corresponded to what Robert Darnton has observed about Old Regime practices in the regulation of the publishing industry. Here again, an eclectic mixture of authors and genres were clustered under the rubric "livres philosophiques." The implications were profound, as Darnton argues, for "what a state of affairs! A regime that classified its most advanced philosophy with its most debased pornography was a regime that sapped itself, that dug its own underground, and that encouraged philosophy to degenerate into *libelle*."[75] In the same way, the policing of attitudes and gestures toward the crown often backfired. Marie Bonafon emerged from her detention meek and subdued, singing the king's glories. For other individuals, however, arrested for similar types of offenses, incarceration provoked more virulent opposition.

Differences between these two perspectives, that of the police and that of the defendants, offer a glimpse of a wider breach in ideas about the nature of kingship. The official attitude asserted a strict definition of sacred kingship in which any criticism of the king's character was an offense against God. Consequently, even idle chatter or imaginary scenarios merited severe punishment. At the same time, many subjects who demonstrated what was deemed disrespect by the royal police remained convinced of their personal loyalty to Louis XV. They were not calling the institution of monarchy into question, but their vision of kingship was increasingly secular. This shift was significant because it placed kingship on utilitarian grounds. The inability to reconcile the desire to speak freely with the institution of kingship would ultimately alienate many of the crown's steadfast supporters.

The police dossier ends with Bonafon's release from the Bernadine convent in 1759. In many ways it is ironic that she was freed in the aftermath of the Damiens affair, when arrests for crimes of *mauvais discours* reached a record high for the century. Bonafon's case sank into oblivion for more than a hundred years; then, in 1898, the historian and future director of the *Revue des Etudes Historiques,* Maurice Boutry, included a biographical sketch of Marie Bonafon in one volume of the series he edited, entitled Curiosités Bourbonnaises. Boutry emphasized Bonafon's sense of alienation and awkwardness in the privileged milieu of the court. He argued that writing had provided a kind of solace for the maladroit servant girl: "Thoughtless, imprudent, she wrote with passion and she wrote too much . . . but writing with ease, endowed with ideas and imagination, she believed herself to be in a position to be appreciated by the world of letters since the world of the salons was off limits for her . . . she hoped to get rich . . . unaware of the consequences to be feared . . . she resolved to undertake a *roman à clef* concerning the mores and manners of the time."[76] According to Boutry, it was Father Griffet, Bonafon's confessor at the Bastille, who intervened on her behalf and secured her release through his connections with *dévot* circles at the court. After more than a decade in isolation, Bonafon emerged penniless and forsaken. She ended up settling in the region near Moulins in the service of the marquise de La Motte.

Although never a cause célèbre, the case of Marie Bonafon alerts us to issues that shaped discussions of kingship in the mid-1740s and later. The concern *Tanastès* provoked can only be understood within the tense political climate of France in the 1740s. The police interrogations revealed official assumptions about kingship and the respect due the king's person. Bonafon's self-defense demonstrated a mind grappling to reconcile obedience and intellectual autonomy, fidelity to Louis XV and literary ambitions.

Two important points should be retained about Bonafon and the writing of *Tanastès.* First, although she never denied her crime, she failed to grasp how her allegory undermined her claims to fidelity. Bonafon believed herself to be a loyal subject, and there was little evidence to contradict her besides her novel. Furthermore, she never tried to deny her authorial responsibility, even though this might have earned her a lighter sentence. Nonetheless, her decision to satirize the king's sexual conduct suggested an inappropriate degree of familiarity with his person. By casting Louis XV as a character in a novel, Bonafon had, whether intentionally or not, dispelled the sacred aura that had traditionally surrounded his person. She could not retract her text, but she could deny malicious intent, although she would be hard-pressed to convince the police of her good faith.

Second, *Tanastès* demonstrated that by the 1740s attitudes toward the royal figure reflected and refracted changing ideas about fathers and families, sex and marriage. The centrality of the king's mistress and the hostility she aroused can only be understood in terms of broader cultural shifts. These changes would have both social and political implications since the legal foundations of the French absolutist state had been built upon a patriarchal family model that limited a woman's ability to select her own mate.[77] As a companionate model of marriage displaced the more austere patriarchal one, assumptions about the model family in the land, the royal one, would also evolve. French men and women wanted to see Louis XV and Marie Leszczynska enact conjugal affection in their own home. Finally, the values of intimacy, modesty, mutual respect, and devotion to the hearth corresponded to a deeper social shift in French society, the gradual decline of the aristocracy. The rise of an ambitious, educated, and hard-working bourgeoisie was antithetical to the traditional aristocratic ethos of idleness, gallantry, and libertinage. Thus, a king who persisted in pursuing the erotic pleasure of a concubine rather than the cozy devotion of a spouse was swimming against the cultural tide. He was flaunting his attachment to a lifestyle in the process of being devalued, aligning himself with the forces of the past in an era of progress and enlightenment.

Bonafon's novel highlights the difficulty of disentangling these issues by offering an ambiguous, often overlapping set of themes and arguments about kingship. Bonafon's fixation on the figure of the royal mistress was not an isolated instance. In the 1740s and 1750s the mistress more than the monarch occupies center stage in the majority of cases involving *mauvais propos*. Such criticism was important, as recent feminist scholarship has insisted, because it established a pattern of popular attitudes toward women closely attached to the king. Thirty years later they would be transferred to the figure of the queen, and eventually they would be used to justify the exclusion of women from participation in politics, paving the way for the replacement of royal households, where women were prominent figures, by the exclusively male representative bodies of the revolutionary and modern periods.[78]

The evil mistress was a prevalent theme in many of the satirical texts in circulation in the second half of the eighteenth century.[79] This image can be read on another level as a strategy for voicing criticism while simultaneously shielding the king's person from harm. In the 1750s, however, the mistress had not been irrevocably fixed as evil incarnate. Her status was arguably still in flux. This last point is illustrated by the fact that some individuals attempted to capitalize on the king's affection for his female favorite, to manipulate this in the service of their ambition. Rather than attack the mistress, they designed false conspiracy plots that allowed them to distinguish themselves by protecting her. No matter which image of the mistress was used, the individuals involved were arrested and often severely punished.

This analysis of Bonafon's treatment of the royal mistress prompts two conclusions. First, the reputation of the king did not, despite elaborate efforts, emerge untarnished. Second, the reluctance to rebuke the king directly attests to the persistence of loyalty among French subjects even within a historical context of mounting dissatisfaction with the king's performance. These two points suggest that arguments about the desacralization of the monarchy and the breakdown of royal authority need to be viewed with some caution. The process of disaffection was incremental, often imperceptible, and rarely unequivocal. Bonafon's case reflects a growing ambivalence more than anything else. Ambivalence does, however, allow for questioning or doubt, which is incompatible with the transcendental concept of sacrality. When the king lost his sacred status, he was effectively rendered banal, and once banal, he was more readily judged like any mortal man.

Chapter 3

The Lioness and the Ant

*Antoine Allègre's Fable
of Despotic Rule*

· ❧ ·

ON 18 SEPTEMBER 1751 the marquis d'Argenson noted in his journal that "the mistress [Pompadour] is prime minister and grows more and more despotic, more than any other favorite has ever been in France."[1] D'Argenson suggests that the two main themes encountered in *Tanastès,* the excessive power of the royal mistress and the fear of despotism, had not diminished. If anything, recent events had confirmed the words of caution sounded in Bonafon's novel.

Chapter 2 illustrates the growing ambivalence that distinguished attitudes toward the king throughout the 1740s. Louis XV's conduct stirred conflicting emotions in the minds of his subjects: initial misgivings about his capacities as a military leader were supplanted first by fears for his life at Metz and then by euphoria at the news of his recovery. The decade closed on a sour note with the disappointing Peace of Aix-la-Chapelle in 1748, the flaring up of the ongoing controversy over the refusal to administer the last sacraments to suspected Jansenists, and finally, the king's resumption of his libertine habits after an all too brief interlude of remorse and marital fidelity. These concerns, as seen in the case of Marie Bonafon, destabilized the traditional image of French kingship and produced a profound sense of ambiguity about the royal figure. Bonafon attempted to use the royal mistress as a foil for Louis XV's own shortcomings and was only partially successful. She was able to exonerate the king in her novel because the mistress was identified as a foreign intrusion into French political life. Yet the neat solutions of a novelist were unavailable to the crown's servants, who were struggling to stem the rising tide of hostile public opinion. As domestic tensions mounted, the mistress would be perceived less as an aberration and more as a symptom of corrupt government, thus paving the way for a more direct attack on the monarchy itself. This impulse to identify the mistress with the monarch is evident in the unfolding and investigation of the case of Antoine Allègre since it informs both the crime and its repression.

During the winter of 1750 Antoine Allègre, a tutor from Marseilles, wrote to the marquise de Pompadour requesting a private audience. He claimed to have important information regarding a conspiracy plot to poison her and her lover, the king. The marquise sent Allègre to see the comte d'Argenson, who turned the letter over to the police, who promptly launched an investigation to track down and arrest the author. Allègre would eventually confess to inventing the conspiracy plot in hopes of earning financial or honorific recompense. Although the police questioned the veracity of Allègre's claims from the start, they did not dismiss them as wholly fictitious. A variety of interrelated factors, ranging from a poor harvest to the imposition of new taxes, nourished a disgruntled populace's hatred of the royal mistress. Allègre relied on this widespread discontent to give credence to his imaginary conspiracy and succeeded in duping the police, albeit briefly. Little did he know that he would pay dearly for his cleverness, ending his days locked up like a mad dog in a cage at Charenton.[2]

That the police regarded Allègre as a dangerous criminal is initially somewhat confusing given the pretext of his letter. Whereas Bonafon had used the mistress to deflect attacks away from the king, Allègre sought to defend her as a demonstration of his loyalty. Yet both acts alarmed the police because through the clever manipulation of their social superiors, Bonafon and Allègre were implicitly assuming a position of judgment vis-à-vis royal authority. It was evident to the police that the king's judgment was being questioned when his female favorite was attacked, whether verbally or physically. Her name and reputation, as well as her person, were protected by the same laws that protected the king. Thus, the very intimacy between Louis XV and Pompadour that Allègre preyed upon in his letters would require that he be severely punished.

Allègre's police file reveals concerns about the misuse of authority in France in the early 1750s that echo themes that have been identified by historians studying other sources, such as judicial *mémoires* and pamphlet literature.[3] Allègre's decision to denounce a secret plot to poison the king's mistress attests to the continuing hostility toward the royal consort and mounting concern about her role in the polity. It forces us to consider the extent to which such attacks damaged the king's status as well. The dominant figures of authority in Allègre's case were royal appendages, the mistress and her doting ministers. Like Bonafon's novel, Allègre's conspiracy revolves around an invisible or ineffective king. The absence of a charismatic royal figure was arguably indicative of a growing emotional detachment on the part of French subjects toward their sovereign.

Allègre's dossier provides a concrete instance of the shift away from a traditional view of sacred kingship to one that was more critical and aggressively secular. This shift can be studied from various angles, including the depiction of the royal mistress and prominent ministers, the image of Louis XV, and attitudes toward the crown's system of criminal law. Allègre was caught between two worldviews, one based on fidelity and the other on justice. It is illuminating to examine his efforts to reconcile them. Although he adopted a language of natural law and human rights to articulate his grievances, Allègre never questioned that monarchy was the form of government best suited for France.

Louis *Vingtième* or
Louis *Méprisé*

Recent work on the political culture of the Old Regime has identified the decade of the 1750s as a critical turning point in the history of the French monarchy. According to Keith Baker, the crown lost its privileged position as ultimate arbitrator and found itself drawn into the fray of the political arena, where it was simply one competing interest among many.[4] The monarchy suffered an irretrievable loss of authority in the process by repeatedly proving unable to enforce obedience to the royal will. That the crown found itself in an increasingly isolated and vulnerable position helps explain the official response to crimes like those for which Allègre was arrested. The police lost their ability to distinguish between real and imagined threats. In a political climate fraught with tension and uncertainty Allègre's alleged conspiracy appeared explicitly threatening, and he was punished accordingly.

The peace treaty Louis XV signed with Great Britain and Austria at Aix-la-Chapelle in 1748 was in effect an armistice. France renounced all her military conquests and emerged with nothing to show for the substantial financial and demographic losses she had sustained. A popular expression in circulation at the time underlined this derisory view of the diplomatic resolution: "You're as stupid as the Peace."[5] Louis XV's failure to secure either material benefit or glory for his country provoked profound disillusionment. This sense of betrayal undermined the king's credibility as a dutiful paterfamilias who provided for his children and compensated them for their sacrifices.[6]

With the end of the military conflict the French monarchy was confronted by the unpleasant reality of overwhelming debt and an empty treasury. The comte de Machault, appointed controller general of finance in 1745, recognized that drastic fiscal reform was needed to settle the crown's outstanding debts and encourage investment in the sagging economy. It would, however, be difficult to impose new taxes on the king's subjects, who were just emerging from a long and costly military fiasco. If anything, the country expected the crown to eliminate some of the extraordinary taxes that had been imposed during the war to cover increased military expenditures. Yet Machault was determined to fill the royal coffers, and he intended to accomplish this goal by tapping into the reservoirs of private wealth, traditionally exempt from the tax burden in France. The cornerstone of Machault's plan was a uniform levy on private incomes, including those of the nobility and the clergy. In early May 1749, with the king's approval, Machault issued a decree imposing the *vingtième* (twentieth) on all of the crown's subjects. Machault's version of an income tax was based on revenue, designed to target landed wealth, not wages, and it would be proportional to an individual's wealth.[7]

Before presenting his edict, Machault steeled himself for the protests of powerful groups whose interests were threatened by the *vingtième*'s principle of fiscal equality. In this instance the Parlement of Paris was relatively acquiescent, registering the edict with minimal wrangling within two weeks of its presentation on 5 May 1749. By contrast, resistance proved stronger in provinces such as Brittany and Languedoc, where local estates were led by seasoned warriors in the battle against encroaching central government. These provinces were not willing to give up the exemptions and autonomy they had struggled to obtain from the crown over the centuries. While Machault wrestled with the provincial estates, he faced the even fiercer opposition of the clergy, who were unwilling to compromise on their traditional immunity from taxation. The church refused to submit its divinely instituted charge to the inspection of secular officials, claiming that its wealth did not constitute temporal property because it was destined for a spiritual mission. In pamphlets and debates the levying of taxes on church property was presented as a form of sacrilege by a misguided king and his impious minister. For three years Louis XV and Machault struggled to impose the new tax on the clergy, but ultimately the church and its *dévot* allies at the court won the king's conscience and forced the crown to relinquish the assault on fiscal privilege. Louis XV abandoned Machault, who was forced to admit defeat on 23 December 1751, when an order-in-council suspended the imposition of the tax on ecclesiastical lands. Without the contributions of the clergy, the tax failed to raise the anticipated revenues. Moreover, the church's success undermined the crown's credibility by fueling resistance to the tax and the king that made collection of the tax both difficult and unpopular.[8]

The contestation over the *vingtième,* which pitted the crown against the church, the parlements, and the provincial estates, intersected with the other political debacle of the decade: the debates between the clergy and the magistrates over the dispensation of last rites to suspected Jansenists. Louis XV was hard-pressed to arbitrate these disputes, desperately trying to placate both sides and to keep both spiritual and secular authority in their proper place. In both instances the monarchy proved incapable of either resolving the conflicts or suppressing them. Ultimately, the sacraments controversy represented a jurisdictional conflict between priests and magistrates, who were vying for control over civil society through the right to regulate an individual's departure from it.[9]

Under the aegis of the archbishop of Paris, Christophe de Beaumont, a vigorous assault was launched against the Jansenists in 1749–52. Since Beaumont was a zealous partisan of the Jesuit circle and *Unigenitus,* the 1713 papal decree that condemned Jansenism as a form of heresy, he refused to allow the theological dispute to lie dormant. He was ruthless in his pursuit of refractory priests and laymen unable to produce an approved *billet de confession,* a certificate of confession from a priest who had accepted *Unigenitus.*

For a variety of practical and ideological reasons, as Dale Van Kley has demonstrated, the Jansenist cause found an institutional ally in the Parlement of Paris.[10] The magistrates argued that *Unigenitus* was not a rule of faith and thus could not be used to deny Catholics their legal rights to participate in the sacraments. They appealed to the king to intervene, but Louis XV was hesitant, genuinely uneasy about overstepping the boundary between spiritual and secular authority. The king's uncertainty led him to defer to the pressures of Beaumont and the *parti dévot*.

When the Parlement of Paris attempted to bring Beaumont to trial in 1752, they crossed the crown's threshold of toleration. The magistrates were exiled in May 1753 as punishment for their unruly behavior. Both the persecuted Jansenists and the banished magistrates aroused a tremendous amount of popular sympathy. The crown was forced to recall the Grand-Chambre in September 1754, and a month later the Parlement registered Louis XV's Declaration of Silence. This decree provided tacit sanction to the magistrates for their prosecution of priests who refused to dispense the last sacraments. At the same time, Beaumont was exiled to his country house. These decisions amounted to a truce, not a solution, for the battles resumed within the year.

It would be a mistake to see these struggles as confined to the world of high politics. They erupted in a moment of economic crisis and played themselves out in more mundane arenas directly touching the daily lives of working Parisians. For example, Beaumont's campaign against the Jansenists included a plan to reform the General Hospital of Paris. Frightened by the growing sympathy for Jansenists among large segments of the Parisian populace, Beaumont aimed to strike at one of their institutional strongholds. He implemented a series of reforms designed to purge the administration of the hospital system of any Jansenist influences. This included forbidding certain pious laymen suspected of Jansenism from continuing to volunteer their services to succor the poor and needy.[11] From the perspective of *le menu peuple* (the little people), only one message emerged from this policy: individuals who had charitably intervened on their behalf were being punished, rather than rewarded, for their efforts. If they accomplished anything, Beaumont's reforms consolidated popular support for the persecuted Jansenist cause.

Thus, the capital was in an uproar in the early 1750s, especially with the interruption of justice that accompanied the exile of the Parlement in December 1751 and then again in May 1752. The threat of a grain shortage heightened the sense of anxiety and uncertainty. Steven Kaplan has identified the years 1751–53, when rumors of a famine plot agitated the populace and prompted revolts throughout the realm, as one of the critical moments in the eighteenth century. Following a predictable pattern of cause and reaction, panic was triggered by the poor harvest in 1751. Royal efforts to prevent a shortage produced an abundance of low-quality grain at what were deemed exorbitant prices. In this case, popular opinion held certain financiers and friends of Mme de Pompadour, such as the new lieutenant of police, Nicolas-René Berryer, responsible for the dearth and the unfair prices.[12] Ultimately the king was accused of scheming to profit from the sale of grain necessary to his subjects' subsistence. The rumors seemed all the more credible in the context of the crown's persistent financial difficulties.

Tempers were short from hunger when another set of rumors erupted in the capital during the spring of 1750. This time the skirmishes occurred in the streets, pitting le menu peuple against police officers charged with maintaining order. The origins of the affair lay in official efforts to clear the streets of vagabonds and mendicants. These efforts nourished allegations that children found playing or walking unattended were being kidnapped. In an atmosphere clouded with suspicion and fear several incredible tales began circulating in connection with the affair. Some believed the children were being sent off to populate America; others asserted that their blood was needed to cure a leprous prince.[13]

A series of riots erupted throughout the city, culminating on 22–23 May in a ritualistic enactment of popular justice. A constable named Labbé, who was seen arresting an unsuspecting eleven-year-old, was chased by a raging populace and brutally stoned to death. Lieutenant of Police Berryer ordered a full investigation of the incident, thus tacitly acknowledging the existence of some degree of police abuse.[14] The Parlement chose three scapegoats from among the rioters to serve as punitive examples and condemned them to hanging. The incident of the vanishing children left a residue of mistrust between the populace and the crown that was not easily dispelled and heightened the level of tension in the capital.

Amidst this welter of conflicts there emerged a continuity of responsibility in the eyes of the French populace. Keith Baker and Dale Van Kley have emphasized the extent to which the ecclesiastical and constitutional controversies intensified demands for royal accountability at all levels of French society. Louis XV found himself obliged to abandon his role as neutral arbiter and descend into the fray of battle. As a result, he was held responsible for some highly contested decisions, which resulted in the alienation of both his institutional allies and his subjects. Moreover, as Van Kley has recently argued, the crown had founded its authority since the late sixteenth century on its ability to impose and maintain religious peace in the realm. Its inability to resolve the ongoing disputes between Jansenists and Jesuits, magistrates and clerics, directly undermined the principal justification for its absolute authority. The monarchy appeared blatantly ineffective in a century that deemed utility, as opposed to tradition or divine right, the only legitimate basis for the exercise of power.[15]

Yet another figure besides the king was perceived as a key player in these incidents: the marquise de Pompadour. Her involvement was a sensitive issue because the court itself was bitterly divided. Pompadour was seen as the ringleader of the faction that had promoted the appointment of Machault as controller general and stood in opposition to the *parti dévot,* which included the queen, Marie Leszczynska, and the Dauphin. In the case of the incident of the vanishing children in 1750, for instance, the recently appointed Lieutenant of Police Berryer, in charge of the investigation, was recognized as one of her *créatures.*[16] Kaplan has demonstrated that the shadow of the marquise hovered over the famine-plot rumors of 1751–52. Her close friend the tax farmer Etienne-Michel Bouret was credited with a scheme to supply grain to the starving masses that would profit the king and the grain swindlers.[17] Pompadour's beauty and charm did not even serve as an embellishment of royal virility. In popular eyes, the amorous activities of Louis XV, unlike those of his promiscuous ancestor Louis XIV, were viewed critically as signs of a character flaw if not condemned outright as sins.[18] This identification of the king's mistress as a source of misconduct in both the domestic and the political spheres had a profoundly destabilizing influence on the king himself.

It is important to recognize that none of these crises operated as a self-contained unit. Each successive outburst proved increasingly difficult to suppress since the crown was unable to isolate the sources of the conflict. The debates over taxes, refusal of the sacraments, and reforms of the General Hospital were intertwined. Louis XV had to reckon simultaneously with the remonstrances of his parlements, the resistance of his clergy, and the protests of his subjects. The net result was the gradual but undeniable erosion of traditional symbols of authority such as the church and the crown. The king was no longer able to define the parameters of public discussion. In a desperate attempt to reassert the royal prerogative, Louis XV tried to stem the opposition by imposing a Declaration of Silence in 1754. This decision reflected above all Louis XV's nostalgia for the days when government was conducted as what Keith Baker refers to as "le secret du roi."[19]

Nostalgia it was destined to remain because secrecy was no longer a viable option in the mid-eighteenth century. Louis XV's subjects had access to more information than his predecessors' subjects had had due to a rise in literacy and the increased availability of printed material in more affordable formats. Too many tongues were accustomed to discussing topics that previously had been the reserve of the privileged few.[20] As Arlette Farge has demonstrated, in the course of the eighteenth century the way the king's subjects viewed their role in the polity was transformed. They claimed as a fundamental right the freedom to formulate and exchange opinions about the issues that concerned them, what Farge has called "a right to know and to judge."[21] These newly discovered rights of the uneducated and unprivileged were not recognized by the crown or its officials. Individuals who challenged the traditional boundaries of silence and obedience were quickly arrested, guilty of crimes of opinion if not *lèse-majesté*. Yet as the case of Antoine Allègre demonstrates, imprisonment was not the most reliable solution, for once the process of politicization had been set in motion, the Bastille would only accelerate it.

The Road to Versailles

Allègre was twenty-four years old and living in Marseilles when he was arrested in May 1750. He was born and raised in Barroux, a village near Carpentras, in the Comtat Venaissin. He described his family in one of the forged letters as being "noble, but reduced to the bourgeoisie by the hardship of the times."[22] Thus, his was the experience of social decline in the eighteenth century, a family pushed down into the Third Estate while others grappled their way out. Both his parents were alive and lived off their income, which provided for ten children.[23] Such a large family imposed financial constraints and encouraged the sons to seek their fortunes beyond the confines of the paternal roof. Allègre's oldest brother had moved to St. Domingue six years earlier, the colonies providing one of the rare opportunities for young, single men willing to accept risks in hopes of earning a fortune. Allègre was closest to his older brother Joseph, who was a member of the Fathers of the Christian Doctrine.[24] Joseph taught rhetoric at a college in the village of Nant, in the neighboring Rouergue district.

Allègre's writings indicate that his parents had been wealthy enough to provide him with considerable formal education. When he was nine years old Allègre was sent off to study with the Jesuits at Carpentras. After four years he moved to Orange, where he studied rhetoric with the Fathers of the Christian Doctrine and acquired a solid educational foundation. Twelve months later he prepared for his novitiate with the Fathers of the Christian Doctrine in Avignon. Soon thereafter, however, he abandoned the order and his ecclesiastical aspirations. This decision cost him the financial support his parents had been willing to provide while he was preparing to be ordained. Since then, he had ceased writing to his mother and father but received occasional family news from his brother Joseph.

From Avignon, he wandered to Lodève and Tarascon, eventually settling in Marseilles in early November 1747. Finding himself penniless, he offered his services as preceptor to a local merchant, Sieur Amalric. Allègre hoped to acquire knowledge and experience in Amalric's trade while tutoring the merchant's four children. His dreams of becoming an associate were quickly dispelled, however, and Allègre moved on to try his luck elsewhere.

By July 1749 Allègre had decided to set up a boarding house with his friend, the abbé Tournel. Since the number of *maîtres de pension* was limited in Marseilles, he purchased the privilege from Sieur Perrier for 1,800 livres. He paid half the sum on borrowed money, mainly from Tournel, and the rest was placed on account, to be paid when he began earning money for his services. The pension had twenty-two boarders and brought in a revenue of approximately 8,000 livres per year. But Allègre had many debts to settle before he could begin amassing a fortune.[25] After his arrest Allègre's pension was dismantled to pay off impatient creditors.

In the winter of 1750 Allègre wrote to Mme de Pompadour, Louis XV's official *maîtresse en titre*, requesting a personal audience.[26] When he received permission to see her, Allègre put his affairs at the school in order and left Marseilles in early April. He arrived in Paris three weeks later and presented himself at the door of the royal favorite. Allègre explained that he had come to warn her to take precautions because he had uncovered evidence of a secret plot to poison both her and the king. When the marquise heard these allegations, she immediately sent Allègre to see the secretary of state, the comte d'Argenson.

Allègre met with the minister the next day and repeated his story about the conspiracy. In addition, he deposited a packet of letters on d'Argenson's desk substantiating his claims. The letters constituted an incomplete correspondence among three prominent figures in mid-eighteenth-century France: the comte de Maurepas, recently dismissed from office at Pompadour's behest; Dominique II de la Rochefoucauld, the archbishop of Albi; and Monseigneur de Souillac, bishop of Lodève. The epistolary exchange outlined the assassination that was being plotted.

D'Argenson thanked Allègre for the documentation, promised to review it carefully, and sent the tutor on his way. As Allègre journeyed back to Marseilles, d'Argenson turned the letters over to the police, who were concerned because the details of the conspiracy were highly plausible in the current political climate. Since 1749, Pompadour's name had been linked to that of her *créature* General Machault, the new controller, and his unpopular tax, the *vingtième*. Although the police found the allegations contained in the letters credible, the evidence itself was dubious. Close scrutiny revealed that all the letters had been written by the same hand. The most obvious suspect, indeed the only one, was the man who had turned the letters over to the marquise, Antoine Allègre. Thus, Allègre was arrested and detained in Montpellier, from where he was transferred to the Bastille on 31 May 1750.

During his first interrogation by Lieutenant of Police Berryer, Allègre denied the charges and protested his innocence. He insisted that the letters had been given to him in February by an unknown sailor in Marseilles. The sailor had come to his doorstep and asked, "Are you the one they call Al-lègre?" When Allègre answered in the affirmative, the stranger had handed him a package, explaining that he had been sent from Lodève. The unknown man had disappeared as quickly and mysteriously as he had arrived. Allègre had been alarmed by the contents of the letters, which included a plot to kill the king and his mistress with poisoned paper. He immediately wrote Pompadour to request a private audience. He had not discussed this incident with anyone because he did not want the assassins to suspect anything.[27]

After forwarding the letters to Versailles, Allègre declared, he had received a response indicating that he would be welcome at the royal palace if he were able to manage the journey. He had left Marseilles on 8 April 1750 and arrived in Versailles three weeks later. He claimed that the marquise had directed him to the comte d'Argenson, the secretary of state, who had been shocked by the letters. Nonetheless, d'Argenson had explained that since these letters were copies of the original, they could not be used as proof to convict the conspirators. With this news, Allègre had opted to return to Lodève, hoping to turn up additional evidence to substantiate his claims.

On 8 June 1750, during his second interrogation by Lieutenant of Police Berryer, Allègre was shown the packet of letters and asked to identify them. Berryer suggested to Allègre that he was in fact the author of the anonymous letters because they "had been written on precisely the same size and type of paper . . . as the two sheets of paper that had been found in his pockets at the time of his arrest."[28] Although Berryer was confident that he had captured the author of these forged epistles, he needed evidence to confirm his suspicions.

Nine months after his initial interrogation Allègre confessed to his crime. He had invented the conspiracy plot, and after seeing the marquise de Pompadour on 29 April 1750 he had written the letters to substantiate his allegations. He had been inspired by rumors he had overheard earlier in the year denouncing Pompadour and blaming her for the *vingtième*.[29] These rumors had persuaded him that Pompadour, and by implication her lover, the king, were in danger. Allègre had decided "to warn the marquise, who was being publicly slandered, and urge her to take greater precautions in looking after her personal safety." He explained to Berryer that he had selected Maurepas as the ringleader since he was a highly visible enemy of the royal mistress, who had engineered his dismissal from the court the preceding year. Allègre explained that "in recompense for this service rendered, I hoped to obtain from her a position or the promotion of a project I had drafted concerning commerce."[30]

By the time Antoine Allègre confessed, on 3 March 1751, the police were not surprised since they had pursued all of Allègre's leads and found nothing to substantiate his initial allegations. They had briefly arrested his brother Joseph, the rhetoric professor, to see if he had been involved in the plot but had released him due to lack of evidence. In his confession Allègre explained how he had pieced his plot together. Many of the details had been suggested by actual events that increased the verisimilitude of his false accusation. For example, he had incorporated rumors he overheard regarding Pompadour into the letters he drafted as evidence of the plot. Regarding another detail he explained: "If I mentioned that the poison was to be supplied by a nun in Auxerre, it was because on passing through Auxerre by stagecoach, I learned that a monk skilled in the composition of poisons had been taken to the local prison."[31]

Like Bonafon, Allègre drew upon overheard conversations and bits of information to patch together a seemingly credible narrative of events. However, whereas Bonafon commented on incidents in the recent past, Allègre predicted those in the near future. Their success in fashioning convincing and compelling stories made the police profoundly uneasy, especially since both tales focused on the king and his female favorite. The stature of their protagonists was mirrored, ironically, in the severity of their punishment, when delinquent acts were classified as treason.

Like Bonafon, Allègre was educated and literate. Both came from impoverished minor noble families who found themselves ranked as members of the unprivileged Third Estate, obliged to work for a living. In both instances, the police were disturbed by the fact that the accused would direct their intellectual curiosity and endeavor to such deviant ends. Whereas Bonafon left a novel as an indication of her literary interests, Allègre bequeathed a police dossier containing book requests, *mémoires*, and notebooks filled with mathematical calculations.

Allègre's book requests reveal his intellectual interests and ambitions.

They fell within a spectrum of Enlightenment interests slanted toward mathematics and mechanical sciences, as the following list of requested titles indicates: *L'architecture hydraulique* and *La science des ingenieurs,* both by Belidor, *La nouvelle mécanique,* by Varignon, *La science du calcul et l'analyse demontrée par le père Reynaud, La table des sines secantes et tangentes, Les commentaires de Polybe,* by the Chevalier de Folard, *Les oeuvres* of Mariotte, *Nouvelle méthode pour apprendre à dessiner,* and *Un traité d'arpentage et de navigation,* by Father Perenan. He also had a subscription to the *Mercure de France* because a concerned postmaster in Marseilles forwarded some back issues to him in prison in 1751.[32] Like many of his contemporaries, Allègre was a dilettante scientist and engineer. He was constantly demanding treatises such as *La science des ingenieurs* or *La nouvelle mécanique.*[33] He was especially interested in mathematics and its practical applications, such as hydraulics and navigation.[34] The evidence suggests, furthermore, that Allègre was not a passive reader. The texts provided the materials for his own inventions: his notebooks were filled with drawings of machines, algebraic equations, and geometric theorems.[35]

Perhaps the most significant of his projects was the treatise on commerce he had hoped to present to the king if he succeeded in securing a royal audience on the pretext of the conspiracy plot. Entitled "Essai sur la Marine," this text makes a convincing case for France's need to invest in the development of a powerful naval force. The essay opens with paeans to the multiple benefits of commerce, which Allègre defines as the free circulation of "the products of nature and the human spirit."[36] The free exchange of goods and ideas echoes themes found in the works of Montesquieu, Mandeville, and Hume, the school of "le doux commerce," whose proponents emphasized the civilizing benefits of trade that followed naturally when commercial exchange replaced military conflict. He insisted that France needed to promote commerce, especially exports of its wines and silks, in order to generate wealth and accrue power in comparison with other countries. Allègre explained that "if France needs commerce, commerce in turn needs a navy." Thus, he outlined a proposal for setting up a royal construction yard at Havre de Grace with sawmills and a labor force recruited from criminals condemned to forced labor on naval arsenals *(peine des galères)* and undeployed soldiers. He was convinced that without a strong navy

France would find itself fighting long and costly wars with unfavorable results. In hindsight, Allègre's project seems prescient given the fiasco of the Seven Years' War with England, which lay just ahead.

Nobody would ever read Allègre's naval project during his lifetime. Yet his name would acquire momentary notoriety in 1756, when his fate was briefly intertwined with that of one of the Bastille's legendary prisoners, Jean Danry, who later renamed himself vicomte de Latude. Allègre entered history as one of seven people who succeeded in breaking out of the Bastille. On the night of 25 February 1756 the two cellmates managed to escape from the royal fortress (see figs. 5 and 6). Both were recaptured within a month, Latude in Holland and Allègre in Brussels. After this second arrest Allègre was placed under stricter surveillance and stripped of all privileges, such as walks around the fortress ramparts and books. Latude was more fortunate than Allègre: he lived to publish his account of their extraordinary feat and saw himself hailed as a hero by the crowd that liberated him on 14 July 1789. Allègre was less fortunate and died by the time history had caught up with his jailers.[37]

The success of Allègre's conspiracy scheme ultimately depended on his ability to produce a story sufficiently plausible to prompt an official response. That the police did not immediately dismiss Allègre's allegations as preposterous was an acknowledgment that they *could* have been true in the current political climate. Moreover, threats against the king and his mistress, whether real or imaginary, could not be lightly dismissed. Under French law, imagining or alluding to the king's death constituted an act of *lèse-majesté*.[38] The police instinctively sensed that by coupling loyalty with regicide, these fictitious scenarios were detrimental to the crown's interests in the long run. Thus, like Bonafon, Allègre was treated with far greater severity than he had anticipated.

The Language of Loyalty

As with Marie Bonafon, Antoine Allègre's attitudes toward Louis XV must be explored in the context of the royal mistress because Allègre's crime involved an alleged threat to her person. Allègre's case differed from that of Bonafon in that the king's consort was a more ambiguous figure. For the author of *Tanastès,* the mistress was evil incarnate: she was a foil for the king,

Figure 5.
Il s'échappe de la Bastille avec Dalègre.

*(Courtesy of the Bibliothèque Nationale de
France, Collection Histoire de France)*

Figure 6.
26 Février 1756: Seconde évasion de Masers de Latude.

*(Courtesy of the Bibliothèque Nationale de
France, Collection Histoire de France)*

a scapegoat for the kingdom's woes, a sign of despotic rule. Allègre's attitudes toward Louis XV's mistress were more ambivalent. Initially, he addressed Pompadour with humility and respect, as an extension of the king's person, a channel of access, a fountain of favor.

There is considerable irony in Allègre's case regarding the royal mistress. He relied on public hostility to substantiate his fictitious plot while simultaneously premising his own intervention on professed loyalty. To succeed, his crime needed to tap into two distinct sets of concerns, one popular and the other official. He drew upon this material when drafting the letters he produced as evidence of his allegations. Moreover, he had to be equally convincing in two antagonistic roles, as would-be assassin and valiant defender. Despite his efforts to distance himself from these disrespectful opinions, Allègre was ultimately implicated by them. His ability to convince the police of a threat meant that the information he provided was plausible. Could he have achieved this level of verisimilitude if he had not shared or at least been sympathetic to the views he so deftly attributed to his conspirators?

In confessing his crime Allègre described its genesis in the following terms: "During the months of January and February 1750, at the time of the publication of the edict for the *vingtième*, the public was attributing this imposition to Mme la Marquise de Pompadour. I heard it said that this could bring her some misfortune and inspire some of her enemies, without mentioning any specific names, to hatch a plot . . . in the course of my journey from Marseilles to the court I heard several people, mainly soldiers I did not know, saying the same things."[39] Allègre's reasoning confirms evidence from other sources concerning the state of public opinion circa 1750. As Thomas Kaiser has shown, there was a consensus among disparate segments of the French populace that the imposition of the *vingtième* was directly linked to excessive artistic expenditures by Pompadour. Drawing upon a long tradition that associated royal mistresses with corrosive luxury and ruinous pleasure, and nourished by the somber reality of the royal deficit, hungry pamphleteers and embittered courtiers mobilized considerable hostility to the marquise, which Allègre then tailored to his own agenda.[40]

It is important to note Allègre's efforts to distance himself from the criticisms of Pompadour mentioned in the quotation in the preceding paragraph. He attributes them to "the public" as a way of shifting responsibility for the offensive attitudes off himself and onto society at large. This rhetorical strategy was not unusual among individuals summoned to defend themselves against charges of *mauvais discours* in the mid-eighteenth century.[41] The tactic allowed for the repetition of seditious remarks while simultaneously legitimating the public as an agent of political discussion and criticism. Although it rarely exonerated the accused, it did testify to the existence of a new force in French political culture well before magistrates and philosophes established it as a tribunal for checking royal authority. The police refused to acknowledge references to the public as legitimate explanations, insisting that *mauvais propos*, no matter where they originated, were criminal utterances even if they were merely overheard or related to others.

Allègre's references to "the public," like Marie Bonafon's, made the police uneasy because the public was by definition amorphous and omnipresent and hence difficult to monitor. Such references testified to their own limitations as effective agents of control in a society where information was no longer a rare commodity but circulated freely on an open market. The accused were attempting to turn the table on their accusers, suggesting that they, the accused, could not be held responsible for misusing information the police had failed to suppress. Moreover, there was an implicit link between information and opinion because access to information was the prerequisite for formulating a defensible opinion. The increased availability of information, in printed and oral forms, enhanced the level of political awareness across the spectrum of French society. By augmenting the development of the critical faculties of the governed, information fueled demands for political accountability that emanated from individuals lacking any institutional or historical basis for such claims.

Allègre's fictitious conspiracy reflected a nuanced understanding of French politics in 1750 by an individual whose station in life precluded any form of legitimate participation in the decision-making process. Two of the individuals whom Allègre selected to mastermind the plot, the comte de Maurepas and the archbishop of Albi, La Rochefoucauld, were publicly recognized enemies of the marquise. Maurepas had been dismissed from the court in 1750 in part because he was reputed to be the author of scurrilous verses about Pompadour's gynecological problems.[42]

Struggles among court rivals were no longer confined to residents of the palace, as Allègre's explanation made clear:

> I planned to draft in the form of letters certain satirical traits that were circulating at the time and to insert a kind of conspiracy plot against the person of Mme de Pompadour; to pass off M. de Maurepas as the perpetrator because this gentleman had always been regarded as the enemy of Mme de Pompadour . . . and the love of vengeance could have easily inspired him to form a violent resolution . . . M. D'Albi because everyone said that he had been strongly opposed to the *vingtième* . . . and also M. de Lodève because since I had lived in this city, it made sense that I would be more likely to be informed of what was happening [here] than in some other place.[43]

The police were startled and disturbed by Allègre's lucid account. His reasoning revealed a surprising level of political acumen for a tutor from Marseilles.

Allègre's police file includes the letters he had forged as evidence of the correspondence among Maurepas, Souillac, and La Rochefoucauld. The three men revealed a conscious plan to take advantage of the discontent provoked by the imposition of the *vingtième* and the growing hostility toward Pompadour. Writing on behalf of Maurepas to La Rochefoucauld, Allègre had emphasized: "Here is the *vingtième* I told you about. The people are groaning under the weight of an extortionist, a slut who leads our Sardanapolous by the nose. Let us seize the occasion to rile up his subjects. I am going to foment, stir up discord among the members of his estates of Brittany, some of whom are devoted to me. You should do the same for those in Languedoc. The people will open their eyes."[44] With this paragraph Allègre tapped into prevailing assumptions that revolts were directed from above: discontented elites stirring up popular sedition. Thus, Allègre suggested that an embittered former minister in exile from the court was sowing discord in the service of personal vengeance.

Allègre not only tailored his allegations to conform to these official convictions but substantiated them with actual instances of contestation that had erupted in specific provinces, such as Brittany and Languedoc, in response to the crown's effort to impose the *vingtième*. These allusions struck a sensitive chord, especially since in 1750–51 the disputes remained unresolved. In this particular passage the parlementary protests are presented as necessary and just responses to a corrupt ruler and a despotic mistress. Louis XV is portrayed as a debauched ruler from antiquity, Sardanapoulos, and his mistress as a whore and an extortionist. The same links between sexual infidelity and political despotism that played a central role in Bonafon's *Tanastès* are reinforced as paradigms for evaluating and criticizing royal authority. Maurepas's letter captured the popular sentiment that the power of Louis XV's mistresses reflected the king's own weakness and emasculation rather than his virility. One of the distinguishing features of a tyrant was the lack of an independent will; corruption and self-indulgence allowed others to seize control of the reins of state.[45]

In the reign of Louis XV, royal lubricity was no longer applauded but was rebuked as a defect if not outright condemned as a sin. Pompadour followed in a long line of women selected by the king to sate his lust.[46] The three villains in Allègre's plot portrayed Louis XV as having an insatiable appetite for women, who were offered in quick succession like sacrificial lambs. The court was transformed into a brothel under the duc de Richelieu's supervision. In one letter La Rochefoucauld wrote to Maurepas: "I have heard that Richelieu is a clever pimp. He has proposed a heifer. I hope it works. He would spare us the death of the financière."[47] The word *financière* refers to Pompadour, whose father had been a steward to the Pâris brothers, who served the crown as bankers and munitions suppliers. The mistresses held sway over the king's mortal body: they catered to his basest cravings in the privacy of the boudoir. As beneficiaries of royal favor, the mistresses had direct and unlimited access to the king's ear. They were supreme instances of arbitrary authority, for their ascent and descent was determined exclusively by the king.

Mme de Pompadour was rarely named directly in this fictional correspondence among her conspiring enemies. Allusions to her assumed two forms, each drawing upon a different linguistic register. On the one hand, Allègre relied on imagery derived from antiquity and the reigns of despotic rulers, for example, when he described Louis XV as Sardanapoulos and Pompadour as Messaline. Such figures were recognizable allusions to the decadence of late antiquity and the collapse of republican traditions into tyranny. They also adhered to the prevailing model of despotism, which held it to be a form of government that was removed in either time or place. They were common parlance in eighteenth-century France to convey fears of despotism, readily comprehensible across the social spectrum.

On the other hand, Allègre selected from a crude and vulgar vocabulary, one associated with *les chansons poissardes* and carnivalesque farce. In these instances Pompadour was referred to as a slut, "une catin," or as a broodmare, "cette jumant poulinière."[48] These terms operated on a different register than those lifted from antiquity. They served as a gauge of popular attitudes, echoing the vulgar expressions overheard in the streets. Despite their distinct features, both vocabularies shared a common goal to demean the character of the woman whom Louis XV had selected as his most intimate companion. In addition, the king emerged as ineffectual and debauched, bearing all the trappings of a despot.

In an unsigned letter intended to reflect the views of one of the two ecclesiastics involved, Allègre referred to the pattern of misconduct Louis XV had established early in his reign:

> Nothing is more striking than the conduct of our prince, born with the most promising inclinations. Hunting absorbed him completely. When he grew older we saw him pleasing himself at private banquets, at which, it was suspected, the rules of propriety were not observed, but scarcely was he disgusted by this that he seduced three sisters in succession, a terrible thing, a scandalous example that had not been seen under any of our kings except one who had been excommunicated by St. Germain. Ah! where are those days when zeal animated the servants of our Gallican church, when kings listened respectfully to pious remonstrances?[49]

The three sisters referred to were the three daughters of the marquis de Nesle. Beginning in 1737 with Mme de Mailly, Louis XV had affairs with three of the five Nesle sisters.[50] The last of these, Mme de la Tournelle, was the unpopular duchesse de Châteauroux discussed in chapter 2. This quotation draws on *dévot* critiques of the king's licentious behavior and their emphasis on his duty to provide spiritual leadership to the kingdom.

Allègre's emphasis on this particular aspect of Louis XV's behavior is telling. It echoes themes from the Bonafon case as well as the ongoing ecclesiastical and constitutional struggles that kept the capital in a state of turmoil. The king's sexuality was a political issue because it placed his sacred status at risk and threatened to delegitimate both his personal authority and that of the church that sanctioned it. Moreover, it was a central argument in the *parti dévot*'s opposition to royal policy on several fronts, including Jansenism, the Parlement's remonstrances, and the *vingtième*.[51]

Both cases confirmed what the police most feared: ribald references to the king's sexual conduct were spreading beyond the intimate circle of court gossip and eroding the awe and mystery that had traditionally adhered to his person. The king's decision in 1737 to seek pleasure outside of the conjugal bed, hardly exceptional in the history of the Bourbon monarchy, prompted an unusually vociferous and hostile response among the populace. Absorbed in his amorous pursuits and uncomfortable in large gatherings, Louis XV eschewed public occasions and rites of state whenever possible. His sexual infidelities prevented him from confessing, which meant that he was unable to perform the royal touch. The ceremony of touching for scrofula was an especially endearing aspect of French sovereignty. It provided a rare moment of direct interaction between the sovereign and his most humble and distressed subjects. The mystical healing power manifested the king's sacredness in familiar and immediately accessible terms. In a crude way the royal touch had been reversed in the reign of Louis XV since both the marquise de Vintimille and the duchesse de Châteauroux had died shortly after being "touched" by Louis XV. Thus reverence and affection gave way to resentment and mockery of a king who was rarely seen, tenuously loved, and therefore easily suspected and maligned.

The forged epistolary exchange among the three conspirators revealed tensions regarding appropriate attitudes toward Louis XV. The conflicting interests that Allègre attributed to Maurepas and the bishop of Lodève perhaps reflected his own uncertainties about the royal person. Bonafon had expressed her ambivalence toward the king by doubling the fictitious figure of the king in her novel; Allègre conveyed the same ambivalence through his imaginary dialog among three correspondents. Allègre established Maurepas as an individual who resented the ingratitude with which the crown had compensated his years of service. He was determined to seek vengeance and blamed Pompadour for his ill-treatment. As he explained in a letter to Souillac: "Yes, Monsieur, I was disgraced, and I was grateful for the letter. You honored me by writing on this subject, but it is not enough to pity me; you must help me seek revenge for myself. You know who is responsible, let her die by our hands. The Châteauroux died, why will this one not die as well?"[52] Attached to this letter were some satirical verses Maurepas had composed to vent his frustration. Like Bonafon, Allègre authenticated his fictional characters with verifiable historical details. Maurepas was, in fact, reputed to be the author of scurrilous verses mocking Pompadour.

Maurepas wrote this letter to persuade Souillac to support the coup he was secretly plotting. Souillac's initial reply was hesitant and noncommittal: "I will not deny, Monsieur, your grievances, but I do not approve of your schemes . . . it is not wise to decry the king . . . it is not for us to judge our master. I will keep your secret, but I would advise you to moderate your language, especially against the king."[53] Although sympathetic to Maurepas's plight, Souillac was unwilling to assume the power to judge the king. As an ecclesiastic, he believed that only God could legitimately depose his appointed viceroy. Mere mortals should not assume responsibility for such judgments. Souillac would need to be persuaded to cooperate.

Maurepas did not temper his critique of Louis XV; nevertheless, he assured Souillac that he was motivated by zeal for his country's welfare. In addition, he indicated that the archbishop of Albi was supporting him. Souillac finally acquiesced, but with reservations: "I am making a mistake, but I was unable to withstand your resentment and the entreaties of M. d'Albi. Do what you will, I consent as long as you do not undertake anything against the king, whom I implore you to treat with greater consideration."[54] As will be seen, the cautious and ambiguous tone of this letter, its reluctance to involve the king directly, corresponded most closely to Allègre's own views about Louis XV.

At the time of his arrest Allègre was brimming with fidelity toward both the king and his official mistress. Fidelity provided the pretext for Allègre's scheme to gain favor, recognition, perhaps even a pension. In denouncing the fictitious conspiracy, Allègre claimed to be fulfilling the duties of a *fidèle sujet*. Thus, Allègre drew attention to evidence that confirmed his loyalty, arguing that his being entrusted with the secret was a testament to his integrity. One of the documents he identified during his interrogation was the cover letter for the package he claimed to have received from the unknown sailor. Ostensibly written by a guilt-ridden member of the conspiracy who had decided to clear his conscience, the letter opened with the following lines: "Although a stranger, sir, you are not lacking in zeal for the state, and this is what has determined my choosing you in preference to anyone else to reveal a great secret. . . . I will not be able to rest until everything has been revealed; do not disappoint . . . my trust . . . go, serve me, save the king, save the state: the letters I am sending you will explain the danger."[55]

Playing upon the familiar trope of a humble servant designated to convey a secret message to the king, Allègre emphasized that he had been carefully selected for this mission of saving the king and his companion. This theme of "touching the king," or speaking to him directly, was an underlying structure of the *mauvais discours* throughout the eighteenth century and exercised considerable popular appeal. It was a dangerous rhetoric from an official perspective and rigorously policed if only because the notion of "touching" was simultaneously empowering and easily distorted to justify illusory missions of sacrificial regicide, a point that would be vividly illustrated several years later by Damiens's coup.[56] As a gesture of loyalty it was therefore notably ambivalent, as likely to confirm suspicions as to allay them.

In his efforts to establish the truth of his allegations Allègre described his initial response to the contents of the letters, stressing that upon "seeing all the vile things these letters contained against the sacred person of His Majesty and that of Mme la Marquise de Pompadour threatened, he did not think it appropriate to bury this package in silence, especially since he did not want to render himself guilty by association."[57] Allègre's insistence that he had reacted with appropriate indignation to a *mauvais discours*, in this case written, not spoken, recurred throughout the discussions between the police and the defendants. The police constantly reminded the accused that a loyal subject was expected to express his anger and repulsion when confronted by a *mauvais propos*. Silence was the equivalent of approval; one was guilty by association with the tainted text or utterance.

This definition of loyalty highlighted the extent to which the theory of French kingship rested on the individual's identifying himself with the king, his honor with the king's. Allègre had clearly internalized this message and incorporated it into the staging of his crime, as the following excerpt from a letter to Louis XV confirms: "The reading of these abominable letters had the same effect on me as they would on all other good French men. I was seized by horror and indignation at the sight of so many heinous crimes."[58] As part of his own defense Allègre had to distance himself from the offensive sentiments expressed in the letters by aligning himself with the principle of loyalty. Alluding to the king's death, as Arlette Farge reminds us, was like playing with fire: it was difficult to approach the topic without getting burned in the process.[59]

The letter Allègre wrote to Louis XV describing the circumstances of the conspiracy and his involvement in it provided a testament of his loyalty. He accounted for his willingness to risk his life "because I would only be too happy to spill my blood in the service of your Majesty."[60] This image of self-sacrifice was omnipresent in the language of fidelity in mid-eighteenth-century France. These subjects believed that just as the king had been appointed by God to protect his subjects, it was their duty to offer their life in their sovereign's defense.[61]

Interestingly enough, Allègre extended the topoi of self-sacrifice to include the king's mistress. Implicit in the terms of the conspiracy was the assumption that attacking what the king held dear was an indirect means of attacking him. It followed from this premise that in protecting the royal favorite, one was protecting the king. Allègre relied on the same image of personal sacrifice in justifying his decision to approach the marquise. As he explained in a letter written to Pompadour from the Bastille on 26 October 1750, "To explain everything in one word, the preservation of your life, for which I would gladly sacrifice a thousand lives if I had that many, was the mainspring for and object of my imprudence, no matter what the motive that pushed me in my error."[62] Even though Allègre's gesture of fidelity was premised on a lie, he claimed that his intentions had been good.

Could loyalty withstand such twisted logic and emerge unscathed? In his confession Allègre described his decision to alert Pompadour about a threat to her life. He emphasized that the prevailing climate of opinion had clouded his judgment. Once he was "persuaded that these rumors could have some foundation, I resolved to warn the Marquise, who was being slandered by them, so that she would be more concerned with her own safety."[63] He had merely elaborated on the truth, presenting vague rumors as real threats. This hardly constituted a criminal act.

Allègre was guilty of lying, not treason, since "as a reward for this service I hoped to obtain from her some employment or the promotion of a project I had drafted concerning commerce."[64] Money, honor, recognition, and
revenge—these were the motives that inspired the majority of false conspiracy plots. Ultimately, this manipulation of the authorities under the
guise of fidelity augmented suspicion and misunderstanding between the
crown and its subjects. Individuals resorted to desperate means to press
claims within a social structure that refused to accommodate their desires,
needs, or grievances.

Allègre had hoped to receive a financial reward or an audience during
which he could present his naval project. He believed that Mme de Pompadour had enough enemies to merit a warning that her life was in danger. By
telling a small lie, he had aimed to protect the royal favorite and profit from
it. It was, he insisted, his ardent loyalty that had first raised his concern and
led him astray. In a supplicatory letter written to d'Argenson from his
prison cell several months earlier he had implored the minister: "Deign, I
beseech you, to forget the fault without forgetting he who is guilty; and if I
sinned, consider that it was less from malice than from misguided imprudence. My zeal produced my errors."[65] The problem for Allègre, however,
was not so much the choice of Pompadour as a target but the decision to include the king, which he would be hard-pressed to justify.

The last of the anonymous letters detailing the coup indicated that both
Louis XV and his mistress would die after coming into contact with poisoned stationery: "These poisoned letters will poison the fingers of the king
and the Marquise, spreading their venom easily if one sniffs them too
closely or if one takes snuff immediately after touching them."[66] This is the
only document that spells out the design to kill the king. The silence suggests that Allègre was reluctant to include the king. His decision may reflect
his belief that by generating greater concern, he would secure a more generous reward.

From the time of his arrest, despite his miserable situation, Allègre maintained his allegiance to Louis XV. Although he would become increasingly
defiant over time, his support for the king remained intact. As late as 1762
Allègre was still writing to d'Argenson: "To please the king, you, the court,
this is the unique object of my ambition, and of all my efforts . . . give me

the opportunity to demonstrate my good intentions other than through words and syllables. . . . I will congratulate myself less on the pleasure of being free than on the pleasure of faithfully serving His Majesty because one cannot attain perfect happiness except through the perfect fulfillment of one's duty."[67] Allègre yearned to demonstrate his fidelity, rectify his error, and restore himself to the king's good graces. Yet, as a prisoner Allègre had nothing but impassioned prose to plead his cause. He searched desperately for a way out of this impasse.

As the preceding chapter demonstrates, Marie Bonafon's primary goal was to reestablish her credibility as a loyal subject. This proved to be Allègre's overriding concern as well. He was willing to tolerate material discomfort if it would allow him to obtain royal retribution: "I am not asking for leniency. All that matters to me is to sense that the court deigns to admit me to the ranks of its most loyal subjects; that is all I need to make my lot bearable."[68] Allègre demanded psychological or emotional reassurance from the king, for fidelity required acknowledgment on the part of its recipient. If the king failed to recognize Allègre's loyalty, then Allègre ceased to exist as a royal subject, a category that posited unqualified obedience and submission to the royal will.

Allègre's persistent attempts to demonstrate his fidelity were part of his effort to secure a pardon. Initially Allègre believed that if he could somehow compensate the king and his mistress for the offense he had provoked, he would be forgiven. He constantly sought to minimize the gravity of his crime, emphasizing the distinction between mischief and malice, criteria that weighed heavily in penal judgment: "I know that what I did was wrong: but my intentions were not malicious . . . my case is one of thoughtlessness and not of malice. It is fitting that His Majesty exercise his justice and that I be punished. But it is also natural to his grandeur to assign limits to the punishment."[69] Thus, Allègre was not denying the sovereign's right to punish his subjects. Yet punishment should be proportional to the gravity of the crime or else it became arbitrary and abusive. Like the police, whose approach to criminal repression was shaped by ecclesiastical definitions of sin, Allègre focused on the issue of intention to minimize his offense.

From his prison cell in the Bastille Allègre attempted to plea-bargain with his captors. He offered his inventions as tributes to his sovereign: "You must believe . . . that I am devoted to France. Even as a captive there is not a day, and often not a night, when I do not try to imagine or invent something that might contribute to His Majesty's glory: liberated, I would willingly dedicate to his service the little bit of youth and talent that remained to me."[70] Allègre designed one invention for the marquise de Pompadour, the woman he held responsible for his fate. He proposed building her a machine that would pump water into her gardens at her château Bellevue. He hastened to clarify that his suggestion was not motivated by self-interest: "In all of this my only goal . . . is to please you with my zeal and fervor . . . deign, illustrious Marquise, to remember the state in which I find myself: please grant me the grace of an exile to my native land or send me to America. . . . I sinned without malice: I repent my error."[71] Allègre was convinced that Pompadour was responsible for his fate since she had been most offended by his actions. Thus, he attested to widespread perceptions that the king's mistress exercised real power through her *créatures*, such as Berryer, whom she had strategically positioned in key offices.

By emphasizing the power of the marquise, Allègre was acknowledging her control over the king. Louis XV would pardon Allègre if his mistress persuaded him to do so. In addressing Pompadour, Allègre recognized the considerable authority she exercised as the king's titled mistress:

It is not worthy of you, Madame, that I should die miserably for you. I rendered myself guilty and unhappy, only in aspiring to be admitted among your clients . . . in this way, Madame, even if you are not the ultimate arbiter of my fate, humane and kind in accordance with the inclinations of the fair sex, on the model of and under the auspices of His Majesty . . . please concern yourself with my fate. Become my mediator . . . the Bastille cannot withstand your eyes . . . just one of your gazes would suffice to open its doors and release me. I am demanding this gaze as a mark of recognition, which you owe, Madame, to the king's glory, to yourself, and to nature.[72]

In this paragraph Allègre both confirms and subverts a traditional language of deference and courtesy. He stresses that it is undignified for someone of elevated station to abuse her position: Pompadour is simultaneously betraying her rank and her sex by refusing to mediate between a prisoner in the Bastille and an angry king.

In his plea Allègre calls specific attention to the power of the royal gaze, and by extension that of the royal mistress. This emphasis on the connections between seeing and power speaks directly to the ceremonial culture of French absolutism as it had developed in the reign of Louis XIV. According to Norbert Elias, the court society was a specific configuration of power in which vision established and legitimated status, rank, and title. Vision not only conferred power, which is why it was constantly sought, but could also negate it through deliberate denial. The symbol of Pompadour's gaze opening the Bastille's bolted doors simultaneously highlights the power of vision and the profound inequality embedded in its deployment under the Old Regime. For Allègre could not lay claim to the same constitutive power of vision as his social superior; he could only demand to be the object of her benevolent gaze. Thus, he implored her to cast an eye to his fate, recognizing that he did not even exist as long as he remained outside her field of vision.

Although Allègre deferred to the marquise's station, he did not place her on a par with Louis XV. The king retained his hold on the reins of his state. Pompadour was still working, at least in Allègre's mind, under royal auspices. Pardon would ultimately spring from one source, that of the royal figure, God's viceroy on earth. Pompadour was a channel to this source; the comte d'Argenson was another. Allègre was convinced that the king, who was by definition merciful and just, remained ignorant of his situation. The idea that if the king only knew, he would help, kept Allègre attached to his sovereign as he grew increasingly desperate about his fate. According to this logic, Louis XV could not be aware of his plight, for if he were, he would not have allowed such injustice to be perpetrated in his name.

In the files of both Allègre and Bonafon the main characters are mistresses, ministers, and police officials. Authority was physically separated from the figure of the king himself. The image of the king took shape in the shadows of these figures; his virtues emerged in contrast to their vices. For Bonafon, the royal consort was used to warn Louis XV that he risked becoming a despot. For Allègre, the female favorite provided a vehicle for self-promotion and, ultimately, self-destruction. In both cases the king was displaced from center stage and left hovering in the wings. He was neither charismatic nor indispensable. With such a diminutive role, Louis XV lost the trappings of invulnerability and omnipotence. Whereas Bonafon regretted her offense and sought repentance, Allègre gravitated in the opposite direction. He assumed an increasingly defiant stance toward forms of authority he saw as arbitrary and unjust. Although he would never attack Louis XV directly, the arguments he developed raised implicit questions about the legitimacy of the king's power.

Fidelity and Justice

Dena Goodman has argued that a distinguishing feature of the early Enlightenment was a shift from fidelity to justice as the conceptual paradigm for maintaining social order and justifying the exercise of authority.[73] Relying on a close reading of Montesquieu's *Persian Letters*, she demonstrates the crucial role played by definitions of loyalty in the theoretical articulation of absolutism. Through the eyes of two foreigners visiting Paris during the Regency, Montesquieu explored the ways interlocking circles of fidelity culminated in the person of the king. Goodman suggests that close analysis of Montesquieu's satire reveals inherent tensions within the concept of loyalty. She refers to "systems of fidelity" that came into conflict with one another, fostering disputes and instability. According to her thesis, the purpose of the *Persian Letters* was to provide a solution to this dilemma through the construction of a new system based on justice. An absolute, transcendental notion of justice would replace the particularistic and subjective value of fidelity. As Goodman argues, justice, unlike loyalty, was not inherently attached to the royal figure. Thus, this transition paved the way for a radical break with traditional divine-right theory in favor of polities founded on principles of law and natural rights.

Goodman's analysis of the *Persian Letters* provides a useful backdrop for charting Allègre's political trajectory during his imprisonment since fidelity and justice constituted the two poles of his political universe. Moreover, the emphasis on Montesquieu is appropriate given Allègre's reliance on the concept and language of despotism in his criticism of Old Regime justice. Like so many French men and women in the 1750s, Allègre feared that the French monarchy was becoming despotic in the hands of a weak and negligent king. The key emblems of this transformation were the domineering mistress, the autocratic ministers, and the invisible king who figured in Allègre's understanding of his plight.

After three years in the Bastille the grim reality of life imprisonment smothered Allègre's flickering hopes for a pardon. This crushing sense of despair and frustration is indicated by a noticeable shift in the tone and tenor of his writings, which grew more violent and aggressive. A subjective vocabulary of fidelity and deference was replaced by the universal claims of justice and natural rights. With these arguments Allègre became a *mauvais sujet* who threatened the regime that had locked him away. Arguably, this was a category the police had created for him, whose criteria he came to fulfill.

Initially Allègre had approached Mme de Pompadour with humility and deference. Since he had threatened her personally, he needed to secure her forgiveness if he was to be released. Unfortunately, Pompadour displayed none of the merciful attributes of either the fair sex or the king. On the contrary, as he explained in a letter to Lieutenant of Police Berryer, she appeared indifferent to his plight: "But I have suffered for three years now and it is as if I had not suffered at all. Nonetheless, if Mme la Marquise de Pompadour were no longer at court, I would be free. Thus, it is not my error that detains me in irons; the will of one powerful person determines my crime since she alone deems it necessary to punish me."[74] With this assertion Allègre shifted the focus from the implications of his crime to the injustice of his punishment. The accused, in effect, became the accuser, denouncing the judicial system he perceived as arbitrary and unjust.

Allègre's emphasis on "the will of one powerful person" draws directly upon the vocabulary of despotism. *Volonté*, or will, was the flag for despotic authority, a system based on force rather than law. In addition to Pompadour's *volonté* Allègre stressed that "she alone deems it necessary to punish me." Here too Allègre was contrasting the arbitrary will of the despot to the legally constituted and constrained will of the French king. Pompadour had circumvented the legal channels and procedures to keep him locked away. Unlike the king, she was unchecked by principles of divine mission or constitutional restraint. Thus, Allègre was consciously relying on a specific vocabulary to transform Pompadour into a despotic symbol. In the process, however, he began to question the political structure of the Old Regime that permitted such misuse of power to occur in the first place.

Fear of despotism was a prevailing and obsessive concern in eighteenth-century France. Starting in the 1770s the word became a powerful weapon in the hands of the crown's opponents. Yet the evidence from this study and others suggests that despotism was an underlying concern throughout the second half of Louis XV's reign. Magistrates and philosophes, hack writers and artisans, drew careful distinctions between the theoretical foundations of absolute monarchy and despotism.[75] French men and women were united in their conviction that their king, unlike a despot, ruled according to law. By midcentury one can identify terms and images that constituted a veritable language of despotism, some of which were already evident in Bonafon's *Tanastès*. The configuration of despotism in French political culture, according to Alain Grosrichard, entailed arbitrary authority that was signaled by the eroticization of power, on the one hand, and its effeminization, on the other. These fears were conveyed rhetorically through a constellation of terms, including *will (volonté)*, *force*, and *caprice*, and images, including debauchery associated with carnal excess and indulgence and indolent and effeminate male rulers paired with ambitious and domineering mistresses. The language was pervasive, used by magistrates as well as artisans, who relied on it to send warnings to the king and his ministers. It provided a tool for criticizing the monarchy without undermining its institutional legacy.

Allègre grew exasperated waiting for responses to his requests for books, for audiences, for a pardon. He found it ridiculous that an individual as elevated as the marquise might perceive him as a dangerous threat and mused, "It is surely enough for her that you are detaining me with an absurd amount of security, which I do not merit. Can a lioness fear an ant? Why, therefore, are you crushing me? Why are you confusing me with a guilty person?"[76] The image of the lion and the ant deftly captures the deeply embedded notion of hierarchy that circumscribed the conduct of men and women in eighteenth-century France. Allègre was acknowledging the distance that separated two ends of the animal kingdom, or two ends of the social spectrum. By pushing this distinction to its logical conclusion he highlighted the absurdity of his imprisonment. A lowly tutor was hardly a serious threat to a member of the royal entourage.

Allègre's resentment of one individual, Pompadour, eventually incited his hostility toward the political regime she represented. At about the same time that Allègre began decrying Pompadour's arbitrary handling of his fate, he also launched a critique of the Old Regime's penal system. He continued to rely on a similar language, borrowing from traditional discussions of despotism, in order to articulate his complaints. Each stage of his argument brought him one step closer to the sacred sphere of kingship.

Allègre initiated his attack on the penal system by focusing on its most visible representative from his perspective, Lieutenant of Police Berryer: "But, sir, king as you are of the Bastille, you are not accountable to anyone for your actions here."[77] Thus Berryer was assimilated, along with Pompadour, into the despotic universe. He had the power of the king but none of the legal constraints since he answered to no one for his conduct. That Berryer had free rein implied that Louis XV was negligent, for the king was expected to make sure that those who exercised authority in his name did not abuse it. Like Uzbek in the *Persian Letters,* Louis XV was ultimately responsible for the behavior of his appointed servants.

In the same letter to Berryer, Allègre railed against the arbitrary distribution of favor under the Old Regime: "For two years I have not received the smallest favor from you ... these favors are arbitrary. They are bestowed on that man over there, they are refused to this one here. One congratulates himself, the other must remain silent."[78] After his arrest, Allègre had assumed that he would be able to secure a pardon by playing the game according to the rules. Thus, he had attempted to work through the appropriate channels, writing contrite petitions and begging for forgiveness. Yet his letters remained unanswered, his situation unchanged. Lacking both wealth and status, Allègre was unlikely to attract much attention languishing in the Bastille. The futility of his situation provoked rage against a judicial system that held him captive with no recourse for his own defense.

In 1755 Allègre wrote a letter to Berryer that marked a personal turning point. In it he shed the trappings of humility and deference and adopted a language of justice and natural rights. Furthermore, he addressed Berryer with unprecedented vehemence: "I see in you neither a judge nor a commissioner. You offer me an enemy whom the most humble prayers would not know how to appease. .... I do not believe that in Fez, in Tunis, in Morocco, or on our galleys slaves are treated with greater inhumanity than I am at the Bastille. The most barbarous peoples place limits on their vengeance, and you put none on yours, even though I have done nothing to provoke it."[79]

As Montesquieu had demonstrated, the subjects of a despot were enslaved men, whereas the subjects of a king were free. By drawing the parallel between his situation as a prisoner and that of slaves in North Africa, Allègre was identifying France as a despotic regime.

Allègre's criticisms drew upon Enlightenment principles of natural law and universal rights. Allègre had read and heard enough to know that cruel treatment of criminals was a glaring eyesore in an age proud of its progressive temperament. His litany against Berryer advanced, gathering force and conviction: "If your dog or cat were ill, you would be more concerned than you are for me. . . . I humbly beseech you that I need to breath some clean air. You are without ears, without eyes, without a mouth, without sensitivity; is this how you should treat a man [*est-ce donc que vous devez traiter un homme*] who is detained in irons by a detestable *I want it thus*."[80] Thus Allègre articulated his demands for material necessities, arguing that criminals deserved to be treated as members of the human species with fundamental rights.

Allègre's decision to use the verb *devoir* in the phrase "est-ce donc que vous devez traiter un homme" is significant. In this context it meant more than "should." *Devoir* conveys a sense of duty, of moral obligation. Posing the question in these terms, Allègre shifted the implications of his condemnation from the particularities of his own case to a broader moral issue. As a man, as a human being, he possessed inviolable rights. The concluding flourish, "I want it thus," framed Berryer as Pompadour's lackey: he served the despotic mistress as opposed to the benevolent king. Here Allègre reflected widespread perceptions that Berryer, along with other ministers, was part of Pompadour's vast patronage network, through which she exercised her illegitimate but nonetheless considerable authority.[81]

Allègre pursued his critique with an appeal to the laws of nature: "I am a man. In creating me, the Being to whom I owe my existence had no intention of creating a miserable wretch. He put me on this earth so that like other men I could enjoy the prerogatives a kind God has granted to humanity, and it is to curtail the most sacred laws of nature to deprive me of my life, my health, and my freedom without any justification."[82] This paragraph displays Allègre's mastery of a new set of political terms and arguments. The king no longer has an exclusive claim to sacred status because Allègre

had extended the category to include the "laws of nature." These laws asserted a new source of justice grounded in the fundamental right to life and
liberty. Allègre's language confirms Roger Chartier's argument that attitudes toward the French king changed in the second half of the eighteenth
century as a result of the king's losing his monopoly on the attribute of sacredness. According to Chartier, the process of desacralization did not entail direct assaults on the king's sacredness so much as the willful expansion
of the category to encompass institutions and concepts besides the king.[83]

Although Louis XV is not mentioned in Allègre's letter to Berryer, he
was not invulnerable to the assault. By establishing equality among men on
the basis of their shared humanity, Allègre directly threatened the theory of
divine-right kingship, which assumed inherent differences between individuals. All men enjoyed fundamental rights derived from universal laws of
nature; any violations were inexcusable. Allègre was not challenging authority in an anarchistic fashion; he was attempting to bring it into line with
the principles of justice and rights. Reason would replace favor as the arbiter of human destiny.

Allègre was not contesting the state's right to punish transgressors but
rather the methods currently employed. He raised two objections, issues
that would be central to the campaign for criminal-law reform in the 1770s
and 1780s. First, he condemned the inhuman conditions of prison life. Second, he decried the penal system's intolerance and severity, its inability to
calibrate the degree of punishment to the crime. Christianity taught men to
forgive and allowed sinners to mend their ways. Yet under the Old Regime,
criminal law made no allowances for errors of judgment nor for repentance.[84] A crime was never dismissed as aberrant behavior; rather it was
viewed as an index of delinquent character. As Allègre explained, he was
troubled "that a youthful folly implicates me in a pattern of vice from which
there is no turning back."[85]

Although he did not realize it immediately, Allègre had almost no chance
of obtaining a pardon from the moment of his arrest. The threshold of toleration for crimes of *mauvais discours* was extremely low given the risk involved both for the king, who was threatened, and for the kingdom, which
would suffer from his loss. The police could justify their rigor not only on
the basis of royal sacredness, which rendered *mauvais discours* the equiv-

alent of blasphemy in the secular realm, but also on the more utilitarian ground of the public good. To think certain thoughts, let alone utter them or act upon them, was a grave offense. The police could not relax their policy toward *mauvais discours* without calling into question both the king's sacredness and their own effectiveness as promoters of public order. Thus, judicial reform could not be initiated without a necessary and prior reformulation of the theory of French kingship, the image of the king and the basis of his authority.

As Allègre's thinking evolved, there was an abrupt shift in his attitudes toward Mme de Pompadour as well as a mounting hostility toward the crown's penal system. In both cases, the presence of the king was implied but never explicitly evoked. Both Pompadour and Berryer were seen as extensions of the royal figure because of their proximity to the king either through intimacy or office. The fact remains, however, that Louis XV was ultimately responsible for the decisions of his mistress and the actions of his ministers. A weak king was a dangerous king, as Montesquieu had insisted, precisely because his power was easily usurped and abused. Weakness paved the way for despotism. Yet Allègre refused to condemn Louis XV along with his representatives. This insistence on loyalty to Louis XV reflected both his understanding of French history and his responses to the contemporary political scene. It must be viewed in tandem with his vehement denunciation of Pompadour, Berryer, and the Bastille in order to grasp the range and complexity of his beliefs. Allègre's ideas were often contradictory. For instance, his talk of natural law and human rights did not lead him to challenge the monarchy directly. He remained a steadfast supporter of the crown, encouraging it in its manifold struggles against the parlements throughout the kingdom. Thus, while he feared despotism, he believed monarchy was the most suitable form of government for France. Like Bonafon's, his criticism was a call for reform, not revolt.

A Blueprint for the Future

The last documents in Allègre's dossier are seven letters he wrote in July and August of 1763. Two are addressed to Louis XV, three to Machault, the former controller general of finance, and the remaining two to a muse whom Allègre referred to as Urania.[86] Allègre attributed many of his observations and suggestions for reform to this imaginary figure. The letters to Urania are difficult to decipher, reflecting the toll prolonged incarceration had taken on Allègre's mind. By contrast, the letters to the king and Machault offer lucid responses to specific problems. For example, Allègre was aware that France was embroiled in an ongoing and increasingly disastrous war with England. He also seemed to know that the king's attempt to levy new taxes to support the military effort had provoked widespread judicial resistance. As a result, he tailored his advice to extricate Louis XV from this web of military fiascos and political miscalculations.

In the debates between the king and his parlements Allègre was a staunch supporter of the crown. Allègre had little sympathy for the magistrates, who in his view cloaked their greed and self-interest in lofty rhetoric to justify their frondish agitation: "The King is too Good: his Goodness will be his undoing. He must banish, disperse the Parlement, in order to enjoy perfect tranquillity; the authority and the preservation of the sacred person of His Majesty depend on it."[87] Rather than work for a compromise, the king should exercise his full authority and send the unruly magistrates into exile, thereby stifling their opposition without ceding to their demands. Such a move would not be unprecedented: the crown had been obliged to resort to such drastic measures in 1753 and would do so again in 1770. It did, however, align Allègre with an absolutist definition of kingship as opposed to a constitutional one. He was perceptive, nonetheless, in identifying the law courts as potentially serious threats to the monarchy's authority.

Of Louis XV's ministers Allègre singled out former Controller General Machault for praise. In so doing he sided with one of the most controversial figures of eighteenth-century French politics. Machault's financial reforms were opposed by all those vested interest groups who refused to renounce economic privileges in order to salvage a bankrupt crown. Machault's version of a proportional income tax, with no exemptions, would have appealed to someone who had never benefited from the privileges of the traditional system, conferred through birth or office: "M. de Machault above all has administered your financial affairs with fidelity . . . you could not find a more qualified person to direct your navy in this time of trouble and division. You must support him as well as the members of your inner council, who are very attached to you; you are in effect being attacked in their name:

by defending them, you are in effect defending yourself."[88] If anything, Al-lègre was in favor of enlightened absolutism as opposed to constitutional monarchy. He supported government by qualified ministers and select councils under the direction of a single man, the king.

Allègre was particularly astute in his observation that Louis XV should be wary of attacks on his councilors. Royal authority was effectively undermined when any of its agents or institutions was called into question. Allègre urged Louis XV to crack down on his rebellious officials in order to consolidate power and ensure order. His opinions on contemporary issues drew upon his understanding of chronic problems in French history: "Because the unrest that France is experiencing at present does not stem uniquely from the Parlement's decree vetoed by your Council at Your Majesty's behest: it is an ulcer that renews itself at every instant in the soul of this body, like the liver of Prometheus, which kept regenerating after it had been gnawed away by a vulture, and from this comes a new system for toppling your authority."[89] The metaphor of Prometheus's regenerating liver for contemporary political conflicts conveyed a warning that the situation was endemic and insurmountable. In July 1763, when this letter was written, relations between Louis XV and the magistrates were rife with tensions over the military fiasco with England and the status of the Jesuit order in the kingdom. The point Allègre sought to impress upon Louis XV was that the pattern of strife could be broken by eliminating the primary institutional source of the conflict.

Louis XV, according to Allègre, needed to restore domestic peace in order to defend the country from foreign invasion. Like so many of the king's subjects in this period, Allègre was obsessed with international plots and intrigue involving England, Brussels, and domestic spies. Allègre inferred that the Parlement of Paris was a bastion of enemy activities, controlled by foreign interests whose goal was to topple the French monarchy: "It was murmured to me in hushed tones in Brussels that the Parlement of France was supported by foreign interests, and this is true. It was the Parlement that urged you to go to war, while they wove a chain from which it will be difficult for you to disentangle yourself as long as it subsists. I am unable to give you more complete proof of this secret information regarding the activities between your subjects and the English; but in these types of cases, doubt

and suspicion are as good as certitude."[90] If the royal mistress was responsible for his personal misfortunes, it was the Parlement that was to blame for
the kingdom's woes in the Seven Years' War.

In Allègre's view, the situation did not allow for compromise. Louis XV
would have to assert his will and crush the Parlement if he was to survive:
"You risk your undoing if you let the Parlement have its authority at the
present moment. It is imperative that you suspend the magistrates; it is the
only way to assure your own authority . . . the only way to restore harmony
at the court and dispel the schemes of your enemies from the north, because
it does not seem that Your Majesty can fight and vanquish them as long as
you fear an uprising or a tempest on the part of your subjects."[91] For Allègre, international politics were linked to domestic ones, and the obstacles
confronting the king were considerable on both fronts. Louis XV had to ensure domestic peace and unwavering obedience on the home front if France
was to face the challenges across her borders.

Louis XV probably never received any of Allègre's advice. Much of
what Allègre ranted about from the time of his arrest actually came to pass.
France suffered severely in the Seven Years' War owing to a lack of naval
power and fiscal instability. The parlements played a fundamental role in
destabilizing the monarchy in the second half of the eighteenth century.
The financial reforms envisioned by Machault were eventually enacted in
the last years of Louis XV's reign under the aegis of the new controller general, the abbé Terray.

Allègre's extended incarceration transformed an essentially loyal but
misguided petty crook into a defiant and violent critic of the regime that had
deprived him of his liberty. As he reached to embrace a new language of
justice, he never relinquished the older language of fidelity. He claimed universal rights and hailed natural law, yet he refused to forsake the myth of an
omniscient and benevolent king. If he questioned the monarchy, it was implicitly through the arguments he raised concerning crime and punishment,
favor and arbitrary authority. His explicit political stance, however, as presented in his letters, was staunchly absolutist in an age that offered other options for envisioning royal government. Until the end he signed his letters
"the very humble and very loyal and very devoted servant and subject Allègre." According to Allègre, the king could rectify injustices by dismissing

those who betrayed his trust and instituting humanitarian reforms in the sphere of criminal justice. The problem, however, as in Bonafon's case, was that the king never remained untarnished when his servants and favorites were attacked.

· 🎨 ·

Over the years, Allègre snapped under the strain of life in the Bastille. Regular memoranda were forwarded to the new lieutenant of police, Gabriel de Sartine, indicating that Allègre had become an unruly and disruptive prisoner. He tore his sheets, broke his plates, and was prone to violent outbursts. The police decided that Allègre should be transferred to Charenton given his mental deterioration. They sent a doctor to examine him to confirm their assessment of his condition.

After examining Allègre, M. Boyer, one of the Bastille's physicians, reported: "I have just finished examining the condition of Sieur Allègre, whose body is in perfect health . . . he has reached the point where he can no longer be put up with at the Bastille unless he is kept enchained . . . because iron clamps on his feet and hands do not prevent him from unfettering himself. . . . I would suggest that you place him somewhere where he [   ] only by stones, denying him the use of his hands and feet with which he does what he wants."[92] Following the doctor's recommendation, Lieutenant of Police Sartine decided on 1 July 1764 that Allègre was "good for Charenton as a crazy."[93] Inspector Roullier was entrusted with the mission of conducting Allègre to his new accommodations. The transfer of prisoners required precautions since escapes could and did occur. In addition, the police tried to prevent the prisoner from agitating the populace along the way with appeals for mercy and help. Roullier had been warned by Chevalier to be extremely cautious since Allègre was clever and dangerous. Nonetheless, it appears from the inspector's account that Allègre was docile: "During the journey he kept talking to me pressingly; he told me how he had been brought up, . . . he assured me that he was by no means crazy and that by acting crazy he only wanted to change his situation."[94] Yet Allègre had grossly miscalculated, as he realized only moments later.

Allègre arrived at Charenton with some enthusiasm. He had no idea what was in store for him, assuming that nothing could be worse than the Bastille.

Roullier's dry and official account of Allègre's reaction to the iron cage captured the bleak poignancy of the situation: "He was led to the room assigned to him. . . . Still convinced that he was going to be put in a comfortable room, he said to me in the presence of several people, *All right,
Monsieur, we will not be breaking any more plates and we will not tear up any
more of our linens.* Upon entering his room he protested that they were putting him in a cage and that he might as well have been left where he was before" (see fig. 7).[95] The dossier of Antoine Allègre ends with his entry into
the iron cage, and thus so, too, must this narrative. He died at Charenton, a
broken man, some time before the Revolution; the precise date cannot be
verified.

Allègre, like Bonafon, was a product of an enlightened age. He believed
in stretching his mind through reading and writing, observation and invention. Initially Allègre accepted his incarceration with stoic resolve, eloquently framed in the letter he sent to his partner in Marseilles, M. Tournel:

Figure 7.
Latude retrouve Dalègre, fou, à Charenton.
*(Courtesy of the Bibliothèque Nationale de
France, Collection Histoire de France)*

"After all, what a machine is man: nothing is so weak and fragile; a thousand cares are needed to raise him and yet a single breath can blow him down.... fortunately philosophy has taught me to endure with firmness the most disagreeable conditions in life, and history, to recognize that man, no matter where he may find himself, is always capable of finding happiness within himself."[96] These were not the words of a lunatic nor a villain; their author did not deserve to end his days in an iron cage. The crown would have done itself a service if it had tried to accommodate the needs of such subjects rather than crushing them. Yet hindsight speaks to the future, not the past.

The Old Regime was arguably responsible for transforming Allègre into a *mauvais sujet* through prolonged incarceration. If there had been some outlet for his creative spirit and his desire for mobility, he might never have undertaken his dangerous scheme. Furthermore, if the police had dealt with him less rigorously, giving him a reprimand instead of a life sentence, he might have emerged repentant for his false allegations and reconciled to the political regime that had punished him. Allègre was reluctant to abandon his king-centered vision of politics despite the increasingly radical tendency of his thought. He remained loyal to Louis XV, denouncing the barbarity of his oppression, not the injustice of his oppressor.

Allègre's harsh treatment by criminal officers reveals the extent to which definitions of crime and punishment were bound up with definitions of royal authority itself. Leniency in the repression of *mauvais discours* entailed an admission that the king was neither sacred nor above criticism. Thus, rather than seeing police repression as evidence of the crown's absolute power, it may be more appropriate to view the exaggerated response to Allègre's misdemeanor as symptomatic of a breakdown of royal authority. Historically, regimes have become most repressive when they sensed that their power was slipping from their grasp. Eighteenth-century France was no exception to this rule. The severity and rigor meted out to the likes of Bonafon and Allègre are evidence of official anxiety and vulnerability more than confidence and efficiency. The task of maintaining public order had assumed dimensions and forms that had never previously existed and would ultimately require new forms of control.

Although the details of Allègre's crime were unique, the underlying structure of his project conformed to a pattern that can be discerned in the files of individuals arrested for *mauvais discours*. The desire to gain money, honor, or notoriety led disgruntled or ambitious individuals to test the boundaries between loyalty and subversion. Their failure to recognize either the risk or the gravity of their actions frightened the crown's officials. Such manipulative schemes revealed the extent to which the king's name was losing its ability to inspire and command respect. The police were alarmed less by the crimes of Bonafon and Allègre than they were by the possibility that such acts could escalate into something more dangerous. These fears would be confirmed on 5 January 1757, when a servant named Damiens attempted to stab Louis XV. In the aftermath of Damiens's trial and execution judicial authorities were bombarded by false threats and calumnious accusations.

Chapter 4 examines one instance of this broader phenomenon through the case of Auguste Claude Tavernier, a former munitions officer who used allegations of a conspiracy plot to manipulate officials in an effort to secure his release from prison. His case illustrates the ways individuals attempted to prey upon police paranoia to promote their own interests. In most cases, including Tavernier's, the king's name was deployed in the service of private ambition or the settling of scores. This manipulation was significant because it suggested a degree of familiarity that was incompatible with the traditional notion of sacredness. Like Allègre, Tavernier would base the king's power in secular concepts of justice and law as opposed to divine sanction. Moreover, he attacked the principle of patriarchy itself, another cornerstone of royal absolutism, thus paving the way for a broader reconsideration of the foundations of legitimate authority, be it in the family or the state.

Chapter 4

The Imagery of Regicide
in the Mind of Auguste
Claude Tavernier

· 🎴 ·

ROBERT FRANÇOIS-DAMIENS'S attempt to stab Louis XV on 5 January 1757 left a deeper scar on the monarchy than the superficial wound it inflicted on the king. Damiens's trial and execution rekindled smoldering ecclesiastical and constitutional conflicts that had obstructed the workings of justice in the capital for much of the decade. The regicide dominated public discussion for a year; Damiens was the subject of choice for songs, sermons, engravings, and news.[1] Since Ravaillac's assassination of Henry IV in 1610 there had been no attempts to murder a French king. In the shadow of Damiens's dagger allusions to the king's death appeared distinctly more ominous and encouraged officials to redouble their repressive efforts. By highlighting the vulnerability of the king's mortal body, the Damiens affair intensified debates about the nature of royal authority and revealed growing ambivalence, if not hostility, toward absolutism.

The police of Paris mobilized the kingdom in a crusade to extirpate all *mauvais propos*. The criminal archives attest to their zeal: more individuals were arrested for crimes of *mauvais discours* in the two years following the Damiens affair than at any other moment in the reign of Louis XV.[2] Yet investigative efforts produced unpredictable results when the police found themselves bombarded with unfounded accusations and imaginary plots. As one exasperated official remarked in reference to the case of Claude Mirlavaud and Claude Horsel, which involved a dispute over land that prompted Mirlavaud's mendacious charge: "It is extremely important that we do not allow such calumnies to proliferate. We have already seen several instances inspired solely by vengeance and personal animosity; at present it seems that it suffices to make an enemy in order to be immediately accused of *mauvais propos*."[3] Unable to stem the flow of false information they had unwittingly inspired, criminal authorities reacted with severity. Calumny involving an allusion to the king was often defined and punished as treason in an effort to shore up flagging respect for his sacred person.[4]

Among the hundreds of denunciations investigated between 1757 and 1759 one finds two cartons of documents devoted to Auguste Claude Tavernier.[5] A former munitions officer, Tavernier had been locked away on the Ile Sainte-Marguerite since 1749 by parental request. After a decade of incarceration Tavernier devised a risky scheme in the hopes of securing his liberty: he claimed to have information about a conspiracy to kill Louis XV. Tavernier's allegations surfaced in the midst of the Damiens trial and therefore could not be ignored by judicial officials determined to find accomplices of the domestic servant. Tavernier was quickly transferred to the Bastille for questioning. Although they failed to extract a confession, the police were soon convinced that Tavernier was lying and left him to languish in the Bastille, where he remained until triumphant crowds released him on 14 July 1789.

Tavernier's case illustrates a pattern of delinquent behavior that can be detected in the police archives from the mid-eighteenth century. This pattern consisted of individuals' manipulating official paranoia in the service of private interest and personal vengeance.[6] It attests to mounting confidence among some members of the French populace who were willing to risk their liberty to secure a desired end when no other options were available. It also reveals a growing rift between the police and the people concerning the meaning of fidelity. All the individuals arrested presented their accusations in the guise of fidelity. They failed to see the offensive implications of their decision to use loyalty to raise doubts about the king's safety. Tavernier's dossier illustrates the extent to which this abuse of fidelity fundamentally undermined its capacity to serve as an affective bond between the king and his subjects.

As the populace grew more irreverent in its references to the king's name and person, the police enforced increasingly rigid definitions of fidelity and treason. This rigor on the part of the criminal authorities addressed two sets of concerns. On the one hand, it reflected an official policy to uphold a tra-

ditional definition of sacred kingship in the face of its conceptual dismantling. Thus, *mauvais propos* were judged by standards similar to those con-
ventionally used in definitions of blasphemy. Imagining the king's death
was deemed equivalent to an actual assassination attempt.[7] Yet, arguably,
more than the crown's authority was at stake in the years following 1757, for
the police themselves had suffered a public humiliation in their failure to
prevent a disgruntled domestic servant from stabbing the king. Their repressive zeal should therefore also be viewed as a display of corporate solidarity in response to the recent blow to their prestige.

That individuals resorted to these ruses reflects their personal dissatisfaction not so much with Louis XV as with the constrictions imposed upon the
unprivileged members of Old Regime society. Lacking legitimate channels
for airing grievances or challenging official decisions, the socially undistinguished were forced to scheme to make their voices heard. Most, including
Tavernier, did not see their demands or their actions as an attack upon the
king. Tavernier lamented many things about the Old Regime, but his plans
for social reform never included a call to topple the monarchy. He believed
that he would purify and reinforce the king's power by putting a stop to the
abuses being perpetrated in his name.

Like so many French men and women reared under the monarchy, Tavernier placed his faith in the king as the instrument of reform. Nonetheless,
in attacking privilege, *lettres de cachet,* and patriarchy Tavernier struck at
the institutional and ideological foundations of the French king's authority.
Thus, official concern may not have been as exaggerated nor as misplaced as
it might initially appear to have been. Although Tavernier failed to perceive
it, the police detected an implicit link between his ability to allude to the
king's death and his critique of practices integral to the functioning of the
monarchy itself.

Islands of Exile

The Damiens affair erupted in the midst of a full-scale political crisis that
left the king visibly shaken and intent upon recovering his lost authority.
During the 1750s the controversy over the refusal of the sacraments to Jansenists entered its most prolonged and intractable phase. The net result was
that the theological dispute of a religious minority within the Catholic

Church fused with a juridical language of constitutional resistance to royal absolutism, producing a formidable set of opponents to the monarchy. The *parti janseniste,* which emerged from this longstanding struggle, not only had the institutional support of the highest court in the land, the Parlement of Paris, but also enjoyed considerable favor among the Parisian populace.[8] The crown intervened reluctantly and ineffectively, uncertain how to proceed through the morass of theological and juridical disputes. When the king did act, as in the exile of the magistrates in 1753–54 or in his *lit de justice* of 13 December 1756, his decrees appeared arbitrary and despotic to a populace long since won over to the Parlement's cause. The events of the 1750s were significant because they eroded both the king's personal popularity and the traditional alliance between the church and the throne. It would be difficult for the monarchy to sustain and enforce its authority without one of these pillars intact.

On 13 December 1756, in a notorious *lit de justice,* Louis XV attempted to force the Parlement of Paris to register a royal declaration concerning the papal bull *Unigenitus,* designed to reinforce its condemnation of Jansenism as a law of church and state without going so far as to call it a rule of faith. The decree would have prevented the magistrates from intervening in cases in which sacraments were refused to individuals lacking a *billet de confession.* This decision was accompanied by a disciplinary edict intended to restrain judicial agitation. The crown's actions prompted the immediate resignation of most of the magistrates, whose protests were seconded by a barristers' strike shortly thereafter. This collective resistance left only twenty-five magistrates to administer justice in the capital city. The turmoil in Paris was accompanied by resistance in several provincial parlements to the crown's attempt to impose a second *vingtième.*[9] Finding itself ineluctably drawn into war with England and Prussia, the government needed to raise the money to pay for it. The parlements of Rouen, Bordeaux, Besançon, and especially Rennes had all proved intractable. Thus, the administration of justice was in a state of chaos when the need for an exemplary trial presented itself in the form of a regicide named Robert François Damiens.

These outstanding grievances were temporarily overshadowed by Damiens's coup. Although the king's wound was minor, the assassination attempt and its outcome captivated national attention for a year. Louis XV recovered quickly but remained depressed for weeks. Intrigue flourished at the court, with members of the *parti dévot* anticipating a royal conversion similar to the scene at Metz in 1744. The Dauphin eagerly awaited the disgrace of the king's favorite, Mme de Pompadour. The mistress was uncertain whether to pack her bags or await an official dismissal. Louis XV put an end to these speculations within a week by paying his old friend a visit. The king was visibly relieved when he returned from Pompadour's chambers, and there was no more talk of banishing the mistress from the court.[10]

Despite the interlude provided by Damiens, the crown's problems remained unresolved. On 1 February Louis XV dismissed two of his most skilled and experienced ministers, Machault d'Arnouville, minister of the navy, and the comte d'Argenson, minister of war. The king's decision, encouraged by incessant court intrigue, left the government temporarily lacking effective leadership. By this time France was deeply immersed in the Seven Years' War, in which it was pitted against the formidable army of Frederick II on the Continent and the superior British navy at sea. France suffered severe defeats, especially in 1759, when it lost significant amounts of overseas territory in Canada, India, and the West Indies to the British. France's poor showing in this war was directly linked to an endemic financial crisis that Louis XV had never succeeded in mastering.

In order to wage war the crown needed money. The common method for raising revenue was taxation, but taxes had to be approved by the parlements. Thus, the registration of taxes inevitably became embroiled in the ongoing disputes over royal sovereignty and legislative prerogative. The crown had been only partially successful when it had attempted to impose a second *vingtième* in 1756. In order to get his taxes approved, Louis XV would be forced to cede ground to his magistrates on other issues, something he was loathe to do. Rather than face a showdown, the king took a risky financial gamble and decided to fund the war through credit, not revenue.[11] The consequences of this decision were numerous and costly. In 1759 the government was forced to default on its payments for publicly held stocks and annuities. Worse than that, Louis XV saddled his country with an enormous debt whose specter would come back to haunt his successor three decades later.

One other aspect of the Seven Years' War that bears mentioning is its

diplomatic significance. The war signaled a fundamental shift in French foreign policy. When Louis XV signed the Treaty of Versailles with Austria in
May 1756, he abandoned France's traditional ally, Brandenburg Prussia, for
its former enemy, Habsburg Austria. Frederick II of Prussia, it should be recalled, had personal ties in Enlightenment circles in France, established
through his patronage of writers and thinkers. He was hailed as a model of
enlightened despotism by many of the philosophes and counted Voltaire
among his admirers. Thus, to proponents of Enlightenment thought the reversal of alliances appeared to be a distinctly reactionary move. France had
linked her destiny to that of absolutist Catholic monarchies and abandoned
the path of enlightened administrative reform.

Together these conflicts created the charged political climate within
which Tavernier's case unfolded. Born in 1728, Auguste Claude Tavernier
was the son of Nicolas and Marie Charlotte Tavernier. Nicolas Tavernier
had served as Pâris de Monmartel's porter since 1713. The Pâris brothers
were Louis XV's principal bankers, and Tavernier's parental connections to
this household placed him on the threshold of a powerful and privileged
world, much like Bonafon. Monmartel was appointed *garde du trésor* in 1730,
and his brother, Duverney, was named *directeur général des vivres* in 1733.
During the 1750s they enjoyed unimpaired rule over royal finances owing to
the protection of Louis XV's mistress, Mme de Pompadour. Pompadour's
father, François Poisson, had been one of Pâris-Duverney's chief buying
agents for the army during the 1720s.[12] The shadow of the two brothers
hovers over this entire dossier, although there is no evidence to confirm
Tavernier's accusations that they were responsible for his detention. Nonetheless, their perceived interference would fuel Tavernier's resentment of
their power and the inegalitarian society that bestowed it.

Pâris de Monmartel helped launch Tavernier's career by securing a minor
position for him in the munitions section of the Royal Treasury. His parents
had worked hard to get him this office and were mortified when he quit his
job and abandoned his career. As they insisted in a letter to Lieutenant of
Police Sartine, their son was "unrecognizable as a result of the change that
had taken place in his manners, given over to excess; it is no longer possible
to get him to do any kind of work."[13] According to the police, once Tavernier returned to Paris, "he devoted himself to libertinage and drunkenness

and all sorts of debauchery and threatened to mistreat his father and mother."[14] Confused by this abrupt and unexplainable change in their son's temperament and fearing for their lives, Tavernier's parents requested a *lettre de cachet* in 1746. He was locked up at Charenton for five months.

Thus the gradual but inexorable process of removing Tavernier from civil society was set in motion. In April 1747 Nicolas Tavernier decided to give his son a second chance. Tavernier was released but managed to get himself arrested within two years, "having been found drunk at dead of night on the rue Saint Antoine" (see fig. 8).[15] Upon learning of his son's arrest, Nicolas Tavernier wrote to Sartine requesting a second *lettre de cachet:* "The supplicant will no longer hide the fact that although he provided his son with an education capable of preparing him for an honorable office according to his station, he has become so deranged that the supplicant fears vexatious consequences."[16] This time Tavernier was sent to Saint Lazare for a year. During his detention his parents pressured Pâris de Monmartel to resolve the problem of their unruly son.

Monmartel's original idea was "to have him sent to the islands in the service of the Compagnie des Indes, where he [Monmartel] had secured a position for him."[17] Tavernier initially agreed and then changed his mind, refusing to accept the post. By this point his options were limited, and Monmartel arranged to detain him in the military fort on the Ile Sainte-Marguerite, off the southern coast of France, near Cannes. His parents agreed to pay 300 livres a year to cover the costs of their son's detention. Since Monmartel was removing Tavernier from the king's expense account, he had little trouble securing the *lettre de cachet* to have Tavernier locked away.

Little information is available about Tavernier before his first arrest in 1749. His parents asserted that they had furnished him with "all the education they were capable of providing." The quality of Tavernier's writings, his literary tastes, and his command of the language suggest a substantial amount of good instruction. He claimed to have been educated by a "lugubrious Jansenist" whose teachings he later rejected, although traces of it can be discerned, for instance, in his vehement hatred of the Jesuits. As for his religious convictions, Tavernier described himself as a deist. According to his parents, by 1749 Tavernier was "possessed by irreligion. He no longer recognized his Christian duty; all our efforts and pleas to bring him back to

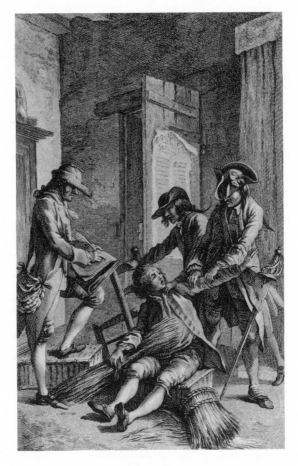

Figure 8.
La Police, 1760.
*(Courtesy of the Carnavalet
Museum)*

his senses were useless."[18] Tavernier frequently cites Voltaire as his intellectual mentor, and one detects the affinity, for instance, in his notion of deism as well as in his denunciation of religious fanaticism: "If fanaticism, as M. de Voltaire says in that letter he wrote to His Prussian Majesty . . . does not always manifest itself in the excesses of serious crimes . . . it produces all the small evils imaginable in the heart of society."[19] Tavernier tossed accusations of fanaticism around rather loosely, including ecclesiastics of all per-

suasion among his targets. He shared Voltaire's hostility toward institutionalized religion and referred to men of the cloth as "Tartuffes," after Molière's timeless symbol of clerical hypocrisy and lechery.

This virulent anticlericalism is consistent with what Dale Van Kley sees
as the distinguishing feature of the mid-century temperament in French culture. It was one significant consequence of the controversy raging between
the church and the parlements over the refusal of the sacraments to Jansenists. As Van Kley has demonstrated, the heated disputes of the 1750s and the
monarchy's inability to impose a satisfactory resolution effectively led to a
desacralization of the clergy, which paved the way for the subsequent desacralization of the monarchy. Anticlericalism had a popular as well as a philosophical constituency, as evidenced by the increase in irreverent and derisory remarks toward the church found in police archives.[20]

In keeping with the tenor of the time, Tavernier directed his hostility toward the church at the individuals who served and represented it. Ecclesiastics were familiar figures at all levels of French society. Tavernier claimed
to have been raised in a household run by priests: his mother was enslaved to
her Jesuit confessor, his father to a Capuchin friar. He could not contain his
contempt for his parents: "There are two things to consider . . . the first
being the extravagance and stupidity of my father and mother. The one believed in all good faith that it was possible to be bewitched, and the other
believed you could read the future with a basin of water and some cards."[21]
Although it is impossible to substantiate his allegations, Tavernier believed
that his parents had turned against him once these "bougres de moines"
(buggers of monks) had insinuated themselves into his home. Expressions
of suspicion and loathing of ecclesiastics, especially Jesuits, run throughout
his dossier. He asserted that one of his primary goals was "to exterminate
them in every corner of the kingdom or have them banished in perpe-
tuity."[22] He would certainly have found echoes of support for such views
among his contemporaries. The magistrates were gathering strength in their
crusade against the Society of Jesus, and it would not be long before they
forced Louis XV to sign a decree expelling the order from the realm.

Although Tavernier never identified himself as a Mason, he made several
allusions to the lodges that flourished in eighteenth-century France and England. There is no evidence that he was a Mason; nonetheless, he was a dis-

tinctly sympathetic observer. He referred to Freemasons as "sincere Deists like me" and insisted that "they should be regarded as the throne's strongest pillar of support and as the preservers of peace and political tranquillity . . . because they are absolutely incapable of betrayal and treason."[23] In Tavernier's mind, Masons stood for liberty and reason, Jesuits for despotism and fanaticism. He believed that "Masons had no other goal than to spread the natural religion . . . purified theism and to perfect understanding."[24]

Tavernier's writings reveal an articulate and cultivated individual, and these qualities were remarked upon by everyone with whom he came into contact. In a 1761 report concerning Tavernier, Lieutenant of Police Sartine observed, "He writes well, he has been educated, he signs his letters."[25] Like Marie Bonafon, Tavernier was proud of his literary skills. He admitted to working hard to perfect his style. He could not resist admiring the results, remarking at the end of one of his *mémoires:* "I write like a master when I care to take the trouble. As for style, all that is needed is clarity, precision, and good sense; rhetoric is unnecessary in this instance because the case speaks for itself from one end to the other."[26] Fully convinced that the injustice of his plight was self-evident, Tavernier believed in the power of the written word to rally readers to his defense.

Tavernier was not only a skillful writer but also an avid reader. His letters were strewn with literary and historical references, and he was constantly requesting books. His literary tastes ranged widely, from the collected works of Molière and Voltaire to volumes of the *Spectator, L'histoire du maréchal de Saxe,* and abbé Nollet's *Les leçons de physique.* His allusions reflected more than a superficial familiarity with the texts and authors in question. He had clearly spent time reading through and reflecting upon the texts he invoked. His responses to police interrogations revealed a firm command of legal theory as well as an understanding of French history. He did not hesitate to cite precedents when analyzing contemporary politics or defending himself.

It is difficult to reconcile this image of a cultured man with that of a violent criminal. Yet by all accounts Tavernier possessed a brutal and volatile temperament. The police described him as having a "savage character" and insisted that "he is a very bad subject: a libertine, an idler, a drunkard, and violent."[27] This unpredictable behavior had prompted his parents to request a *lettre de cachet* and would keep him in prison until 1789. His outbursts would attract the attention of both his captors and his fellow prisoners.

When Tavernier arrived on the Ile Sainte-Marguerite in March 1750 he encountered his future partner in crime, Louis-Auguste d'Esparbès, the chevalier de Lussan. It is not surprising that the two men were initially drawn to each other given the similarity of their backgrounds. Like Tavernier, Lussan had a checkered past that included a substantial criminal record. He too had been locked away by *lettre de cachet* at the request of his parents. Both men were determined to get off the island at any price and were viewed with suspicion by the fort's guards, who described them as "deux grands coquins" (two major rascals) and thoroughly "mauvais sujets."

The youngest of four children, Lussan was thirty-five in 1759. He came from a well-to-do family in Bordeaux, where his father owned several large pieces of property as well as two windmills.[28] He described himself as belonging to a family having "a name recognized in Paris and at the court with parents who maintained a distinguished household."[29] As the youngest son, Lussan was destined for the priesthood. This decision was not uncommon in large landed families as a strategy to prevent their fortune from being divided among too many heirs. Unfortunately, Lussan was an unwilling candidate for the cloth. His resistance to the parental plan led his mother to request a *lettre de cachet,* and he was locked up for five months in the Château de Lourdes at age sixteen.

Lussan engineered an escape from the royal fortress and enlisted as a lieutenant in the Regiment of Provence. On leaving the army he sought reconciliation with his family and attempted to comply with his mother's wishes. He spent several months studying with the Cordeliers in Ayen and then at a Jesuit seminary in Auch. He abandoned his training, however, when one of his spiritual directors warned him that "to embrace the priesthood without a true calling" would cost him his salvation.[30] His disobedience led his family to request another *lettre de cachet* in 1749, but this time Lussan fled rather than face another prison cell.

He headed for Marseilles, where he intended to board a ship sailing for Canada. When he attempted to arrange his departure, the mounted constabulary tried to arrest him. Lussan killed an officer in his efforts to resist arrest. He claimed that he had acted in self-defense. He was tried by the parlement of Aix and sentenced to death. His parents managed to obtain a royal pardon stipulating that Lussan be locked away on the Ile Sainte-Marguerite. He arrived four months after Tavernier, in July 1750.

These biographical sketches reveal that this case involves two men of dubious integrity whose evidence must be handled with care. Both were desperate and resentful after years of detention; neither had ever relinquished hope of resuming life in civil society. They were prepared to take enormous risks since they had nothing left to lose. Although Tavernier's fictitious conspiracy did get them off the island, it did not radically improve their respective situations. The ruse merely confirmed the assessment of the marquis de Fénelon's, lieutenant general of the king's armies in Marseilles, that the two men were "thoroughly disreputable subjects, capable of even greater crimes. It would be, I believe, a great service to society to keep them in separate prisons, without any communication with the outside world."[31]

Secrets and Lies

Tavernier's affair was investigated in two phases. The first took place on the Ile Sainte-Marguerite in May and June 1759. It was directed by the island's lieutenant, M. de Latil, with the assistance of the fort's major, M. de Robaud. The gravity of the subject matter, a conspiracy to kill the king, quickly drew the attention of authorities in Paris. After a series of reports were exchanged, Lieutenant of Police Bertin decided to take charge of the case. The two prisoners were transferred to the Bastille in early August 1759, where a second round of depositions and interrogations began. The case was difficult to unravel because Tavernier denied Lussan's allegations and was constantly contradicting himself.

The plan was set in motion when Lussan brought Tavernier's conspiracy to official attention in a letter addressed to the maréchal de Belle-Isle, minister of war, on 22 March 1759: "The blood that flows in my veins is too pure for me to guard in silence the danger that pursues His Majesty. I have important information concerning a plot to kill the king . . . which will be carried out some time next November, . . . the warnings I am giving you Monsieur are not to be scorned; deign, I beseech you, to warn the king about this." In order to substantiate his allegations Lussan needed to compensate for his dubious status as a convicted criminal. He prefaced his allegations by emphasizing his noble ancestry as a badge of honor and fidelity. Having established his credentials and piqued official curiosity, Lussan stipulated: "I don't want to reveal my secret to anyone but you or the king. If he sends to fetch me in a post-chaise it would be useless to assign anyone to question me since I will always be on my guard." He hastened to add that if the danger had been imminent, he would have disclosed the information immediately since "I would risk a thousand lives if it were within my power to protect the sacred days of a monarch who is the delight of his subjects."[32]

Despite the vague language, Lussan's allegations could not be dismissed with the shadow of Damiens's knife hanging over the country. When the island's intendant, Latil, forwarded the letters to Belle-Isle after reading through them, he emphasized that he was doing so "even though I must regard everything the Chevalier de Lussan puts forward as pure inventions imagined as a way of obtaining his transfer to some other prison." He justified his caution, adding that "nothing that touches the Sacred Person of the King can knowingly be concealed."[33] Latil was in a bind: his instincts told him that the conspiracy was a ruse, Yet in all good conscience he could not simply let the matter drop. Lussan sensed the lieutenant's dilemma and subtly preyed upon his fears: "I offer warnings that have nothing to do with the pure chimera of a prisoner trying to get himself out of trouble . . . let time pass and it will, unfortunately, justify the events, and then you will regret not having believed me . . . you are failing in your duty if you neglect matters regarding the king's person."[34] Lussan needed Latil to contact authorities in Paris if he was to succeed in getting himself recalled from the island for questioning.

Lussan, however, would have to be patient. As his letters ascended the hierarchy of royal officialdom, they were subjected to multiple delays. Latil showed the letters to the marquis de Fénelon, who was visiting the island for a routine inspection, and Fénelon took the opportunity to question Lussan in person. He too was convinced that the allegations were "the visions of an overheated mind" but felt that "the matter in question is too important to neglect even the most implausible allegations." According to Fénelon, Lussan had repeated his allegations but refused to reveal the source of his information. Fénelon advised Latil to hush up the matter and "prevent the spread of such ideas."[35]

Fénelon's meeting with Lussan aroused Tavernier's suspicions and prompted him to write a letter telling his version of the story. He sought to undermine Lussan's credibility as a witness, emphasizing that Lussan was a convicted murderer who had only escaped a death sentence through family connections. Tavernier demanded that he be given a full hearing and offered to pay the cost of his voyage to Paris if necessary. He warned the authorities that Lussan could not be trusted because "he [Lussan] fancied that he would land at the king's feet by accusing me of wanting to stab His Majesty as soon as I am released. He bases all this on an outburst of despair I had more than five or six years ago." Tavernier proceeded to recount the incident in question. Several years earlier, on a sweltering hot day, he had asked his porter for a salad and some wine. These were luxuries he could procure because his father occasionally sent him extra money in addition to the fees for his board. When his request was ignored, he apparently exploded with rage: "Outraged by such a rude refusal, the memory of all my troubles past, present, and future came rushing back. . . . I was overcome by a blind fury, and in this agitated state I blamed God, the king, M. de Monmartel, my father, finally, all of nature, and in my rage I drove a knife into the door, a knife I was holding in my hand all the time, screaming like a miserable wretch against *lettres de cachet* and those who administered them."[36] Tavernier was convinced that his violent declamations against Louis XV had inspired Lussan's subsequent accusations.

In the meantime, Lussan was summoned on 29 May to give an official deposition to the fort's major, François de Robaud. Lussan recounted a conversation he had had with Tavernier four months earlier, in January. Echoes of Tavernier's outburst can be heard in Lussan's description, according to which Tavernier had said "that with his father and mother being dead he would infallibly have his liberty, and then he would let M. Louis Quinze know that if Damiens had missed him, he [Tavernier] would not miss him and that he would make known for centuries to come his [Louis XV] project to exterminate innocent people between four walls with *lettres de cachet*, [and that he had] promised Lussan, in order to prevent him from revealing the secret, that he would have his liberty along with all the other prisoners."[37] The impassioned rhetoric and grievances contained in Lussan's account were characteristic of Tavernier, and certain issues, such as the injustice of *lettres de cachet,* recur throughout the dossier.

Lussan claimed that he had tried to dissuade Tavernier from pursuing this malicious scheme, reminding him that if he were caught, he would be subjected to torture before being executed. Tavernier had scoffed at Lussan's warning and responded by demonstrating his ability to withstand pain. Taking a brick from Lussan's fireplace, he had lit a package of matches and used it to burn his hand. Then he had driven a large pin deep into his thigh. Lussan had been so disgusted by these exploits that he refused to continue the conversation. In his deposition Lussan explained that initially he had been inclined to dismiss these discussions as "vague ideas." The incident with the matches and the pin had changed his mind because "having reflected upon the serious nature of the matter, he decided to search for ways to communicate what he knew to the minister and ask to be taken to the Bastille in order to be available to declare what he knew before his secret leaked out." Lussan said that he had pressed Tavernier to reveal the details of his plan and that Tavernier had explained that he intended to rely on Monmartel's connections at the court in order to gain entry to Versailles. Tavernier had boasted that "it would be easy for him when the king passed, surrounded by his guards, to shoot his brains out with two pistols." When Lussan interjected that this plan was very risky, that he was sure to be arrested, Tavernier had replied that this was his intention since "his goal was to create a scene in the Parlement of Paris as a means of getting the magistrates to revoke all the *lettres de cachet* used to imprison family members."[38]

Lussan's deposition was sent to Fénelon, who forwarded it to Lieutenant of Police Bertin in Paris. Three weeks later, on 20 June, Lussan was summoned by Latil for further questioning. This time he revealed more information concerning the alleged plot. Although Tavernier had consistently refused to identify his accomplices, he had indicated that they were former prisoners on the island. There were supposedly twenty-one men involved, three of whom were based in Paris. Tavernier had insisted that he would disclose the names of his partners only if the magistrates swore to spare him from being tortured. When Lussan had reproached Tavernier for joining the plot in exchange for his liberty, Tavernier had asserted that he was acting in the king's best interest. His acquiescence was intentional since "he wanted to use them in order to get to the bottom of their feelings, and to have his liberty, and once free, he would have gone immediately to the captain of the Royal Guard and denounced the plot."[39] Thus the tale grew more convoluted as the two men competed to display their loyalty.

This last point provides an important clue for understanding the investigation of the case. Both Lussan and Tavernier presented their crimes and accusations as gestures of fidelity. Each insisted that protecting the king was his primary motive. In the aftermath of the Damiens affair information concerning *mauvais propos* and plots was a valuable commodity, and the police were avid buyers. Members of the French populace were eager to profit from their loyalty while the market was favorable. Yet, as many would discover to their horror and chagrin, calumny that involved the king's name was no small prank. It was a heinous crime and often earned its perpetrators life imprisonment if not death.

Before turning our attention to Tavernier, it is useful to pause and consider Lussan's efforts to establish his credentials as a *fidèle sujet*. In a *mémoire* written on 23 June 1759 Lussan explained that Tavernier's plot offered him an opportunity "to demonstrate my zeal and love for the interests of my king." Such occasions were rare for persons serving a life sentence on the Ile Sainte-Marguerite. He emphasized that upon discovering Tavernier's plan, he had repeatedly sought to dissuade him: "Tavernier, I said to him, you have confided in me such an awful project that no matter what advantages are in it for me, I would not be an honest man, nor worthy of living for one moment, if I did not exhort you with all my force to renounce it completely. I pointed out the enormity of the crime, the horrors of the torture he would suffer." These efforts testified to Lussan's loyalty because they constituted an active defense of the king's honor under the onslaught of offensive utterances. He hastened to add that he had hesitated for three months before denouncing Tavernier, knowing that "it was in my best interest not to raise a false alarm without the necessary proof because that would have enabled Tavernier to deny everything." The ultimate proof of his integrity was that he had gained nothing but harsh treatment for his efforts: "This affair has procured me no gain except more abuse, whereas I ought to be seen as the savior of the king and the state and the instrument God is using to have

Tavernier summoned before the Parlement of Paris." He closed this letter by urging Belle-Isle to "allow us to work together for the greater good of the king and the state."[40] In the meantime he would make every effort to discover the names of Tavernier's accomplices.

Lussan's relentless pressure augmented official concern and intensified the investigative efforts of Latil and Robaud. Their anxiety was heightened by Tavernier's decision to provide more specific information. On 28 June Tavernier called for the arrest of several individuals, all of whom were allegedly involved in the conspiracy. Among the accused were two soldiers formally stationed at the fort, Courmés and Giroux, and a captain of the port named Felix Coulomb. In addition, he requested that "all Franciscan friars or men of the cloth, coming to France from the side of the papal states or via the Beauvoisin bridge or through Briançon or by sea . . . be arrested and detained with as little disturbance as possible." By providing a partial list of suspects that included an allusion to disgruntled ecclesiastics, Tavernier sought to enhance the *vraisemblance* of his conspiracy. Yet he refused to reveal "the most important details" until he stood before his judges. In this same statement he claimed to have sealed his agreement with the regicides by signing his name in blood. In exchange for his services as a hired assassin, he was to receive his liberty, a reward of 96,000 livres, and employment in the service of an unidentified foreign country.[41]

In this outline of the conspiracy Tavernier incorporated details guaranteed to arouse official concern. Two examples will serve to illustrate this strategy. First, in the list of suspects Tavernier included Franciscans and men of the cloth coming from Rome, a reference to Jesuits in the aftermath of two recent assassination attempts, one against Louis XV in 1757, a second against Joseph I of Portugal in 1758. Enemies of the Jesuits had mounted a successful campaign to vilify the order as papal agents who condoned regicide. Links between Jesuits, fanatics, and conspiracy theories were common parlance in mid-eighteenth-century French political culture. This hostility was a cornerstone of the judicial Jansenist position, based in the Parlement of Paris, whose systematic pressure on the crown culminated in the order's dissolution and expulsion from the kingdom in 1763–64.

Tavernier's allusion to working for a foreign power was equally timely. In 1757 France had entered into the Seven Years' War against England and

Prussia. It was not inconceivable, at least from the government's perspective, that enemy tactics included a plot to kill the French king as a means of forcing the country to make peace.[42] Thus, Tavernier's suggestion that he was working for foreign agents can be seen as a conscious strategy to manipulate official concerns in a time of military conflict.

A few days later Tavernier revealed the logistics of the planned coup. He explained that "it was not until the end of September, when the king went from Choisy to hunt deer in the woods of Venar, that the coup was to be executed in Villeneuve Saint George, and that the assassins would leave from the house alongside the house of either Monsieur le prince or Monsieur le duc, and that it was extremely important that this minister prevent His Majesty from passing hereafter in the said Villeneuve Saint George, in his coach or any other vehicle."[43] In a later deposition Tavernier specified that he would identify his accomplices on two conditions: that he would not be tortured and that he would be heard "before the princes of the blood, the peers of the realm, and the Grande-Chambre of the Parlement." He insisted that he had refused to join the conspiracy at least three times before accepting. His decision to cooperate had been prompted by the receipt of two letters from his family "which deprived him of all hope of being delivered from his detention."[44] Thus, he had seized upon the conspiracy as his last chance for freedom. When Latil pressed him to clarify how he had communicated with his accomplices, Tavernier alluded to a network of former prisoners, merchants, and guards who had served as intermediaries.

By 4 July 1759 Latil was visibly distraught and requested that the case be taken out of his hands: "I am so troubled by . . . the enormity of the conspiracy plot set forth in the depositions that it seems to me . . . necessary that the wretched Tavernier be transferred immediately, determined as he is to reveal the identity of his accomplices only before his judges." Latil complained that he lacked reliable guards since many of the fort's officers were in liaison with the prisoners, facilitating the exchange of letters and contacts with the outside world. He was at his wit's end: "The pain and bitterness I suffer, . . . there is nothing sadder than the lot of a commander or a major of this fort here."[45] He was visibly relieved when he bid his captives farewell on 28 July, reporting that "Lussan and Tavernier . . . left at 10:00 this morning; I gave to . . . Sieur Prevost all the original depositions of these two prisoners as well as the letters Tavernier had written to me. . . . Tavernier is leaving here with considerable debts."[46] The two criminals were full of hope as they boarded the ship that was to carry them away from their island of exile. Although the future remained uncertain, both men were confident that things could only improve.

Plotting the King's Death

Upon their arrival at the Bastille, Lussan and Tavernier were subjected to intensive questioning. Lussan's first interrogation stretched over two days, 9–10 August, and was remarkably consistent. This uniformity suggests that he was repeating things, perhaps with some elaboration, that Tavernier had confided in him. Tavernier, by contrast, was continually wavering in his account. He initially confessed to having invented the plot but subsequently contradicted himself. The records of the interrogations are useful because they highlight the assumptions and concerns of both the police and the defendants.

After summarizing the events that had culminated in his detention on the Ile Sainte-Marguerite, Lussan recapitulated his version of the story. He added details to enhance the dramatic qualities of his narrative. For example, he described the elation with which Tavernier had greeted the news of his parents' death in November 1758: "Upon learning the news . . . Tavernier exclaimed, 'Very well! they were mortal and they have died with the crime of having succumbed to the entreaties of the Tartuffes who strengthened their implacable hatred for me. I have nothing else to settle. I will get my revenge some day and I am going to drink an extra jug of wine to celebrate.'"[47] Lussan's goal was to vilify Tavernier to make him credible as a regicide. To accomplish this, he played on police assumptions that crime was the product of character, not circumstance. Thus, he aimed to convince them that Tavernier had a long history of malicious behavior.

It was but one step, Lussan insisted, from Tavernier's resentment of his parents to his hostility toward the king. The two were interconnected since parents relied on royal intervention to enforce their authority over their children. On that same day in November Tavernier had continued, "My father and mother are dead. I will surely be released; several people are working to help me obtain my liberty. Then M. Louis XV will feel the consequences of his wrongdoing in exterminating honest men who have committed no crimes between four prison walls. If Damiens missed his target, I will not. . . . I have suffered too much for too long, I must have vengeance. I will arrange to have all *lettres de cachet* revoked for the children of families; there will be no more except for state criminals."[48] Lussan explained that having no witnesses to this exchange, he had decided to write a confidential letter to the minister of war, maréchal de Belle-Isle.

Individuals such as Lussan who came to the police with denunciations found themselves in a double bind. They had to present enough evidence to make their case convincing. At the same time, they had to delineate boundaries between themselves and the person they were accusing. Personal contact could not be allowed to blur these distinctions. *Mauvais discours* were viewed as contagious diseases; exposure increased the risk of infection. Commissioner Rochebrune was skeptical because Lussan had delayed several months before reporting to the authorities. Lussan defended this lapse: "In order to avoid alarming the state unnecessarily, he needed to extract as much information from Tavernier as was possible, and despite the purity of the defendant's intentions in denouncing the plot, which he, himself, had difficulty believing, he knew that he risked being mistaken for a calumniator and an imposture if . . . Tavernier had not made statements that attested to the veracity of all the defendant has put forth."[49] Rochebrune had difficulty accepting this line of reasoning. He suggested that the two men had invented the plot as a means of getting off the island. It was, he observed sardonically, unlikely that anyone would have selected "a man deprived of his liberty and locked up in a fort" as a reliable accomplice in a plot to kill the king.

Lussan said that after several months of listening to Tavernier he had become convinced that there must be some underlying truth: "He had good grounds for believing in the existence of the plot that had been confirmed too many times by Tavernier, an enterprising man capable of masterminding the most complicated schemes and of ensuring their successful execution." Lussan explained that once he was persuaded that the king's life was in danger, he knew that he had to report to the authorities. He supported this reasoning with an allusion to the notorious conspiracy of Cinq Mars in the reign of Louis XIII, asserting that "silence is criminal in such cases."[50] He recalled that François de Thou's failure to alert the king to his friend's plot to assassinate Cardinal Richelieu had cost him his head.

Tavernier had warned Lussan that he would deny everything if denounced to the police. Yet, as Lussan repeatedly insisted, his loyalty left him no choice: "As a good citizen, I believed myself indispensably obliged to reveal this abominable assassination plot that was being hatched against the precious days of our august Master . . . prejudice is always against a man deprived of his liberty, . . . but nothing was capable of stopping for an instant the course of my fidelity and my attachment to the interests of His Majesty. I can . . . flatter myself with the glory of having fully sacrificed my happiness, which I would not exchange for all the goods of the world."[51] Lussan framed his denunciation of Tavernier in a language of fidelity because it was the only legitimate excuse for repeating subversive utterances. Lussan's statements revealed fundamental assumptions about the meaning of fidelity as well as the ways it could be manipulated by a royal subject in the late 1750s. Even though the police doubted his integrity, he stood before them in this instance as the accuser, not the accused. Consequently, he was in a less defensive position than most individuals subjected to questioning. His motives were ambiguous. He may or may not have believed in the existence of Tavernier's plot. Whatever his personal convictions, he was determined to use this information to barter for his freedom. He perceived a rare opportunity to force judicial officials to reevaluate his character and reduce his sentence.

Lussan assumed that his loyal service would be recognized by the king and appropriately rewarded. His confidence revealed the residual strength of fidelity as a bond between subject and sovereign. Yet the language he used to formulate his allegiance was not entirely traditional because it explicitly denied a paternalistic model of royal authority. As he proclaimed, "I no longer belong to my family but entirely to the state, and I am counting on the state to ensure my happiness."[52] Thus, on Lussan's part one detects a subtle but perceptible shift in the image of the French king from a benevolent paterfamilias to the judicious administrator of an impersonal entity known as the state. The family model of politics, founded on principles of patriarchy and dutiful submission to the monarchy, was breaking down just as the authoritarian family was being redefined in more affective terms, culturally and legally, in the eighteenth century. Lussan's statement captures this transition as the king/father figure gave way to a juridical entity, the state, to which obedience was presumed to be voluntary, even contractual, rather than compulsory.

Lussan directed his zeal toward a sovereign whose person embodied the interests of the state rather than a divine trust. When he offered to serve in the colonies in exchange for his liberty, Lussan emphasized, "I would willingly sacrifice my life in the service of the state, I would fulfill my duty with dignity, never losing sight of the fact that a good citizen must always hold the interests of his Sovereign and his fatherland dearer than his own."[53] This image of self-sacrifice was omnipresent in expressions of fidelity. Nonetheless, Lussan had shifted it slightly by introducing elements of a distinctly different vocabulary, such as "citizen" and "fatherland." The fusion of state and sovereign suggests that Lussan understood monarchy in administrative rather than sacred terms, as a system of government rather than a divine mandate. Lussan's loyalty not only affirmed the superiority of the state over the family, the institutional over the personal, but also suggested a principle of civic, as opposed to filial, duty.

Lussan's revolt against paternal authority, although directed against his own father, was not without its implications for Louis XV. French absolutism rested on a theoretical composite that included divine right, fundamental law, and paternalism. Recent work by Lynn Hunt, as well as the art historian Carol Duncan, has argued that conflicting images of father figures in fiction and painting of the later eighteenth century played a significant role in eroding the legitimacy of the king's power.[54] Both Tavernier and Lussan undermined the paternalistic basis of kingship in their refusal to sanction the authority fathers could legally exercise over their children's fate. Lussan stressed that fidelity to the king, as representative of the state, transcended all other allegiances, including those between fathers and sons. He clearly distinguished this bond with the king from one of filial obligation, grounding it in principles of reason and choice rather than nature and religion.

As final evidence of his loyalty, Lussan emphasized that Tavernier had guaranteed him his freedom in exchange for his trust. Yet, Lussan asserted, he was willing to forgo his liberty rather than "fall short in his duty."[55] Despite his efforts to establish his credentials as a loyal and obedient subject, Lussan was unable to convince the police of his integrity. From an official perspective, nobody involved in such ventures remained untainted. Although he was not shipped back to the Ile Sainte-Marguerite, his only recompense was a transfer in 1762 to another royal fortress, Pierre en Cise, whose walls marked the end of his involvement in this case.

After the initial examinations, the police fixed their attention on Tavernier, who was guilty of the more serious crime since he had actually imagined the king's death. Tavernier's story was difficult to unravel. He was a shrewd and resourceful man who could not immediately be dismissed as crazy. He had invented a plot to assassinate Louis XV and cast himself in an instrumental role. Finding himself temporarily occupying center stage, he used the opportunity to denounce a penal system whose abuses he had personally suffered, transforming his particular grievance into a broader political critique.

Imagining the king's death assumed multiple guises in Tavernier's mind. At times he claimed to be the member turned informant of a large conspiracy. In other instances he was an individual operating on his own, a martyr whose sacrificial coup would provoke social and political reform by alarming the king and his subjects. His arguments reveal a conflicting set of images and attitudes concerning royal authority and fidelity. The contradictions embedded in Tavernier's case are significant since they were simultaneously being played out on a much larger scale throughout the kingdom. Part of regarding the king as a father figure entailed reprimanding him when he failed to fulfill his paternal obligations.

Tavernier's initial interrogation at the Bastille by Commissioner Rochebrune stretched over three days. Rochebrune rehearsed Lussan's allegations in his first questions and instructed Tavernier to respond to the accusations. Tavernier recalled the incident of his violent outburst that had culminated in his plunging a knife into the door. He said he regretted the incident and dismissed it as a passing fit of rage. At the same time, Tavernier attempted to undermine Lussan's credibility as a witness. He depicted Lussan as an agitated and unpredictable character, asserting that Lussan had suggested that the two of them murder Lieutenant Latil and Major Robaud. Tavernier insisted that he had invented his regicidal plot to divert Lussan from such dangerous thoughts. He recounted the details more or less as Lussan had presented them.

Rochebrune, visibly frustrated by Tavernier's convoluted narrative, rebuked him harshly. Tavernier reiterated several times that the conspiracy was "purely fictive" and "that he never had any accomplices planning to assassinate the king and that it was a fable he invented to get himself transferred from the Ile Saint-Marguerite to the Bastille." The fact that Tavernier was explicitly retracting a statement made under oath several months earlier was not reassuring. Rochebrune was wary about accepting a confession because Tavernier might simply be covering up for his accomplices. He insisted that the idea of going to such extremes "to calm Lussan's raging temper" was preposterous. Recalling the incident in which Tavernier had burned his hand and pierced his thigh with a pin, Rochebrune had trouble believing that "the defendant was enough of an imbecile to suffer such pains in the hopes of appeasing Lussan."[56] Rochebrune remained convinced that even if the conspiracy were a ruse, Tavernier had resolved to kill the king in a spirit of vengeance.

Tavernier explained that ever since his outburst in 1755 he had been convinced that Lussan was scheming to denounce him. He had decided to provide additional bait in order to accelerate the process of getting himself transferred off the island. When pressed to clarify what he hoped to achieve once he had arrived in the Bastille, Tavernier replied "that he hoped he would be duly tried . . . that if he were found guilty, death would put an end to his sufferings, and if he were found innocent, he flattered himself that the magistrates would look into the reasons for his incarceration these past nine years."[57] This response draws attention to two significant themes: first, Tavernier's overwhelming sense of the futility of his situation and his desire to end his life as the only means of alleviating his suffering; and second, his tenacious belief that justice would ultimately prevail. Tavernier was convinced that if he were given the chance to present his case before the king and the magistrates, he would be vindicated and his oppressors duly punished. He still believed in the inherent justice of the king's rule.

Commissioner Rochebrune hastened to point out that "it is truly criminal for a subject to conceive of an assassination attempt against his sovereign or to pretend that a plot against his king exists even when the project has no reality."[58] Rochebrune was obliged to reiterate this dozens of times in the aftermath of the Damiens affair. The police had responded to their perceived incompetence in preventing the attack by redoubling their efforts to eradicate *mauvais discours.* Their efforts to clean up the state of French public opinion triggered a surge of calumnious accusations and false plots and created a whole new category of crimes and criminals. The police detected a dangerous precedent in this matrix of personal vendettas and public interest. Both the sovereign and his representatives were being manipulated by abject members of the populace, and nothing could be done to stop it.

Criminal officials responded to this unexpected turn of events by enforcing the most rigorous definitions of *lèse-majesté.* In essence, they turned the tables on the populace they were charged with monitoring. If the perpetrators of these crimes failed to distinguish true threats from false ones, then so, too, would the law. As Rochebrune reminded Tavernier: "The defendant is criminal if he wanted to assassinate the king and is equally so if he wanted to make others believe that such a plot existed . . . because in either case he generated anxiety concerning the safety of the king, whose days are cherished by his people."[59] The official view upheld a strictly sacred theory of the monarchy. The king's name was hallowed precisely because his person was sacred. Since the king was no ordinary mortal, certain thoughts were impermissible in connection with his person, and the misuse of his name constituted a criminal offense of the highest order.

The police were guided by the principle that "words are the expressions of our feelings."[60] Consequently, certain thoughts, once uttered, could not be simply retracted. The fact that Tavernier had conceived and discussed an assassination plot, for whatever reason, unequivocally suggested malicious intent. It revealed an insufficient amount of awe and respect for the king's sacred person since such sentiments, if properly instilled, would deter the production and dissemination of *mauvais propos.* Tavernier's case illustrates the extent to which these values had been eroded and transformed. Since he would not be released from the Bastille until it was destroyed in 1789, Tavernier had time for reflection. His prison writings offer evidence of his conflicted attitudes toward Louis XV and the institution of kingship.

Unworthy Fathers and
Rebellious Sons

Writing staved off the boredom and isolation that filled the long days of the unfortunate denizens of the Bastille. Furthermore, writing provided the only opportunity most prisoners ever had for justifying their actions. This relative freedom of expression contrasted sharply with the verbal interrogations, in which the accused could only speak in response to the interrogator's questions. As official interest in his case waned, Tavernier sought to rekindle it by elaborating upon his initial story. By 1760, however, Tavernier's credibility as a witness was so low that the police were inclined to dismiss his assertions since, as one official suggested, "it is not easy to figure out whether or not this man writes all this to amuse himself and for the sole pleasure of creating intrigue."[61] Despite the rambling quality of these later writings, certain recurring themes and images allow us to situate Tavernier's thinking within the spectrum of Old Regime political culture.

Tavernier's critique of royal authority arose in response to his personal experience as the victim of a *lettre de cachet*. Although these decrees had always been unpopular, they became a central issue in the campaign to check the powers of the monarchy, which gathered strength as the century progressed. In the hands of philosophes and magistrates the *lettres de cachet* became glaring symbols of the crown's despotic tendencies. Nonetheless, while the system was notorious for its abuses, it was also relied on by families and officials as a stopgap mechanism for a variety of social ills.[62] These royal decrees made it possible to detain troublesome or unruly individuals indefinitely in a royal prison or hospital at their family's expense. After ten years of suffering at his parents' request, Tavernier channeled his anger and frustration into a personal crusade to abolish the use of *lettres de cachet* as an institution of Old Regime justice.

Tolerance of abusive paternal power diminished over the course of the eighteenth century as affection replaced the principles of force and subjugation within the conjugal family. Since the family metaphor was so pervasive in the rhetoric of the French monarchy, it was not surprising that filial resentment was readily translated into rebellion against the preeminent paterfamilias, the king himself.[63] This process of transferal from the particular wrong to the broader injustice is explicit in Tavernier's description of his ultimate goal, that is, being summoned before the Parlement of Paris: "I am going to avenge my personal quarrel, and my quarrel will be that of the entire nation, or should I say, that of the entire human race."[64]

Tavernier's "personal quarrel" stemmed from his experience as the victim of a *lettre de cachet*. To begin with, he held his parents responsible since they had repeatedly requested that he be locked away. After viciously mocking "the extravagance and stupidity of my father and my mother," he questioned the rationale of a society that upheld the unconditional authority of parents: "Is it right that in a well-policed state [*un état policé*] like ours and in a century as enlightened as the one in which we live such creatures should have the right of life and death over their children?"[65] It should be noted that Tavernier's reference to France as "un état policé" was directly linked both rhetorically and conceptually to the concept of enlightenment that followed.[66] The existence of a sophisticated police force was the sign of a civilized or culturally advanced society that reinforced the ensuing reference to an "enlightened" century. It should not be confused with the twentieth-century notion of a police state. The point of Tavernier's query was to highlight the contradictions between the arbitrary, unenlightened practice of *lettres de cachet* and a century renowned for its progressive temperament.

Since Tavernier was neither ignorant nor insane, he could not be easily dismissed. His meticulously logical arguments could be disarming. His attitudes concerning penal reform were consistent with those of the great thinkers of his age, such as Voltaire and Montesquieu. Even though his conspiracy theories were constantly shifting, his underlying assumptions about criminal justice and royal authority were not. At times he described himself as the ignorant member of a mysterious regicidal plot. In other instances he asserted that he alone had been planning an assassination attempt as a means of attracting attention that would enable him to pursue his crusade to abolish the *lettres de cachet*. No matter what the narrative, there was no disputing the intensity of Tavernier's anger nor the strength of his resolve to bring about judicial reform.

In tracing his accumulated resentment, Tavernier used vivid and forceful language to convey the deprivation he had suffered as a prisoner on the island:

> I was arrested against the law and taken from the Châtelet to Saint Lazare by virtue of a *lettre de cachet* obtained on the basis of my unworthy father's false testimony, brought back to the Châtelet within sixteen months, and taken to the Ile Sainte-Marguerite with 74 *livres* of iron chained to my body. From

then on I was systematically cut off from all contact with the courageous men who would have been able to help me. The first five years of my captivity in that place, they made me endure the utmost horrors of nudity, plague, and famine. I watched my blood flow as profusely as their injustice and cruelty. It seemed that the Chevalier de Villefort made it his pleasure as well as his duty to sully and dishonor my reputation in the eyes of everyone who approached the island by delivering long speeches in which he attributed to me the vilest thoughts and the most evil crimes.[67]

Even if we allow for some distortion in the aim of stirring Sartine's sympathy, the litany provides ample cause for complaint. Tavernier was outraged more by the lack of a single channel for legal redress, however, than he was by all the suffering.

Tavernier did not restrict his wrath to his mother and father. After all, his parents had died in 1758, and his situation remained unchanged. His understanding of his world, like that of most of his contemporaries, was informed by a deeply ingrained sense of social hierarchy. He was convinced throughout his life that persons of greater distinction than his parents were responsible for his plight. The most logical suspects were Pâris de Monmartel, his father's employer, and his brother, Pâris-Duverney. Tavernier believed that the intervention of the Pâris brothers accounted for the severity and rigor with which he continued to be treated.

During his incarceration on the Ile Sainte-Marguerite, Tavernier had tried on two occasions to secure a legitimate conversion of his sentence. As he explained, "I wrote to M. Duverney beseeching him to make my father see reason. My brother indicated to me that he was absolutely opposed to my release. A ship was being fitted at Toulon to go to America. I begged M. de Monmartel with all possible humility to have me taken with the chains on my feet and hands aboard one of the ships in the squadron, where I could have served as a sailor or a soldier, but I was told that I was not worth a shot of gunpowder."[68] It is impossible to determine how much, if any, time and effort the Pâris brothers may have expended on the disorderly son of a member of their domestic staff. Nonetheless, Tavernier perceived their hands directing his fate, and this conviction nourished his resentment of *les grands* and the regime that sustained them. At the very least he demanded the right to be informed of their charges in order to be able to refute them:

"As it is you, M. de Monmartel, who requested the *lettre de cachet,* I would
be infinitely grateful if you would be so kind as to write down the grievances you have against me and give them to the lieutenant of police in order
that I may respond to them."[69] In a language of deference, Tavernier demanded accountability on the part of his social superior. The polite rhetoric
was a thin veil for his radical presumption.

Tavernier stressed that the accumulation of resentment and hardship had
led him to include the king in his plans for reform. In fact, he explicitly
shifted responsibility for his fate away from Louis XV and onto the king's
appointed servants: "As for the crime I am guilty of, if the king's sacred
name had not been used to sacrifice me with impunity to sweet Jesus while I
was still alive, I would never have had a bone to pick with this prince."[70] He
was turning the accusation that had been leveled against him back onto his
accusers. He had arguably been guilty of abusing the king's name by
spreading a false alarm. Yet he asserted that a similar, more serious abuse
was being perpetrated by those entrusted with enforcing the crown's policies, that in effect the crown's servants were establishing a pattern of behavior deleterious to the sanctity of the king's name.

Tavernier's arguments were riddled with contradictions. On the one
hand, he was acutely aware of his inability to effect the changes he desired.
Classified among the criminal rabble and lacking an honorable birthright,
Tavernier was constrained by his *état:* "I can accomplish nothing on my
own, being nothing but a man from the dregs of society, but I am going to
do as the sapper who uses gunpowder. I will stir up the political scene."[71] Yet
he was unwilling to accept the reduced sphere of action allotted to him. He
was determined to find a way to command official attention, however
briefly, before he died.

This resiliency reflected his deeply embedded elitism. He took pains to
distinguish himself from the disreputable characters with whom he had
been mistakenly and unforgivably lumped. He was a cultivated and literate
man and did not hesitate to reveal his scorn for the majority of his peers,
whom he dismissed as incredulous fools: "Nothing is more common among
the bourgeoisie and the rabble than these impertinent remarks lacking
rhyme or reason."[72] In fact, his inflated self-confidence encouraged delusions of grandeur such as those expressed in the following outburst: "For

my liberty . . . it will be glorious for me to receive it from nobody but the king. I recognize nobody in this world as my superior except His Majesty and the brave men who represent him at the head of the army or in the tribunals. I don't give a damn about the rest of the world."[73] These extravagant claims reveal both arrogance and insecurity: Tavernier boasted precisely because he was profoundly aware of his impotence. His plans for reform revealed a utopian vision. The abolition of *lettres de cachet* was the cornerstone of a program for sweeping social change. He explained that the assassination attempt against Louis XV had been designed as a means of achieving this higher goal. He never expected to succeed in executing his scheme, especially since he had no desire to kill the king. It was part of his plan to get arrested so that he could secure a judicial hearing. He would use his trial as a forum for exposing the injustices he had suffered, which were rotting the core of absolutism. He did not anticipate a pardon but would be content to die once he had voiced his proposals for reform.

Tavernier intended to abolish some institutions and refashion others while leaving the king's authority intact. In the process Louis XV would be transformed from an ignorant and abusive ruler into a benevolent but impotent father. This point is significant because, as Lynn Hunt argued in her analysis of paternal images in the late eighteenth century, "the shift toward the good father undermined absolutist royal authority" by stripping the king of any real power. In her reading of plays and novels of the last decades of the Old Regime, Hunt demonstrated that as benevolent fathers replaced authoritarian ones, what she terms "the domestication of fatherhood," they were also being effaced.[74]

Tavernier planned to enact a general amnesty for all the innocent victims of *lettres de cachet*. In abolishing the royal decrees, however, Tavernier did not seek to invalidate the rule of law. He proposed the erection of "a new Tribunal" whose members would be entrusted with, among other tasks, the dispensation of justice and the eradication of fanaticism:

> It should be hoped for the nation's welfare that a tribunal similar to the Spanish Inquisition be established . . . whose sole purpose was to chase away all those sacrilegious cheats who are contained in the class of Tartuffes, and this tribunal would also concern itself with juvenile offenders. Paternal author-

ity, which is too widespread, would find itself limited, as it should be; it would no longer be whim and passion that determined punishment in such cases. It would be reason and equity . . . near each capital there would be a house administered by a philosophe designed specifically for those cases when temporary seclusion from the world proved necessary.[75]

It is difficult to comprehend why Tavernier would compare his tribunal to the Spanish Inquisition. A symbol of religious persecution and intolerance, the Inquisition was hardly an appropriate model for a tribunal entrusted with enlightened reform.

Like many utopian schemes, Tavernier's proposal failed to specify the actual mechanics of government in his reformed state, such as how leaders would be selected and how power would be distributed. The only specific promise Tavernier offered was that "the Sovereign who would establish such an institution in this country would be adored by present and future generations and could flatter himself . . . with having secured peace, honor, and tranquillity for his country forever."[76] Tavernier failed to see that in challenging paternal authority as it was embodied in the *lettres de cachet* he was necessarily undermining one of the theoretical premises upon which the French monarchy rested its claim to rule. It was impossible to decry the abusive power of fathers without disparaging the preeminent paternal symbol in the kingdom.

Despite his grievances, the toppling of the monarchy never figured in Tavernier's designs for reform. On the contrary, he sought to reinforce the king's power by eliminating the abuses being perpetrated in his name. Moreover, he expected the initiative for reform to come from the king himself. His tenacity in clinging to the royal figure as the deus ex machina attests to the difficulty of breaking with a king-centered vision of the world even when calling for radical social change. For an individual accustomed to seeing all power flowing from this one source, it was difficult to conceive of alternative or multiple channels of authority. Thus, Tavernier, like Bonafon and Allègre, placed his hopes in Louis XV as the logical catalyst for political reform.

Tavernier was convinced that Louis XV's wrath would give way to gratitude once he understood the goals that were to be achieved:

What would the king have said, the day after the execution of this terrible project, when he would have been informed of my principal desire in making such a sacrifice and received a full account of all the abominations that took place on the Ile Sainte-Marguerite. Wouldn't he have been all the more struck by this gesture of generosity on the part of a miserable wretch who had been provoked beyond measure as I had been than if he had been wounded by a true assassin? He would have digested all the evidence that would have been shown to him that day with so much wisdom and prudence that I would bet a hundred to one that I would have obtained what I wanted to have, the erection of this new tribunal, assuming for one minute that the king had consented.[77]

Clearly, Tavernier had premised the success of his plan on the assumption that the king was a benevolent and enlightened leader. Once the king was fully informed, his natural goodness would guide him in pursuit of the just cause. Thus, he was not attacking paternal authority so much as he was re-configuring it, emphasizing affection and voluntary duty rather than forced obedience as its distinguishing attributes.

Tavernier's discussion of paternal authority was riddled with ambiguity. Although he condemned the *lettres de cachet* both in principle and in practice, he was unable to strip the French king of his paternal attributes. Rather than eliminate the father, he was determined to reform him. He sought to correct one instance of abusive paternal authority without challenging the more fundamental principle on which it rested: "Thus, with a single blow, paternal authority restrained without being degraded or debased, irrepressible youth contained by duty without our being obliged to lock it away or dishonor it, as has been the custom until the present."[78] Tavernier recognized the inherent legitimacy of paternal authority as well as the social problems posed by rebellious and disorderly youths. What he was criticizing, then, was not the motives that had inspired the *lettres de cachet* but their inability to cure social ills. Prone to abuse, they marred the exercise of royal authority and deserved to be eliminated.

Tavernier was not one for modest claims; he insisted that the establishment of his tribunal would usher in an age of unprecedented harmony,

a general confederation into which the entire nation would have necessarily entered. All social divisions would have melted away and been swallowed up therein; the farmers from the country; the city dwellers; the two classes of the nobility, the Robe and the Sword. The soul of this large body would be nothing other than an inviolable and unwavering fidelity to the person of Kings and an implacable hatred for, and deadly aversion to, all persecutors and all persecution, an ardent and sincere love for everything that contributed to social order and public tranquillity. The nation was going to be re-fashioned in terms of character and style; cured of that mad frenzy that has possessed it until the present . . . inspired by this new spirit of reason, gentleness, and humanity, our compatriots would henceforth form one immense family of which kings would be regarded and expected to serve as the true fathers.[79]

Here is Tavernier's Enlightenment utopia, echoing the language of reason and progress, as well as the model of the family held together through bonds of love rather than force. It is significant that Tavernier chose to reinforce his model society with a traditional language of fidelity. It reveals the limits of his visions for change and the persistent power of loyalty. This decision represented a conciliatory gesture toward the existing political order. He consciously avoided an outright confrontation, assuring Louis XV that his critique was not intended as a threat to the monarchy.

Theoretically, Tavernier could have abolished the monarchy or transformed Louis XV into a constitutional or a puppet king. He chose, rather, to restore the natural relationship between king and country: the good father and loving family. His emphasis that "henceforth . . . kings would be . . . true fathers" implied that such was not the current situation. Louis XV was currently a bad father because he had abandoned his sons and exposed them to the cruel abuse of his servants. Tavernier's argument upheld the important distinction between negligence and malice. Like Bonafon's satire, Tavernier chided the king for being remiss while deliberately avoiding the accusation of intentional wrongdoing.

Tavernier found convincing the police of his attachment to Louis XV to be more difficult than he had anticipated. From an absolutist perspective, one that by definition precluded consultation, there was never justification for questioning either the king or his ministers. Commissioner Rochebrune could not have been more explicit when he reminded Tavernier "that he should not complain about His Majesty or the minister who deemed it necessary to deprive the accused of his liberty . . . that he is truly criminal to have formed in his heart the project of assassinating His Majesty."[80] Tavernier could not refute such arguments, despite the higher ideals he claimed to be serving. The ability to imagine murdering the king and the audacity to share such thoughts with others were the indisputable marks of an evil character.

Longevity was one of fidelity's distinguishing features, from both an official and a popular perspective, and Tavernier spoke to this assumption when he emphasized "that in the home where the defendant [Tavernier] was raised, children were imbued with feelings of love and fidelity for the person of the sovereign, . . . that the defendant had spent his life in military camps and among the king's troops, where this prince was adored equally by soldier and officer." From birth, Tavernier had been instilled with love for his sovereign and surrounded by models of *fidèles sujets*. These experiences had reinforced and intensified his personal allegiance to the king. Tavernier admitted that he had erred in directing his wrath against the king since Louis XV was not directly responsible for his plight. He explained that "today he [Tavernier] recognized clearly that he bore a grudge less against the king than against the cowards who had abused the sacred name of His Majesty to strip the defendant of his honor and life and then abscond with his fortune."[81] As this excerpt illustrates, Tavernier believed he had mistakenly assimilated the person of the monarch with the institution of monarchy. A natural confusion, one might add, since the theory of absolutism had encouraged a conflation of state and king in rhetorical and practical terms. Yet Tavernier was now attempting to disassociate the person from the institution in order to extricate the man, Louis XV, from the political system over which he presided.

In several instances Tavernier suggested that monarchy's fundamental flaw was its susceptibility to abuse. Like Montesquieu, he argued that the king needed to be aware of this danger because it threatened to undermine his authority. The tribunal Tavernier proposed erecting was designed to counteract this tendency toward corruption and decline. Tavernier clarified that his assassination attempt had been designed to warn the king of "the great risk he incurred by allowing his name to be prostituted as it had been up until the present."[82] The use of the verb *prostitute* suggested a sordid commercial transaction that threatened to devalue the king's image. Since ministers and officials exercised their authority in the king's name, every miscarriage of justice redounded on his person.

Throughout his incarceration Tavernier clung to the topos of an inherently good king who was unaware of the hardships being inflicted upon his devoted subjects. If the king only knew: there was nothing original in this refrain. What was striking, however, was that an individual whose resentment and frustration was so acute refused, nevertheless, to turn against the king. In a *mémoire* addressed to Lieutenant of Police Sartine, Tavernier recalled a conversation with a fellow prisoner on the Ile Sainte-Marguerite named Gautier. Apparently, said Tavernier, Gautier was dumbfounded "when he heard me say that the king was the best man in the world and that if he knew what was taking place in our prison, he would have put an immediate stop to such abuse, that is to say he would have brought Villefort to trial and rendered justice to all of us wretches." Moreover, almost as if he detected a glimmer of sympathy in Sartine's eye, Tavernier appended the following lines: "Certainly when a man says that the king is the best of men, when he is speaking to a friend and not to one of the crown's officials . . . this is proof that this same man is not inclined to slaughter this same king."[83] The proof of his integrity lay in this unguarded conversation with a friend, in which he had expressed his sentiments without an ulterior motive.

Tavernier's fidelity was not unconditional even in prison. It possessed a sharp critical edge that cut into his effusive discourses of devotion and self-sacrifice. This point is most clearly illustrated in his variations on the theme of the king's ignorance. At times Tavernier transformed the traditional language of "if the king only knew" into a much more aggressive assertion that "the king should know better." In a *mémoire* drafted in July 1761 his rebuke of royal authority was noticeably more aggressive: "Give me . . . some sign of life . . . otherwise you will drive me to some desperate act. I am in a place where I breathe in poisoned air . . . your *Bien-Aimé* should know better than to detain his most loyal subjects in conditions he would be embarrassed to use for his own assassins. He makes me envy Damiens's fate."[84] According to Tavernier, Louis XV had a moral obligation to keep abreast of what was occurring under his aegis. Moreover, like Allègre, Tavernier argued that even criminals deserved to be treated with dignity and justice.

Tavernier's anger exploded periodically in vitriolic language. In these instances he relied on animal imagery, depicting the king as a savage hunter and his subjects as his beasts of prey: "It is truly astonishing that Louis XV, who got himself titled the *Bien-Aimé*, renders the condition of the men whom he has the honor to command more deplorable than that of the deer and the wild boar who roam his forests. At least the latter are not skinned alive; they are allowed to die before they are stripped of their hides."[85] He concluded this statement with a request that the king provide him with the means to kill himself. He threatened to starve himself to death if all else failed.

The allusion to Louis XV's passion for hunting was neither random nor innocuous. Arlette Farge has demonstrated how the king's favorite sport became an object of popular contempt early in his reign, reflecting deep anxieties about the new king's military capacities.[86] Hunting was seen as a complement to military struggle, yet Louis XV seemed to prefer chasing the deer in his forests to pursuing his kingdom's enemies in armed conflict. There was a sense that the king's passion for hunting interfered with his duties as sovereign leader. Moreover, the young king was portrayed as an exceptionally cruel and rapacious hunter. It was a parody of conquest to display one's dominion over the unarmed beasts who roamed the forests, and the king's violence was seen as exaggerated and misplaced. Tavernier drew an analogy between his captivity and the fate of the king's prey. In both instances the challenge did not merit the severity of the response. It revealed cowardice and brutality more than it signaled glory.

Despite his confinement, Tavernier demonstrated a keen interest in contemporary politics from his island retreat, especially the unfolding of the Damiens affair. Tavernier was fascinated with Damiens and wrote one long *mémoire*, entitled "Réflexions sur l'Affaire de Damiens," in which he attempted to trace the genesis of the crime. He was most interested in determining what or who had motivated Damiens's coup, and he offered his own hypothesis. He began his analysis with a review of those individuals or groups who stood to gain by the king's death. He dismissed in rapid succession the princes of the blood, including the ever suspicious Conti, the magistrates, and the clergy. He asserted that the princes were "upright and honorable men . . . who truly loved the king." As for the magistrates and ecclesiastics, Tavernier claimed that despite an unending series of disputes, "there have not been any of those huge disturbances that occurred under preceding reigns."[87] This left two possibilities: either Damiens acted as an independent agent or he acted as the hired hand of a foreign plot.

For Tavernier, the most plausible explanation was that Damiens had been driven to his rash act by religious fanaticism: "Before being employed by a man of distinction, Damiens frequented colleges and pensions, where he acquired that bad habit of pedants of judging definitively without taking a minute to consider things more deeply. He also . . . brought away with him that stupid credulity that accepts all rumors as facts no matter what they are . . . all Picards are hotheads and never think twice after forming their first impression."[88] The reference to "colleges and pensions" alludes to Damiens's highly publicized connections to the Jesuits. He had been educated by Jesuits and had worked as a servant in the Jesuit college of Louis-le-Grand. Even after being dismissed, Damiens had maintained close contacts with a couple of his former employers. For Tavernier, as for many French men and women, the Jesuits were linked both to religious fanaticism and to regicide.

Having established Damiens's predisposition for rash and impulsive judgments, Tavernier sought to determine the catalyst. He proposed the following as an account of what had transpired in Damiens's mind: "A little while later, he came to serve at a table where the conversation turned to the subject of the king of Prussia . . . lots of praise . . . from then on his heart was divided . . . between love and hate. He felt nothing but scorn and loathing for his sovereign and tenderness and esteem for this foreign king. And thus he became a zealot . . . because fanaticism is nothing more than a redoubling of zealotry."[89] What made Tavernier's analysis intriguing was his effort to uncover the psychological motives that underlay Damiens's decision. He wanted to understand the criminal mentality as well as the mechanism by which fanaticism usurped rational thinking.

One is struck not only by Tavernier's penetrating gaze but also by the elitism that pervaded his evaluation of Damiens's character. He had immediately decided that Damiens was far too impressionable, that he reacted impulsively rather than allowing time for reflection. These qualities corresponded almost exactly to depictions of *le menu peuple* by officials and elites of the Old Regime. Perhaps Tavernier was consciously attempting to draw a sharp distinction between himself and Damiens, especially since he stood implicated in a similar crime. Tavernier's elitism emerged most strikingly in his discussion of the possible connections between Damiens's project and Voltaire's description of Ravaillac in his *Tableau général de l'Europe*. Tavernier could not help speculating on the erroneous conclusions Damiens may have drawn from a cursory reading of the philosophe's text.

> If, unfortunately for the king, a copy of Voltaire's *Tableau général de l'Europe* fell into his [Damiens's] hands and his eyes happened upon the chapter concerning Ravaillac . . . his imagination, which was already unbalanced, would have created monsters out of all this. If I could do the same as Ravaillac, he would have said to himself, . . . I would bring about a revolution in the current political system and I would put Frederick at his ease. Thus, he formulated his assassination project and did not delay in executing his plan. It all follows naturally.[90]

It is ironic to find a prisoner of the Bastille confirming the official argument that reading was a dangerous activity for the majority of the king's subjects. As the response to Bonafon's case demonstrated, literary activities were believed to pose great risks for men and women who lacked the education and critical faculties necessary for disciplining their potentially unruly imaginations.

Like the police, Tavernier perceived a causal link between reading and criminal activity. He even went so far as to urge Lieutenant of Police Sartine to be more rigorous in controlling the literature in circulation:

> As the king's lieutenant of police for the kingdom, you should urge M. de Voltaire to suppress from his history the entire article on Ravaillac, and especially the remark at the very end, "is it possible that such a man changed the face of Europe?" This remark is worthy of a philosophe such as M. de Voltaire since one can never inspire too much contempt for such wretches; however, it is dangerous in that it teaches any man inclined toward that fanaticism which engenders these sorts of crimes that he can do as much if he is willing to make the effort.[91]

In calling for stricter censorship Tavernier echoed prevailing arguments that printed matter was dangerous precisely because it made information available to an unprepared populace. He clearly believed, moreover, that restrictions were necessary only for the inferior segments of society. For some strange reason, Tavernier seemed to identify more with his oppressors, the police, than with the oppressed in expressing his concerns about the dangerous power of print.

A quick glance at Voltaire's discussion of Ravaillac's assassination of Henri IV clarifies the basis of Tavernier's interpretation of Damiens. It is apparent that Tavernier relied heavily on Voltaire and his notion of fanaticism. Even Tavernier's condescending tone toward Damiens echoed Voltaire's description of Ravaillac as "one of those miserable wretches from the dregs of society for whom the fanaticism of the rabble of leaguers and monks alone inspires such frenzy." Furthermore, Voltaire was convinced that Ravaillac had acted independently, dismissing conspiracy theories as unfounded rumors. "It is an established fact that Ravaillac had no other accomplices besides the rage of superstition."[92] Voltaire had played an important role in shaping Tavernier's ideas concerning fanaticism and royal authority. It is rare to find such an explicit example of an individual's appropriating information from a cited text and tailoring it to his own intellectual intent.

In at least one instance Voltaire's influence was perhaps greater than Tavernier ever acknowledged. Recall that Tavernier once asserted that he had designed an attack against Louis XV guaranteed to fail as a means of warning the king that a real attack was likely to follow unless he improved the lot of his subjects. Tavernier's description—"My primary objective in this simulated assassination attempt was to prevent a real one by impressing upon the king with as much force as possible the great risk he incurred by allowing his name to be prostituted as it had been up until the present"[93]—sounded remarkably similar to Voltaire's portrayal of Damiens: "Damiens conceived of his project all alone and did not share it with anyone, . . . the craziest idea that ever fell into the head of any man . . . he imagined to strike the king with a penknife, not with the intention of killing him, because such an instrument would have been incapable of that, but to serve as a lesson and to make him fear that another citizen might try the same thing with a more deadly weapon."[94] There could hardly be more substantial proof of a text's providing inspiration, practically a script, for a crime. Thus, when

Tavernier speculated about Damiens's reaction to reading Voltaire, he may have been speaking from personal experience.

On 1 May 1760 Lieutenant of Police Sartine vented his exasperation with Tavernier's case in a note he sent to the major of the Bastille with instructions concerning the prisoner: "Since Tavernier is untrustworthy and crazy and has abused the privilege I had the kindness to grant him, the permission to write to me after he had insisted, I refuse to consider his most recent request on this issue. Do not, under any circumstances, give him paper or ink or pen; this man is making a mockery of us."[95] The mention of mockery is significant. It suggests an acute awareness on the part of the police that their authority had eroded considerably in the aftermath of the Damiens affair. Moreover, it undercuts the assessment of Tavernier as crazy since a mentally unfit person could hardly exert such power over the forces of order and reason.

By enlisting popular support in their efforts to keep themselves informed, by conflating loyalty with policing, criminal officials had unwittingly made themselves the prey of the very populace they were charged with monitoring. They found themselves bombarded with alarming reports of *mauvais propos* and conspiracy plots arising in every corner of the kingdom. As a general rule, at least one of the individuals involved was lying. Although the scenarios varied endlessly, they always drew inspiration from a common pool of financial intrigue, personal vendetta, and private interest. What transformed these otherwise petty crimes into serious offenses was the allusion to the king's death as the primary motor. Too many French subjects were transgressing the boundaries of permissible thought and speech with their allusions to regicide.

Damiens's attempt to assassinate Louis XV momentarily destroyed those carefully wrought boundaries because it forced every one of the king's subjects to think the unthinkable. If familiarity breeds contempt, it is possible that the king's death lost some of its ability to horrify the more it was discussed and contemplated. At no moment in the reign of Louis XV was the vulnerability of the king's mortal body more keenly felt. Lynn Hunt detects a growing interest on the part of artists and writers after 1760 to explore the problem of a world without fathers.[96] She argues that this shift undermined royal authority by mentally preparing French men and women for a polity that was no longer centered on the king. It may be that Damiens's aborted coup provided the impetus for this cultural transition by making the issue of the king's disappearance palpably real.

As in the case of Antoine Allègre, Tavernier's extended incarceration fueled his resentment against the society responsible for his captivity. His bitterness and anger, however, were directed at specific targets. He attacked individuals and institutions whose authority struck him as illegitimate. One year after his arrival in the Bastille, in September 1760, Tavernier realized that his plans had failed. He was still waiting for an opportunity to air his grievances before a court of law. He condemned the politics of power and privilege, which condoned his plight: "I have been refused a trial. Why? because the wealthy M. de Monmartel does not deem it appropriate. The condition of a man born under a monarchy is deplorable! In a republic a private person, no matter how rich he may be, cannot attack the life, the honor, and the liberty of another citizen and go unpunished."[97] Monmartel was the symbol of the most sinister aspects of monarchy as a system for the exercise of authority: opulence, individual tyranny, arbitrary power, and corrupt justice.

Tavernier's reference to the rights enjoyed by members of a republic was not unusual in the context of public discussion in France in the 1750s and 1760s.[98] Comparisons between the governments of France and England were popular topics in philosophical and enlightened circles. Like many of his contemporaries, Tavernier found himself distinguishing the institution of kingship from the person of the king. He decried the injustices of absolute monarchy in order to reform it and tried to exculpate the monarch himself. He believed the change he proposed would ultimately strengthen and glorify royal authority. Tavernier was firmly convinced, however, that the king ran a great risk if he failed to check abuse because he stood at the pinnacle of the Old Regime's hierarchy of privilege and power.

He made this point emphatically in regards to his brothers, whom he accused of absconding with his share of his parents' inheritance: "My assassins of brothers . . . are guilty in this case of a crime of *lèse-majesté* in the first degree: by the prostitution of the king's sacred name to strip me with impunity of my honor and my life. In the first *mémoire* I will be sending you, I will prove clearly and neatly that they along with many others who hold prominent positions in society are among the primary causes that led to Damiens's attempt to stab the king."[99] With this passage, Tavernier warned Louis XV that Damiens was not so much an aberration as he was an expression of widespread grievances. The strength of popular affection for the king exacted a heavy toll. The sovereign, if he was to merit this love, had to protect the interests of *all* his subjects. The king could not allow crimes to be perpetrated in his name without endangering his legitimacy. By pointing to the accumulation of resentment against the Old Regime's elites, Tavernier identified one major cause of the monarchy's eventual collapse. The crown's unwillingness to distinguish itself from bastions of privilege concurrent with its failure to court the affection of the disadvantaged members of the populace placed it in a narrow bind. As it became more closely identified with the interests of the elites, the monarchy increased the likelihood of finding itself indicted on the same charges as those leveled against them.

From an official perspective, Tavernier's false allegations concerning a conspiracy against the king were symptomatic of an unbalanced and malicious mind. There was no threshold of tolerance for speculation or allegations concerning the security of the king's person. The police articulated these assumptions most clearly in their definition of fidelity. Rigorous standards had to be upheld as a means of bolstering the sacredness of the monarch in an increasingly secular age. Both Lussan and Tavernier offer instances of this evolution, Lussan through his notion of patriotism and Tavernier through his attack on paternal authority. These efforts can be seen as part of a broader process that gradually secularized politics. More precisely, these divergent opinions would coalesce into a new model for political and social relations based on a contract rather than on nature, tradition, or religion.

For the moment, however, the police were primarily concerned with their ability to maintain social order. They were convinced that there was a direct link between thoughts and actions since "words are the expressions of our feelings." Utterances, whether printed or verbal, could be monitored, collected, and eventually eliminated. For the police, the prevention of crime required that all of the king's subjects be prepared to restrain their own imaginations. After all, how much distance separated the imagining of the king's death and its literal enactment? As the case of the soldier Paul René du Truch de La Chaux, in chapter 5, demonstrates, it was but a very small step.

Chapter 5

Staging Loyalty

A Criminal Performance
by Paul René du Truch
de La Chaux

· ·

THERE WAS A LARGE CROWD at Versailles on the evening of 6 January 1762. Local residents pressed for a glimpse of Louis XV, who was dining at a banquet table before his assembled court to celebrate the Epiphany. This year, however, the festivities were abruptly interrupted at 9:30 P.M., when one of the king's personal guards, Paul René du Truch de La Chaux, was discovered wounded near the entrance to the palace kitchens. La Chaux said that he had been attacked by two armed men who intended to murder the king and the Dauphin.[1] The company was immediately dismissed, and the royal family was advised to withdraw into private chambers. While police officers began combing the palace for the two assassins, the victim was taken to the infirmary. He appeared to have been stabbed since his clothes were slashed in several places, yet the doctor who examined La Chaux was struck by the superficial quality of the wounds and remarked that La Chaux was fortunate to have escaped without more serious injuries.

Several arrests were made over the next few days, while La Chaux lay convalescent in the palace infirmary. As the investigation proceeded the police grew increasingly suspicious about the soldier's story. For instance, none of the witnesses in the neighboring apartments had heard any noise at the time of the alleged struggle. After four days La Chaux, who was fully recovered, was arrested and taken to the Bastille for further questioning. Initially he recapitulated the story as recounted so far. Two days later, however, he had a change of heart. He asked to see the lieutenant of police, Gabriel de Sartine, and with tears in his eyes he retracted his prior statement.

On his knees, he begged for pardon, explaining that he had invented the entire story. There had never been two men, nor had there been any threat to the king's life. Sartine was stupefied by La Chaux's confession, unable to comprehend such self-destructive behavior.

The police were not the only ones trying to sort out what had taken place on the night of 6 January 1762. News of the attack flew from Versailles to Paris and was the topic of endless speculation. Sartine had his inspectors monitoring the cafés and submitting daily reports summarizing the public discussions. Opinions varied widely as the following sampling suggests:

> In the cafés of Dubuisson and Brigarne near the Comédie-Française many different things were said, and it is difficult to establish what actually occurred; nonetheless, the public appears greatly saddened by this event.
>
> Some say that the wounded guard is the same one who first laid hands on the wretched Damiens when he committed his horrible crime, in recompense for which His Majesty had awarded him a pension, and that wanting to augment his fortune he invented this shameful stratagem of stabbing himself with his own dagger.
>
> Others say that it was a dispute this soldier had begun with two men he did not know while having his dinner at an inn.
>
> Others say that the two unknown men were, without doubt, the envoys of a sect whose roots needed to be cut, meaning the Jesuits.[2]

Thus, from the outset La Chaux's contemporaries established connections between his incident and more sensitive political issues such as the Damiens affair and the parlementary efforts to expel the Jesuits from France. Such conjecture was neither random nor coincidental because La Chaux had factored in public opinion when calculating his crime. He had consciously incorporated references to current affairs into his script to heighten its verisimilitude, and this decision would ultimately cost him his life.

La Chaux executed his coup against a backdrop of political and social tensions that he relied on to give credence to his story. That his case generated such concern indicates that, like Bonafon, Allègre, and Tavernier, he had correctly identified sources of tension between the crown and its subjects. Exploring how La Chaux constructed his story to make it as persuasive as possible provides a window onto the problems confronting the French monarchy in a particularly difficult moment.

The official reaction to La Chaux's crime reflected the crown's heightened sense of vulnerability in a troubled era. Military defeat combined with
uninterrupted constitutional and ecclesiastical struggles had eroded much of
the king's personal authority. Consequently, the government was more sensitive to incidents such as La Chaux's, which confirmed fears that popular
affection for Louis XV was wavering. Moreover, La Chaux had instinctively recognized official paranoia about religious fanatics, particularly disgruntled Jesuits, and manipulated these fears for his own purposes. Although he managed to dupe the authorities only briefly, he would be
severely punished for his false alarm.

Even though it was an invented tale, La Chaux's initial success in convincing authorities of a real threat to the king lay in his ability to invent a
scenario that could have been true given the political context. This rapprochement between the actual and the plausible, between the *vrai* and the
vraisemblable, was the central strategic element of his plan. Thus, even
though it was an invented tale, it permits us to establish plausible ways of
talking about Louis XV in 1762, both positively and negatively. Moreover, it
clarifies official guidelines for distinguishing between appropriate and inappropriate attitudes toward the royal figure. These two sets of criteria are
significant because they reveal considerable disagreement between La
Chaux and royal officials over the definition of loyalty.

This gap between the two perspectives hinges on the term *fidelity,* which
is omnipresent in the police dossier. Fidelity was the pretext for the imaginary scenario since La Chaux claimed to have been injured in attempting to
protect the king. It was used to manipulate the authorities because he hoped
to be generously compensated for his efforts. Finally, fidelity played a central role in his confession and his efforts to exculpate himself. Like Bonafon
and Allègre, he saw his lie as a personal misdemeanor, not a capital offense.
Unfortunately, neither the crown nor its officials shared his benign interpretation of the incident.

Fidelity was an integral part of the institutionalization of absolutism in
France. As an ethic of personal loyalty and service, fidelity had historically
been harnessed to the person and cause of the king. Yet by the 1760s the evidence from the police files suggests that there was no longer any agreement
about what fidelity entailed or how it should be directed. La Chaux's failure

to recognize the subversive implications of his actions demonstrated that the crown could not rely on fidelity as a source of consensus between the king and his people. La Chaux was appalled to find his crime classified as high treason. From the police's perspective, however, allusions to the king's death, especially when dramatized to such effect, were profoundly irreverent and overtly malicious. They merited the most severe punishment available if only to set an example that would deter future offenders. The confusion surrounding the definition of fidelity in this dossier suggests an even deeper conflict over the nature of royal authority and the person of the king in France in 1762. As Louis XV was learning in the ongoing conflicts with his parlements, the language of loyalty could be deployed in the service of causes directly opposed to the interests of the crown itself.

Hard Times

The early 1760s constituted one of the most trying moments in the three decades of Louis XV's personal rule. By 1762 the war with England was drawing to a close. This costly and disappointing military adventure had taken its toll economically and demographically. Taxes had been increasing since the beginning of the war, and in 1760 a third *vingtième* had been imposed, along with a doubling of the capitation. The government's finances were in such bad shape that the French would continue paying for this military fiasco long after the fighting had ceased.[3] The new taxes provoked serious confrontations between the crown and its parlements, especially in the provinces, where members feared the loss of customary privileges and fiscal autonomy that implementation of the proposed measures promised. Stormy debates and published remonstrances not only delayed the registration and collection of the taxes but also undermined the monarchy's authority at home and, more seriously given the military situation, weakened France's image abroad. This deadlock culminated in the crisis of 1763, when various parlements united forces and refused to register the fiscal edicts. This entrenched resistance forced the needy crown to retreat and marked a critical shift in the governmental balance of power in favor of the magistrates, who were not only claiming but confirming their right to limit the king's authority.[4]

Combined with the hardships imposed by war was the mounting tension between Louis XV and his law courts over the status of the Jesuits in the kingdom. Legal disputes reached a crescendo in 1761–63 as parlements throughout the country used debates over the Jesuits to check royal power and assert their own prerogatives. A core group of Jansenists in the Parlement of Paris engineered the expulsion of the Society of Jesus by royal decree in 1764. The crown was forced to acquiesce since it needed legislative support for the unpopular fiscal measures it was obliged to implement after four years of uninterrupted warfare.[5] The vilification of the Jesuits had a serious impact on the image of the French monarchy because the Society of Jesus was one of the historical symbols of Bourbon absolutism. The fate of the crown was inextricably linked to that of the Jesuits since the kings of France had promoted the order and traditionally relied on it to supply their confessors. In the course of the controversy over the sacraments the Jesuits became a convenient rallying point for Jansenist, Gallican, and enlightened opposition to the crown. By 1762 this united front posed a formidable challenge to royal authority.

The expulsion of the Jesuits was a decisive blow to the *parti dévot* and the church, while it marked a triumph for the Gallican and constitutional arguments of the magistrates. By the mid-1750s the Jesuits had become the scapegoats in the controversy over the refusal of the sacraments, and the magistrates concentrated their efforts on expelling the society from the kingdom. The Jesuits were denounced for spreading ultramontanist and despotic tendencies through their teachings and their influential position at court as confessors. Most seriously, their enemies charged them with condoning regicide as a result of their oath of obedience to the pope. Since the sixteenth century the Society of Jesus had been linked in the minds of French men and women to the killing of kings. The Jesuits had been publicly implicated in the Damiens affair, and they were immediate suspects, as the police report shows, in the case of La Chaux.

It would be a mistake to assume that these ecclesiastical and constitutional debates were contained within the palace corridors where they were fought. Recent research by Dale Van Kley has demonstrated the extent to which this controversy spilled out into the streets and influenced the attitudes of working Parisians. The Jansenist newspaper *Nouvelles Ecclesiastiques* and the legal briefs published in connection with the debates allowed ordinary men and women to follow the battles and choose sides. These controversies irrevocably damaged the prestige not only of the clergy but also of the king himself and the institution of the monarchy because religion, politics, and finances were inextricably linked.[6]

It should be recalled that Jesuits occupied prominent places near the throne and throughout the kingdom. They had a small circle of devoted supporters at the court itself, including the Queen Marie Leczszynska, the Dauphin, and Chancellor Lamoignon, who was dismissed in the fall of 1763, a victim of the judicial conflict. They exerted considerable influence as secondary-school teachers, especially in areas outside large urban centers. By 1761 they were responsible for operating 111 colleges and 21 seminaries in France.[7] Thus, many individuals who appeared before the police, including La Chaux, had encountered Jesuits and their teachings either during their formative years or later in their lives.

This summary of contemporary politics highlights the vulnerability of the crown's position when La Chaux staged his coup. At the time of his arrest in 1762 La Chaux was twenty-nine years old and had been a soldier in the king's army since 1754. He was a native of La Tourdure, eighteen miles outside of Bordeaux, a region where his family had lived since the early seventeenth century. His family belonged to the lesser robe nobility; the first of his ancestors to come to France had been a gentleman to Henri IV. His father, who had died in 1751, had been a cavalry captain. In spite of this respectable lineage, the family's fortunes were declining in the eighteenth century. By the time we meet La Chaux he was a *hobereau*, enjoying some privileges and a minor title but economically bankrupt. Although most nobles who entered the military acquired positions as commanding officers, La Chaux clearly lacked the financial and possibly the social resources to obtain such a place.[8] As a *garde du corps* (bodyguard) he occupied the lowest rank within the nobility, that of squire, which, given his impoverishment, gave him little more than a toehold in the prestigious Second Estate.

La Chaux was the child of his father's second marriage. When he was still young La Chaux's parents had separated, and his mother had retired to a convent in Bordeaux. Although both his parents were Catholic, he had been raised by a Protestant aunt after his parents' separation, and he had adopted her faith. La Chaux reached the third class in his schooling at a pension in Bordeaux. At age seventeen he was obliged to interrupt his studies since his father could no longer afford to pay the fees. During the next few years La Chaux appears to have wandered a good deal, first spending time with his father and then moving in with his mother for a couple of years after his father's death. He went to Paris for the first time in 1753 and was rejected when he applied for a company in the cavalry. He returned a year later and after considerable petitioning managed to obtain a position in the Maison Militaire du Roi as a bodyguard. The troops attached to the royal household did not constitute a fighting unit but a separate guard assigned to protect the king and to participate in royal ceremonies.[9]

In October 1761 La Chaux converted back to Catholicism, something his father had long urged him to do.[10] This checkered religious history made La Chaux more suspicious from a police perspective. Throughout the eighteenth century there was a reservoir of anti-Protestant sentiment among French Catholics that linked Protestantism with disorder, revolt, and treason. These fears had crystallized in 1756 in the murky dealings of the king's cousin, the prince de Conti, with the Languedocian Protestants on the eve of the Seven Years' War. Although the dreaded revolt never materialized, the Huguenots had allegedly been relying on Conti to negotiate with William Pitt's ministry to land a fleet on the French coast and launch a combined assault.[11] These rumors, however unsubstantiated, were all the more plausible in the context of the losing war France was waging against the Protestant kingdoms of England and Prussia.

La Chaux immediately strove to allay official concerns about his Protestant background. He explained that he had started attending mass upon entering the king's service. He had decided to convert but delayed until 1761. The police were anxious to know how he had prepared for his conversion, for example, what books he had read. One suspects that they were pressing to uncover possible Jansenist leanings since the two groups, Protestants and Jansenists, were drawing closer at just this time to make common cause of their separate struggles with the crown.[12] La Chaux explained that he had received primarily oral instruction in Catholicism from the bishop of Amiens. He admitted to having perused some devotional books, as well as the New Testament.[13] He insisted that he intended to die a good Catholic.

Religion was not the only element in La Chaux's past that raised questions about his integrity. At the time of his arrest in 1762 La Chaux was over his head in debt with no obvious means for repaying his creditors. The police attributed this dire financial predicament to an "excess of libertinage." He owed money everywhere—at Versailles, in Paris, as well as in his native province. The interest he earned on his dwindling fortune was not enough to keep up with these mounting debts. According to La Chaux, he had an income of 400 livres and debts amounting to 1,400 livres.[14] In the months preceding his crime he had been pressuring the captain of his regiment to help him obtain a pension or benefice from the court. When these efforts failed to produce any results, La Chaux resolved upon his dreadful coup.

In the course of their investigation the police discovered that La Chaux had succeeded once before in obtaining financial reward for services rendered to the crown. On 17 January 1757, less than two weeks after Damiens's attempt to stab Louis XV, La Chaux had met a Sieur du Breuille de Chantreza while dining at an inn in Orléans. During their conversation Chantreza had referred to a lame peasant he had encountered on his way to Paris a month earlier. This peasant had claimed to be transporting packages from the Jesuits in Bourges to those in Paris. The anonymous peasant had asserted that he was not alone, that there were others like him commissioned by the Jesuits to serve as go-betweens. La Chaux explained that Chantreza's words "gave him occasion to draw conjectures against the Jesuits, and he saw it as essential to declare this event and bring it to light; consequently, he wrote a letter to the major of the King's Household from the inn at Orléans." When La Chaux had attempted to track Chantreza down, he had been unsuccessful. Nonetheless, he had received one hundred pistoles from the crown in 1759 in recognition of his efforts. La Chaux used this episode as proof of his devotion to the king, asserting "that he only undertook these steps to demonstrate how strongly he was attached to the person of his master, whom he had always loved."[15]

Perhaps the memory of his good fortune in 1759 had inspired him to try a similar maneuver in 1762. Yet this time the stakes were higher since the king's life was more directly threatened. Whatever the connection between the two incidents, one thing is clear from La Chaux's biography: he was a desperate man by 1762. After repeated attempts to petition members of the court had failed, La Chaux saw no other options but the risk of raising a false alarm. Like the defendants in the preceding chapters, he failed to grasp the gravity of his offense and hence never envisaged the severity of his punishment. Arguably the most fascinating element of this case is the theatrical staging of an assassination attempt, which briefly succeeded in convincing officials of a real threat to Louis XV. Yet La Chaux's imprudent decision to simulate regicide was viewed as a very dangerous form of performance that merited the most severe punishment.

Staging Loyalty

Commissioner Rochebrune was the first official assigned to investigate this strange and problematic case. Rochebrune interrogated La Chaux on 12 January, two days after his arrival at the Bastille. At this point La Chaux maintained the statement he had given to the king's personal envoy, Lieutenant Davour, on the evening he was discovered. He explained that at approximately 9:00 P.M. on 6 January he had gone to purchase some tobacco. On his return he had passed the Office of Foreign Affairs, where he had noticed two strangers, one dressed as a clergyman in a dirty black coat, the other in a green suit. The two had approached him and requested to be shown to the king's banquet table, to which La Chaux had replied that this was impossible without special permission from a captain on duty. Furthermore, he had added in reference to the stranger in green, "you are improperly dressed." The two men had pressed their demands, explaining that they had come from far away and were obliged to leave the next day. They had asked La Chaux at the very least to indicate a place where they might glimpse the king as he passed on his way to or from dinner.

When La Chaux remarked that he found their requests most extraordinary, the assailants had exclaimed, "We have no evil intention; we are only acting to restore the power it deserves to a religion that has been destroyed and liberty to an oppressed people. If you comply with our request, we will offer you as a token of our appreciation anything you might desire."[16] La Chaux had been shocked by these suggestions, but not wanting to provoke the strangers, he had pretended to acquiesce and told them to follow him. He had led them into the palace via a small staircase near the entry to the kitchens. As they were mounting the stairs, the two had stopped and asked him where he was taking them. La Chaux had spun around and hurled back,

"Rogue, to arrest you," at which point he had attacked the man in green. Outnumbered two to one, La Chaux had ended up on the ground, his mouth bound with a handkerchief to muffle his cries. He had fainted under the barrage of blows, and when he regained consciousness, the strangers had disappeared. He had stumbled to get up, fallen down, and been rescued by two guards, Sylvain Mesle and Jean Philippe de Launay, shortly thereafter.

La Chaux's capacity to raise an alarm, however briefly, attests to the verisimilitude of his carefully planned and executed performance. His story was plausible precisely because it provided a scenario that addressed prevailing concerns and expectations in contemporary France. The fact that so many people were willing to believe that such an event had occurred indicated a state of affairs in which it *might* have occurred. Thus, La Chaux displayed a dual awareness: one, of the political context; and two, of the field of plausible action within it. An examination of those elements of La Chaux's dossier that investigators found most troublesome makes this point clear.

The police and the court, as well as the general public, did not fail to notice the ominous coincidence with Damiens's thwarted assassination attempt of exactly five years earlier. All were perturbed by this, including Louis XV, who was rumored to have said upon learning of the wounded guard, "It is thus decided that I will die by the hand of an assassin."[17] Commissioner Le Noir asked La Chaux in one of his later interrogations whether he had specifically chosen the festival of the Three Kings for his project, hoping to substantiate the alleged threats to the king by stirring memories of Damiens's prior attempt. La Chaux admitted that "since the month of October the idea had come to him that several years earlier the king had been assassinated on Twelfth Night, that he had thought that if his project were executed on that day [Twelfth Day], this would give it greater weight and would cause a bigger sensation."[18] To Commissioner Le Noir it made perfect sense, given the nature of the crime, that La Chaux had been inspired by Damiens. La Chaux explained that he had been ready since 1 January; however, he waited for a night when the king was dining at a banquet table. He sheepishly remarked that he had not realized that the date of 6 January "would make such a striking impression."[19]

Whether La Chaux was willing to acknowledge it or not, the ghost of Damiens haunted the public imagination on Twelfth Night in 1762 and heightened the impact of his crime. Nevertheless, five years separated La Chaux from the infamous regicide, and the details chosen to structure his narrative reflected the altered contours of the political landscape. One clear example was the presence of the two strangers with their grumblings about an oppressed religion and their intention to seek revenge. When Commissioner Le Noir asked La Chaux to review the actual process of planning his crime, La Chaux explained that "initially he only imagined to attack himself with his sword and to impute the blows to two individuals seeking vengeance on the king," but later, "on the spur of the moment the idea came to him that to stir people, it was necessary to present the two individuals as extraordinary men talking of religion."[20] Both the query and the response in this exchange mask ulterior motives. For Le Noir, the issue of planning was important because it was directly linked to the question of intentionality, so critical in legal definitions of crime. Moreover, planning would indicate whether La Chaux might have had time to discuss his project with others. As always in cases involving a threat to the king's life, officials faced the double constraints of a desire for secrecy and the need to verify that no accomplices had escaped their grasp. By contrast, it was in La Chaux's best interest to downplay the plotting element in order to minimize his guilt. A contrived crime revealed more deliberate malice than an act of passion because one had consciously harbored evil intent without seeking assistance through confession. Thus, La Chaux strove to emphasize spontaneity rather than protracted furtive scheming when answering his interrogators.

The police refused to accept La Chaux's claim that he had fleshed out his two assailants upon being discovered by his colleagues in the darkened corridor. As Le Noir insisted, "If all the circumstances were his invention, it is natural to think that he had given considerably more reflection to his declaration to give it more verisimilitude [*vraisemblance*]." La Chaux replied that "he had not imagined the circumstances in advance but in response to the different requests that were made of him."[21] Thus, in describing his assailants, he explained that one of them had to be dressed in a manner inappropriate for an audience with the king. This clothing would conform to his refusal to show the strangers into the banquet hall. The choice of an ecclesiastical costume for the second was necessary to substantiate the assailants' alleged motive for killing Louis XV.

The most significant detail of La Chaux's invented story was his description of what the two men said. In one version, he quoted them as saying, "We are only acting to restore power to a religion already destroyed and liberty to an oppressed people,"[22] and in another, "that they wanted to convey to the king some reports or some observations concerning his people's welfare and to obtain some tranquillity for a province currently troubled by religious disputes."[23] The two phrases refer explicitly to the Protestants, whose civil status was being debated at the time. Arguably, the "province" in question was Languedoc, traditionally a Huguenot stronghold and experiencing widespread unrest in the early 1760s. The Huguenots were, after all, both a "religion" and an "oppressed people," to borrow La Chaux's words, and they were "already destroyed" in 1762. The call for liberty echoed the rhetoric of French resistance literature dating back to the sixteenth century.

Yet La Chaux's allusions were ambivalent, for if the language suggested disgruntled Protestants, the clerical garb implied that the assailants might be Jesuits. Either La Chaux was undecided about the identity of his imaginary assassins or he intentionally supplied ambiguous clues, open to multiple interpretations. The Jesuits were the more appropriate scapegoats in this instance given their precarious status in the realm in 1762 and the perception that they condoned regicide. At the same time, since La Chaux was raised by a Protestant aunt, he would have been familiar with the Huguenot plight and the vocabulary of rebellion. No matter which interpretation was chosen, La Chaux's regicides were credible figures to the king, his officials, and his subjects. Both Jesuits and Protestants had ample cause for resentment vis-à-vis the monarchy in the early 1760s, and both were thorns in the crown's side, vexing reminders of unfinished business.

Commissioner Le Noir was anxious to establish the depth of La Chaux's understanding of the issues at stake in the ongoing debates over the status of French Protestants and Jesuits in the realm. To what extent did his actions reflect his commitment to a larger cause? When pressed to explain the precise source of inspiration for these imaginary assassins, La Chaux was deliberately elusive, explaining that "whenever assassination attempts were made on kings, he had heard that the evildoers and assassins had religious systems, and thus by making these two strangers speak like fanatics, he assumed that everyone would suppose that the assassins who had stabbed him were real human beings who intended to attack the king."[24] Thus, La Chaux carefully avoided identifying himself with a specific religious faction by playing on the consensus that acts of regicide were committed by fanatics. His references to the two strangers possessed a dual meaning, both parts of which were plausible in the tense political climate of 1762.

Commissioner Le Noir tried to turn La Chaux's false tale back on him by asking "if he thinks that the religion [*la religion*] was already destroyed" as his assassins had declared. La Chaux deliberately misunderstood the question, choosing to interpret "la religion" as religion in general as opposed to a specific religion, namely, Protestantism. He responded "that on the contrary, he firmly believes that religion [*la religion*] is always honored as it should be and that he conceived of attributing this phrase to his two assassins in order to give his assassination attempt greater verisimilitude [*vraisemblance*]."[25]

La Chaux clearly grasped enough about the debates concerning the Jesuits and the Huguenots, as well as the Jansenists, to incorporate such references into his fictitious scenario. Yet when he found himself accused of a capital offense speaking before a police officer, he retreated into the safer refuge of ignorance, insisting upon the limits of his understanding of contemporary politics. He stressed "that he never took sides in all of the divisions religious matters were capable of producing, that he had never read the books that might have been produced by one side or the other, that he does not even know what stakes divided minds in that regard, that he never knew what the papal bull *Unigenitus* was, never meddled in other people's quarrels, and was never persecuted by anything except the wretched ambition that led him to execute his evil project."[26] It is difficult to swallow his protested ignorance regarding issues he was able to rattle off with such precision. This quotation suggests that he was consciously feigning ignorance as part of a defensive strategy to downplay his guilt in the eyes of his accusers. Once he was in the Bastille, it was in his interest to distance himself as much as possible from the political debates that had circumscribed his performance in order to avoid the suspicion of having acted in conjunction with more powerful opponents of the crown.[27] On the other hand, he may have lacked a firm command of the distinct grievances in the current polemical literature, which would explain his confusion about his assailants, who dressed as Jesuits but spoke like Protestants.

Whether his knowledge was superficial or profound, however, is almost besides the point. The evidence does not allow us to identify La Chaux with a specific cause, such as judicial Jansenism or Protestantism. What mattered was not his personal involvement in the battles being waged but his decision to take advantage of them to enhance the plausibility of his fictitious attack. He knew enough about the principal actors and issues to fashion a real threat to Louis XV. He might have been better off, however, if he had been less successful in convincing officials because he ultimately paid a heavier price for his scheming. Even though officials had trouble at first comprehending and later classifying La Chaux's crime, they were unanimous in perceiving it as flagrantly offensive to the king and hence treasonous.

That the police took La Chaux's initial accusations seriously was evidenced by their efforts to track down his assailants in the days following his attack. They combed the environs of Versailles and made several arrests based on La Chaux's description. On 8 January Jacques François de Castelnault, a chaplain from Chaillot, was arrested with his neighbor Bartelemi Coeppé, a merchant. The two men had come to Versailles on business and were waiting for a coach to take them home when they were seized by the police. Castelnault was wearing his ecclesiastical garb, and Coeppé was dressed in a green suit. When the two men were presented to La Chaux for identification, he said that he did not recognize them. His response suggested that he was already having second thoughts about his scheme and his ability to make his argument convincing.

A Criminal Performance

Doubts about the veracity of La Chaux's tale were first aroused by the doctor who examined him. In his deposition Doctor Auger explained that when he arrived in the palace infirmary he found La Chaux lying on a bed confessing to a priest. Upon examining the victim, the doctor "could not prevent himself from saying, 'Well, he will not die,' and he dismissed the confessor and then bandaged La Chaux's wounds, which he noticed were all superficial . . . not one appearing to him to be dangerous, and . . . the bandaging he performed was more or less a formality, not a necessity." Dr. Auger

had immediately suspected that La Chaux was an impostor, and this frightened La Chaux, who then tried to play up his pain and suffering. The doctor
was not surprised when La Chaux confessed his ruse.[28] In addition, the servants in the apartment of the marquise de Saint Sauveur had heard nothing
even though the struggle allegedly occurred right outside their doors.

Thus, there were parts of La Chaux's story that did not hold together
from the start. Still, a staged regicide required extra precautions. Even after
La Chaux retracted his statement, he continued to be harangued in order to
determine whether he was concealing a secret plot. For the judicial authorities, denial of an initial statement could merely be an attempt to dissemble
the truth and protect accomplices. It was essential to extract a full and accurate confession before sending a criminal to the scaffold.[29]

Despite their professed desire for the truth, police officials were often
blinded by their own assumptions about crime and criminality. These rigid
categories shaped questions designed to elicit answers that would conform
to their predetermined criteria and assessments of the case under investigation. For instance, it was difficult for police officials to acknowledge, despite
mounting evidence to the contrary, that individuals lacking wealth, education, and status were capable of staging elaborate crimes on their own.[30]
Criminality, like so many aspects of Old Regime society, was understood in
terms of hierarchy. In the view of the police, only sophisticated people were
capable of conceiving and executing sophisticated crimes. This conviction
weighed heavily in cases involving clandestine publication, like Bonafon's,
or references to contemporary politics, such as La Chaux's.

From the start the police assumed that La Chaux had been guided or paid
by someone of more elevated status, presumably at the court, whose identity needed to be uncovered. Commissioner Le Noir refused to abandon this
line of questioning even after La Chaux had confessed to lying. One month
after the incident Le Noir returned to the alleged statements of the would-
be assassins and summoned La Chaux "to tell whether the speech had not
been inspired by someone else, and if so, by whom, when, and under what
circumstances."[31] Le Noir's words echo those of Lieutenant of Police Marville two decades earlier in his interrogation of the palace chambermaid
Marie Bonafon. As with Bonafon, despite their determination, the police
failed to uncover a secret conspiracy in La Chaux's case because one did not

exist. Yet, they remained baffled and visibly uneasy when confronted by La Chaux and his tangled skein of lies. They kept pointing out contradictions in his testimony, refusing to believe that he had assembled his story so incompetently. They were convinced that some key fragment was missing that, once revealed, would complete the puzzle.

La Chaux started having second thoughts about his actions when he found himself under arrest. The authorities were not responding according to his plan: instead of a pension from the court he had received a cell in the Bastille. Two days after his arrival in the royal prison, on 14 January 1762, La Chaux threw himself at the feet of Lieutenant of Police Sartine and begged for mercy. With tears in his eyes, La Chaux confessed "that having only 400 livres in income and more than 1,400 livres in debt both in his native province and in Paris and Versailles and wanting to receive a pension in order to pay off his creditors, at the beginning of last October he conceived the plan of stabbing himself and making believe that he had received the blows from persons who had designs on the king's life."[32] He explained that he had delayed executing his project because he kept hoping that he would succeed in procuring a pension from the court.

La Chaux had apparently been pressuring both the captain of his regiment, the maréchal de Luxembourg, as well as the king's daughters, through a Mme Bosquin, who was first lady-in-waiting to Mme Louise. By December, when he realized that no one, not even the maréchal de Luxembourg, was actively soliciting in his favor, La Chaux decided to act. On 30 December he made one last visit to Mme Bosquin:

> and had shared his grief with her, fearing that he would not obtain anything in terms of the rewards and pensions he was hoping for, that he saw clearly that the maréchal de Luxembourg had been unable to do anything for him, that the Dame Bosquin, before whom he appeared quite moved, strongly exhorted him to be patient and to console himself by telling him that many people were in the same situation as he was and had been waiting for a long time, she promised she would renew her efforts with Mesdames to obtain a pension of one hundred écus for him, . . . and that he had left dissatisfied with everything the Dame Bosquin had told him and in leaving had resolved to execute his plan.[33]

He had initially planned to stage his coup on New Year's Day, a day "when there would be lots of people at Versailles; that in effect he went alone to the palace at 8:15 in the evening with the intention of executing his project, that he mounted a small staircase leading to the king's for entering the little apartments, and left by the door that opens onto the Marble Courtyard. In the course of this walk he changed his mind and returned to his lodgings without speaking to anyone."[34] It took La Chaux five days to recover his nerve to try again, and this time he succeeded.

In describing his performance La Chaux drew upon the language and context of the sacrament of confession. He cast himself as a repentant sinner, if not to justify, then to excuse, his actions. He implored the monarch's mercy in several ways. To begin, he described his struggle to master his evil thoughts, insisting that "he had not ceased to be tormented by the same idea. He shed tears several times in his room, where he prostrated himself more than twenty times since October to ask God to remove this thought from his spirit."[35] La Chaux depicted himself as the victim of a malicious external power that had invaded his soul. That he had failed in his first attempt to carry out his plan on New Year's Day was, moreover, evidence of his good conscience.

He chose his words carefully to conjure up his disturbed state of mind. He had not slept a wink on the night of 5 January, he said, and had awakened early on the sixth "no longer knowing himself, being out of his mind" and "blind, knowing no other goal but that of procuring himself some benefits . . . to accelerate the pension he had been promised."[36] Thus, La Chaux sought to distance himself from what he had done by establishing a split identity: the man who had executed this crime was not the same individual who had served in the king's army nor the one standing before the police that day. This detachment fulfilled two functions for La Chaux: it minimized his responsibility while simultaneously clearing a path for his profession of loyalty to Louis XV.

In relying on the language of confession to excuse his actions La Chaux was treading on familiar ground. This was a shared vocabulary, one the police frequently resorted to in formulating their questions. They used it to challenge the veracity of La Chaux's statements as well as to test his religious conviction. Commissioner Le Noir could not understand why La

Chaux had failed to seek moral guidance from a confessor and reminded him "that our religion, into which he had entered, provided him with the means to destroy such a criminal idea . . . that his aversion to addressing himself to learned persons, whom he could have sought out without being personally acquainted with them, makes clear that he wanted to nourish and sustain his evil design inside him."[37] According to Le Noir, La Chaux's actions belied his statements. His unwillingness to seek out a confessor *before* his crime indicated that he was truly evil. His avoidance of the one sacrament that could have saved him also suggested that his recent conversion back to Catholicism had been a sham. La Chaux had taken no active measures to dissuade himself from his project; he had secretly nurtured it for three months. His subsequent avowal had been spurred by fear, not true remorse.

La Chaux rallied to his own defense, explaining that "he would never have dared to open himself to anyone about his evil project, that the shame of confessing such a fault would have distanced him from the confessional, that he would have liked to hide his evil thoughts from himself, that he had used all his strength for that but was never able to succeed and never managed to banish his evil project, which was stronger than him, that he did not have a regular confessor."[38] This outburst was clear confirmation of the church's waning effectiveness as a moral guide to the French populace in the second half of the eighteenth century. One of the indirect victims of the controversy over the refusal of the sacraments was the sacrament of confession itself, which got trampled in the protracted struggle. The confusion surrounding confessors, especially those suspected of Jansenism, in an era of declining religiosity offered powerful reasons to avoid the already undesirable confessional. La Chaux's lack of a trusted confessor alarmed a police force that viewed its tasks in moral as well as administrative terms. The police looked to the church as an ally in the struggle against crime and counted on confession as a deterrent. The grim fact remained that religion had failed to dissuade La Chaux and, as we shall see, La Chaux was less concerned about offending God than about offending his king.

Once he realized how seriously he had miscalculated the gravity of his offense, La Chaux attempted to atone for his actions with a full avowal. Like Marie Bonafon, he consciously fashioned an image of himself that relied on Christian teachings concerning sin and repentance. He insisted that although he may have acted selfishly and recklessly, he harbored no ill will toward Louis XV. Yet La Chaux failed to convince the police of either his remorse or his loyalty because criminal officials were committed to enforcing rigorous definitions of fidelity. Their standards were shaped by a traditional view of the king as a divinely appointed absolute monarch. For these reasons, verbal utterances and imaginary threats could not be casually dismissed. They were overtly disrespectful of the sacred principles upon which royal authority rested its claim to rule. La Chaux did his best to challenge these standards in impassioned declarations of fidelity to Louis XV. The dialogue between Le Noir and La Chaux concerning the meaning of fidelity is historically revealing because it allows us to identify two distinct, often irreconcilable positions on the issue. The clash between Le Noir and La Chaux over loyalty was arguably symptomatic of a more fundamental disagreement about the nature of kingship in mid-eighteenth-century France.

The Ambiguities of Fidelity

La Chaux insisted that despite appearances to the contrary, "there is no subject more loyal than he or more devoted to the king's service." To substantiate these claims, La Chaux sought ways to demonstrate his loyalty to sway his accusers, whom he told

> that if he had to give his life a thousand times for his master, he would give it willingly, that he often searched out the opportunity to acquire glory and reputation for himself as part of his duties serving His Majesty, that he often desired to know whether there existed in the world some enemies so that he might demonstrate the ardor of his zeal for His Majesty's interests, that he had never committed a wrong in his life except for the wretched project of which he was guilty, that for this he was more unhappy than criminal since he had been constrained to execute his project almost in spite of himself and by a wretched idea he could not surmount.[39]

With this long declaration La Chaux sought to establish his credibility as a loyal subject. Given his goal, it can be assumed that he selected proof that he believed would conform to official expectations regarding fidelity.

The quotation above suggests that fidelity was understood as an active, not a passive, condition. Verbal assertions of fidelity, no matter how eloquent or insistent, were insufficient; fidelity had to be demonstrated to be convincing. Thus, La Chaux relies on strong verbs such as *donner, chercher, s'attirer* and *demontrer* to emphasize his efforts to distinguish himself in the king's service. Moreover, they help bridge the gap between his impoverished status as a prisoner and that of the dedicated soldier with whom he sought to identify himself. Not only did he offer to sacrifice his life a thousand times for his king but he argued that he had always looked for such opportunities to distinguish himself and to demonstrate his attachment to his king.

This last point is significant because it opens up the question about the boundaries of fidelity. There were limits to what was deemed credible, and the police became skeptical if one pushed fidelity too far. Since the Damiens affair there had been a growing tendency to use fidelity as a foil for personal vendettas and calumnious accusations.[40] La Chaux was treading on shaky ground when he explained that "he often desired to know whether there existed in the world some enemies [of the king] so that he might demonstrate the ardor of his zeal." The police distrusted those who professed too much. After this assertion Commissioner Le Noir returned to the incident with Chantreza in 1757, which now cast an unfavorable light on La Chaux's dilemma. Viewed together, the two affairs established a pattern of manipulation and self-promotion that undermined La Chaux's credibility as a loyal subject.

According to La Chaux, fidelity was not only an active condition but also an ongoing commitment, part of a lifelong endeavor. Relying once again on language borrowed from confession, La Chaux endeavored to define a dual criterion whereby he should be judged. He insisted that one misdemeanor within a lifetime of loyalty should not be given disproportionate weight in evaluating criminality. As he explained, "he had never committed a wrong in his life except for the wretched project of which he was guilty."[41]

Implicit in this emphasis on the enduring quality of fidelity was the belief that a lapse in one's sense of duty, a *manque de fidelité*, did not leap out of a vacuum. Fidelity was an absolute value; if one had always been a *fidèle sujet*, one would continue to be one. If an individual could demonstrate a pattern of appropriate behavior, he was more likely to find a sympathetic ear when justifying a temporary blunder. Police officials understood both criminality and loyalty as moral and ontological categories that manifested themselves as character traits and patterns of behavior established in youth. La Chaux used his denunciation of Chantreza to play on these official assumptions. He stressed that he had expended so much time and effort to track him down "in order to demonstrate the extent to which he was attached to the person of his master, whom he had always loved."[42] The contrary also held true: if evidence could be found of prior delinquency or disrespect, then the offense became a logical outcome of a malicious character.

In his efforts to defend himself La Chaux drew sharp distinctions between the representatives of spiritual and temporal authority. He articulated his understanding of fidelity in decidedly secular terms. He never went so far as to deny the divine basis of kingship; nonetheless, in arguing that his actions had offended God but not Louis XV he undermined traditional divine right theories of kingship, which had sought to fuse juridical and sacred sources of authority in the person of the king. According to the jurists, the French king was God's appointed vice-regent on earth, charged with upholding the Catholic faith and the fundamental laws of the realm. Given this hierarchy, it was impossible to sin against the Lord without necessarily offending his chosen minister on earth.[43]

When describing his predicament La Chaux emphasized that he never would have gone through with his plan if he had thought it would offend the king because "throughout the different agitations which continually persecuted him, he saw clearly that he was offending God, but he never saw that he was offending the king, that certainly he never had any intention to offend such a good master, and that all the people who had witnessed his service to His Majesty could render him justice on this count."[44] This passage reveals La Chaux's determination to separate spiritual faith from allegiance to the king and the radical implications of this decision. For it not only attests to a dwindling respect for the sacred but also appears to diminish the deference traditionally felt for the king.

By 1762 royal sacrality had lost the force and conviction it had succeeded in establishing a century earlier. Alternative definitions of royal authority and the constitutional workings of government were vigorously debated and diffused in the pamphlet material circulating in the streets of Paris. Louis XV may have derived his authority from God, and this imposed a divine trust, but he was no longer unaccountable to his subjects for his actions. He was constrained by the law and its representatives like any other man. This point is important in terms of assessing the impact that the desacralization of the monarchy had on the institution of kingship in eighteenth-century France. By basing royal power on secular as opposed to sacred foundations, individuals like La Chaux were not necessarily calling for the dismantling of the monarchy. Upon close examination, it appears to have been the crown's sacred claims more than its legitimacy as a political institution that were becoming unpalatable to its opponents in the second half of this enlightened century. Definitions of kingship and the corresponding legitimating discourses may have shifted in the course of the century without undermining popular affection and respect for the royal figure.

The impassioned language La Chaux relied on to protest his loyalty to Louis XV reveals something deeper than an attempt to evade the police. La Chaux's desire to excuse himself before the king even when he knew his fate was sealed needs to be recognized and explained. When asked what had motivated him to confess the truth, he responded "that he currently had no other project in mind than to try to expiate his fault by a sincere repentance and by his submission to the king's will."[45] He was making a direct appeal to Louis XV for pardon, reaffirming the intimate and personal relationship between subject and sovereign through one of the few remaining channels.

The articulation of absolutism as the ideological basis of the monarchy had been accompanied by a dizzying growth in bureaucratic procedures and officials. One immediate and significant consequence of this development had been to erode the fiction of the king's imagined accessibility in the eyes of his subjects, who increasingly encountered the royal will in a legislative decree or a minister's antechamber. Individuals who found themselves hauled before the police had the distinct impression that the traditional lines of communication between the king and his subjects had been blocked or eliminated. These perceptions were often vented to the refrain "if the king only knew." The notable exception to this rule, and one clung to with tenacity, was the royal grace of mercy. The king's pardon was an attribute of his divinity, a gift he shared with God, who had appointed him to rule. It was the necessary theoretical counterpart to his power to judge and punish. Each act of sovereign grace was a public gesture that reinforced the concept of accessibility by momentarily collapsing the distance separating the French king from his subjects, all the more powerful because it involved those who had been delinquent.[46]

Kingship is best understood as a set of reinforcing images that coexisted in the person of the king. These images, which included the lawgiver, the warrior, the father, and the pardoner, had accrued over the centuries. Each one had given birth to a corresponding language, including forms of address and metaphors, that sharpened and strengthened the image. When individuals or *corps* expressed praise or grievances, they usually directed their voices at one of these faces. Therefore, it is important to specify which facet of the king was the focus of attention when *the* king was being addressed. If Bonafon rebuked the king for being a philandering husband and negligent father, La Chaux was now turning to him as a merciful judge.

Over time some of these languages and the roles they defined had been attacked, and often they emerged from the scuffle with diminished appeal and authority. Yet the model of a merciful king continued to command respect late into the eighteenth century, especially among those whose education did not permit them to articulate demands through alternative sources of power. The association of clemency with royal majesty, which stretched back to Saint Louis, possessed enormous persuasive power. Moreover, judicial grace was a royal monopoly, a prerogative of the king alone, symbolic of his distinct status and sacred mission.[47] It is helpful to keep this framework in mind when looking at the breakdown of royal authority in the second half of the eighteenth century. Rather than a sudden collapse, it should be seen as the progressive erosion of an interlocking system of images and expressions that had traditionally inspired awe and obedience. Different groups in French society attacked different facets of kingship, but the cumulative effect was the dismantling of a complex ideological structure in which some layers held out longer than others. Understood in this fashion, the role of the king as grand pardoner was one of the last, if not the very last, to give way.[48]

La Chaux demanded pardon for the crime he had inadvertently committed. When asked what had inspired him to confess, he answered, "The remorse of his conscience and the affliction he experienced for having provoked anxiety about the king's welfare, which he had not anticipated." It was the last part of this avowal that troubled the police, and Le Noir asked, "How could he fail to anticipate the alarm he would cause in everyone's mind, since the minute he was lifted off the floor his first words had been that the king's life was in danger?"[49] The most disturbing aspect of La Chaux's false alarm was the seeming flippancy with which he had treated the king's life. By integrating the most serious criminal offense, regicide, into his schemes to secure himself a pension, La Chaux had demonstrated a detachment and disrespect that could only be qualified as dangerous.

The concern of the police was heightened by La Chaux's insistence that "he had not imagined the consequences of his wretched project and the consternation it would produce."[50] Perhaps, as Commissioner Le Noir secretly feared, La Chaux had failed to anticipate the anxiety his crime would generate because the king's popularity among his subjects was declining. Otherwise he would have known that his lie would create panic. The ineluctable conclusion was that public opinion was characterized by an unwelcome measure of indifference toward the royal figure. Le Noir was not alone in his reasoning. His concern was shared by the magistrates who tried La Chaux and sentenced him to death. If La Chaux's crime had raised the possibility of an affective gap between Louis XV and his subjects, the magistrates worded their *arrêt* to deny this interpretation. By condemning La Chaux for threatening the welfare of both the king and the kingdom, the judges implicitly reaffirmed the strong reciprocal bonds of love that bound the two together.

La Chaux's confession that he had invented his story only rendered his case more problematic from an official perspective. To begin with, it was unclear how to classify the crime in order to establish judicial precedents for determining an appropriate sentence. In a memo of 16 January the king's secretary of state, the comte de Saint Florentin, asked "whether there is a law against such roguery and for what the Sieur de La Chaux could be condemned."[51] Everyone agreed that La Chaux had played a dangerous game, but nobody was sure which rules had been broken. The Parisian lawyer Edmond-Jean François Barbier noted in his journal that the search for judicial precedents unearthed two cases from the early seventeenth century and that copies of these cases from the reigns of Henri IV and Louis XIII were being printed and sold by street vendors to an inquisitive public.[52] Barbier's comment suggests that La Chaux's case drew considerable attention, a source of evident concern on the part of the authorities, whose primary desire was to hush up the incident and prevent a scandal. Saint Florentin was hesitant about sending the case before the Parlement of Paris because "one fears the noise it will generate."[53]

The Theater of Punishment

La Chaux's case was first judged at the Châtelet, the principal municipal courts for the city and faubourgs of Paris, on 26 January 1762. Although the term *lèse-majesté* does not appear in the wording of the sentence, his case was treated as the equivalent in terms of his punishment. La Chaux was to be broken on the wheel and left to die. According to the procedure in serious crimes judged by the Grand Criminel, La Chaux's verdict was automatically appealed for final decision by the Parlement of Paris. At 7:30 A.M. on 1 February 1762 La Chaux appeared before the criminal chamber, the Tournelle, of the Parlement of Paris, where he was examined for five hours. The magistrates then withdrew to discuss the case in private for more than two hours. The new sentence found La Chaux guilty of the same crime but converted his punishment to hanging, the most common form of execution under the Old Regime. The conversion of La Chaux's sentence was not unusual since the agony of the wheel, like the death penalty overall, was rarely inflicted during the eighteenth century within the jurisdiction of the Parlement of Paris.[54] As was customary in cases involving capital punishment, La Chaux would be interrogated one last time just prior to his execution and tortured to extract a final confession.[55] It is striking that La Chaux, who had injured nobody but himself, was sentenced to death at a time when capital punishment was under attack in theory and on the wane in practice. To comprehend the severity of the sentence requires a closer look at the legal concept of *lèse-majesté* which clearly influenced the magistrates' interpretation of the affair and the wording of the sentence.

The legal definition of *lèse-majesté* had been formulated by jurists as part of the elaboration of Bourbon absolutism in the seventeenth century. These efforts reflected the crown's ongoing struggle to assert its sovereignty in the face of constant opposition at all levels of French society. The royal declaration of 27 May 1610 proclaimed *lèse-majesté* to consist in overt and covert acts against the person of the king, members of his family, or the safety of his realm. Under Richelieu, as the monarchy attempted to consolidate its power, definitions of *lèse-majesté* were expanded to cover a wider array of criminal activities. At the time, Richelieu was concerned primarily with the problem of conspiracies and assassination plots on the part of the nobility. Among the provisions he added to the list of crimes punishable as *lèse-majesté* in the Code Michaud of 1629 were the publication and dissemination of defamatory libels.[56]

It is important to recognize the extent to which the theory of *lèse-majesté* was centered on the person of the king. This point is most clearly illustrated by Cardin Le Bret's treatise *De la souverainété du roy,* first published in 1632.[57] Le Bret, councilor of state during Richelieu's government, devoted considerable space to the issue of *lèse-majesté*. His arguments would be extremely influential in shaping legal definitions of the crime for subsequent generations of French magistrates. What is most important for our purposes, Le Bret insisted that any criticism of the king, whether serious or derisory, qualified as an attack on his person and therefore as *lèse-majesté*. Moreover, Le Bret offered a sweeping interpretation of what constituted a threat to the king's life. He argued that a guilty verdict could be rendered in cases where individuals were involved in failed or unrealized plots. By extension, it was a criminal act to contemplate or allude to the king's death in private or public because such thoughts explicitly challenged the divine basis of royal authority. Only God had the power to determine the life or death of his appointed sovereign.[58]

These were the judicial principles and precedents that guided the magistrates who were presented with the results of the police investigation of La Chaux's case. They had to determine a legal category for his crime in order to assign an appropriate sentence. La Chaux had not only contemplated and alluded to the king's death, he had staged it before witnesses. By his own admission, his crime was premeditated, which made it more serious than a spontaneous act of passion. It was imperative that La Chaux be punished for his false alarm primarily to deter others from such schemes. This argument reflected fundamental assumptions that guided the Old Regime's ideology of punishment. The logic underlying criminal justice was primarily pedagogical, combining secular concerns for public order with Christian teachings on sin. The purpose was to dissuade potential offenders through horrific example, thereby avoiding similar threats in the future and reinforcing social cohesion.[59] Like Damiens's, La Chaux's execution was an instructive spectacle, choreographed to demonstrate that royal authority could not be injured without the gravest consequences. Marching to his death, La Chaux carried signboards explaining his crime to crowds watching in the streets. These pedagogical and political imperatives were explicit in the wording of the Parlement's sentence, which held La Chaux guilty on two accounts, for he had offended both the king and the nation.

After his trial the Parlement of Paris condemned La Chaux as a "fabricator of impostures against the security of the king and the fidelity of the nation" because his actions were "capable of alarming the king about the sentiments of love and fidelity of his subjects, and his subjects about the safety of his sacred person."[60] La Chaux's crime was perceived as twofold: he had raised doubts in the king's mind about the loyalty of his subjects and provoked widespread anxiety by indicating that the king's life was in danger. This argument was not unprecedented in 1762; it had been mobilized five years earlier in the outpouring of printed matter that accompanied the Damiens affair. As Pierre Rétat and his collaborators have demonstrated, when Damiens knife pierced the king's skin it inflicted a deeper wound on the body of the nation than on the body of the king himself. The attempted regicide triggered a surge of effusive proclamations of fidelity throughout the kingdom to heal the breach opened by Damiens's blow.[61] A similar logic informed the official response to the case of La Chaux: the wording of the court's decree reinforced the conviction that royal power rested on popular affection and allegiance, not fear and force. Like Damiens, La Chaux had offended both king and kingdom with his rash act because he had violated the contract of love and duty that was ideally supposed to govern relations between the French sovereign and his subjects. In their culpability both men implicated the society that had produced them, and therefore they had to be expelled if trust and harmony were to be restored.

The inclusion of the nation in the trial's verdict indicates that by 1762 French jurists were articulating a conception of royal sovereignty that did not reside exclusively in divine sanction. Describing La Chaux's crime as an offense against the king and the nation implicitly gives equal weight to the two subjects. His actions threatened to dispel the fiction of a love contract between Louis XV and his subjects because he effectively ignored or denied the existence of popular affection for the king. Perhaps La Chaux was judged with such severity because his case erupted in the midst of an acute judicial crisis. His trial offered the magistrates a chance to demonstrate their solidarity with the crown despite their ongoing opposition to many of its policies. Ironically, La Chaux may have paid for the tense political climate that had enhanced the plausibility of his crime in the first place.

· 🌣 ·

The spectacle of La Chaux's execution on 4 February 1762 attracted a huge crowd. It was an extended ritual of retribution and expulsion from the body social.[62] It began with La Chaux making amends in front of the doors of Notre Dame and ended with his hanging in the Place de Grève. One police official observed in his report that "everything went as planned. There was as much of a crowd gathered, from all walks of life, as there had been for Damiens's execution."[63]

Public opinion was divided over La Chaux's fate. Many of those who waited at the Place de Grève expected, as did La Chaux himself, that the king would intervene with a pardon at the last minute. The Parisian lawyer Barbier, who chronicled the age and especially its legal disputes, noted in his journal:

> There was no discussion of the judgment until Thursday morning, 4 February, when it was hawked and sold. Everyone believed that there had been disagreement in the council concerning the possibility of a pardon, because one section of the public was waiting for it to come through until the last moment; nonetheless, no reprieve. Thursday afternoon, he [La Chaux] left the Grand Châtelet, where the Court had sent him, in a tumbrel to make his honorable amends, after which he returned to the [Place de] Grève, where he was, in fact, hung at 4:30, in front of a huge crowd, who witnessed a very great resignation to God.[64]

The anticipation of a royal appearance in the final act in which the king would display his mercy added an element of suspense that was not dispelled until the cord was firmly fitted around La Chaux's neck. The expectation of a pardon suggests that La Chaux's punishment seemed severe at the time even by Old Regime standards.[65] No such ambivalence, for instance, had surfaced in the sea of spectators gathered for Damiens's execution five years earlier.

Damiens had been subjected to horrific punishment, but he had actually stabbed Louis XV. La Chaux, on the other hand, never even intended to harm the king, let alone murder him. Yet La Chaux was viewed and judged as an equally serious threat. Problematic as it was, La Chaux's case had to be exemplary precisely because such an irreverent performance could not be tolerated. Moreover, he had betrayed the sacred trust of his office as a soldier, charged with the mission of defending the king and the realm. The significance of this connection was noted in the judicial summary of the affair: "the author [La Chaux] . . . rendered himself all the more guilty given that he belonged to one of the most distinguished and cherished corps intimately attached to His Majesty's service."[66] If the king could not rely on his personal guards to protect him in his own palace, then whom could he trust? La Chaux's case threatened to dispel the ethos of loyalty, service, duty, and love that underlay and structured relations between the French king and his subjects. It thus replayed in miniature the same struggles confronting the monarchy in the much broader fields of fiscal legislation and government.

Imagining the king's death or staging it, albeit in simulated form, was legally defined as the equivalent of a direct physical assault. Yet the decision to enforce such rigid definitions of *lèse-majesté* was a problematic and ultimately costly one because it narrowed the already circumscribed field of permissible speech and action in reference to the king in an age in which other cultural developments made it impossible to enforce such restrictions. The police, however, could not ignore the subversive implications of these accusations, which played freely with the king, his name, and his person. There can be no doubt that the haphazard tossing around of the king's name was a crime of the gravest nature. Not only did it demonstrate disrespect for the king, it also strained the frame of the social body of which the king was the theoretical head. On the day of his execution La Chaux was obliged to carry signboards inscribed with the message "Fabricator of impostures against the security of the king and the fidelity of the nation."[67] The idea that La Chaux had harmed both the king and the French people reflected the fundamental view of the authorities regarding the nature of these offenses. In case after case police commissioners indicated that these crimes injured the body social, an interpretation that reaffirmed the ideological basis of the monarchy. A model of mutual affection was vigorously upheld and deployed by officials in the face of an individual whose actions explicitly threatened to dispel this fiction simply by ignoring its very existence.

The problem posed by La Chaux was that he believed he was a loyal subject. His impassioned declarations of fidelity suggest his own refusal to acknowledge the legitimacy of contesting royal authority despite his delinquent act. Like the defendants in the preceding chapters, La Chaux juggled incompatible convictions concerning kingship, loyalty, and personal ambition. He failed to recognize that fidelity was irrevocably distorted when it was harnessed to the service of personal ambition. Yet, he shared with Bonafon, Allègre, and Tavernier the frustration of having no other options. He had the distinct sense that he had tried the few available channels and had failed. His gesture, like Damiens's, was a desperate effort to touch the king, to bring his service and his grievances directly to the foot of his sovereign. In the process, he aimed to distinguish himself, an impoverished soldier, by linking his fate to that of his sovereign. The audacity of his decision lay in his assumption that such connections were conceivable, let alone possible, within the strict hierarchy of Old Regime society. The police and the magistrates recognized the subversive implications of La Chaux's simulated regicide, which threatened to collapse the distance separating a humble subject from a divinely appointed king, inevitably challenging the latter's sacred status in the process. These assessments were confirmed by La Chaux's own testimony, which revealed a distinctly secular definition of both fidelity and kingship. In response, royal officials enforced strict definitions of loyalty and *lèse-majesté* in an effort to restore the king's momentarily injured sovereignty and display it in its full glory. Hence the need for public punishment and expiation in La Chaux's case given the vivid impression he had made and the speculation he had generated.

La Chaux's case marks a rupture within the traditional language of loyalty. The dramatic distortions entailed in La Chaux's criminal performance effectively depleted fidelity's effectiveness as a bond between sovereign and subject. Chapter 6 demonstrates that the gradual secularization of French kingship left the actual incumbent on the throne more vulnerable to attack. Increasingly, the king would be summoned to account for his decisions by individuals as well as institutional bodies, and royal authority would be firmly rooted in the law both to define and restrain it. As the case of the retired lawyer Pierre Denis de La Rivoire suggests, the language of loyalty would be transformed into a language of criticism when the king's performance failed to meet popular expectations. Fidelity would be transferred from the person of the king to the unwritten fundamental laws embodied in historic institutions such as the Parlement of Paris and the Estates General. This displacement of trust would not have been so threatening if the French king had not been simultaneously losing the obedience of his representative institutions.

Chapter 6

"A King of Beggars"

Pierre Denis de La Rivoire's Critique of Absolutism

· ❧ ·

IN 1770 THE BARRISTER Pierre Denis de La Rivoire reminded Louis XV in an anonymous letter, "You are not king for nothing, you are king for the welfare of your people."[1] He returned to his harangue in a later letter, insisting that "it is justice that makes kings; without it they are nothing but tyrants, usurpers, and oppressors, whose power, founded on violence, finishes with their force and never passes on to posterity."[2] This rhetoric is noticeably more aggressive and radical than that encountered in the preceding chapters. It was fueled by the constitutional debates that preoccupied the crown and the French public in the last four years of Louis XV's reign. It suggests that by 1770 the level of verbal hostility directed toward the king and his authority had escalated considerably. The deterioration in the king's personal popularity was sadly evident when the affectionate title *Bien-Aimé* conferred at Metz in 1745 was replaced by the jeers of *Mal-Aimé* that greeted his funeral procession in 1774.

The souring of relations between Louis XV and his subjects reflected an accumulation of grievances and crushed hopes, many of which are identified in the preceding chapters. These concerns about authority and its abuse climaxed in the Maupeou crisis of 1770–74, a protracted and controversial effort by the crown to impose judicial reform on the kingdom's law courts. In defending their resistance to the king and justifying their own role in government the magistrates emphasized the concept of royal accountability and made it a cornerstone of public political discussion. From that point on, French kings could only ignore this demand at their peril. The government's effort to tamper with the judiciary provoked a storm of protest, and

the king's image as a benevolent paterfamilias was damaged under an onslaught of pamphlets and flyers denouncing him as a despot. The police
were unable to control the abundance of printed matter that accompanied
and intensified the struggle. One aggrieved scribbler who failed to elude
their grasp was the former barrister Pierre Denis de La Rivoire, who was
taken to the Bastille on 28 April 1771. He was suspected of being the author
of six offensive letters addressed to Louis XV that he had been observed
mailing. When the police searched his apartment, although they did not find
copies of the letters in question, they did confiscate enough incriminating
printed evidence to substantiate their charges.[3]

The documents constituted an unabashed critique of Louis XV's performance as king, accusing him of financial corruption and negligent leadership. In the process of evaluating the king, La Rivoire constructed a new definition of royal authority based on principles of law and governmental
accountability. The impassioned rhetoric reflected his profound disappointment with a sovereign from whom he expected great things. His efforts to delineate Louis XV's failings and his suggestions for reform provide clues to
the limited range of political compromises available to the crown in this turbulent era. La Rivoire's vision of kingship was distinctly secular, consciously
avoiding any association with the divine or the mystical. Based on what La
Rivoire wrote and said, this chapter clarifies the assumptions, arguments, and
contradictions that underlay his theory of constitutional monarchy as a proposed solution to the political crisis triggered by Maupeou's reforms.

It is important to establish this position since it was repeatedly exploited
by groups contesting royal authority during the early 1770s. Moreover, it
drew upon the residual fears of despotism that had figured so strongly in the
cases of Bonafon and Allègre. These accusations of despotism peaked during the Maupeou crisis and were leveled at the crown with unprecedented
vigor and frequency. They permeate La Rivoire's dossier and played a crucial role in his definition of royal government. His bitter opposition to despotism was inseparable from his staunch support for the monarchy. Despotism allowed La Rivoire to criticize Louis XV in the name of a higher ideal
without destroying the foundation of the king's rule itself. As previous
analysis has demonstrated, despotism was strategically employed as a language of reform, not revolution.

The cumulative effect of the contents of this dossier was a sweeping challenge to traditional theories of divine right kingship. La Rivoire fashioned his conception of royal government from broad strands of Enlightenment political thought concerning the secular basis of authority, natural law, and popular sovereignty. He relied on vivid and historically informed language to defend the banished magistrates and their cause from an unjustified and misguided assault. Distinct rhetorical and thematic affinities can be detected between La Rivoire's position and what Dale Van Kley has referred to as judicial Jansenism, a language of loyal opposition based in the Parlement of Paris and ideologically allied to the Jansenist cause.[4] This discourse was identified with historical, legal, and philosophical arguments that aimed to restrain the exercise of royal authority through traditional institutions such as the parlements and principles such as the fundamental laws. It was guided by a dual concern with defining legitimate authority as well as the limits of obedience in cases where the sovereign's will conflicted with the terms under which he held his trust to rule. It sought above all to protect both the crown and the country against the omnipresent threat of despotism. Many of these themes found their way into La Rivoire's thinking, with its emphasis on law, contract theory, and moderate monarchy. This influence is not surprising given La Rivoire's background and familiarity with the legal culture of the Old Regime. Although the possibility of Louis XV's fulfilling such a role remains debatable, it is instructive to examine La Rivoire's efforts to navigate a political path between absolutist ideals and constitutional tenets because they highlight the ideological and emotional dilemmas that confronted any French subject in the 1770s who was bent on restructuring, but not overturning, his government.

A King of Beggars

In the last four years of Louis XV's reign parlements throughout the kingdom mounted a relentless assault on royal authority. Since the volatile clashes of the early 1760s the magistrates had consistently triumphed over the crown in the battle to speak for and lay claim to the voice of public opinion. The crown's persistent efforts to disarm the law courts had backfired, and the parlements had emerged as the undisputed defenders of the nation's interests in the face of royal despotism. Like many of his contemporaries,

Pierre Denis de La Rivoire was personally and intellectually embroiled in these debates.[5] Caught up in the pamphlet wars that riveted public attention, La Rivoire overstepped the boundaries of loyalty when he opted for active political engagement by taking up his pen in defense of the Parlement's cause. As the previous chapters confirm, official responses to these cases reflected the crown's heightened sense of vulnerability in a turbulent political era. This connection was made explicit by Inspector d'Hémery, who noted that La Rivoire's was "an important affair in the present circumstances."[6]

D'Hémery's comment suggests that an analysis of La Rivoire's dossier must begin with a survey of the political and cultural landscape that contained it. The personal unpopularity of Louis XV reached its zenith in 1770–74. Public opinion was merciless in its scorn for the king's newest *maîtresse en titre*, Jeanne du Barry. She was deplored as a narrow-minded, vulgar, greedy woman and was commonly referred to as a whore. An illegitimate child from Toulouse who never knew her real father, Jeanne Bécu had acquired the reputation of a great beauty from the Parisian salon circles in which she moved. A series of distinguished and not so distinguished lovers brought her to the attention of the anti-Choiseul faction at the court, including the marechal de Richelieu, the duc d'Aiguillon, and the *parti dévot*. She appeared to be the perfect means for unseating the duc de Choiseul, secretary of war and foreign affairs and a trusted royal adviser, if she could win the king's affection. The wager was successful, and the king was smitten by the summer of 1768, when she became his official mistress, guaranteeing her promoters direct access to the king's ear. Richelieu arranged for her to marry Guillaume du Barry, the brother of her former lover, which would endow her with both title and husband, necessary prerequisites for presentation at court. Once ensconced as *maîtresse en titre*, she became a rallying point for opposition to Choiseul and the legislative resistance to the crown with which he was associated. A curious marriage of convenience between d'Aiguillon supporters and the *parti dévot* was effected through Du Barry, who allowed them to pass their concerns and criticisms directly onto the king. Although Du Barry was less politically ambitious than her predecessor, Pompadour, had been, she was committed to defending those who had secured her fortune and position and would use her intimacy with the king to influence decisions and appointments even if she failed to oust Choiseul.[7]

Outside of these court struggles, the new mistress had a reputation for greed, and the king's expenditures on his favorite outraged a populace well informed of the treasury's bankruptcy.

In addition to the persistent public hostility directed at his mistresses, Louis XV suffered one other serious failure on the front of public relations at the end of his reign. During the spring of 1770 elaborate festivities were staged throughout the realm in celebration of the Dauphin's marriage to the Austrian princess Marie Antoinette. The marriage marked a triumph for Choiseul's pro-Austrian foreign policy and the diplomatic reversal it entailed, since the Habsburgs had traditionally been France's enemies. The wedding ceremonies culminated in an enormous fireworks display organized in Paris on the evening of 30 May 1770. Municipal authorities had attempted to provide security and ensure traffic flow around the Place Louis XV in anticipation of the enormous crowds the pyrotechnic spectacles were expected to draw. Despite their precautions, 132 people were trampled to death as they streamed away from the ceremony and collided with coaches blocking the adjoining streets (see fig. 9).[8] This tragic outcome to public rejoicing blackened the authorities, who were charged with negligence, and boded ill for the nuptials that had inspired it.

The timing of the accident was particularly inopportune because it occurred in the midst of a subsistence crisis. From the initial planning stages, the crown's decision to dispense exorbitant funds on marriage celebrations had been invoked as evidence of Louis XV's indifference to the needs of his subjects.[9] With the specter of famine looming on the horizon, the crown's lavish expenditures appeared flagrantly inappropriate. Royal profligacy nourished rumors of a plot to starve the people, an accusation that had surfaced periodically in preceding decades. In 1770, public opinion focused blame on the crown's recently appointed controller general, abbé Joseph-Marie Terray.[10] Even though the government had returned to a policy of grain control after an unsettling experiment with deregulation under L'Averdy's ministry in the mid-1760s, the persistence of high prices and dearth nourished suspicions of a famine plot. The transition from laissez-faire to regulation was difficult, and Terray organized a *régie*, a public corporation designed to buy and store grain, as a way of regulating supply in times of dearth. Veiled in mystery, Terray's policy of purchasing grain in large

Figure 9.
Feu d'artifice tiré à l'occasion du mariage de Louis XVI
et accidents arrivés sur le bord de la Seine, 30 mai 1770.
*(Courtesy of the Bibliothèque Nationale
de France, Collection Hennin)*

quantities was easily misunderstood, provoking resentment, rumor, and finally panic. Wild allegations of a plot to starve the people inevitably redounded on the king, who appeared rapacious, if not cruel, in the public eye.

In conjunction with the misery provoked by dearth, the royal treasury
found itself on the verge of bankruptcy. Although lack of liquidity was a
chronic problem for the French monarchy, rarely had the possibilities for
borrowing money or raising revenues seemed so limited as in 1770.[11] The
Seven Years' War had strained the country's resources, and financial difficulties continued throughout the 1760s. The inability to restore budgetary
equilibrium led to the crisis of 1770, which was unusual since it erupted in
peacetime. Terray was once again at the center of things, implementing
some drastic and risky measures to clear up outstanding debt and enforce a
more equitable distribution of the tax burden. To begin with, in an edict of

November 1771 he succeeded in transforming the first *vingtième* into a perpetual tax and prolonging the second one until 1781. Assessment of payment would be proportional to taxable wealth, in keeping with Machault's original proposal of 1749. Terray succeeded on this front where his predecessors had repeatedly failed, and the reform of the *vingtième* was a relative success.

The second cornerstone of his fiscal policy was more dangerous both for the crown and for its creditors. In January 1770 Terray introduced a series of edicts that constituted a declaration of government bankruptcy. The crown's decision to default on its debt had two precedents in the reign of Louis XV, the first in 1720, during the liquidation of Scottish financier John Law's inflationary banking system, and the second in 1759, as a result of the military expenditures incurred during the Seven Years' War with England. In all three instances the remedy was arguably worse than the disease. The public lost confidence in the government, credit grew even tighter, and the treasury remained desperately short of funds.[12]

In 1770, the crown's bankruptcy affected individuals like La Rivoire who had large sums invested in government paper. Broadly speaking, Terray suspended reimbursement payments on government bonds and arbitrarily converted them into nonredeemable *rentes*. In addition, he reduced the interest rates on various types of public securities, or *effets royaux*. Thus, La Rivoire saw half of his fortune demolished with the stroke of a ministerial pen. The crown's decision to default on its debt appeared all the more unjust because it coincided with the exile of the Parlement of Paris. The one institution capable of defending private property and raising legitimate objections to royal fiscal policy had been disarmed and effectively silenced.

The immediate catalyst for the constitutional crisis of 1770, however, was the reopening of an old wound: the bitter conflict between the parlement of Brittany and the duc d'Aiguillon. The parlement's attempt to bring the king's representative to trial was quashed in a *lit de justice* on 27 June 1770. This royal resistance to normal judicial procedures was spearheaded by Chancellor Maupeou, who was strategically allied with d'Aiguillon and committed to defending the interests of the crown even if it meant appearing despotic. This move provoked a storm of remonstrances, prompting another royal edict imposing strict constraints on parlementary activities. When this edict was forcibly registered in a *lit de justice*, the magistrates of the Parlement of Paris called a strike. As punishment for their behavior, Chancellor Maupeou revoked their offices and sent them into exile on the night of 20–21 January 1771. Maupeou was arguably pressured into adapting a hard line by d'Aiguillon supporters and the *parti dévot,* whose disapproval he risked incurring if he proved too lenient toward the rebellious magistrates.[13]

The temporary suspension of judicial activity threw the capital into a state of turmoil. By 1770 the magistrates commanded bastions of support among the Parisian populace, whose interests it had claimed to represent successfully in two decades' worth of published remonstrances. The crown was unprepared for the public outcry provoked by Maupeou's seemingly brusque and authoritarian reforms. In the pamphlet warfare that ensued the issues of public finances, despotism, famine, and royal negligence became hopelessly entangled. The judicial cause provided a vehicle for launching a general assault on the crown's authority under the banner of patriotism, the ideological label that came to identify Maupeou's opponents, known as *patriotes.* For many of the king's *fidèles sujets,* such as Pierre Denis de la Rivoire, the Maupeou era marked a political rite of passage that mobilized them to stake claims and voice grievances with unprecedented boldness in defense of traditional laws, customs, and institutions. The fact that the Parlement could be abolished and new courts established and staffed revealed the weakness of the Parlement in the face of a determined onslaught by the crown. It confirmed the arguments that had been circulating for two decades in Jansenist and judicial circles that the country lacked an effective check on royal authority. Maupeou's coup made the need for an immediate solution to this problem painfully clear.

The World of the Law

As a member of the Old Regime's legal culture, La Rivoire had a personal stake in the heated debates prompted by Maupeou's attempt to restructure the courts and their officials. His father had been a *procureur* (solicitor) attached to the Châtelet, an administrative body that included the principal municipal courts in Paris, and his brother, Louis Etienne, was a prominent barrister who had been a substitute for the *procureur general* on the king's Grand Conseil. Pierre Denis was a barrister and former *procureur* for the

Châtelet. Chronic illness, including digestive disorders, had obliged him to sell his office as *procureur* in 1765.[14] By 1771 he appears to have been more of a titular barrister than an active one, which was common in the eighteenth century.[15]

At the time of his arrest in 1771 Pierre Denis de La Rivoire was forty-three and lived alone in a small apartment on the narrow rue de la Harpe in the parish of Saint-Severin. Both Pierre and his younger brother Louis had studied jurisprudence and practiced law. Pierre had inherited from his father the office of *procureur au Châtelet* along with some municipal bonds. The earnings from these secure investments, combined with the sale of his office, enabled him to live comfortably while restoring his health. During his first interrogation he explained that he had eliminated all activity from his life except reading and daily promenades, which were "necessary to his health and aids to his digestion."[16] These walks included visits to the Paris Bourse to follow the stock market's activities and monitor his investments.

With the money and *rentes* inherited from his parents, La Rivoire had pursued the riskier side of Old Regime investment practices. Contrary to the traditional path of social mobility, whereby individuals gradually shifted their assets into land, office, and *rentes* bearing modest but secure interest, La Rivoire had moved in the opposite direction. He had sold off his office and was eager to move his money into less secure but potentially more lucrative forms of speculation. He was less interested in long-term stability than in flexibility and a high rate of capital turnover. For instance, he decided to purchase new government bonds, issues called *rentes à porteur,* which were readily transferable with no additional fees, as opposed to the preexisting perpetual or lifetime annuities. The documents reveal a pattern of shifting capital to take advantage of incentives to buy government securities.

In describing his speculative activities, La Rivoire alluded to a world of protocapitalist finance operating on the margins of the crown's established forms of raising revenue. During his first interrogation La Rivoire indicated his willingness to take risks in pursuit of profit when he explained that "his current income consists of more than 100,000 livres he had invested in a government security, of which approximately half was transferred in the name of one of his friends . . . that he also had stocks payable to the bearer at '2 sols pour livre' at 10 percent and that he liquidated these at the time of the fourth Royal Lottery, and with these earnings he acquired about two years ago . . . 100,000 livres in capital on a loan of 50 million."[17] Thus, La Rivoire was a member of a burgeoning minority of nascent capitalists taking advantage of what George Taylor labeled court capitalism.[18] He saw capital as a tool of advancement and believed it was inviolable. He was deeply attached to his wealth and held mobile capital as well as land to be a sacred trust and a guarantee of personal liberty. These convictions explain the acute sense of betrayal he felt when the crown defaulted on its financial obligations in 1770.

Although his speculative activities can be qualified as modern, socially La Rivoire was firmly ensconced in one of the Old Regime's most venerable professional milieus. The legal field encompassed a broad spectrum of officials ranging from humble clerks to prominent barristers and powerful judges. As solicitors and attorneys, La Rivoire's family stood at the threshold of the robe nobility, an elite stratum of royal officials whose status was historically linked to the purchase of office. La Rivoire represented the second generation in his family to hold the position of *procureur au Châtelet*, an office that granted the holder personal nobility.[19] It is unclear from the evidence whether La Rivoire's father held the office long enough to acquire hereditary nobility. If not, La Rivoire would have lost his privileged status when he sold his office in 1765. From the figures he mentioned when describing his financial operations, his wealth can be estimated at roughly 100,000 livres, the minimum required to maintain a noble style of life and placing him among the upper third in a profession where the average fortune was 50,000, with some considerably lower.[20]

Despite the socioeconomic heterogeneity of the eighteenth-century legal profession, individual members shared a distinctive outlook shaped by education, a common culture, and corporate pride. La Rivoire's views were an outgrowth of this milieu and its attachment to a judicial, as opposed to an administrative, monarchy. He defended the historical role of the parlements as royal councilors, upholders of the law, and organs of government. This conviction explains his scorn for useless courtiers and ambitious ministers, who threatened to displace the authority of the courts and their officials. As a lawyer, La Rivoire was imbued with a sense of public responsibility that he would tenaciously defend.

Lawyers as a group had considerable libraries by eighteenth-century standards, and literary activities served to unite and define their interests. La Rivoire was no exception. He was well educated, and print was an integral part of his personal and professional life. Literature had assumed greater prominence in his life since his retirement because, as he explained, "he abstained from all activities with the exception of reading through the journals and works that had recently started appearing and were intended for diversion."[21] Throughout the dossier, his arguments reveal familiarity with classic texts of antiquity and French history as well as the works of contemporary authors such as Linguet. Among the manuscripts seized in his apartment was a translation he was preparing of Homer's *Odyssey*. La Rivoire's literary proclivities inevitably raised the suspicions of the investigating officials, who considered reading a dangerous and undesirable pastime. Commissioner Mutel's notes on the case indicate that he perceived a direct connection between La Rivoire's reading tastes and his delinquent behavior. He would make a point of questioning the defendant closely on this topic.

La Rivoire was interested in contemporary politics and made a concerted effort to keep himself informed of issues that concerned him personally as both a barrister and an investor in public securities. He regularly stopped in at the cafés of the Palais Royal to read through the published legal briefs of the Parlement, or factums, that circulated freely and constituted an informal source of political and legal news. The factums played a critical role in the Maupeou crisis, mobilizing support and disseminating information as well as ushering in a new role for the lawyer as a public crusader in a theater of corrupt politics and immoral characters.[22]

La Rivoire instinctively sensed that his literary and political interests were a liability for his defense and hastened to assure the police that his reading was recreational, not criminal. In reference to the seditious pamphlets discovered when his apartment was searched he insisted that "all that was found was literature concerning public affairs and politics, this being my diversion and my taste; I inform myself of things concerning my personal affairs and don't meddle with the rest of it. If I refer to it in passing discussions, it is with reason, not passion, and always with due respect to persons of distinction. I know, moreover, that the king is the master."[23] This quotation suggests that La Rivoire understood that his desire to be politi-

cally informed was viewed by the police with suspicion and required qual-
ification. He explained that he was a prudent and selective reader who relied
on print to monitor his investments, interest rates, currency, and bond issues. Surely there was no harm in such practices, he suggested, for "can
these tastes concern the state?"[24] Despite his disingenuous air, La Rivoire
was well aware that literary tastes did interest the state and were viewed by
its policing agents as threatening given their inability to regulate them.

Although Inspector d'Hémery and Commissioner Mutel were convinced
of La Rivoire's guilt, they lacked sufficient proof and needed a confession
to close the case. Their search of La Rivoire's apartment had turned up no
drafts of the letters in question. In his first interrogation, on 2 May 1771, La
Rivoire was asked to examine a packet of documents containing the offensive letters to Louis XV. Although he conceded that the handwriting bore a
striking resemblance to his own, he denied authorship. When Mutel pressed
him, observing that besides the handwriting the paper was the same as that
found in the apartment, La Rivoire protested

> that he had told the truth, that there were historical examples of physical re-
> semblances so close, most notably in the case of Martin Guerre recounted in
> the *Causes célèbres,* that it was not impossible that there could also be perfect
> handwriting similarities between different hands . . . that one finds examples
> of persons who were condemned on the basis of such similarities and whose
> innocence was later recognized. As for the similarity of the paper, this paper
> is so common that it can be found everywhere and that handwriting is so easy
> to imitate that there are at least a hundred examples of people who have been
> deceived.[25]

This effort to muster historical precedent and draw analogies in his defense
was based on readings both in French history and in the extremely popular
Causes célèbres of the eighteenth century, a collection of famous criminal trials and their proceedings.[26] The appeal to legal precedent as a defensive
strategy was not surprising given his education and experience.

La Rivoire stood before his accusers as a man who was familiar with both
the theory and the practice of the law. He would use this information to his
advantage. Since the evidence against him was inconclusive, La Rivoire referred to the notorious sixteenth-century case of mistaken identity, that of

Martin Guerre, to strengthen his defense.[27] By drawing this parallel he depicted himself as a persecuted innocent and cast a shadow of doubt over the official interpretation of the case.

Despite La Rivoire's efforts, Commissioner Mutel remained unconvinced. To begin with, La Rivoire had been identified mailing one of the anonymous letters the Friday before his arrest. In addition, when the *maîtres écrivains* were summoned to compare the handwriting in the letters to La Rivoire's confiscated translation of *The Odyssey,* they concluded that the two were written by the same person.[28] La Rivoire was undeterred by the verdict, exclaiming: "But here is handwriting similar to my own. This is not proof, my crime cannot be to have handwriting similar to that found in these papers. . . . I am not familiar with the criteria for judging handwriting, but . . . you would have had to catch me in the act of writing them, or at least to discover them on my person or in my home. Nothing of the kind."[29] La Rivoire had identified loopholes in the official case against him and was exploiting them.

Since the evidence was circumstantial, La Rivoire concentrated on emphasizing his honesty and integrity, qualities associated with his profession and useful to the crown: "I cannot believe that the security of the state requires the removal of a citizen who served it so faithfully according to his rank as long as he was in good health. Honorable and peaceful sentiments have always inspired me. . . . I was useful as long as I could be . . . I never harmed anyone."[30] La Rivoire hoped to remove suspicion by reminding the police that he had dedicated his life to upholding and enforcing the law. Reputation was a source of marked pride within the legal culture of the Old Regime, as manifested in judicial dynasties and the symbolic weight of the oath barristers took upon entering the order. It also weighed heavily in police assessments of crime and criminality. There was an official consensus that guilt and innocence were absolute moral categories conferred at birth and manifested in conduct both public and private. La Rivoire mobilized family background and professional identity to turn this assumption in his favor.

La Rivoire contrasted his irreproachable conduct in the past to the tone of the offensive letters. Like all *fidèles sujets,* he protested that "I suffer because I appear to be guilty, even though nothing be so certain for me or God as my innocence."[31] He added that "one would have to be crazy to have written them. I have always conducted myself wisely and prudently and never dreamed of such craziness." He insisted that there was no motive for his crime because "only those who have nothing to lose have nothing to fear from fomenting trouble. I have much to lose, especially because my fortune is invested in lifetime or perpetual public annuities [*rentes*] and I desire peace."[32] That La Rivoire's fortune was directly linked to the solvency of the royal treasury did not escape official notice. On the contrary, the police knew that La Rivoire had recently suffered severe financial losses as a result of the crown's decision to repudiate part of the government's debt. His brother, Louis Etienne, confirmed this interpretation when he wrote Lieutenant of Police Sartine to ask for his brother's release and suggested that Pierre's crime be dismissed as a passing rage brought on by bankruptcy. Both the police and La Rivoire's family believed that the economic blow provided a plausible motive for La Rivoire's anger and subsequent actions.[33]

La Rivoire ascertained the direction of official suspicion and sought to deflect it. Six days after his arrest he wrote a justificatory letter to Sartine's secretary, M. Gobron, explaining, "I have lost a great deal in public securities because I had a large number of them. But my restrained conduct, which encouraged me to put a little bit aside in savings each year, combined with my remaining funds, means that this loss has not disturbed me at all."[34] The lack of financial information makes it difficult to determine the severity of La Rivoire's losses. His portfolio indicates that he lost more than 100,000 livres as a result of Terray's measures. Thus, he must have been more concerned than his complacent tone would indicate. He was certainly not so wealthy that he could watch half his income disappear without wincing. Furthermore, the purpose of this letter was to secure his release in order to prevent further financial loss that might result from his absence. Despite his protestations to the contrary, La Rivoire had serious financial worries. Once he had sold his most solid assets, his solicitor's office, he could no longer count on regular returns. He was obliged to play the market and keep a close watch on interest rates and discounts on bills of exchange to supplement his income.

From the moment of his arrest La Rivoire regarded the loss of his personal liberty and fortune as intrinsically linked violations of his rights. He implored Lieutenant of Police Sartine, "Why make these letters an excuse for depriving me of my liberty, and by consequence the pursuit of my affairs, which will necessarily entail the loss of my fortune?"[35] This perceived connection between personal freedom and material possession would play a significant role in La Rivoire's critique of kingship. In order to prevent the crown from abusing its power, through either profligacy or mismanagement, La Rivoire believed in the necessity of institutions such as the Parlement of Paris to represent the interests of the nation and protect property and freedom. Without intermediary bodies the country would be at the mercy of royal tyranny. A king who consistently encroached upon and mismanaged the wealth of his subjects would ruin his country and become "a king of beggars."[36]

Crimes and Confession

Even before La Rivoire confessed his crime the police were sure they had identified the right man. Their confidence was reinforced by the intervention of Pierre's younger brother, Louis Etienne de La Rivoire. Louis wrote several letters on his brother's behalf emphasizing the honor and integrity of a family distinguished by its service in the king's judiciary. He implored the police to release his brother, promising to look after Pierre at his country house in Sucy-en-Brie, near Boissy. From the moment he learned of Pierre's arrest Louis accepted his brother's guilt. Rather than deny it, he sought to justify it with extenuating circumstances and pleas for royal mercy. He explained that Pierre had been noticeably depressed for the past few months and that he had "proposed several times to bring him [Pierre] to his country house to restore his spirits, since he had come often last year and enjoyed himself a great deal."[37] But Pierre had repeatedly refused the invitations, insisting that he had to stay in Paris to monitor his affairs.

According to Louis, this melancholy state left Pierre mentally weak and unstable, prompting his violent reaction to the news of the crown's default and the severe losses he expected to incur as a result. Louis insisted that his brother had overreacted since he had enough income "to live according to his taste" despite the losses. Thus, Louis acknowledged his brother's guilt but attempted to extract a pardon by demonstrating that his brother was mentally unfit, thereby diminishing the charge of premeditation. He also emphasized that Pierre was "a man of little consequence" and therefore not a grave threat to the regime. He assured the police that he could vouch for his brother's behavior in the future since "he had always demonstrated perfect honesty until the moment of his cruel breakdown."[38]

La Rivoire himself, however, rejected his brother's defensive strategy in favor of another option available to individuals by the mid-eighteenth century. Like Marie Bonafon, he attempted to shift responsibility for his crime onto a vaguely defined source of information—the public—in an effort to exculpate himself. This tactic guided the written confession he sent early in August 1771 to Chancellor Maupeou and the duc de la Vrillière, one of Louis XV's *conseillers d'état*. Following the ritual of confession, he opened with an avowal that culminated in a plea for absolution:

> A citizen of the lowest order, who has until now always conducted himself with the respect and submission owed to authority and the powers that be, forgot himself to the point of interfering with the ministry, fighting your laws and grievously offending you in anonymous writings that he dared to address to the king. The extraordinary circumstances of the time, the losses he incurred on public securities, the rumors of another crash and the stoppage of payments even on the most stable annuities, the writings and public discussions, led his simple and straightforward soul astray for the first time in his life. He begs for grace, and his grateful heart will not cease to work to repair his errors.[39]

In identifying "writings and public discussions" as the sources of his irreverent scribbling, La Rivoire sought to minimize his guilt by denying evil volition. Moreover, he cast his avowal in a language of fidelity, choosing words and allusions to promote his image as an essentially loyal and dutiful subject who had unwittingly erred.

Many of the components of fidelity touched on by La Rivoire are now familiar. He set the scene for his confession by establishing the enormous distance that separated him from the throne. By emphasizing his humble condition he sought to garner sympathy and leniency from his superiors. Weaker souls were impressionable and more likely to be led astray by base instincts and passions. This image of "a simple and straightforward soul" being swept away by "public discussions" was a necessary prerequisite for his appeal to royal mercy.

La Rivoire did not deny the offensive nature of his crime but rather attempted to demonstrate the sincerity of his repentance to merit a pardon. Like La Chaux, he stressed that he had not been himself when he undertook this project, that "he had forgotten himself" to the point of offending a sovereign he had always cherished. He relied on the excuse already provided by the police when he acknowledged the anxiety provoked by his financial losses. Speaking as a truly *fidèle sujet*, he asserted that if he received grace, he would spend the rest of his life atoning for this one lapse. Unfortunately for La Rivoire, royal officials believed that once forsaken, the path of loyalty was irretrievable.

The language used to fashion pardon requests was borrowed directly from the confessional rite. Emphasis was consistently placed on the suffering experienced by the accused as a result of his or her misdemeanor. Shortly before his avowal, La Rivoire addressed Lieutenant of Police Sartine with the mixture of deference, hope, and trust normally bestowed on a confessor: "Monseigneur, you are my judge, my master, but you would also like for me to regard you as a protector and a father. Your renowned kindness does not permit you to ignore these two qualities that temper the harshness others would show an unfortunate wretch like me . . . rest assured that the mercy you show me will not incline me to any abuse and will inspire my eternal gratitude."[40] From the confines of his cell La Rivoire invested Sartine with all the qualities of a stern but loving father. He had to believe in Sartine's capacity for mercy and beneficence before he could unburden his guilty conscience.

The problem with reproducing the confessional dialogue was that it offered the defendant false hope. Since most of the individuals arrested for *mauvais discours* were deemed dangerous to the interests of the royal state, there was little chance of their being released. Unlike the penitent, a prisoner's decision to divulge his guilt did not prompt an immediate gesture of absolution from the crown. La Rivoire was bound to be disappointed, so thoroughly convinced was he of his imminent pardon when he urged Sartine, "Please do not hold back any longer the absolute pardon for my faults, for which I am sincerely repentant, in order that my brother can take me tomorrow, the eve of several holidays, to the country. I will stay there as long as you deem necessary. . . . I have never harmed anybody and cannot even bear the thought of doing harm."[41] Yet acknowledgment of his errors could not retract the offensive statements found in his letters.

La Rivoire added that he should be rewarded for his voluntary confession when the evidence against him was inconclusive. As he explained, the police were indebted to his honesty given "that these papers . . . were not found in my apartment . . . it follows that since my confessions lacked substantiating proof, they were inspired by deference and blind submission that my habit of obeying and respecting authority will always lead me to render."[42] He believed that his decision to tell the truth at the expense of his liberty testified to his integrity and loyalty.

The words La Rivoire chose to mask his offense recall those chosen by his predecessors in these pages. He constructed a dichotomy between his imagination and his heart. This split corresponded to his public actions and his private thoughts, or what the police referred to as external and internal forms of respect. He emphasized that "my imagination may have been led astray. My simple and upright heart was not at all corrupted. I respect and submit myself to the authority and powers that be."[43] This language of duality allowed him to proclaim his fidelity to the king while blaming his vivid imagination for his delinquent behavior.

He distanced himself from his imagination by describing it as an intoxicating force that had invaded and overwhelmed him. La Rivoire's description of his state of mind recalls La Chaux's attempt to evoke his altered mental condition on the eve of his crime. He claimed to have written the offensive letters in a frenzy: "I beg you to grasp the circumstances in which these letters, whose contents are totally unknown to me, were written; it was a rapid instant of an unfortunate intoxication of the imagination that produced and dispersed them as soon as they had been formulated, leaving no traces in my brain or my memory, and that I never discussed with anyone."[44] The metaphor of intoxication and its accompanying loss of memory allowed La Rivoire to account for his persistent denial of the charges during the first two months of his incarceration.

He explained that his feverish psychological condition had been provoked by a combination of poor health and the turbulent state of affairs in the city. He stressed his susceptibility to the circumstances reported in the foreign press, other printed matter, the proceedings of the judicial courts, all the public and private discussions, and all those minds captivated by the extraordinary revolutions present in the state and throughout the realm, [which] were able to lead me astray without removing my capacity for remorse. My previous readings were entangled with the ideas of these tracts and discussions and led me to take advantage of my obscurity by writing rapidly in a flush of enthusiasm, writing I should have wanted to throw in the fire as soon as it had left my hands.[45]

In this statement La Rivoire not only recognizes the dangers associated with publicly available information but also implicitly blames his accusers for their failure to monitor it more effectively. Thus, he succeeds in shifting blame, first, onto external factors, such as public discussions, printed matter, and an agitated political climate, and second, onto the very men holding him prisoner.

In protesting his allegiance to Louis XV, La Rivoire highlighted fundamental tensions within the concept of fidelity. From a police perspective, fidelity entailed internal and external forms of submission and respect. Ideally, fidelity possessed a religious dimension, a belief manifested and reinforced by faith in ritualized utterances, gestures, and actions. La Rivoire acknowledged that he had violated this primordial and mystical bond of loyalty when he wrote his offensive letters: "I meddled in things that did not concern me, but at a time when all the journals and pamphlets and discussions were focusing attention on these issues. These circumstances of medical disorders left me prey to the disorderly workings of my imagination, led me astray in secret without changing my public conduct, which remained as ever submissive, honest, and tranquil. Simplicity, ignorance, and inexperience made me believe that I was indifferent to such freedoms."[46] La Rivoire failed to recognize that the very notion of a distinction between public conduct and private belief was subversive of absolutist discourse. Fidelity entailed a state of harmony or transparency in which words, gestures, and outward behavior were reflections of the soul. From an official perspective, public conformity alone did not qualify as true allegiance.

La Rivoire's efforts to justify his crime were flawed in two respects from an official perspective. First, admitting to subversive activities in private made him no less guilty than if he had participated in public protests. Second, the decision to send a dozen vituperative letters to Louis XV was a highly public and visible act. His emphasis on the dichotomy between the two realms of action to exculpate himself was significant and supports scholars who identify the Enlightenment as the critical moment in the emergence of a separate sphere of privacy or intimacy that corresponded to a heightened sense of subjectivity. Both Jürgen Habermas and Reinhardt Koselleck have insisted on the connection between the development of a private sphere, of moral inquiry for Koselleck and subjectivity for Habermas, and the formulation of critical attitudes toward royal authority. For Habermas, this private sphere was the necessary underpinning of the corresponding emergence of a public sphere, an essential component of a modern civil society.[47] La Rivoire's description of his crime as being inspired by public discussion but enacted within a private realm confirms the interconnections between the two, especially in relation to a hostile attitude toward the French monarchy. It revealed the dangers of an uncontrolled private domain and helps explain why the police sought to enforce a definition of fidelity predicated on the denial of the existence of a separation between public and private.

In pleading for clemency La Rivoire stressed that "my heart never shared these illusions of my deranged mind, which nobody ever saw or knew about."[48] He asserted that he had acted against his will when he wrote the offensive epistles: "I had the misfortune, without wanting it, without even knowing it, of offending all that I ought to respect, even in loving it and wanting to serve it, and by a principle of love and zeal so true and sincere albeit thoughtless . . . there are no atonements I am not ready to make. . . . Give me back the life I am losing with each passing day . . . I will dedicate it to acknowledging and blessing unceasingly so much goodness and generosity."[49] Nevertheless, La Rivoire's efforts to portray himself as an essentially loyal subject who had been temporarily led astray were incompatible with the radical tenor of the evidence found in his apartment.

The Lessons of History

By combining the letters sent to Louis XV with the papers confiscated in his apartment and the justificatory letters he wrote from the Bastille, it is possible to reconstruct the key elements of La Rivoire's political views. His analysis of contemporary politics relied heavily on his interpretation of French history and the place of the monarchy in that interpretation. To guide his critique of kingship, La Rivoire established two poles of princely conduct, the Roman emperor Nero and the first Bourbon king, Henri IV. He repeatedly invoked these two rulers as standards for gauging Louis XV's performance. It was significant that the paragon of a just and generous ruler was rooted in the tradition of French kingship. La Rivoire's decision to use Nero as the countermodel of correct rule reflected the eighteenth-century view that despotism was alien to French political culture in both time and place. The genesis of La Rivoire's ideas about royal authority, in particular his grievances regarding Louis XV, can be traced through his references to these two historical figures. This information provides the basis for his formulation of an alternative definition of kingship.

La Rivoire's litany of charges against Louis XV echoes themes encountered in the preceding chapters. The most salient features of this criticism are evident in a fable entitled "La Queue du Chat," discovered among the papers in his apartment. It recounts the story of an "honest bourgeois" who falls asleep one night in the corner by his fireplace while waiting for his wife to return home. Curled up next to the man is a cat intent on warming itself. While the master of the house snores, the cat's tail catches fire, and the town is soon reduced to a heap of ashes.

The narrator of the parable offers the following summary of its meaning: "Such is the prince, who instead of governing falls asleep, indolent from his dirty lecheries. The cat is the minister. His tail is all the evils whose crushing weight is pushing the state into its grave. You, who are among the best of men, are a very bad king, Louis, perfidious traitor, infidel of the faith. All the universe knows that in your projects for peace or battle you are inspired solely by your indolence [*mollesse*], and as a result, under your fatal rule, there are only *ministres chats*."[50] This fable was followed by one of the anonymous letters dated November 1771. Thus, La Rivoire had either written the story himself or copied it down because it resonated with his own concerns and grievances. Even if his authorship cannot be demonstrated, it is safe to assume that La Rivoire was sympathetic to the sentiments it expressed given his decision to include it in his letter.

The parable identifies by now familiar flaws in Louis XV's character—indolence and sloth—that prevented him from properly exercising his charge as sovereign. In language reminiscent of Montesquieu's and d'Argenson's charges against the court and the aristocracy, the king was condemned for his *mollesse*, or softness. *Mollesse* was a loaded term in the political lexicon of eighteenth-century France.[51] It implied a lack of moral resolve and was associated with the self-indulgence, or *sales voluptés*, of a despot. It accounted for Louis XV's betrayal of his oath to serve as protector of the Catholic faith by his lax personal conduct. Moreover, it was the distinguishing attribute of effeminate men or men who allowed themselves to be controlled by women. By calling the king's virility into question and suggesting that the traditionally separate categories of masculinity and femininity were confused, if not reversed, the fable revealed the inability of patriarchy to provide a solid theoretical foundation for the king's sovereignty in the age of Enlightenment. The collapse of patriarchy had ushered in a reign of political corruption and moral decadence, as signaled by the figures of effeminate men and virile women. Authority was not only feminized but eroticized, and these were the symbolics of despotism as configured, for instance, in Montesquieu's *Persian Letters*.

In La Rivoire's parable the town caught fire because the master of the house was negligent and failed to monitor his pet's activities. Translated into the language of contemporary France, La Rivoire was suggesting that Louis XV could be faulted for his ignorance and laziness, not malicious intent. Although this distinction was important, the consequences for negligence were so tragic that the king could not be fully exonerated. It was, after all, his responsibility to supervise the activities of his appointed ministers, his "ministres chats." The choice of a cat, moreover, was not haphazard in the context of early modern culture. Cats were viewed, not as innocuous domestic pets, but as symbols of sloth, sensuality, self-indulgence, deception, and witchcraft.[52] These same traits were traditionally gendered female; hence here again the principle of male rule was undermined through its submission to a creature defined as lascivious, irrational, and deceptive.

The fable was attached to an explanatory letter in which the critique of the king's chief ministers was directly linked to chronic fiscal mismanagement and instability. In a reference to the current financial crisis, La Rivoire alluded to two prior instances in Louis XV's reign, in 1720 and 1756, when the crown had been forced to default on the national debt. He argued that the speculative bubble of 1720 was excusable because it occurred when the king was still a minor. Yet in regard to the instances of 1756 and 1770 La Rivoire observed: "This reveals the danger of public loans by the facility with which parvenus or beggarly ministers can abuse them under an indolent king who does no good except for those he fears, with the result that the only friends he can find are scoundrels who ruin his people."[53] Not only was the crown bankrupt but Louis XV had committed an egregious error in failing to protect his people from his rapacious councilors. La Rivoire was condemning the crown's practice of filling its coffers through systematic public borrowing rather than true fiscal reform or reduced expenditures.

La Rivoire directed his wrath at specific individuals in the government whose names were associated with the policies he was decrying. "Your Terray is a firebrand, your Choiseul a vainglorious fool, your chancellor [Maupeou] a rascal; it is not good that a little Ramses from the thoughtless masses should reign as master simply because he can afford to buy an office."[54] Although La Rivoire identified Choiseul as part of the triumvirate, he had been dismissed from the government in December 1770 and replaced by the duc d'Aiguillon. Abbé Terray, d'Aiguillon, and Chancellor Maupeou were responsible for a reversal of traditional policy in the realms of public finance, foreign affairs, and the judiciary. In the last four years of his reign Louis XV was intimately linked to the controversial and often unpopular policies of these ministers, whose careers he had promoted.

According to La Rivoire, ministerial tyranny threatened to transform the king into a despot. The king's desire for tranquillity, his perceived indifference, left too much responsibility in the hands of the men appointed to serve him. "But is it appropriate that while you are occupied with your pleasures, ignorant of the financial affairs you detest, like all who are debauched and idle, your ministers [   ] have courtesans more savage, cruel, and wicked than highway robbers, govern unrestrained by rivals or by the rules of law and equity? Do you want them to make a despot out of you, to make your ministers into viziers and absolutist Pachas? Send them the rope and the *muets* they have deserved for a long time now."[55] La Rivoire felt that Louis XV had seriously erred in siding with these three ministers at the expense of his natural allies, the parlements, who provided the sole barrier between monarchy and despotism. His argument recalled concerns Montesquieu and d'Argenson had voiced about the monarchy during the Regency of the duc d'Orléans at the beginning of the century. More explicitly, La Rivoire's language echoed the vocabulary and arguments of the judicial remonstrances articulated by Jansenist barristers and publicists that had accompanied successive stages in the clashes between the crown and its law courts. As a member of this legal milieu La Rivoire would have followed these discussions closely and been imbued with their rhetoric and interpretation of current affairs.[56]

Although ministers were prominent villains from La Rivoire's perspective, the court of Louis XV also merited reproach. In his continuing evaluation of the king La Rivoire referred to the figures of Henri IV and Nero to illustrate his points. He discussed both rulers in the context of the courts over which they had presided. La Rivoire contrasted the character of the nobility under Henri IV and Louis XV: "The court was composed of the ancient nobility, whose founders were the peers of the realm. They were not parvenus, products of luxury or libertinage, with sentiments as vile, as destructive, as their source."[57] Here La Rivoire was attacking the monarchy's practice of ennobling wealthy commoners through the sale of offices, an important source of royal revenue but costly in terms of service since such men owed allegiance to the king, not to the realm. Consequently, the personal example and principles of the reigning monarch played a crucial role in establishing discipline and enforcing right conduct.

La Rivoire lavished praise on Henri IV's ability to escape the corrosive effects of the court: "It was not that he did not have any sycophantic enemies who made themselves into playthings for debauchery and all the crimes it engenders. He shielded himself from this evil inherent to all courts through his heart and his virtuous friends." Yet, this golden age of court life was short-lived, according to La Rivoire, because Cardinal Richelieu had systematically dismantled it. Richelieu's efforts to strengthen the crown vis-à-vis provincial grandees and princes of the blood had been misguided, and it had succeeded in destroying the "ancienne noblesse" and replacing it with an aristocracy "d'argent et de maquerelage" (of money and pimping).[58] La Rivoire's analysis of the French court, emphasizing the importance of the ancient nobility as a political body and vilifying Richelieu and the drive to absolutism he had instigated, displayed a firm command of French history as well as an aristocratic or constitutionalist interpretation of it. By situating his critique of Louis XV's court within a historical framework, La Rivoire's identified patterns in French political culture that guided his analysis of contemporary affairs.

In this extended digression on Richelieu's policy toward the nobility in the early seventeenth century La Rivoire perceived a precedent for Maupeou's strike against the Parlement of Paris in 1771. He drew a parallel between the plight of the ancient nobility and that of the ancient magistracy. After describing Richelieu's tactic of substituting an order of parvenus for the true aristocracy, he asserted:

> He [Richelieu] conceived of a project that was destructive for the entire nation. It resembled the current effort to destroy the ancient magistracy in order to replace it with an assembly of persons of obscure origins, the rubbish of honest societies. But the goodness of the national constitution resisted Richelieu's assassination attempt; it will resist again the current ambush that is a direct consequence. Do not think for one minute that the noble created by money or whoring is more noble afterwards than before; nobility acquired by such means only renders the bearer more ignoble.[59]

This analogy revealed the residual elitism of La Rivoire's social outlook and its accompanying faith in the magistrates as the king's natural councilors and guides. He believed the crown had violated the fundamental laws of the realm when it exiled the unruly magistrates in 1771.

Using the Roman emperor Nero as a countermodel to Henri IV, La Rivoire suggested that Louis XV's behavior resembled that of the imperial despot more than it resembled that of his Bourbon ancestor on the throne. He emphasized the current king's debauched sexual behavior, describing the court as a seraglio under the direction of the duc de Richelieu: "The division he [Richelieu] drove between you and your deceased wife through the ministry of his Jesuit confessor and the prostitution to which he delivered you, beginning with the three sisters in succession, then, after an infinity of others, the first arrivals in your *parc aux cerfs,* like the seraglio of an Oriental despot, in contempt of the religion whose superstitious trappings you

affect."[60] From the earliest years of his reign, Louis XV's sexual peccadil-
loes had been a constant source of concern. They provoked consternation at
all levels of French society as glaring symbols of duplicity and betrayal
because Louis XV had broken his vows to his wife, his people, and his
church. How could a king who never went to confession uphold the faith he
had sworn to defend at his coronation? This question was all the more em-
barrassing in the context of the intractable religious controversies that had
plagued the reign and that royal intervention had repeatedly failed to resolve. Moreover, his marital infidelity may have rankled his subjects less
on religious grounds than on sentimental ones given the century's cult of
the conjugal family and the accompanying values trust, reciprocity, and
fidelity.[61]

The image of Nero was especially powerful because it expressed dissatisfaction with Louis XV for both his personal and his political conduct. Not
only was the Roman emperor notorious for his debauched lifestyle but his
name was linked to destructive political tyranny. The image of the fire in
"La Queue du Chat" implicitly recalled the great fire that erupted in Rome
in A.D. 70 and read historically as a symbol of Nero's selfish and cruel reign.
With the references to Nero, La Rivoire found evidence to support his conviction that financial profligacy, corruption, and abuse of authority were
ineluctably linked. He established these connections when describing the
despot: "Nero, enemy of the Romans and the entire universe over which he
was Emperor, having ruined the country's finances with his wasteful indul-
gences, his excesses, proscribed the rich in order to confiscate their wealth
. . . he came to hate the Senate to the point of wanting to destroy it; he was
warned, declared an enemy of the state, and condemned to be hung like a
traitor."[62] Just as Nero had attacked the Senate, Louis XV had dismantled
the kingdom's most prestigious and powerful law court, the Parlement of
Paris. Both rulers had betrayed their subjects, and if the analogy held, Louis
XV, like Nero, would pay for his crimes with his life. This recurring theme
of betrayal is significant and highlights La Rivoire's belief that authority
was ultimately a trust between ruler and ruled. More strongly than his
predecessors in this study, La Rivoire explicitly condemned Louis XV for
his blind and misdirected rule. He asserted that by violating this trust Louis
XV had effectively abrogated his right to rule.

The king's treachery was most visible in his recent attack on the parlements. Like the Roman senators, the magistrates were entrusted with protecting the laws of the land. By elaborating an extended parallel between the Roman Senate and the Parlement of Paris, La Rivoire sought to root the French law courts within a republican political tradition. He hoped to use this as a historical counterweight to the monarchy and the political theory of absolutism as it had been elaborated in the course of the seventeenth century. As he insisted in a letter addressed to Louis XV: "You will suffer the same fate as Nero, who wanted to destroy the Roman Senate, even though the French Senate, far from condemning you to be hung as an enemy of the country, has only fought you out of a sense of duty and refused to follow orders contrary to that same duty, orders that emanated from you because you had blinded yourself to their consequences."[63] Refrains of judicial Jansenism and legal remonstrances are evident in La Rivoire's emphasis here on the limits of obedience as well as the language of a "duty to resist" the king if his wishes conflicted with the express purposes of the fundamental laws. La Rivoire reminded Louis XV that the crown's legitimacy depended on the existence of the parlements. By attacking the Parlement the king undermined the important distinction between monarchy and tyranny. The magistrates had been justified in their resistance because they had been protecting the king's true interests. Failure to reinstate them would be detrimental to both king and kingdom.

Poverty and Glory

La Rivoire had specific ideas about kingship. He believed that despotism could only be avoided if customary and time-honored rules were respected. Despite his dissatisfaction with Louis XV's performance, he remained convinced that monarchy was the most appropriate form of government for France. La Rivoire's grievances, like those of his predecessors in this book, reflected his profound disillusionment with a sovereign figure he yearned to revere but was obliged to criticize.

To begin with, La Rivoire chided Louis XV for setting a bad example for his subjects. He reminded the king of his unique role as the preeminent public figure in the realm: "If you were a private person, you would need only private goodness, but you are public, and the first public man in the realm;

therefore, you need a benevolence that prefers the public good [*le bien public*] over the particular."[64] Keith Baker has shown that a central component of traditional absolutist theory was the idea that the king was the only public person in the land.[65] According to Baker, no other individual or institution besides the king could legitimately arbitrate on behalf of the community. All of the king's subjects were clustered in aggregates of particular interests, such as the *corps* and corporations subordinate to the crown. As the quotation confirms, La Rivoire held the imperative of the public good to be essential to the proper exercise of royal authority.

In light of the charges directed against Louis XV in the preceding cases, La Rivoire's rebukes sound familiar. Time and again Louis XV was criticized for his personal misconduct and self-indulgence. The implication was that the king had subordinated his public responsibility to his private interest at the expense of the kingdom's welfare and prosperity. In the view of La Rivoire and many others, the king did not have a choice: he must devote himself exclusively to promoting "le bien public."

The monarch had to be circumspect because his actions were looked to as standards of conduct. It followed that the king's tolerance of corruption and mismanagement in his government served to condone such behavior. La Rivoire was especially concerned about the crown's financial profligacy: "And when a king sets the example for his subjects of paying his debts as opposed to declaring bankruptcy, he will be more magnificent than Solomon in all his glory."[66] For La Rivoire, a king who impoverished his country, whether through vainglory or ignorance, had committed a fundamental act of civic betrayal. By this point in time the languages of moral and fiscal integrity were no longer distinct strains but merged into a single powerful critique of royal government.

In this conception of royal authority the monarch was essentially an administrator of resources that had been entrusted to him on the assumption that he would use them to promote the prosperity of his subjects. La Rivoire condemned the king for dissipating funds on excessive ceremonial festivities, such as the Dauphin's marriage in May 1770, and in the court, among "your whores, your pimps, your wicked courtesans such as Richelieu, d'Aiguillon."[67] Ultimately, La Rivoire was calling for financial accountability on

the part of the crown and thereby refusing to accept government as "le secret du roi."

In this same letter La Rivoire reminded Louis XV that "the magnificence
of a king is the happiness of his people, that the peasant should have a
chicken to put in his pot every Sunday, as the good king Henry IV said."[68]
The health of a kingdom reflected the wisdom of its leader and was his true
glory. A bankrupt treasury and a starving populace belied all claims to grandeur. "You enrich monsters who despoil you, who will ruin you and your
descendants, and who will eventually offer to foreigners or turn against you
the powers they have acquired through your weakness; remember that the
wealth of a king is to be found neither in a wicked court nor in the immen-
sity of his taxes but rather among the people, equally in the cities as in the
countryside."[69] The problem, according to La Rivoire, was not a lack of national wealth but governmental corruption that perpetuated an inequitable
distribution of the tax burden. He was emphatic that the king's primary duty
consisted in promoting wealth and ensuring its dissemination.

Spurred by his fiscal predicament, La Rivoire used his notion of financial
accountability to construct a radical theory of kingship, arguing that the
king held his authority on a mandate from the people. This power was del-
egated with the understanding that it would be deployed to protect and promote the public good. Louis XV's exploitation of his subjects, his profiting
from the sweat of their labor, was a betrayal of this primordial trust. With
respect to this last accusation, La Rivoire accused Louis XV of plotting to
starve his people and linked this famine plot to the Maupeou reforms of the
judiciary. La Rivoire asserted that the Parlement of Paris had been disbanded because it had been on the verge of revealing the scandal of a royal
grain monopoly. "You publish texts in which you accuse it [the Parlement of
Paris] of keeping bread prices high. It [the Parlement] no longer exists, is
bread any cheaper? When you rushed to exile it, it had just declared the
names of three more hoarders who would have revealed the extent to which
you, your monster of a chancellor, the deceased comte d'Etrées, in whose
possession they found a stash of grain, your entire wicked court, all were
profiting from this vile exploitation."[70] The rumor of a famine plot was an
undercurrent of popular protest throughout the eighteenth century, erupt-

ing in moments of dearth and political crisis. Generally, panic spread when the populace anticipated a shortage or when scarcity was experienced in the midst of apparent abundance. On the whole, the rumors spared the king and focused on those who surrounded him, including ministers, mistresses, and financiers.[71] La Rivoire's audacious decision to place Louis XV first in the line of attack reveals the intensity of his anger as well as the magnitude of the king's unpopularity by 1771.

La Rivoire's critique of the crown's policy, whether it had to do with the grain trade, public finance, or debt management, focused on its inequality and inefficiency. Despite the fiscal hardships imposed upon a struggling populace, the crown was perpetually on the brink of bankruptcy. According to La Rivoire, the treasury was chronically short of funds because revenues from taxes were being diverted into the hands of parasitic ministers and courtiers. With distinctly physiocratic echoes La Rivoire observed, "What a sad country where the bourgeois pays one amount and the peasant pays double. Consider how he [the peasant] can live and raise the children necessary to sustain the population and fill the armies. And you say that you are obliged to declare bankruptcy."[72] Although he lacked practical experience in government, La Rivoire intuitively perceived causal connections between the economic and political problems confronting the country in 1771. By impoverishing the working populace and the peasantry the crown was undermining its ability to survive in an increasingly competitive world.

It was rare for La Rivoire to cast his glance this far from the familiar confines of the legal world. On the whole his allusions to the misery of *le menu peuple* were couched in abstract terms. He was far more concerned with his plight and that of his professional colleagues, drawing upon his own grievances to launch a broader social critique.

Your Majesty, you are a good man who has done much bad for some time in order to give temporary relief to the idle rich who surround you . . . why should five million reserved for the state's welfare be squandered in ostentatious displays and delivered to the pillage of courtiers? Should Choiseul receive fifteen hundred thousand francs simply because he asks for it? While your subjects, victims of their faith in your edicts and declarations, your promises and oaths, are reduced to half of their expected returns on their investments and the rising cost of living, not counting that it will rise further because one misery always brings another. Let's not be nasty; that is unfair. But what would you call the theft you committed against your creditors, national and foreign? The commerce that you tolerate and that is conducted by your ministers at the price of the bread and life of your subjects and all the depredations that are imposed on your people in the shadow of your weakness and incapacity.[73]

No doubt, La Rivoire's wrath had been provoked by the heavy losses he had incurred in the wake of the crown's decision to default on the public debt. His trust had been abused, his capital literally "stolen." He refused to exculpate Louis XV and held him personally responsible for his misfortune and that of others in similar positions. He saw himself as one victim among many and demanded compensation or at least a guarantee for the future.

La Rivoire ended this same letter with a list of specific proposals for change, reforms intended to improve the monarchy and ensure its survival. The following passage highlights the concerns and expectations about kingship found in other police dossiers from the period:

Nonetheless, beware, your apparent friends are cheats. Terray and Maupeou don't have that much power, even though they deserve no better . . . choose Chalotais, disband your court, cultivate your family life like your cousin, as much a king as you, the king of England, let your parlements execute the laws, punish iniquitous judges with impunity, give the collection of taxes back to the cities, send military officers back to their families with the charge to rally at the first command, reform everything that is costly to the state and prevents it from applying its revenues to their intended objects, reestablish the public bonds at full value and pay their dividends regularly. Live off of your domains like your predecessors by respecting customs, knowing that your end becomes what was your beginning, . . . The true and only source of wealth for a state, its inner and outer strength, is the happiness of its people and its leaders.[74]

With conviction and fervency La Rivoire calls for a sweeping overhaul of public finances as well as royal conduct.

Taken together, these proposed changes represented a conscious effort to resist the monarchy's evolution into an omnipotent and arbitrary ministerial apparatus. In this sense, La Rivoire was echoing the most powerful currents in *parlementaire* opposition to royal authority. His vision of kingship posited a sovereign who did not interfere with the judicial and municipal bodies charged with administering the realm. The king need only intercede when necessary to arbitrate between contesting factions. On the whole, however, the collection of taxes and the dispensation of justice should be left to local authorities and institutions.[75] The king's most important role was to establish a protocol of upright conduct both in his personal lifestyle and in the management of his estate.

As in the cases of Bonafon and Allègre, the themes of personal debauchery and financial corruption were intrinsically linked for La Rivoire. Both were attributes of despotic rulers, and both signaled a character that lacked restraint and was therefore untrustworthy. Louis XV's failure to organize his household and manage the royal domain was symptomatic of his incompetence in ruling his kingdom. The appeal to the king to "live off of your domains like your predecessors" attests to the persistent, if unrealistic, belief that French kings should live directly off their personal holdings in land and dues. By carefully managing their resources, they could support themselves without resorting to an eternal cycle of taxing and borrowing.[76]

For La Rivoire, Louis XV's failure to respect the traditions and precedents established by his ancestors on the throne was a serious flaw. The king was not solely responsible; he was the tool of evil men who had usurped the reins of state: "The realm is full of monsters such as d'Aiguillon, covered in royal crimes, charged with satisfying your despicable inclinations; but rest assured, the time of your crimes is finished, you will no longer be free to continue, either you will have virtues and repair the past or you will perish as ignominiously as you have lived."[77] There was an ominous tenor to La Rivoire's message: Louis XV would not go unpunished if he remained unrepentant. La Rivoire was worried about the future not just for himself or his sovereign but for his country.

Law, Property, and Authority

In the process of rebuking Louis XV for his shortcomings as king, La Rivoire fashioned a contractual and secular conception of royal authority by combining Enlightenment political philosophy with strands of judicial Jansenism and *patriote* opposition to Maupeou's reforms. He elaborated this theory in a language that fused vaguely defined notions of popular sovereignty and contract theory with Montesquieu's ideals of limited monarchy.[78] Like his former colleagues in the law courts, La Rivoire never called for the dismantling of the monarchy. Nonetheless, he insisted that kings derived their authority from a combination of legal sanction and popular sovereignty. A king who failed to respect the fundamental laws of the realm, whether through willful intent or ignorance, violated his mandate and effectively relinquished his sovereignty.

La Rivoire systematically refuted the traditional tenets of absolutism. In his opinion, the notion of a divinely appointed sovereign accountable to no earthly authority was nothing more than a euphemism for a despot. *Despotism* was a pivotal term in the language of criticism that had developed in response to the crown's absolutist claims. It acquired heightened visibility and significance in the last years of Louis XV's reign, when the crown appeared to be acting despotically or at least was portrayed as such in the pamphlet literature that flooded the capital.[79] An analysis of the term in the police dossier on La Rivoire will clarify its implications for attitudes toward royal authority and its resonance with ongoing constitutional discussions. La Rivoire applied *despotism* more to the king's policies than to his misconduct, reflecting his conviction that the monarchy was above all a judicial institution, not a personal mandate.

In the entire dossier there is only one explicit reference to popular sovereignty as the basis of royal authority. For the most part, La Rivoire spoke of law and justice as the foundations of the French monarchy. He constantly referred to the sovereign's duties and obligations toward his people but avoided the logical conclusion that Louis XV owed his crown to his subjects. He discussed this idea most specifically in a statement concerning the exiled Jesuits and the possibility of their seeking revenge: "See whom you ought to favor, either the Jesuits, whom you banished and who want to revenge themselves on you and your people, or your people, who make you king and will glorify your race when you preserve their property, which can only be done by their laws, their Parlement, including its officers and customs, the safeguard of property."[80] This passage touches on several issues, especially La Rivoire's manifest concern for the protection of property. For the moment, however, the words "your people, who make you king" deserve attention because they constitute an explicit refutation of divine-right kingship. They highlight the secular direction of La Rivoire's arguments and their implications for his conception of French kingship.

Although the popular basis of royal authority was hinted at more than expounded, La Rivoire emphatically rooted royal authority in the fundamental laws of the realm. He asserted that the king was the product of law and was bound by oath to respect it. Once again calling for the return of the exiled magistrates, he insisted: "Take back your absolute orders, the product of an arbitrary authority forbidden by the laws to which you must be faithful, as your people are loyal to you, because you are the product of those same laws."[81] La Rivoire was not only shifting kingship from sacred to secular ground but also supplying a new definition of fidelity in which allegiance to the fundamental law transcended all other obligations and loyalties.

La Rivoire expanded and transformed the traditional notions associated with fidelity. Loyalty had always been envisioned as a dynamic and reciprocal relationship between the king and his subjects. The growth of absolutism had promoted half of the equation, emphasizing the obligations of subjects. By 1770, however, a century of enlightened inquiry and constitutional debate had begun to redress the balance. Individuals who found their own interests at stake in these conflicts felt justified in reminding Louis XV what he owed his people: "You are not king for nothing, but for the good of your people, and good lies only in the performance of your duties, which consist in maintaining the order you swore to observe and uphold."[82] In a curious rhetorical twist La Rivoire reversed the official line concerning fidelity and momentarily traded positions with his captors. Instead of police officers dictating the duties of loyal subjects, here was a subject reminding his sovereign of his obligations.

La Rivoire implied that a king's performance not only could be monitored and continually evaluated but in fact demanded it. This argument presupposed that the coronation oath constituted a contractual agreement between king and people.[83] In La Rivoire's view, it obliged the king to respect and uphold the fundamental laws of the realm and their sacred guardian, the Parlement of Paris. He reminded Louis XV to follow "your decrees and those of your predecessors, registered validly and freely by the Parlement, which makes the fundamental laws of the realm, decrees you swore to respect when you came to the throne."[84] The phrase "validly and freely" was a reference to the crown's recourse to forcing its legislation through the Parlement in a *lit de justice*. Since the crisis in the 1750s over the refusal of sacraments and, most recently, the Brittany affair, Louis XV had resorted to what was theoretically an extraordinary procedure on a far too regular basis. The *lit de justice* had proved to be the crown's last weapon in its battle to regain control over its judiciary in the second half of the eighteenth century. The king's growing reliance on the *lit de justice* was viewed by many observers, especially in the legal profession, as a dangerous precedent for the arbitrary exercise of authority. Like La Rivoire, these men believed that only the Parlement was qualified to debate and validate laws proposed by the king, and consequently they took up arms to defend it when it was under siege.

Contract theory, with its emphasis on popular consent and rule in the interest of the public good, underlay La Rivoire's conception of social and political organization. In contrast to moderate *patriotes,* who suggested that the sovereign should comply with constitutional guidelines, La Rivoire adopted a stronger position, insisting that these obligations were the basis of the monarch's authority and that violations were a breach of contract that effectively released men from their social and political obligations. In an undated letter to Louis XV, La Rivoire expounded upon this last point: "You yourself swore an oath to the Parlement at your accession to the throne and cannot destroy it [the Parlement] without breaking your own oath, the only basis for uniting societies, and when these oaths are overturned, each individual returns to his original rights. Society, which owes you nothing, has nothing to fear but force, but since your force derives from society, and you, on your own, are a poor mortal hardly worthy of the name man, which you dishonor as long as it remains a part of you, this force is not difficult to account for . . . reflect upon this."[85] This quotation makes clear that power is a trust, conditional upon the specific terms of the oath. It implies that popular consent as manifested in the coronation oath is the prerequisite for a legitimate political community. The language borrows from a natural-law tradition that underlay and guided so much of both enlightened and Jansenist efforts to limit the French king's power by the 1770s.[86]

It is important to note that La Rivoire is undermining Louis XV's sacrality on two levels. Not only does he suggest that the king derives his authority from the people as opposed to God but he addresses Louis XV as an ordinary mortal man. Having abrogated his sovereign status by dissolving the Parlement and exiling the magistrates, Louis XV was no different from anyone else. Despite the revolutionary potential of this line of thought, La Rivoire was reluctant to pursue it to the logical conclusion: namely, that kings were disposable appendages. He preferred to design a solution that would bring the crown into line with the law rather than eliminate it entirely.

By identifying the Parlement of Paris with the law, La Rivoire strengthened his argument that the magistrates provided the essential bulwark against abusive power. He also fleshed out a vision of a sovereign who was, like Bodin's, primarily a lawgiver: "It is there [the Parlement], the true court, where your royalty really exists; the greatest right of ruling consists in making laws, and the most essential of your duties is rendering justice to your people . . . you disbanded that court through an enormous abuse of your illegal power. From that moment . . . you are without power to make law. You are thus without royalty."[87] La Rivoire made a direct connection between the attributes of royalty inherent to the king and the legitimacy of his authority. A king who lost his ability to make law because he refused to comply with it lost his majesty and became an ordinary mortal usurping the throne.

According to La Rivoire's understanding of French history, when Louis XV abolished the Parlement in 1771 he effectively deposed himself as king. "No Parlement, no king, that is the law of France, which your interest, bound to that of your people, obliges you to execute in accordance with your coronation oath. Teach, therefore, your ninny of a Dauphin . . . that . . . from the day of the Parlement's exile you ceased to have a tribunal qualified to review and register the laws, ordinances, edicts, declarations that you would want to make for the good of your crown in accord with that of your people."[88] La Rivoire's interpretation of the coronation transformed it into a constitutional ceremony in which the king vowed to uphold the law. He consciously minimized the sacred and mystical dimensions that had accrued as the rite had been passed down over the centuries.

For La Rivoire, legislative power resided in the joint actions of king and

Parlement. Although laws initiated with the monarch, they remained ineffective until they had been reviewed and registered by the sovereign court.
These were the central tenets of the *parlementaire* opposition to the crown
throughout the eighteenth century, first articulated by Montesquieu and
Boulainvilliers and mobilized for the cause of judicial Jansenism and *patriote*
resistance in the 1760s and 1770s. It followed from this theory that despite
the king's decision to exile the magistrates, he had not succeeded in dismantling the Parlement of Paris. As La Rivoire proclaimed, although its
members had been scattered and their offices revoked, the Parlement remained the sole legitimate representative institution for the kingdom: "Even
though exiled, even though its offices have been confiscated, it continues to
exist in its entirety, only it is unable to exercise its functions, to the detriment
of the nation and the throne itself; because these exiles and confiscations are
null according to the fundamental laws of the realm, they can have no legal
consequences, and what is destroyed by them is rendered no less viable."[89]
In this eloquent defense of the exiled magistrates La Rivoire confirms that
the law is the highest power in the land. Moreover, Louis XV's actions toward the Parlement was doubly offensive because he had not only attacked
the seat of justice in the land but also challenged the inviolable right of private property.

Respect for private property depended on the immutability of the Parlement. After an allusion to Louis XV's illness at Metz in 1744, La Rivoire remarked "It is no longer you who are in danger; it is the state, the goods, the
possessions of your subjects, all of which depend on the immutability of the
parlements and the offices of those who comprise it. Save the laws from the
assassination attempts of a madman who rends them and violates them
without scruple, you will restore the state's health, which the current situation has destroyed. The country loved you as a son; it will adore you as a
father."[90] This defense of property can be read as simultaneously progressive and anachronistic. On the one hand, the inviolability of private property was a founding tenet of republics and democracies. On the other, the
property at stake in this discussion, an office, was linked to the archaic practice of venality and an inegalitarian social structure. La Rivoire never for a
moment questioned the legitimacy of venality of office or the privileges it
bestowed. Thus, his critique was spurred by the desire to safeguard the

interests of individuals who, like himself, possessed land and wealth, although it necessarily defended the broader principle as a universal right.

It should not be forgotten that administrators of the Old Regime owned their offices. These *charges* constituted property; revoking them without reimbursing the holder was a form of theft. Many magistrates had turned down compensation for their *charges* because they feared that acceptance would sanction Maupeou's coup. La Rivoire perceived a connection between the assault on these vested interests and his own financial losses. In both instances suffering had been inflicted through arbitrary and unprecedented royal decisions. These abuses, and the lack of an institutional body to correct them, were linked to the king's gravest crime, a plot to starve his people:

> Fraud at all levels of society is less widespread in Turkey than it is in Paris and other parts of France. There [in Turkey], the profit you have made off your monopoly of the grain trade for six years now is completely unheard of. This monopoly, which is stronger and more constant now than before, is responsible for the doubling of prices on all commodities, including tallow and meat; because your desire to profit from these high prices led you to have all the pasture lands converted into grain crops . . . this monopoly, as much as your disputes with d'Aiguillon in Brittany, [is] the cause of your decision to exile the Parlement, executed at the moment when the magistrates had just charged three hoarders who were about to reveal the secret of this vile commerce by a king who trades in the blood and sustenance of his poorest subjects.[91]

This quotation reveals both the complexity and the breadth of La Rivoire's challenge, which extended beyond particular instances of royal negligence or incompetence. La Rivoire establishes causal links between disparate grievances including financial mismanagement, famine plots, royal despotism, and *parlementaire* resistance. By delineating these connections, La Rivoire suggests that they were structural flaws not random occurrences. He thus calls into question the monarchy's capacity and raison d'être as a governing institution. Ultimately, the smooth operation of this cumbersome machine depended upon the skill of one person: the king.

In distinguishing monarchy from despotism La Rivoire was borrowing from Montesquieu's analysis of government based on distinctions concerning the modalities for the exercise of authority. He explained to Louis XV: "You believe, moreover, like your predecessor, out of arrogance or obstinacy . . . that arbitrary authority, unrestrained authority, is the necessary foundation of the people's happiness, or rather your own, and the glory of the state. Thus, in confusing arbitrary or dissolute authority, which destroys the power of sovereigns, with fixed and absolute authority, which constitutes royal power, you sacrifice to this idol your people, your finances, the glory and security of the state, and even yourself."[92] La Rivoire clearly is not denying the legitimacy of the monarchy as a political institution for governing France. He explicitly refers to the appropriate use of authority as fixed and absolute; yet the quandary was how to fix what was, by definition, absolute.

La Rivoire implicitly suggested that royal power was fixed in two ways. First, the Parlement of Paris had historically been responsible for monitoring and checking abuses. Second, the king himself had to act with restraint. By contrast, the more dangerous form of authority was characterized as "arbitrary authority, always ready to crush anything that attempts to resist it, [scorning] the laws and [overturning] them, knowing no guide except for its whims [*caprices*], no rule except for its wills [*volontés*]."[93] The terms *caprices* and *volontés* signaled the realm of despotism to an eighteenth-century reader. They connoted a reign characterized by the unbridled use of force, not the legally constituted authority of an absolute monarch. Ideally, these terms were not part of a lawful king's vocabulary of rule. This concept of fixed authority depended upon rigorous distinctions between public and private spheres. Under despotic rulers these boundaries were dissolved because the desires and ambitions of one man shaped national policy at the expense of the public good.

La Rivoire's fear that the French monarchy was devolving into despotism was linked to an organic social view in which the threat of change was omnipresent. Like many of his contemporaries in the judiciary, influenced by Montesquieu and Jansenist arguments, La Rivoire believed that monarchy treaded a fine line between anarchy and despotism. The only safeguards were the laws and the strength of institutions that enforced them. Monarchy and despotism were linked in the spectrum of political organization: each possessed distinguishing physical and moral attributes. La Rivoire already

detected symptoms of decay in Louis XV's feeble progeny: "You are growing old, debauchery has destroyed your body and weakened your judgment,
your Dauphin and his brothers are themselves puny and of weak constitutions; a stronger race is going to transplant itself onto yours."[94] By substituting the rule of might for right Louis XV had opened the door to enemies
of superior strength who would destroy him and his claims to the throne.
Nobody would defend the king or his dynasty because he had alienated his
subjects through his arbitrary and unjust rule.

The tone of this dossier is apocalyptic in certain letters predicting catas-
trophe unless drastic and immediate measures were taken. La Rivoire
warned Louis XV of the fragility of power based on force: "Justice is the basis of royal authority, without justice kings are nothing more than usurpers
and oppressors, whose authority, founded on violence, ends in violence and
bequeaths nothing to posterity."[95] Such had been the main thesis of Montesquieu's analysis of the seraglio in the *Persian Letters*. As the novel makes
painfully clear, despotic regimes are inherently unstable and self-destructive
because they violate the universal principles of justice and freedom.

Pursuing this train of thought, La Rivoire warned Louis XV that "the
reign that is beginning is that of force, blind power that knows no restraint
or rule, today for you, tomorrow against you, exactly as in Turkey. The
chancellor, your spokesman, will be your sword, your vizier . . . your throne
is nothing but a scaffold on which all those who reign will be sacrificed at the
first whim of the arbitrary power you have allowed to be established."[96] The
gruesome image of a throne transformed into a scaffold on which ministers
would be sacrificed one after the other was meant to shock Louis XV into
acting before it was too late.

For La Rivoire, contemporary France resembled a Hobbesian state of
nature, in which "people are without justice, families without leaders, the
wives of your soldiers no longer have dowries, their children have no inheritance, orders, customs. Everything is violated and destroyed, all this for
one man, a single guilty man who is even against you because he who re-
ceives your unjust orders should heed justice, not you."[97] La Rivoire insisted, and here he was undermining royal authority, that the dictates of justice superseded those of the king if the two should conflict. He was also
blaming Louis XV personally for Maupeou's judicial reforms. Whereas Bo-

nafon and Allègre shielded the king behind his evil mistress or minister, La Rivoire held Louis XV directly responsible for his "ministres chats." The king was no longer an innocent pawn surrounded by conniving councilors but a leader who had to answer for his decisions and, ultimately, pay for them.

· 🜊 ·

After La Rivoire had been incarcerated for a few months, the police perceived that he was deteriorating both mentally and physically. In September 1771, five months after his initial arrest, he was transferred to Charenton as mentally unfit. The persistent efforts of his brother, perhaps combined with the family's distinguished record of legal service, persuaded the police to release him at the end of November and exile him to Lyon. This last decision was revoked on 2 March 1772, when La Rivoire was allowed to return to Paris and resume what was left of his life there. Thus, he spent a total of seven months in prison as punishment for his offensive letters. He evidently kept his opinions to himself from then on, for his name does not reappear in the police files.

La Rivoire embodied the deepest contradictions that riddled French political thought during the latter half of the Enlightenment. On the one hand, he proposed a radical redefinition of sovereignty grounded in the secular concept of fundamental law. The roots of this secular definition of French kingship lay in the religious struggles of the sixteenth century, when the sacred was deemed too controversial a theoretical base for the emerging royal state, which was dedicated to preserving order and unity. When the religious conflicts subsided, however, Bourbon monarchs intent on augmenting their power and ensuring dynastic continuity recuperated the sacral basis of royal authority at the expense of the secular concept of *majestas*, the capacity to make law. That this older political tradition was mobilized so effectively by the magistrates and their supporters in the early 1770s was telling. It suggested that the monarchy, if it were to survive, would have to alter its discourse and accommodate this secular tradition. In many ways, the Maupeou years provided the last window of opportunity for fashioning a compromise between the king and his subjects. If the crown had listened more closely to its opponents, it might have discovered ways to consolidate its power by redefining its authority. It certainly would have been better prepared to defend itself fifteen years later, when an acute financial crisis churned up these same demands, this time with greater intransigence and conviction.

La Rivoire's critique was fundamentally a conservative one; his dissatisfaction with royal authority stemmed from his personal frustrations. A personal grievance inspired a broader attack that was fueled by information and arguments gleaned from the pamphlets and judicial *mémoires* that accompanied political turmoil in the capital. Arguably, La Rivoire was critical of Louis XV precisely because he had high expectations. The vehemence of his charges reflected the strength of his attachment to the royal figure. As the following quotation demonstrates, La Rivoire had specific ideas about what majesty entailed and how Louis XV had deviated from these standards: "Your position sets in front of you a sword for punishment, a hand for rewarding, an eye as a symbol of prudence formed by reason and enlightened by science to direct the sword and the hand. Ignorance, debauchery, crimes without limit have put out the eye henceforth blind. Since that time the hand has only opened in order to take or give to the useless what it took from the useful. The sword strikes the innocent wildly and randomly."[98] A lawful king was surrounded by instruments of rule that could be abused if they were not guided by the light of reason.

La Rivoire's sovereign was not a divinely appointed viceroy of God, nor was he an enlightened despot. Rather, he was a legally constituted leader bound by an oath to promote the public good and respect the fundamental laws of the realm. His mandate was revocable if he failed to comply with these terms. As much as the sovereign, the parlements were intrinsic parts of the French polity, serving as repositories for the legal codes. Only the magistrates could ensure that jurisprudence would be respected by both the king and his subjects. Moreover, La Rivoire insisted on the intrinsic connection between law and property. A regime that failed to uphold the inviolable right of private property was by definition despotic, if only because such incursions enslaved men to fear and deprived them of the sources of their livelihood.

That La Rivoire articulated theories of contractual obligation, natural rights, and the inviolability of property in his defense of the magistrates is significant. It highlights the extent to which the Maupeou reforms mobilized and politicized individuals who heretofore had been compliant subjects of royal authority. In addition, it reveals the revolutionary potential of such engagement. The *patriotes* cast their arguments in a traditional language of loyalty: it was their duty to remonstrate with the king when he made an error of judgment. Yet, as La Rivoire's dossier demonstrates, the struggle obliged individuals to embrace political vocabularies and theories that were ultimately subversive of royal authority. It thus supports recent research emphasizing the crucial role of the law courts in the breakdown of absolutism as well as the impact of legal culture in mobilizing public opinion in the second half of the eighteenth century.

By elevating justice to a supreme position, La Rivoire laid bare the structural problems that would plague French men and women confronted with the task of building a new order once the old one had been declared obsolete. Individuals weaned on absolutism found it difficult to envision a polity in which authority was not highly concentrated. Thus, La Rivoire never shattered the absolutist mode of political thought; he merely substituted the concept of justice and *le bien public* for that of divinely instituted royal will. The execution of power remained the same: it would continue to be concentrated in royally designated hands, imposed uniformly, unfettered by popular discussion or arbitration. Such monolithic and omnipotent conceptions of authority could assume varying guises in French history—crowned heads, revolutionary tribunals, and military dictators. Although the ideological basis would shift with each new regime, the inherent dangers to civil liberties remained the same.

Perhaps this inability to perceive alternative ways of exercising authority helps explain the obsessive fear of despotism in eighteenth-century French political thought. This anxiety pervaded discussions among individuals scattered across the social and professional spectrum of the Old Regime. It was crucial to the arguments of the monarchy's advocates as well as to those of its most entrenched opponents. It is a central theme in each of the cases examined in this book. La Rivoire's conviction that Louis XV was approaching despotic status echoed dominant motifs in Jansenist and *patriote* opposition to the crown, as well powerful currents in *dévot* thought. That both the crown and its critics shared a compulsive need to distinguish monarchy from despotism is important. It reveals an area of consensus within a morass of conflict. It suggests not only the potential for resolving differences but also the profound desire on both sides to work within old traditions rather than carve out wholly new ones.

La Rivoire's experience both before and during his incarceration impressed him, above all, with a sense of his helplessness and insignificance. After all, his carefully constructed fortune had been destroyed without warning or recompense by seemingly arbitrary ministerial fiat. Languishing in prison, he was struck by the disproportion between the severity of his repression and his minimal capacity to provoke change, let alone harm: "I have much to lose especially because my fortune is invested in lifetime or perpetual public annuities and I desire peace, but lacking social distinction, I can only have desires and will never be able to make either war or peace on my own. Despite this, I am perceived as dangerous."[99] In expressing his powerlessness as a man "lacking social distinction" La Rivoire evoked a sentiment shared by his fellow captives in the Bastille. None grasped the gravity of the actions that had landed them in prison nor their capacity to threaten. Yet police repression reflected contemporary governmental perceptions of these crimes as dangerous and irreverent acts within an ideological framework designed to enforce a traditional definition of sacred kingship. Although La Rivoire's voice was temporarily muted while the storm raged in the early 1770s, his arguments prompted unsettling conclusions regarding the traditional theory and practice of French kingship. Moreover, while they may have been undistinguished or impoverished, Bonafon, Allègre, Tavernier, La Chaux, and La Rivoire did discover their capacity to provoke fear, and this awareness, dependent as it was on police repression, was arguably a potential resource for claiming political and social power in the future.

The King Never Dies

· 🐚 ·

ON THURSDAY, 6 JANUARY 1757, a legal clerk named Jacques Roy stopped in at a café across the street from the Comédie-Française. It was 4:00 in the afternoon, and the café was crowded with Parisians busy discussing the alarming news of Damiens's attempt to stab the king the previous day. When Roy entered the room, his attention was drawn to a group of men near the fire whose conversation was particularly animated. As Roy approached, one of the men observed that "only a fanatic could have executed such an attack."[1] This statement elicited a strange response from one member of the group, an abbé, who exclaimed, "Ho! it certainly was not the hand of a royalist."[2] According to Roy, the priest's remark met with a harsh rebuke: "One of the individuals who was there, shocked by the indecency of the priest's statement, retorted, 'Do you know of two parties in France? Monseigneur l'abbé, isn't every French man a royalist?' The priest had immediately spun on his heels and marched off to the other side of the room without a word of explanation, and the same young man had commented, 'You see how such men think!'"[3] When Roy went to the police, his story was corroborated by two other witnesses. Given the circumstances, the incident did not go unnoticed. The police were anxious to identify the disgruntled ecclesiastic whose irreverent remark expressed possible affiliations with either Jansenists or Jesuits, equally suspicious sympathies in the aftermath of the Damiens affair. Within a week they had arrested the priest, Jean Baptiste Mesquet, and taken him to the Bastille for questioning. He would not be released until July 1758, several months after Damiens's trial and execution.

As Roy's account of this exchange makes clear, the word *royalist* had subversive connotations in mid-eighteenth-century France. Nobody who believed himself to be a *fidèle sujet* would have described himself as a royalist.

The term could only be employed by someone who considered support for the monarchy to be conditional. It suggested a pluralistic political culture in which allegiance to the king could be transferred onto or shared with other groups or institutions. Yet absolutism was a political system defined by a principle of unity embodied in the person of the king. Royal government was not designed to accommodate either competing interest groups or an established opposition. These concepts, although they existed in contemporary British political culture, were alien to the French theory and practice of government. The king could delegate responsibility, but he never shared his power.

In the course of the eighteenth century this cherished principle of unity came under attack. The king lost his monopoly on political discourse and was forced to govern through a "politics of contestation."[4] A series of military defeats accompanied by fiscal and constitutional crises pitted Louis XV against his law courts and the representatives of his faith. The king was unable to arbitrate these disputes, and this failing seriously compromised his ability to rule. The monarchy's image suffered irreparable damage during these tumultuous decades if only because its opponents were quickly mastering techniques for mobilizing and swaying public opinion. Taking advantage of rising literacy, cheaper textual formats, and the growing literary market, a collection of articulate Jansenists, lawyers, and philosophes erected a veritable tribunal of public opinion with the express purpose of monitoring the crown by obliging it to justify all of its decisions before it. The increased availability of information opened up the activity of opinion-making to just about anyone who cared to partake, a glaring anomaly in a society that continued to conceive of itself in the restrictive terms of birth, hierarchy, and privilege. This capacity to formulate an informed opinion strengthened demands for governmental accountability and expanded participation in the governing process.

These changes are reflected in Abbé Mesquet's remark, which acknowledged the possibility of political choice within a theory of government premised on a principle of uniformity embodied in the person of the king and his omnipotent will. Mesquet's swift arrest attested to the crown's refusal to compromise its absolutist conception of government. Moreover, the nature of his crime, a controversial use of the word *royalist*, confirms that language was an important source of tension between the crown and its subjects in the reign of Louis XV. The word, whether printed or uttered, was not a free commodity under the Old Regime. It was understood to descend directly from God onto his appointed sovereign as an instrument for communicating law and maintaining authority. Its regulation, through the Académie Française or censorship, was a distinguishing feature of the royal state. A central aim of the Enlightenment program was to dismantle this monopoly on language, which restricted the spread of knowledge and inhibited progress. It is hard to recover the power of words, their ability to threaten, offend, or provoke, from the media-infused perspective of the late twentieth century. Nonetheless, that a criminal category, *mauvais discours*, existed under the Old Regime and was rigorously enforced attests to the perceived power of language and its abuses.

Words such as *royaliste, fidelité,* and *despotisme* had specific connotations in eighteenth-century France that corresponded to a distinctly early modern set of values and assumptions concerning the nature of the world, the purpose of government, and the place of man in society. To penetrate the mental world of subjects living under an absolute monarchy entails recovering the meanings of the terms they used to define it. Under normal circumstances, such meanings were rarely discussed since they were submerged in consensual practices and tacit assumptions. It was only when a rupture occurred, when a *discours* became a *mauvais discours,* that the terms were subjected to heated debate in an attempt to reinforce their presumably fixed meanings. Such moments are recorded in the police records for crimes of opinion, providing singular instances for exploring the perceptions that make for both consensus and contestation.

Through five detailed case studies, this book focuses on the criteria individuals relied on to construct criminal narratives, both true and false, and the responses of the royal authorities to these efforts. I emphasize the interaction in these encounters while recognizing that an unequal balance of power weighed more heavily on the accused than on his or her accusers. The book's structure is significant because it seeks to make a methodological as well as a historical argument. I do not claim that these cases are typical or that they offer statistical studies of criminality. Rather, like the microhistorical work of Carlo Ginzburg and Giovanni Levi, they suggest that by shrinking the scale, one can see things that are often hidden by a more elevated and sweeping perspective. The point is not to choose between two schools of thought but rather to recognize that both offer valid, albeit different, historical insights. Although the cases focus on individuals, the individuals only make sense within larger political, cultural, and rhetorical currents. Thus, I selected cases that highlight prevailing themes and concerns identified in other police dossiers and sources at particular dates in the reign of Louis XV.

Since most of the cases involved elaborate lies and false alarms, it would be misleading to place too much emphasis on the content alone. The analysis, to borrow from Roger Chartier, focuses on forms and practices of expression, representation, and manipulation as much as on content. This decision was a response to the evidence itself. The dossiers do not reflect actual events and utterances as much as they indicate a range of thought and action deemed plausible in a specific historical context. In order to be convincing and to secure the desired advantages, the invented stories had to be *vraisemblable* (seemingly true) even if they were not *vrai* (true). The ability to sustain an illusion of *vraisemblance* determined an individual's success in duping the authorities. Verisimilitude depended on a near perfect fit between text and context. The *mauvais discours* had to echo prevailing concerns and allegations about the king in order to be credible. Thus, the content of the dossier is a revealing but not a transparent source of information regarding attitudes toward the monarchy in the mid-eighteenth century. A critical distance from royal authority can be detected in each chapter, though less through the rhetoric, much of which repeats age-old tropes and complaints about various kings, than through the ways in which language was manipulated and deployed in the service of personal interest.

The story here is perhaps less the fall of sacred kingship than the rise of a new sensibility about the appropriate role of the individual, privileged or not, in Old Regime society. The dilemma for a French subject in the reign of Louis XV was that the claims of the latter necessarily challenged and undermined the authority of the former. The police perceived these implications, and this explains their decision to treat these crimes with severity. The perpetrators arguably found themselves classified as dangerous criminals because the right to form and express an opinion, let alone demand it be recognized as a legitimate contribution to political discussion, did not exist under an absolute monarchy defined in part by the king's monopoly on the written, printed, and spoken word. This monopoly was challenged both institutionally and individually with growing conviction in the second half of the eighteenth century.

Each of the cases examined in this book defies the historian's effort to impose neat political categories since none exhibits the consistency of a recognized doctrine or position. The five individuals considered would hardly qualify as a party of opposition. It would be impossible to define an agenda that united them beyond their belief that monarchy was the best form of government for France. They were moved to criticize the crown precisely because they expected it to meet very high standards. None perceived his or her suggestions for reform as inconsistent with fidelity to Louis XV. Each made elaborate efforts to shield the king from attack, blaming evil mistresses, ambitious ministers, or royal ignorance for abuses of power. Yet their critiques assumed different guises, reflecting diverse personal needs and arguments that often relied on opposing strategies to achieve the intended goals. Thus, for example, Antoine Allègre denounced parlementary agitation for undermining royal authority, whereas Pierre Denis de La Rivoire hailed it as an essential safeguard against royal despotism. Their attitudes reflected an eclectic blend of learned and popular sources, of rumors, myths, facts, and fears, combined to express grievances and articulate needs.

Focusing on individual cases allows us to understand broad historical changes on a human scale. In France, the reign of Louis XV marked the culmination of a centuries-long effort to delineate the boundaries between the sacred and secular realms of authority. The monarchy increasingly looked to arguments based on reason and historical necessity to justify its authority. The evidence gathered from these case studies suggests that this process of secularization was both difficult and disorienting from the perspective of the crown's subjects. Although these five individuals refused to question the legitimacy of the monarchy as a governing institution, they were propelled by the cultural currents of the Enlightenment to adapt a critical stance toward it. They continued to embrace their king but revered him as a decidedly secular figure to be judged by standards of reason, utility, and accountability. Most strikingly, their grievances, demands, and proposals for reform were couched in a traditional language of loyalty.

While the cultural changes associated with the Enlightenment may have provided French men and women with the intellectual tools and vocabulary of democratic politics, they did not fundamentally alter their paternalistic conception of authority. In fact, while the eighteenth century may have delegitimated the sacred as a source of political authority, it arguably reinforced the power of the paterfamilias and the currency of the family as a political model. In a careful analysis of popular works of art and literature, Lynn Hunt uses Freud's psychoanalytical model of the family romance to illuminate changing attitudes toward authority figures, gender roles, and the exercise of power in prerevolutionary France. She demonstrates that in the last two decades of the Old Regime depictions of fathers underwent a radical transformation at the hand of artists and authors. The more traditional image of a cruel and authoritarian father was replaced by a benevolent but impotent one. As fathers were domesticated and the family unit itself was reinforced as a haven of comfort and self-cultivation, they were also divested of their absolute authority, a significant change in France, where the king was referred to as the father of the kingdom and fathers were described as virtual monarchs in their own household kingdoms. According to Hunt, this evolution in attitudes paved the way for the eventual possibility of removing the archetypal paternal symbol, the king, from the political scene. Nonetheless, Hunt insists that although the execution of Louis XVI was momentarily liberating, it was also profoundly disturbing for the revolutionary leaders, who had to swallow the guilt of patricide along with regicide as they sought to fill the void left by the former king. Moreover, as Hunt emphasizes, the real challenge for the future leaders consisted in finding a way to salvage the principle of patriarchy from the executioner's basket after the regicide.[5] Hunt's book reveals, above all, that the killing of the king was highly problematic if only because it exposed the powerful, often irresolvable tensions embedded in the family romance as a political model both during and after the revolution.

This theme of paternalism is not confined to the late eighteenth century, as the historian Michel Winock insists in his long, reflective essay on contemporary France as seen through the lens of the past. Winock suggests that after the execution of Louis XVI in 1793 the French were searching not only for a new regime but also for a new father. He sees this need to "seek unflaggingly the return of a lost father" as a deeply rooted ideological force in French political culture and gives it considerable explanatory weight in his analysis.[6] In a line of argument that descends directly from Tocqueville, Winock insists that the monarchy continued to exercise considerable power over the course of French history long after it had been figuratively and practically beheaded. On the most obvious level, such influence can be seen throughout the nineteenth century in the struggles between royalists and republicans as well as in the success of Bonapartism as a political phenomenon. Yet, less evident but perhaps more problematic is the monarchy's legacy as a mode for envisioning and articulating authority in French history. This influential model manifests itself in a desire for power to be personalized and centralized, as well as in the overwhelming drive for unity at the expense of a truly democratic polity of competing interests. While the continuing force of the monarchy gives France historical continuity and stability, it also accounts for the curiously fragile nature, or at least contradictory tendencies, of French democracy since 1789.

According to Winock, modern France is the product of two traditions, one monarchical and the other revolutionary, that together shape the contemporary political terrain. The two legacies are frequently, but not always, in opposition to one another. This unstable combination of reactionary impulses and radical demands, of liking authority and insisting on liberty, has been a distinguishing feature of French political life. The Revolution's failure to resolve this fundamental conflict helps explain both the controversial nature of the revolutionary legacy and the chronic instability of French government since the end of the eighteenth century. These same issues recently resurfaced in the debates surrounding the commemoration of the bicentennial of the French Revolution, and they can be detected as well in the ongoing discussions about the overweening power of the presidency under the Fifth Republic.[7]

The condemnation of the Old Regime, of its institutions and values, did not completely stifle the monarchy's personal appeal as a model for centralized leadership. The monarchy is inextricably linked to the Revolution in the memory of the French people and remains a highly charged topic.[8] In January 1993, to honor the bicentennial of the execution of Louis XVI, the French leftist weekly *Le Nouvel Observateur* brandished the following caption across its cover page: "Fallait-il tuer Louis XVI?" It was accompanied by a picture of the executioner's hand boldly displaying the former king's head.[9] The purpose of this inquiry by two distinguished historians of the Revolution, François Furet and Mona Ozouf, was to review the controversies surrounding the question of the king's fate in 1792–93. Furet and Ozouf suggested that the decision to execute the king, although politically expedient, was emotionally traumatic. An article by Alan Riding in the *New York Times* describing the bicentennial commemoration of the king's death reported that if a vote were taken among French men and women today, it would result in a draw.[10] Neither of these articles contends that the French are royalists at heart or that they regret the revolutionary experience. Rather, they suggest that the figure of the king remains a compelling symbol of authority even in a world of democratic values. Most recently, Winock has posed the question even more explicitly: "The French, despite appearances, don't they remain royalists?"[11] For Winock, the myth of royalism haunts the French psyche, promising grandeur in times of misery, paternal benevolence in the face of ruthless competition, an idealized past in exchange for a disappointing present.

The influence of the monarchy involves more than the art and architecture it has bequeathed to later generations. It shapes the government's notion of leadership and responsibility in such areas as urban planning, the regulation of baguette prices and wine appellations, and presidential public relations. The French fascination with politics and political discussion is directly linked to the absolutist effort to consolidate royal authority in the seventeenth and eighteenth centuries. The omnipresence of the crown's officers obliged French men and women to accept the interventionist role of their government. The weight of the state engendered ever greater dependency on it and, correspondingly, an instinctive willingness to protest when these expectations were disappointed. Embedded in this statist conception is a corollary fiction of accessibility or unfettered communication that relies on the personification of power, arguably another legacy from the monarchy. Thus, the most popular element of the Fifth Republic is the election of the president by universal suffrage, an affirmation of the indissoluble link between citizens and their leader.[12]

The conviction that the leader and the government are two distinct entities echoes the persistent desire among eighteenth-century French men and women to have access to the king's ear. In his study of early modern popular myths surrounding the existence of "a hidden king," Yves-Marie Bercé demonstrates that the aura surrounding a French leader, be it regal or presidial, has not been entirely dispelled. In the last chapter of his book Bercé includes a sample of letters written by individuals to the president of the Fifth Republic. The letters suggest that individuals in desperate circumstances continue to turn to the president, not the law or the government, as a last resort.[13] The belief that assistance would be forthcoming "if the king only knew" corresponds to the conviction that justice is personalized, not institutionalized, in a world that is often cruel, unjust, or confusing.

An understanding of the eighteenth-century monarchy, of its strengths and weaknesses, is a necessary prerequisite for navigating through France's political landscape today. The monarchy provides a vocabulary as well as a *point de repère* for describing and analyzing the governing process. As Tocqueville observed, the monarchy established patterns of authority from which the French have rarely deviated. The relative stability of the Fifth Republic, in comparison with its two predecessors, arguably resides in the strength of the executive branch. The French president has distinctly regal features in terms of the scope of his authority and his lack of accountability. Clearly, the president is not a king since he is elected by a popular mandate. Yet it is not unusual to find comparisons being drawn between the two sorts of rulers.[14] Moreover, these analogies are most evident in the rhetorical forms and arguments selected for expressing grievances and proposing reforms.

A *dix-huitièmiste* who peruses contemporary journals and publications is struck by the similarity between the critiques of the presidency and the attacks against Louis XV. There are certain traits, such as indifference, indolence, and profligacy, that the French refuse to tolerate in their leaders. These concerns are distinctly French because they speak to a political tradition that emphasizes the individual leader more than the institution he embodies. Their grievances, in both the eighteenth and the twentieth century, invariably play upon one of these three themes. These same qualities were associated with despotic rule, a pervasive and obsessive fear in eighteenth-century France. The vocabulary of this language has not changed much either. Jean-François Revel, a contemporary journalist and writer, re-proached Mitterand for the same failings as those held against Louis XV and, later, Marie-Antoinette. The words *caprice* (caprice), *gaspillage* (waste-fulness), *fastes* (ostentation), and *vie privée* (private life) filled the pamphlet literature two hundred years ago, and Revel relies on them to support his own contentions.[15] More recently, in an uproar provoked by Prime Minister Lionel Jospin's initiative to reform the French language to reflect women's growing role in society as professionals and politicians, Jean Dutourd, a member of the Académie Française, denounced the proposed law as "the re-sults of polygamy by Jospin, who has surrounded himself with sultanesses and, to please his harem, has resurfaced an old idea." These terms, with their lurid fears about the feminization and eroticization of power, are strangely reminiscent of eighteenth-century *mauvais discours*.[16] Alas, there is no Bastille for the immortal M. Dutourd, and even if there were, it is not clear he would be sent there since his concerns arguably strike a chord in French political culture today.

Like many of his contemporaries who specialize in politics, history, or law, Jean-Francois Revel is concerned with the problem of power and its abuses. He is critical of Marxism and looks to America as a model of an open, democratic society. He is alarmed by the authoritarian tendencies he discerns in the Fifth Republic's definition of the presidency. He does not hesitate to draw analogies between Mitterand and the former kings who ruled France. Revel argues, for instance, that one of the key flaws in the French presidency is the lack of political accountability. The president can nominate and dismiss ministers at his will, allowing them to bear the burden of political mishaps and faulty judgment. Revel exaggerates his point to support his fundamental tenet that executive power needs to be more tightly constrained by other branches of government. Nonetheless, his observation is not misplaced because he has identified a structural feature of French pol-itics. As the evidence garnered from the five case studies demonstrates, this desire to shield the sovereign leader from personal responsibility is long-standing. The instinct to transfer blame onto mistresses or ministers or to at-tribute mistakes to ignorance is deeply rooted in French culture. It is un-likely to disappear in the near future. Moreover, French leaders, like their Bourbon predecessors, reveal a marked preference for governing in the tradition of "le secret du roi," Mitterand's hidden prostate cancer being a salient example. History suggests that in order to resolve this dilemma the French will need to devise constitutional restraints that enforce presidential accountability since it will never be volunteered by the government.

As I write these last lines, the French are celebrating, which means debating, the fortieth anniversary of the promulgation of the constitution establishing the Fifth Republic. The leftist daily newspaper *Libération* published a special section on 3–4 October 1998 entitled "Faut-il changer de République?" The text includes excerpts from an ongoing discussion among French journalists, academics, and intellectuals concerning the future of the Fifth Republic and the need for reform. Although the participants ranged widely in their responses, there was a consensus that the exercise of executive power remained the most troubling aspect of the constitution's legacy. Embedded in this discussion of the presidency were the questions of the seven-year renewable term, the efficacy of cohabitation, and ultimately the democratic process itself. Bertrand Mathieu, a professor at Paris I, captured the overwhelming sentiment when he remarked that "we have a problem of sovereignty, not really of institutions." Most of the respondents saw the swollen powers of the executive as symptomatic of a more entrenched set of structural problems, including the lack of truly representative political parties and government accountability, as well as the persistence of a closed political elite dedicated to reproducing itself at the price of eschewing conflict and opposition. These tendencies, according to Jacques Georgel, a retired law professor at Rennes, reflect the fact that democracy has never really implanted itself in French culture. Echoing Bertrand Mathieu, Georgel observed that "democracy is much more a state of mind than a form of government." These comments suggest that, at least for some contemporaries, while France has the institutional and rhetorical trappings of a modern parliamentary democracy, it doesn't yet have the heart and soul of one. The roots of this dilemma are arguably to be found deep in the French past, some two hundred years ago, when a burgeoning democratic consciousness was taking shape in the shadows of an absolute monarchy. This difficult historical transition bequeathed a complex political and cultural legacy whose weight continues to be felt in France today.

NOTES

· ❦ ·

List of Abbreviations

AB	Archives de la Bastille
AN	Archives Nationales
BHVP	Bibliothèque Historique de la Ville de Paris
BN	Bibliothèque Nationale
JDF	Collection Joly de Fleury

Introduction

1. AN Y 10203, interrogation of Jean Moriceau de La Motte by Lieutenant of Police Sartine, Châtelet, 26 August 1758.

2. AN X2A 797, parlementary *arrêt*, 6 September 1758.

3. Barbier, *Chronique de la régence et du règne de Louis XV,* 7:91.

4. Gates, "The End of Loyalty," 34–44.

5. Classic examples of Annaliste scholarship would include the work of Marc Bloch, Lucien Febvre, Ferdinand Braudel, and more recently, Emmanuel Le Roy Ladurie. Representatives of the Marxist tendency in French historiography include George Rudé and Albert Soboul. For a critical overview of the Annales movement, from its inception to the present, see the articles by A. Burgière and J. Revel written on the occasion of the journal's fiftieth anniversary, Burgière, "Histoire d'une histoire," and Revel, "Histoire et sciences sociales"; and Hunt, "French History in the Last Twenty Years."

6. Furet, *Interpreting the French Revolution,* 46–47.

7. Giesey, *Royal Funeral Ceremony in Renaissance France;* Hanley, *The Lit de Justice of the Kings of France.* In this same school, but less successful, are Jackson, *Vive le Roi!* and Mansel, *Court of France.* Most recently, Alain Boureau has posited a critique of the Kantorowicz thesis (see *Le simple corps du roi*).

8. See Baker, *Inventing the French Revolution;* Merrick, *Desacralization of the French Monarchy;* Van Kley, *Damiens Affair;* and idem, *Jansenists.*

9. Chartier, *Cultural Origins of the French Revolution;* Darnton, *Literary Underground;* Farge, *Subversive Words;* Hunt, *Family Romance of the French Revolution;* Maza, "Le tribunal de la nation"; idem, *Private Lives and Public Affairs.*

10. Habermas, *Structural Transformation of the Public Sphere.* Roger Chartier summarizes Habermas's impact on recent French historiography in chapter 1 of his *Cultural Origins of the French Revolution.*

11. Three noteworthy examples are Thomas Crow, *Painters and Public Life in Eighteenth-Century Paris* (New Haven, Conn., 1985); Goodman, *Republic of Letters;* and James Johnson, *Listening in Paris* (Berkeley, 1995).

12. For examples of this type of work, see Cerruti, *La ville et les métiers;* Davis, *Society and Culture in Early Modern France;* Ginzburg, *Cheese and the Worms;* Giovanni Levi, *Inheriting Power;* and Sabean, *Power in the Blood.* A good introduction to microhistory can be found in "L'histoire au ras du sol," Jacques Revel's preface to the French edition of Levi's book, *Le pouvoir au village,* i–xxxiii.

13. Ménétra, *Journal of My Life.*

14. Keith Baker, "Public Opinion As Political Invention," in *Inventing the French Revolution,* 167–202; Merrick, *Desacralization of the French Monarchy;* Ozouf, "Le concept de l'opinion publique du XVIIIe siècle." The bibliography on public opinion is too extensive to cite here, but the following sources provide a good introduction: Goodman, "Public Sphere and Private Life"; La Vopa, "Conceiving a Public"; as well as the articles by David Bell, Daniel Gordon, and Sara Maza in a discussion entitled "The Public Sphere in the Eighteenth Century" in *French Historical Studies* in fall 1992, namely, Bell's "The 'Public Sphere,' the State, and the World of Law in Eighteenth-Century France," Gordon's "Philosophy, Sociology, and Gender in the Enlightenment Conception of Public Opinion," and Maza's "Women, the Bourgeoisie, and the Public Sphere."

15. Representative works of these authors are Cobb, *Police and the People;* Darnton, "A Police Inspector Sorts His Files," in *Great Cat Massacre,* 145–89; Farge, *Subversive Words;* and Kaplan, "Réflexions sur la police du monde du travail."

16. See Baker, *Inventing the French Revolution;* Merrick, *Desacralization of the French Monarchy;* and Van Kley, *Damiens Affair.*

17. For a history of the Bastille and its archives, see Funck-Brentano, *La Bastille et ses secrets.*

18. Carlo Ginzburg addresses this issue in his discussion of his own work on trial records of the Inquisition in Italy (see "The Inquisitor As Anthropologist," in *Clues, Myths, and the Historical Method*).

19. Roger Chartier, "Culture As Appropriation," in Kaplan, *Understanding Popular Culture.*

20. Chartier, *On the Edge of the Cliff,* 21.

21. Ibid., 20.

22. Davis, *Fiction in the Archives,* 112.

23. Cobb, *A Second Identity,* 49.

24. See Darnton, *Literary Underground.*

25. AB 12107, fol. 323, Michel Mitre Touche to Sartine, 1 March 1760.

26. This point is explored by Arlette Farge in her recent study of public opinion, *Subversive Words;* it is also addressed by Chartier in *Cultural Origins of the French Revolution.*

27. Fogel, *Les cérémonies de l'information.* In his biography of Louis XV, Michel Antoine emphasizes the king's secretive nature and visible discomfort in public appearances (see Antoine, *Louis XV*).

28. See Jean-François Revel's scathing critique of what he terms, "l'hypertrophie presidentielle" in *L'absolutisme inefficace.*

29. Davis, *Fiction in the Archives.*

CHAPTER I
Police, Crime, and Public Order in Enlightenment Paris

1. Tocqueville, *The Old Regime and the French Revolution,* 60–61.

2. Much research has been devoted to the police of Paris. A good place to start is with the monographs by Chassaigne, *La lieutenance générale de police de Paris;* and Williams, *Police of Paris.* There is useful information throughout Andrews, *System of Criminal Justice.* See also chapter 1 of Kaplan, *Bread, Politics, and Political Economy;* as well as his articles "Notes sur les commissaires de police à Paris" and "Réflexions sur la police du monde du travail." Arlette Farge explores the use of police records as historical evidence in all of her work; see esp. *Le goût de l'archive* and *Subversive Words.* See also Benabou, *La prostitution et la police des moeurs.*

3. For information on the creation of this office and the duties associated with it, see Piasenza, "Juges, lieutenants de police et bourgeois."

4. Williams, *Police of Paris,* 37–39.

5. Andrews, *System of Criminal Justice,* 9–10, 31–43; Williams, *Police of Paris.* Several scholars have studied the Old Regime's policy toward the poor (see Hufton, *Poor in Eighteenth-Century France;* Kaplow, *Names of Kings;* and more recently, Schwarz, *Policing the Poor in Eighteenth-Century France*).

6. This point is elaborated upon in Gordon, "Philosophy, Sociology, and

Gender in the Enlightenment Conception of Public Opinion"; Kaplan, *Bread, Politics, and Political Economy;* and Williams, *Police of Paris.*

7. Darnton, "A Police Inspector Sorts His Files."

8. Andrews, *System of Criminal Justice,* 34; Williams, *Police of Paris,* 119–25.

9. See, e.g., Cobb, *Police and the People;* Farge, *Fragile Lives;* and Kaplan, "Notes sur les commissaires de police à Paris."

10. Williams, *Police of Paris,* 95.

11. Piasenza, "Juges, lieutenants de police et bourgeois," 1194.

12. The work of Arlette Farge is one of the best sources for understanding the relationship between the police and the populace (see her *Vivre dans la rue à Paris; Fragile Lives;* and, with Jacques Revel, *Logic of a Crowd*).

13. Tocqueville, *The Old Regime and the French Revolution,* 61.

14. Jacques Revel, "Intellectuals and Popular Culture in France, 1650–1800," in Kaplan, *Understanding Popular Culture,* 266.

15. Garrioch, "Police of Paris."

16. Foucault, *Discipline and Punish,* 222.

17. Foucault is explicit on this point when he writes, "'Discipline' may be identified neither with an institution nor with an apparatus; it is a type of power, a modality for its exercise, comprising a whole set of instruments, techniques, procedures, levels of application, targets; it is a 'physics' or an anatomy of power, a technology" (ibid., 215).

18. I am drawing here on Foucault's argument in ibid., 189–91.

19. JDF 2074, fol. 275.

20. JDF 2074, fol. 267. Benabou alludes to this same issue in her discussion of official treatment of prostitutes (see *La prostitution et la police des moeurs,* 155–61).

21. The following cases provide clear statements of the official definition of fidelity: AB 11981, fols. 87–92, Jean-Baptiste Manem, arrested February 1757; AB 11968, fols. 184–86, Alexandre Louis Marchal, arrested November 1757; AB 11967, fols. 159–61, Pierre Liebert, arrested October 1757; and AB 12264, fols. 42–45, Jean-Louis Langlois, arrested October 1765.

22. JDF 2074, fol. 239.

23. Rétat, *L'attentat de Damiens,* 156.

24. AB 12264, fol. 43, interrogation of Jean-Louis Langlois by Commissioner Rochebrune, Bastille, 6 November 1765.

25. AB 12107, fol. 285, interrogation of Michel-Mitre Touche by Rochebrune, Bastille, 7 May 1760. This meticulous attention to details of comportment, the gestures and emphasis that accompanied verbal testimony, recalls Ginzburg's discussion of inquisitorial archives in his essay "The Inquisitor As Anthropologist."

26. "Une science de la police est en place au xviiieme siecle, c'est certain, mais pas vraiment une police" (Farge and Foucault, *Le désordre des familles*, 345).

27. Brennan, *Public Drinking and Popular Culture in Eighteenth-Century Paris;* Farge, *Vivre dans la rue à Paris;* idem, *Fragile Lives;* Garrioch, *Neighborhood and Community;* Garrioch and Sonenscher, "Compagnonnages, Confraternities, and Associations of Journeymen"; Kaplan, "Réflexions sur la police du monde du travail."

28. AB 11964, fol. 56, Pierre-Paul Bouchet de la Croix, Sieur de la Timonniere, arrested 1757, undated letter to the king.

29. JDF 2075, fol. 105, *mémoire* from Joseph Clement and Louis Belleguele, 30 May 1765.

30. AN Y 10203, records of questioning under torture of Jean Moriceau de La Motte by Sartine, Châtelet, 11 September 1758.

31. Ibid.

32. AB 12227, fol. 46, summary of the case of Jean Philippe Paquet by Rochebrune for the secretary of state, the comte de Saint Florentin.

33. AB 11968, fol. 126, interrogation of Alexandre Louis Marchal by Rochebrune, Bastille, 30 December 1757.

34. AB 12227, fols. 37–38, interrogation of Jean Philippe Paquet by Rochebrune, Bastille, 8–9 February 1764.

35. The following cases illustrate both popular and official usages of the term *imagination* and clarify its various connotations: AB 12139, Valerie de Brulz du Tilleul, arrested 18 June 1761; AB 11967, fols. 69, 74, André L'Honoré, arrested 18 February 1757; AB 11981, fols. 195, 265–66, Jean-Baptiste Manem, arrested February 1757; AN Y 10235 and AB 12170–71, Paul René du Truch de La Chaux, arrested 6 January 1757; and AB 12264, fols. 36–37, Jean-Louis Langlois, arrested October 1765.

36. AB 12139, memorandum from Inspector d'Hémery to Saint Florentin, 2 May 1762.

37. JDF 2077, fol. 123, letter from M. Marlot, *procureur du roi* (the king's chief prosecutor), 21 December 1765.

38. Similar concerns were apparent in official attitudes toward prostitutes and cases of libertinage (see Benabou, *La prostitution et la police des moeurs*, 163).

39. JDF 2078, fol. 15.

40. Arlette Lebigre examines the role of punishment in Old Regime France in *La justice du roi*, esp. 133–38; and Farge discusses the ritual of public execution in *Fragile Lives*, 223–33.

41. AB 12010, fol. 25, interrogation of Jerome Michel by Rochebrune, Bastille, 2 August 1758.

42. Andrews, *System of Criminal Justice*, 501.

43. JDF 2076, fol. 108, intendant of Moulins to Saint Florentin, 25 August 1757, concerning the case of Claude Horsel and Claude Mirlavaud.

44. Farge explores this point in *Subversive Words*.

45. AB 11981, fol. 266, interrogation of Jean-Baptiste Manem by Rochebrune, Bastille, 19 May 1757.

46. Foucault, *Discipline and Punish*, 48. For more on this topic, see Michel Bée, "Le spectacle de l'exécution"; Farge, *Fragile Lives*, 223–33; and Lebigre, *La justice du roi*, 133–38.

47. Andrews, *System of Criminal Justice*, 496–98. See also Lebigre, *La justice du roi*, 178–211; and Kaufmann, "Critique of Criminal Justice."

48. In his efforts to debunk what he calls the "black legend" of Old Regime criminal procedure Andrews emphasizes that inquisitorial procedure was not inherently unjust (see *System of Criminal Justice*, 417–24).

49. Ibid., 285–88.

50. Ibid., 302–3.

51. Delumeau, *L'aveu et le pardon*, 109–22.

52. Andrews, *System of Criminal Justice*, 441–67.

53. For a discussion of changing attitudes toward torture and the death penalty in eighteenth-century France from three different perspectives, see Foucault, *Discipline and Punish*, 3–69; Maza, *Private Lives and Public Affairs*, 233–42; and Andrews, *System of Criminal Justice*, 296–306, 383–93.

54. Kaufmann explored the debates surrounding confessions extracted through torture in "Critique of Criminal Justice," 137–57.

55. Andrews, *System of Criminal Justice*, 444.

56. JDF 2074, fol. 252, interrogation of Toussaint Courtin by Rochebrune, Bastille, 20 August 1757.

57. For an analysis of the evolution of confessional practices in early modern Europe, see Delumeau, *L'aveu et le pardon*.

58. AB 12107, fol. 278, interrogation of Touche by Rochebrune, Bastille, 16 March 1760.

59. On mercy, see Andrews, *System of Criminal Justice*, 394–408; and Lebigre, *La justice du roi*, 222–30.

60. AB 11981, fol. 90, interrogation of Manem by Rochebrune, Bastille, 18 May 1757.

CHAPTER 2
Fiction and Authority in the *Tanastès* Affair

1. Anonymous song, BN, Collection Delamare Manuscrits Français 21750, fol. 22.

2. The documents pertaining to the case of Marie-Magdeleine Bonafon (sometimes spelled Bonafous) are located at the Bibliothèque de l'Arsenal, AB 11582. The dossier contains approximately five hundred pages of interrogations, personal correspondence, and police reports. Both the Bibliothèque Nationale and the Bibliothèque de l'Arsenal have copies of *Tanastès*. I cite the Arsenal copy throughout.

3. AB 11582, fol. 20. The titles of her other plays were *Le Destin*, *Les Dons*, and *Le Demi-savant*. Her novel was called *Le Baron de XXX*. I have not been able to locate any of these manuscripts.

4. See Habermas, *Structural Transformation of the Public Sphere*, 31–51. For a discussion of changing attitudes toward the family in eighteenth-century France, see Flandrin, *Families in Former Times;* and Traer, *Marriage and the Family*. For feminist critiques of Habermas, see Goodman, *Republic of Letters;* Landes, *Women and the Public Sphere;* and Maza, *Private Lives and Public Affairs*.

5. The most powerful analysis of the famine plot remains Kaplan's *Famine Plot Persuasion*.

6. Antoine, *Louis XV*, 354–403. For the war itself, see Browning, *War of the Austrian Succession*.

7. Antoine, *Louis XV*, 360–64.

8. For further discussion of concerns about Louis XV prior to 1744, see Farge, *Subversive Words*, 95–109; and Thomas E. Kaiser, "Louis *LE BIEN-AIMÉ* and the Rhetoric of the Royal Body," in Norberg and Melzer, *From the Royal to the Republican Body*. My thanks to Thomas Kaiser for sharing this article with me before its publication.

9. BHVP, MS 720, fol. 91, Lieutenant of Police Feydeau de Marville to Secretary of State Maurepas, 1 May 1744.

10. AB 10029, fols. 147v, 148.

11. Farge, *Subversive Words*, 104.

12. Two classic studies of the theory of sacred kingship in early modern Europe are Bloch, *The Royal Touch;* and Kantorowicz, *The King's Two Bodies*. More recent analyses are provided by Giesey, *Royal Funeral Ceremony in Renaissance France;* and Hanley, *The Lit de Justice of the Kings of France*.

13. Farge, *Subversive Words*, 108. For a discussion of popular concern with the king's sexuality, see Guicciardi, "Between the Licit and the Illicit." Lynn Hunt insists on this point in her introductory remarks to *Eroticism and the Body Politic*.

14. "Finally touched by our prayers / and favorable to our ardent wishes / the sky returns the best of fathers / to the most loyal of children" (BN, "Ode sur le rétablissement de la Santé du Roy," quoted in *Rejouissances faites dans la ville de Soissons les 23 et 24 septembre 1744*, by M. l'abbé Portes, canon of the church of Laon, 34).

15. Thomas Kaiser examines in detail the staging of the king's recovery, as well as the notion of a love contract, in "Louis *LE BIEN-AIMÉ.*"

16. René Voyer d'Argenson, *Mémoires et journal inédit,* 2:296.

17. Changing attitudes toward women and the family in eighteenth-century France are discussed in Hunt, *Family Romance of the French Revolution;* Madelyn Gutwirth, *The Twilight of the Goddesses: Women and Representation in the French Revolutionary Era* (New Brunswick, N.J., 1992); Landes, *Women and the Public Sphere;* and Maza, *Private Lives and Public Affairs.*

18. Antoine, *Louis XV;* and Vignerie, "Le roi et le public." Michèle Fogel analyzes the transformation in royal ceremonies from the sixteenth to the eighteenth century in *Les cérémonies de l'information.* D'Argenson, in his assessment of Louis XV's character, repeatedly referred to "le goût du roi pour le mystère" (see *Mémoires et journal inédit,* 2:300). On *dévot* critiques of Louis XV, see Van Kley, *Religious Origins of the French Revolution,* 114–22, 160–70, 218–34.

19. Françoise Weil cites Bonafon's baptismal certificate from the parish registers of Versailles in *L'interdiction du roman,* 345. On the title *écuyer,* see Marion, *Dictionnaire des institutions de la France,* 197.

20. Kettering, "Household Service of Early Modern French Noblewomen." On domestic servants in eighteenth-century France, see Fairchilds, *Domestic Enemies;* and Maza, *Servants and Masters in Eighteenth Century France.* For the staffing of a royal household, see Kleinman, "Social Dynamics at the French Court."

21. See Kettering, "Household Service of Early Modern French Noblewomen," 64–65.

22. In the 1745 edition of the *Almanach Royal* the Princesse de Montauban is listed as one of the queen's "Dames d'Atours" (113).

23. Minet was the *souffleur* (prompter) for the Comédie-Française (Weil, *L'interdiction du roman,* 346).

24. Officials were convinced that someone had paid Damiens to commit his crime (see Van Kley, *Damiens Affair*).

25. AB 11582, fol. 80, interrogation of Marie-Magdeleine Bonafon by Marville, Bastille, 4 September 1745.

26. AB 11582, fol. 55, interrogation of Bonafon by Marville, Bastille, 29 August 1745.

27. Roger Chartier has written extensively on reading practices, the circulation of texts, and the reception of ideas in the Old Regime (see *Cultural Uses of Print in Early Modern France* and *Cultural History*). In addition, the work of Robert Darnton has alerted us to a world of readers and hack writers outside of the official republic of letters (see *Literary Underground* and *Forbidden Bestsellers*).

28. AB 11582, fol. 80, interrogation of Bonafon by Marville, Bastille, 4 September 1745.

29. The role of domestic servants as cultural intermediaries is examined by Robert Mandrou in "Culture populaire et savante: rapports et contacts," in Beauroy, Bertand, and Gargan, *The Wolf and the Lamb*. See also Maza, *Servants and Masters*.

30. Weil, *L'interdiction du roman*, 137, 151.

31. Paul Hammond has demonstrated how rhetorical familiarity could undermine absolutist ideology during the Stuart restoration (see Hammond, "The King's Two Bodies").

32. AB 11582, fol. 57, interrogation of Bonafon by Marville, Bastille, 29 August 1745.

33. I discuss such references at greater length in Graham, "Crimes of Opinion."

34. It is difficult to determine whether the crown's crackdown on the novel in the 1730s reflected concerns about women as authors or as readers, although it was undoubtedly both (see May, *Le dilemme du roman;* and Weil, *L'interdiction du roman*). Recent scholarship has examined the ways in which the creation of a literary canon in France actively worked to deny and exclude female authors, who had dominated novel production in the seventeenth century (see Dejean, *Tender Geographies;* and Ekstein, "Appropriation and Gender").

35. Weil, *L'interdiction du roman*, 121–38, 385. In addition to Weil, for a discussion of official attitudes toward the novel, see May, *Le dilemme du roman*, 75–105; and Minois, *Censure et culture sous l'Ancien Regime*.

36. AB 11582, fol. 80, interrogation of Bonafon by Marville, Bastille, 4 September 1745.

37. According to Weil, the vogue for allegorical novels, or *romans à applications,* peaked in 1745, when Bonafon published *Tanastès*. She notes that the keys accompanying the circulating manuscripts were not always supplied by the authors themselves (Weil, *L'interdiction du roman*, 151).

38. AB 11582, fol. 80, interrogation of Bonafon by Marville, Bastille, 4 September 1745.

39. Weil devotes an entire section to the publishing industry in Rouen (see *L'interdiction du roman*, 307–50).

40. AB 11582, fol. 77, interrogation of the Widow Ferrand by Marville, Bastille, 4 September 1745.

41. AB 11582, fols. 71–72, interrogation of Nicolas Dubuisson by Marville, Bastille, 2 September 1745.

42. AB 11582, fol. 56, interrogation of Bonafon by Marville, Bastille, 29 August 1745.

43. AB 11582, fol. 79, interrogation of Bonafon by Marville, Bastille, 4 September 1745.

44. AB 11582, fol. 115, interrogation of Bonafon by Marville, Bastille, 9 October 1745.

45. Ibid., fol. 116.

46. Dubuisson apparently unloaded copies of *Tanastès*, along with other samples of forbidden literature, on an acquaintance, the carpenter Guillaume Drouvoy. The police searched Drouvoy's apartment on 26 August 1745 and confiscated all the papers they found (AB 11582, fol. 34).

47. Marville to Maurepas, 29 June 1746, reprinted in Boislisle, *Lettres de Monsieur de Marville*, 3:8.

48. This more graphic and politically explicit pornography prevailed in the 1770s and 1780s (see the excerpt from *Anecdotes sur Madame du Barry* in Darnton, *Forbidden Bestsellers;* and Darnton's *Literary Underground*).

49. Quotations from *Tanastès* are cited in the text by part and page numbers.

50. Farge, *Subversive Words*, 107.

51. Paul Hammond has argued that the proliferation of scandal and gossip under Charles II in England was subversive because the control of means of representation passed from the king to his subjects ("The King's Two Bodies"). Roger Chartier suggests that desacralization is best understood as a process of banalization of kingship ("A Desacralized King," in *Cultural Origins of the French Revolution*, 111–35).

52. Jean de la Bruyère offers a classic example of this position in *Characters*.

53. Grosrichard, *Structure du sérail*, 52.

54. Montesquieu, *Persian Letters*. On despotism, see Richet, "Autour des origines idéologiques lointaines de la Révolution Française"; and Grosrichard, *Structure du sérail*.

55. Baker, "Public Opinion As Political Invention," esp. 178–85.

56. Maza, *Private Lives and Public Affairs*, esp. 111, 169–73, 279.

57. See Weil, "The Crown Has Fallen to the Distaff." Some recent work has focused on the depiction of Marie-Antoinette in prerevolutionary and revolutionary literature (see Lynn Hunt, "The Many Bodies of Marie Antoinette," and Sarah Maza, "The Diamond Necklace Affair Revisited, 1785–1786," in Hunt, *Eroticism and the Body Politic*, 108–31 and 63–89, respectively; and Revel, "Marie-Antoinette in Her Fictions").

58. Maza, *Private Lives and Public Affairs*, 279.

59. Ibid., 169–72.

60. D'Argenson supported this last point when he described the role of Marie Leczszynska at the court: "Son rang est un drapeau de ralliement, et depuis que le

roi a des maîtresses declarées, ceux qui crient au scandale s'attachent à elle, pour dé-plaire au Roi et à la favorite" (*Mémoires et journal inédit*, 2:331). Van Kley notes that sympathy for the queen was a distinguishing feature of *dévot* seditious utterances (see *Religious Origins of the French Revolution*, 186).

61. An interesting comparison can be drawn with the Queen Caroline affair in England in the early nineteenth century. Anna Clark has demonstrated that a de-fense of the queen's cause became a vehicle for popular participation in the political arena ("Queen Caroline and the Sexual Politics of Popular Culture in London, 1820"). In the same vein, Walter Laqueur has emphasized that Caroline "provided a shield behind which to defy and confront authority in relative safety" ("The Queen Caroline Affair," 421).

62. Maza, *Private Lives and Public Affairs*, 111.

63. The analysis in this paragraph was suggested to me by Lynn Hunt in her comments on my paper "A Bed of Misrule: Adultery and Authority in the Reign of Louis XV," presented at the Western Society for French History in Charlotte, N.C., 30 October–2 November 1996, and I thank her.

64. AB 11582, fol. 142, Bonafon to Marville, n.d.

65. For an exploration of the symbolic connections between intimacy and royal power in early modern England, see Starkey, "Representations through Intimacy."

66. AB 11582, fol. 201, Marville to Maurepas, 25 December 1746.

67. AB 11582, fol. 211, Maurepas to Mme Bourdier, 31 January 1747.

68. AB 11582, fol. 265, Bonafon to Berryer, received 1 January 1748.

69. Several historians have developed arguments about the emergence of auto-biographical and confessional literature in mid-eighteenth-century France. See, e.g., Chartier, *Passions of the Renaissance;* Lejeune, *On Autobiography;* and Méné-tra, *Journal of My Life.*

70. AB 11582, fol. 459, Bonafon to M. de Bonafon, Paris, 28 December 1754.

71. Koselleck, *Critique and Crisis.*

72. AB 11582, fol. 460, Bonafon to M. de Bonafon, Paris, 28 December 1754.

73. AB 11582, fol. 506, Bonafon to Lieutenant of Police Henri Baptiste Bertin de Bellisle, 18 January 1759.

74. AB 11582 fol. 499, Bonafon to Bertin de Bellisle, 2 December 1757.

75. Darnton, *Literary Underground*, 207–8.

76. Boutry, *De la cour de Versailles aux Bernardines de Moulins*, 10–11.

77. Sarah Hanley has published several articles on the links between the state building process and the enforcement of patriarchal family structure in early mod-ern France (see "Family and State in Early Modern France," in Boxer and Qua-taert, *Connecting Spheres*, 53–63; and "Engendering the State").

78. Sarah Maza discusses Louis XV's mistresses as an important precedent for

attitudes toward women in the public sphere in the last decades of the eighteenth century (see "Diamond Necklace Affair Revisited").

79. In his *Forbidden Bestsellers* Robert Darnton gives two examples of such texts and discusses the impact of political slander (137–66; see also Merrick, "Sexual Politics and Public Order in Late Eighteenth-Century France").

CHAPTER 3
The Lioness and the Ant

1. D'Argenson, *Mémoires et journal inédit*, 4:49.

2. The documents for this case are located in the Bibliothèque de l'Arsenal, AB 11729. There are scattered references in the following volumes of official correspondence as well: AB 12493, 12494, 12496, 12497, 12499, 12503, 12505, 12506, 12518, and 12527. The primary carton contains approximately five hundred pages and includes interrogations; depositions by witnesses, including Joseph Allègre, Antoine's brother, who was arrested briefly in connection with the affair; and copies of the anonymous letters that served as evidence of the alleged conspiracy, as well as letters written by Allègre during his incarceration.

3. For a discussion of the parlementary disputes, see Rogister, *Louis XV and the Parlement of Paris*; Swann, *Politics and the Parlement of Paris under Louis XV*; and Van Kley, *Damiens Affair*. For pamphlet literature, see Darnton, *Forbidden Bestsellers*; and Farge, *Subversive Words*.

4. Baker, *Inventing the French Revolution*, 167–99.

5. See Farge, *Subversive Words*, 156.

6. Antoine, *Louis XV*, 402–3; Browning, *War of Austrian Succession*; Farge, *Subversive Words*, 153–59.

7. See Antoine, *Louis XV*, 617–42; Egret, *Louis XV et l'opposition parlementaire*, 50–92; Marion, *Dictionnaire des institutions de la France*, 556–59; and Mousnier, *Institutions of France*, 2:611–19.

8. See Antoine, *Louis XV*, 617–42; and Rogister, *Louis XV and the Parlement of Paris*.

9. For a summary of these disputes, see Marion, *Dictionnaire des institutions de la France*, 474–75; Merrick, *Desacralization of the French Monarchy*, 49–104; Mousnier, *Institutions of France*, 2:611–17; and Van Kley, *Damiens Affair*, 36–165.

10. Van Kley, *Jansenists*; idem, *Damiens Affair*.

11. Farge, *Subversive Words*, 48–49; Merrick, *Desacralization of the French Monarchy*, 78–80, 99; Van Kley, *Damiens Affair*, 108–9. For a discussion of Jansenism's appeal to members of the popular classes, see Maire, *Les convulsionnaires de Saint-Médard*; and Kreiser, *Miracles, Convulsions, and Ecclesiastical Politics*.

12. Kaplan, *Famine Plot Persuasion,* 48.

13. For a reconstruction and analysis of this affair, see Farge and Revel, *Logic of a Crowd.*

14. Ibid., 115.

15. Here I am summarizing the argument in Dale Van Kley's important book *Religious Origins of the French Revolution.*

16. Farge and Revel make this point in their analysis of the incident (*Logic of a Crowd,* 41). For further analysis of the factions at the court and Pompadour's patronage network, which included Berryer, see Kaiser, "Madame de Pompadour and the Theaters of Power."

17. Kaplan, *Famine Plot Persuasion,* 46–49.

18. Farge, *Subversive Words,* 159.

19. Baker, "Public Opinion As Public Invention," 172.

20. I discuss this point in Graham, "Crimes of Opinion."

21. Farge, *Subversive Words,* 36.

22. AB 11729, fol. 67, Allègre to Louis XV from Versailles, 2 May 1750.

23. The following biographical data are based on Allègre's first interrogation by Lieutenant of Police Berryer, on 2 June 1750 (AB 11729, fols. 48–51).

24. The Fathers of the Christian Doctrine was a religious order founded in Avignon in 1593 by the Venerable César de Bus that received papal confirmation in 1598. The order continued to thrive after De Bus's death in 1607, occupying itself above all with educating the humble and illiterate residents of the surrounding countryside (*New Catholic Encyclopedia,* 1967 ed., s.v. "Bus, Cesar de, Ven."; *Dictionnaire d'histoire et de géographie ecclesiastiques,* 1938 ed., s.v. "Bus, César de").

25. Information about Allègre's pension is based both on his interrogation of 2 June 1750 and on some notes by Berryer's secretary, M. Duval, at the top of a letter from Allègre dated 21 November 1751 (AB 11729, fol. 147).

26. The following summary of Allègre's activities is based on information from two interrogations conducted by Berryer at the Bastille, on 2 June 1750 (AB 11729, fols. 48–51) and 8 June 1750 (AB 11729, fols. 54–56), as well as a voluntary declaration by Allègre on 3 March 1751 (AB 11729, fols. 180–81).

27. AB 11729, fols. 50–51, interrogation of 2 June 1750.

28. AB 11729, fol. 56, interrogation of 8 June 1750.

29. Thomas Kaiser explores the connections between Pompadour and the imposition of the *vingtième,* as well as the more general campaign to vilify her character by the *parti dévot,* in his article "Madame de Pompadour and the Theaters of Power."

30. AB 11729, fols. 180–81, interrogation of 3 March 1751.

31. AB 11729, fol. 181, interrogation of 3 March 1751.

32. AB 11729, fol. 161, letter from M. Moulars, 3 February 1751.

33. AB 11729, fol. 182, internal memorandum from Rochebrune, 19 March 1753.

34. AB 12518, fols. 51–53. Rochebrune recounted his efforts to locate some of Allègre's requests, including *Un traité d'arpentage et de navigation*, by Father Perenan, and *La théorie de la manoeuvre des vassaux*.

35. AB 11729, fol. 422.

36. AB 11729, fol. 165. The following summary is based on the copy of Allègre's essay located in his police dossier, fols. 165–68.

37. Information about Jean Danry is based on Quétel, *Escape from the Bastille*. Danry is a fascinating subject in his own right, and interested readers should consult Quétel's work, esp. 43–57, for an account of the escape. Latude is also discussed in Funck-Brentano, *La Bastille et ses secrets*, 173–230.

38. For definitions of lèse-majesté in French criminal law, see Church, *Richelieu*, 268–76; and Giesey, Haldy, and Millhorn, "Cardin Le Bret and Lese Majesty."

39. AB 11729, fol. 180.

40. Kaiser, "Madame de Pompadour and the Theaters of Power," 1031.

41. See Graham, "Crimes of Opinion."

42. Kaiser, "Madame de Pompadour and the Theaters of Power," 1030.

43. AB 11729, fol. 180, declaration of Antoine Allègre, Bastille, 3 March 1751.

44. AB 11729, fol. 63v, forged letter from M. de Maurepas to M. d'Albi, La Rochefoucauld.

45. Kaiser makes this point in exploring fears about Pompadour's theatrical enterprises at Versailles (see "Madame de Pompadour and the Theaters of Power," 1038–39; see also Maza, *Private Lives and Public Affairs*, 169–71, 263–311. For a comparative perspective, see Paul Hammond's analysis of the same themes in the reign of Charles II in "The King's Two Bodies").

46. Farge, *Subversive Words*, 159–60; Kaiser, "Madame de Pompadour and the Theaters of Power"; idem, "Louis LE BIEN-AIMÉ"; Guicciardi, "Between the Licit and the Illicit."

47. AB 11729, fol. 63, forged letter from La Rochefoucauld to Maurepas.

48. AB 11729, fol. 65r–v, forged letters between Maurepas and Monseigneur de Souillac.

49. AB 11729, fols. 65v, 66. The rest of this document is missing.

50. For a discussion of Louis XV's mistresses, see Antoine, *Louis XV*, 484–510.

51. The only systematic treatment of the *parti dévot* under the Old Regime is in Van Kley, *Religious Origins of the French Revolution*.

52. AB 11729, fol. 61, forged letter from Souillac.

53. AB 11729, fol. 61v, forged letter, alleged response from Maurepas to Souillac.

54. AB 11729, fol. 62v, forged letter from Souillac to Maurepas.

55. AB 11729, fol. 59, unsigned and undated letter found among Allègre's papers at the time of his arrest.

56. For a discussion of Damiens and his understanding of his mission, see Van Kley, *Damiens Affair*, 19–98. On the theme of sacrificial regicide, see Rétat, *L'attentat de Damiens*, 242–66; and Farge, *Subversive Words*, 133–50. This pattern would persist into the nineteenth century, reappearing during the Restoration in the case of Thomas Ignace Martin (see Boutry and Nassif, *Martin l'archange*).

57. AB 11729, fol. 50, interrogation of 2 June 1750.

58. AB 11729, fols. 67–68, letter from Allègre, 2 May 1750.

59. Farge, *Subversive Words*, 136.

60. AB 11729, fol. 68.

61. Arthur Herman analyzes the role of self-sacrifice in the language of fidelity among the nobility and the officeholders of the Old Regime in "Language of Fidelity." Sacrifice of life was linked to the idea that merit and devotion to the king had to be witnessed by other members of the court (see Smith, "Our Sovereign's Gaze").

62. AB 11729, fol. 128, Allègre to Pompadour, 26 October 1750, from the Bastille.

63. AB 11729, fol. 180, interrogation of 3 March 1751.

64. Ibid., fols. 180–81.

65. AB 11729, fols. 106–7, Allègre to d'Argenson, 19 August 1750.

66. AB 11729, fol. 72, anonymous letter signed "à Montpellier le 13 mai."

67. AB 11729, fols. 366–67, Allègre to d'Argenson, 11 August 1762.

68. AB 11729, fol. 362, Allègre to d'Argenson, 4 July 1761.

69. AB 11729, fol. 351, Allègre to d'Argenson, 12 February 1761.

70. Ibid., fol. 352.

71. AB 11729, fol. 229, Allègre to Pompadour, 4 April 1752. "Your château Bellevue near Sève, being situated on a hill, where it appears that there is not enough water to furnish all the embellishments you might desire; I have recently discovered in my readings of mathematics a hydraulic machine that I have the honor of proposing to construct for you . . . this machine is capable of raising water to whatever heights you desire. It is nonetheless very simple . . . it will cost very little to maintain it."

72. AB 11729, fol. 348, Allègre to Pompadour, 18 May 1760.

73. Goodman, *Criticism in Action*.

74. AB 11729, fol. 287, Allègre to Berryer, 5 August 1753.

75. Besides Goodman's discussion in *Criticism in Action*, two articles that address

the role of despotism in eighteenth-century French political debate are Richet, "Autour des origines idéologiques lointaines de la Révolution Française"; and Venturi, "Oriental Despotism." For an analysis of despotism's place in the eighteenth-century imagination, see Grosrichard, *Structure du sérail.*

76. AB 11729, fol. 310, Allègre to Berryer, 14 December 1755.

77. AB 11729, fol. 286, Allègre to Berryer, 5 August 1753.

78. Ibid.

79. AB 11729, fol. 310, Allègre to Berryer, 14 December 1755.

80. Ibid.

81. D'Argenson, for example, confirms this perception in his *Mémoires* on 23 January 1751 when he notes, "Rien n'est si dangereux que l'usage que l'on fait de Monsieur Berryer, lieutenant de police, qui rend compte à cette dame [Pompadour] de tout ce qui se passe et se dit à Paris."

82. AB 11729, fol. 310, Allègre to Berryer, 14 December 1755.

83. Chartier, *Cultural Origins of the French Revolution,* 111–35.

84. See Lebigre, *La justice du roi,* 70.

85. AB 11729, fol. 354, Allègre to Sartine, 12 February 1761.

86. One of the nine muses in Greek mythology, Urania was the muse of astronomy and celestial forces. She provided comfort to mortals by pointing to the harmony of heaven (Edith Hamilton, *Mythology* [Boston, 1942], 40).

87. AB 11729, fol. 397, Allègre to Controller General Machault d'Arnouville, 23 July 1763.

88. AB 11729, fol. 348, Allègre to Louis XV, 28 July 1763.

89. AB 11729, fol. 398, Allègre to Machault, 28 July 1763.

90. Ibid.

91. Ibid., fol. 399.

92. AB 11729, fol. 411, medical report submitted by Doctor Boyer, 30 June 1764.

93. AB 11729, fol. 412, Sartine to Saint Florentin.

94. AB 11729, fol. 415, report on prisoner's transfer by Inspector Roullier, 17 July 1764.

95. Ibid.

96. AB 11729, fol. 100, Allègre to M. Tournel, 20 August 1750.

CHAPTER 4

The Imagery of Regicide in the Mind
of Auguste Claude Tavernier

1. Two excellent studies of the Damiens affair complement each other more than they overlap: Rétat, *L'attentat de Damiens;* and Van Kley, *Damiens Affair.*

2. Farge discusses the connection between the Damiens affair and a surge in arrests for crimes of *mauvais discours* in *Subversive Words*, 161–75.

3. JDF 2076, fol. 108, police memorandum to Saint Florentin, 25 August 1757, concerning the case of Claude Mirlavaud and Claude Horsel. Mirlavaud falsely accused Horsel of uttering *mauvais propos* during a dinner party at his son's house. Mirlavaud was apparently motivated by an outstanding dispute over land Horsel had prevented him from acquiring. The documents for this case can be found in JDF 2076 and AN X2B 1019.

4. The case of the imprisoned soldier Felix Ricard vividly illustrates this point. Ricard lied about a plot to kill Louis XV in order to secure his release from prison. He was sentenced to death and broken on the wheel when his crime was revealed. Documents for the Ricard affair are in JDF 2078–79, AB 11979, and AN X2B 1362.

5. The relevant documents for this case are AB 12058 and 12059. Additional references in Sartine's correspondence include AB 12500, fol. 15; AB 12502, fols. 6, 12, 163, 257; AB 12503, fols. 62, 157; AB 12504, fol. 257; and AB 12514, fol. 72.

6. The following cases clearly illustrate the ways in which individuals sought to manipulate official concern through false threats and accusations: AB 11979, Alexandre Armand, arrested February 1759; AB 11979, Jean Breton, arrested March 1757; AB 11979, JDF 2074, Toussaint Courtin and Gaspard Ferlin, arrested July 1757; AN Y 15818B, Marie Anne Giroux, arrested April 1757; JDF 2076, AN X2B 1019, Claude Horsel and Claude Mirlavaud, arrested June 1757; AB 11979, JDF 2077, Claude Antoine François Paratre, arrested January 1757; AN Y 15813, Jean Quevillard, arrested February 1757; AB 11979, Joseph Rodier and Jean Antoine Fromonot, arrested June 1758; JDF 2073, 2077, AB 11979, AN X2B 1362, François Roger and Jean Mirault, arrested August 1757; AN Y 10204, JDF 2072, Charles Sourdeval and Bernard Heraut, arrested October 1758.

7. Arlette Farge has elaborated on the implications of imagining the king's death in *Subversive Words*, 132–37, and "La mort du roi et l'imaginaire collectif."

8. See Farge, *Subversive Words*, 22–53; Garrioch, "Parish Politics"; and Van Kley, *Religious Origins of the French Revolution*, 89–100, 108–14.

9. Van Kley, *Religious Origins of the French Revolution*, 147–50. More detailed discussion of these conflicts and their impact on royal authority can be found in Antoine, *Louis XV*, 566–742; Baker, *Inventing the French Revolution;* Egret, *Louis XV et L'opposition parlementaire;* Merrick, *Desacralization of the French Monarchy;* Rogister, *Louis XV and the Parlement of Paris;* and Swann, *Politics and the Parlement of Paris under Louis XV.*

10. Dufort de Cheverny provides a wonderful description of this episode (see *Mémoires de Dufort de Cheverny*, 206–8).

11. This summary of France's role in the war is based on Riley, *The Seven Years War*.

12. Chaussinand-Nogaret, *Gens de Finance*, 59. Connections between Pompadour and the Pâris brothers are also discussed in Kaplan, *Famine Plot Persuasion*.

13. AB 12058, fol. 48, Nicolas and Marie Charlotte Tavernier to Sartine, n.d., requesting a *lettre de cachet* for their son.

14. AB 12058, fol. 31, police notes.

15. Ibid.

16. AB 12058, fol. 51, Nicolas Tavernier to Sartine, Paris, 19 March 1749.

17. AB 12058, fol. 58, police notes.

18. AB 12058, fol. 48, *mémoire* from Nicolas and Marie Charlotte Tavernier to Sartine, 1749, requesting that their son be locked away. Tavernier refers to his education at one point (see AB 12058, fol. 257, fragment of a *mémoire* addressed to M. Pâris-Duverney and written at some point after Tavernier's arrival at the Bastille in July 1759).

19. AB 12058, fol. 336, *mémoire* from Tavernier.

20. Van Kley, *Religious Origins of the French Revolution*, 170–80.

21. AB 12058, fol. 507, *mémoire* from Tavernier, "La Dévote des Jesuites de la rue St. Antoine et la Phitonisse," Bastille, 16 June 1761.

22. AB 12058, fol. 516v, "Suite de ma confession. Affaire des Tartuffes," 16 June 1761.

23. AB 12058, fol. 566, *mémoire* to Sartine, 20 September 1761. For a discussion of Freemasons and their connections to the Enlightenment, see Halevi, *Les loges maçonniques;* Jacob, *Living the Enlightenment;* and Koselleck, *Critique and Crisis*.

24. AB 12058, fol. 493, "Réflexions sur l'Affaire de Damiens," 25 November 1760.

25. AB 12058, fol. 229, Sartine to Saint Florentin, 3 May 1761.

26. AB 12058, fol. 467, "Papier à bruler après la lecture."

27. AB 12058, fol. 167, "Histoire abregée de Tavernier et Lussan."

28. AB 12058, fol. 266, letter from Lussan, 18 August 1759, from the Bastille.

29. AB 12058, fol. 102, undated declaration by Lussan.

30. AB 12058, fol. 327. In a letter of 24 September 1759 from the Bastille Lussan explained that it was "a Jesuitical father who advised me that it was better to risk the cruelest persecutions rather than to embrace the priesthood without a true calling because I would not be able to count on salvation in the afterlife: I thus decided to leave the seminary and returned to my mother's home and explained my dilemma."

31. AB 12058, fol. 111, letter from the marquis de Fénelon, Marseilles, 2 June 1759.

32. AB 15082, fol. 87, letter from Lussan, Ile Sainte-Marguerite, 22 March 1759.

33. AB 15082, fol. 96, letter from Lieutenant Latil, presumably to the maréchal de Belle-Isle, 7 April 1759.

34. AB 15082, fol. 92, Lussan to Lieutenant Latil, Ile Sainte-Marguerite, 1 April 1759.

35. AB 15082, fols. 96–97, Fénelon to Belle-Isle, 6 April 1759.

36. AB 15082, fols. 102–3, Tavernier to Fénelon, Ile Sainte-Marguerite, 19 May 1759.

37. AB 12058, fol. 104, deposition of Lussan by Major Robaud, Ile Sainte-Marguerite, 29 May 1759.

38. Ibid.

39. AB 12058, fols. 115–16, deposition of Lussan by Latil, Ile Sainte-Marguerite, 20 June 1759.

40. AB 12058, fols. 120–21, letter from Lussan, "Contenant quelques détails sur l'affaire," Ile Sainte-Marguerite, 23 June 1759.

41. AB 12058, fol. 130, deposition of Tavernier by Latil, Ile Sainte-Marguerite, 28 June 1759.

42. Woodbridge, *Revolt in Prerevolutionary France.*

43. AB 12058, fol. 133, deposition of Tavernier by Latil, Ile Sainte-Marguerite, 1 July 1759.

44. AB 12058, fol. 138, deposition of Tavernier by Latil, Ile Sainte-Marguerite, 2 July 1759.

45. AB 12058, fol. 151, letter from Latil, Ile Sainte-Marguerite, 4 July 1759.

46. AB 12058, fol. 159, letter from Latil, Ile Sainte-Marguerite, 28 July 1759.

47. AB 12058, fol. 184, interrogation of Lussan by Rochebrune, Bastille, 9–10 August 1759.

48. Ibid., fol. 185.

49. Ibid., fol. 191.

50. Ibid. On the Cinq Mars conspiracy against Richelieu under Louis XIII, see Church, *Richelieu and Reason of State.*

51. AB 12058, fol. 265, letter from Lussan, Bastille, 18 August 1759.

52. AB 12058, fol. 269, Lussan to an unidentified cousin, Bastille, 14 August 1759.

53. Ibid., fol. 270.

54. Hunt, *Family Romance of the French Revolution;* Duncan, "Fallen Fathers." See also Merrick, "Fathers and Kings," 289.

55. AB 12058, fol. 324, letter from Lussan, September 1759.

56. AB 12058, fol. 211, interrogation of Tavernier by Rochebrune, Bastille, 14–16 August 1759.

57. Ibid., fol. 219.

58. Ibid., fol. 217.

59. Ibid., fol. 224.

60. Ibid., fol. 222.

61. AB 12058, fol. 496, police comments on Tavernier's *mémoire* of 20 December 1760.

62. For the history of *lettres de cachet*, see Farge and Foucault, *Le désordre des familles;* and Quétel, *De par le Roy*. Maza discusses the campaign to abolish the practice in the 1770s in *Private Lives and Public Affairs*, 279–81.

63. Lynn Hunt, "The Rise and Fall of the Good Father," in *Family Romance of the French Revolution*, 17–52.

64. AB 12058, fol. 454, "Plan de la conspiration formée par un prisonnier," 20 September 1760.

65. AB 12058, fol. 507, *mémoire* from Tavernier, "La Dévote des Jesuites de la rue St. Antoine et la Phitonisse," Bastille, 16 June 1761.

66. See Gordon, "Philosophy, Sociology, and Gender in the Enlightenment Concept of Public Opinion."

67. AB 12058, fol. 126v, "mémoire à bruler" to Sartine.

68. Ibid.

69. AB 12058, fol. 424, Tavernier to M. Pâris Duverney and to M. de Monmartel, Bastille, 13 April 1760.

70. AB 12058, fol. 333, undated *mémoire* with misnumbered pages.

71. Ibid.

72. Ibid., fol. 491, "Réflexions sur l'affaire de Damiens," 25 November 1760.

73. Ibid., fol. 467, "Papier à bruler après la lecture."

74. Hunt, *Family Romance of the French Revolution*, 21–40.

75. AB 12058, fol. 454, "Plan de la conspiration formée par un prisonnier," 20 September 1760.

76. Ibid.

77. AB 12058, fol. 126v, "Mémoire à bruler après la lecture."

78. Ibid.

79. AB 12058, fol. 336, undated *mémoire* with misnumbered pages.

80. AB 12058, fol. 356, interrogation of Tavernier by Rochebrune, Bastille, 16 October 1759.

81. Ibid., fols. 353–54.

82. AB 12058, fol. 127r, "mémoire à bruler" to Sartine.

83. AB 12058, fol. 256, undated *mémoire* from Tavernier to Sartine.

84. AB 12058, fol. 526, *mémoire*, 17 July 1761.

85. AB 12058, fol. 572, letter from Tavernier, Bastille, 19 December 1761.

86. Farge, *Subversive Words*, 102–3.

87. AB 12058, fol. 492, "Réflexions sur l'Affaire de Damiens," 25 November 1760.

88. Ibid., fol. 491.

89. Ibid.

90. Ibid.

91. Ibid.

92. Voltaire, *Histoire du Parlement*, 7.

93. AB 12058, fol. 127r.

94. Voltaire, *Histoire du Parlement*, 93.

95. AB 12503, fol. 62, Sartine to the major of the Bastille, 1 May 1760.

96. Hunt, *Family Romance of the French Revolution*, 40.

97. AB 12058, fol. 383, letter from Tavernier, 20 September 1760.

98. Keith Baker has explored the ways philosophes, especially Montesquieu, relied on comparisons between France and England in their analysis of the monarchy and the role of public opinion in political debate (see Baker, "Public Opinion As Political Invention"). Voltaire had set the precedent for this type of critical analysis in 1734, when he published his *Letters on England*.

99. AB 12059, fol. 3, letter from Tavernier, Bastille, 15 January 1762.

CHAPTER 5
Staging Loyalty

1. Documents for La Chaux are located at the Bibliothèque de l'Arsenal, AB 12170, and at the Archives Nationales, Y 10235.

2. AB 12170, fol. 6, report submitted by Inspector Beauvillegaudin, 9 January 1762.

3. Riley, *The Seven Years War*. For an analysis of the war's negative impact on the king's image and the crown's efforts to respond, see Rombouts, "Art As Propaganda in Eighteenth-Century France."

4. Antoine, *Louis XV*, 790–800; Hudson, "Parlementary Crisis of 1763 in France and Its Consequences"; Swann, *Politics and the Parlement of Paris under Louis XV*, 218–50.

5. Van Kley, *Jansenists*, esp. 163–207. See also Egret, "Le procès des Jesuites."

6. The impact of Jansenism on the Parisian popular classes in the first half of the eighteenth century has been effectively demonstrated (see Farge, *Subversive Words*, 22–53; Garrioch, "Parish Politics"; Kreiser, *Miracles, Convulsions, and Ecclesiastical Politics;* and Maire, *Les convulsionnaires de Saint-Médard*). On the links between the

legal battles and popular perceptions of the monarchy, see Van Kley, *Religious Origins of the French Revolution,* 180–90.

7. Van Kley, *Jansenists,* 148. See also Dominique Julia and Daniel Milo, "Les ressources culturelles," in Revel, *L'espace français,* 375–406.

8. For information on the social composition of the military under the Old Regime, see Corvisier, *Armies and Societies in Europe;* and idem, "Hiérarchie militaire et hiérarchie sociale."

9. On the Maison Militaire du Roi, see Forrest, *Soldiers of the French Revolution,* 26–30; and Marion, *Dictionnaire des institutions de la France,* 352–56.

10. There was some confusion concerning the precise date of La Chaux's conversion. In the second part of his interrogation of 24 January 1762 he asserted that he had converted in October 1761. However, in an examination one day later he changed the date to May 1760. Since the police referred to a certificate of conversion from the bishop of Amiens dated 3 October 1761, found among La Chaux's papers, I am inclined to rely on that as an indication of the correct date.

11. On attitudes toward Protestants in eighteenth-century France, see Bien, *Calas Affair,* 43–76; Van Kley, *Religious Origins of the French Revolution,* 151–66; and Woodbridge, *Revolt in Prerevolutionary France.*

12. Van Kley traces the rapprochement between the Protestant and Jansenist causes in *Religious Origins of the French Revolution,* 154–56.

13. AN Y 10235, interrogation of La Chaux by Commissioner Le Noir, Châtelet, 24 January 1762.

14. AB 12170, fol. 85, interrogation of La Chaux by Sartine, Bastille, 14 January 1762.

15. AN Y 10235, interrogation of La Chaux before the Criminal Chamber of the Châtelet, 26 January 1762.

16. AB 12170, fols. 52–53, interrogation of La Chaux by Rochebrune, Bastille, 12 January 1762.

17. AB 12170, fol. 7, police report, 9 January 1762.

18. AN Y 10235, interrogation of La Chaux by Le Noir, Châtelet, 23 January 1762.

19. Ibid.

20. AN Y 10235, interrogation of La Chaux by Le Noir, Châtelet, 24 January 1762.

21. Ibid.

22. AB 12170, fol. 53, interrogation of La Chaux by Rochebrune, Bastille, 12 January 1762.

23. AN Y 10235, deposition of La Chaux by Commissioner Davour, Versailles, 7 January 1762.

24. AN Y 10235, interrogation of La Chaux by Le Noir, Châtelet, 24 January 1762.

25. Ibid.

26. Ibid.

27. I thank Jotham Parsons for his useful comments on an earlier version of this chapter.

28. AN Y 10235, deposition of Doctor Anger by Le Noir, 22 January 1762.

29. Arlette Lebigre discusses the importance of the defendant's confession in the criminal justice system of the Old Regime in *La justice du roi*, 178–211.

30. This line of reasoning shaped the trial of Robert François Damiens in 1757. Damiens was alternately suspected of working for the Jesuits and working for the Jansenists (see Van Kley, *Damiens Affair*. I discuss this same issue in Graham, "Crimes of Opinion").

31. AN Y 10235, interrogation of La Chaux by Le Noir, Châtelet, 4 February 1762.

32. AB 12170, fol. 85, interrogation of La Chaux by Sartine, Bastille, 14 January 1762.

33. AN Y 10235, interrogation of La Chaux by Le Noir, Châtelet, 23 January 1762.

34. AB 12170, fol. 86, interrogation of La Chaux by Sartine, Bastille, 14 January 1762.

35. Ibid.

36. AN Y 10235, interrogation of La Chaux by Le Noir, Châtelet, 23 January 1762.

37. AN Y 10235, interrogation of La Chaux by Le Noir, Châtelet, 25 January 1762.

38. Ibid.

39. AN Y 10235, interrogation of La Chaux by Le Noir, Châtelet, 23 January 1762.

40. See Farge, *Subversive Words*, 161–75; and Rétat, *L'attentat de Damiens*.

41. AN Y 10235, interrogation of La Chaux by Le Noir, Châtelet, 23 January 1762.

42. AN Y 10235, interrogation of La Chaux by Le Noir, Châtelet, 26 January 1762.

43. Merrick, *Desacralization of the French Monarchy;* Van Kley, *Religious Origins of the French Revolution*, 15–49. For discussions of traditional theories of kingship in early modern Europe, see Bloch, *The Royal Touch*, and Kantorowicz, *The King's Two Bodies;* more recent works are Boureau, *Le simple corps du roi*, and Giesey, *Royal Funeral Ceremony in Renaissance France*.

44. AN Y 10235, interrogation of La Chaux by Le Noir, Châtelet, 24 January 1762.

45. Ibid.

46. On royal mercy, see Andrews, *System of Criminal Justice*, 394–409.

47. Ibid., 394–95. For a discussion of royal mercy in the sixteenth century see Davis, *Fiction in the Archives*, esp. 52–57; and Smithers, "St. Bartholomew's Day Massacre and Images of Kingship in France."

48. The last chapter of Yves Marie Bercé's *Le roi caché* suggests that the appeal of royal mercy continues even today.

49. AN Y 10235, interrogation of La Chaux by Le Noir, Châtelet, 24 January 1762.

50. Ibid.

51. AB 12170, fol. 97, Saint Florentin to Sartine, 16 January 1762.

52. Barbier, *Chronique de la régence et du règne de Louis XV*, 8:5.

53. AB 12170, fol. 97, Saint Florentin to Sartine, 16 January 1762.

54. Andrews, *System of Criminal Justice*, 59, 383–86.

55. AB 12170, fol. 185, police report submitted by Inspector Bouton, 1 February 1762. The parlementary sentence, of the same date, can be found in AN X2B 1027.

56. Church, *Richelieu*, 113.

57. The discussion of Cardin Le Bret draws primarily from Giesey, Haldy, and Millhorn, "Cardin Le Bret and Lese Majesty." Church also considers Le Bret in *Richelieu*, 268–76.

58. See Church, *Richelieu*, 274; and Ranum, "Lèse-Majesté Divine."

59. Andrews, *System of Criminal Justice*, 296–306.

60. AN X2B 1027, Parlement's decree against La Chaux, 1 February 1762.

61. Rétat, *L'attentat de Damiens*, 101–44, 340–46.

62. Arlette Farge has described the rites of punishment and execution in the Old Regime in *Fragile Lives*, 177–204. See also Lebigre, *La justice du roi*.

63. AB 12170, fol. 195, police report sent to Sartine, 4 February 1762.

64. Barbier, *Chronique de la régence et du règne de Louis XV*, 8:7.

65. On Old Regime criminal law, see Andrews, *System of Criminal Justice;* Bée, "Le spectacle de l'exécution"; Kaufmann, "Critique of Criminal Justice"; and Strayer, "*Lettres de Cachet* and Social Control in the *Ancien Régime*."

66. AN Y 10235, parlementary indictment including complaint and ruling of 21 January 1762.

67. AN X2B 1027.

CHAPTER 6
"A King of Beggars"

1. AB 12395, fol. 169, Pierre Denis de La Rivoire, unsigned letter "To the King of Unhappy France," late March 1770.

2. AB 12395, fol. 177, La Rivoire, undated letter "To the King Himself."

3. The documents for this case are located at the Bibliothèque de l'Arsenal in the Archives de la Bastille, dossiers 12395 and 12513.

4. Van Kley, *Religious Origins of the French Revolution*, 210–18.

5. For a discussion of individuals arrested in the aftermath of Maupeou's coup, see Dupieux, "L'agitation parisienne"; and Farge, *Subversive Words*, 184–92.

6. AB 12395, fol. 2, internal police memorandum concerning La Rivoire's dossier.

7. Swann, *Politics and the Parlement of Paris under Louis XV*, 315–23.

8. The following summary is based on Kaplan, *La Bagarre*, 1–25. The incident is also described by Farge in *Fragile Lives*.

9. Kaplan, *Bread, Politics, and Political Economy*, 2:491–676.

10. Kaplan, *Famine Plot Persuasion*, 58–61.

11. A general introduction to French finances in the eighteenth century is provided by Bosher, *French Finances;* as well as Riley, *The Seven Years War*. See also Marion, *Histoire financière de la France;* and Guery, "Les finances de la monarchie française."

12. On the crisis of 1770, see Antoine, *Louis XV*, 945–49; Swann, *Politics and the Parlement of Paris under Louis XV*, 286–90; and Velde and Weir, "Financial Market and Government Debt Policy in France."

13. Swann, *Politics and the Parlement of Paris under Louis XV*, 346–50. See also Antoine, *Louis XV*, 957–82; Doyle, "Parlements of France"; and Egret, *Louis XV et l'opposition parlementaire*. On the Maupeou crisis, see Echeverria, *Maupeou Revolution;* and more recently, Van Kley, "Religious Origins of the Patriot and Ministerial Parties in Pre-Revolutionary France."

14. Information about La Rivoire's family and background is based on the transcriptions of his first interrogation by Inspector Mutel, Bastille, 2 May 1771 (AB 12395, fols. 18–21). His descriptions of his physical maladies were vague, yet he consistently described them as digestive disorders, for example: "Il y a dix ans qu'il a quitté sa charge pour raison de santé: estomac derangé, dissenterie, et maladie de genre nerveux dont il n'est que peu soulagé" (AB 12395, fol. 156).

15. Bell, *Lawyers and Citizens*, 31–32.

16. AB 12395, fol. 18, interrogation of La Rivoire by Mutel, Bastille, 2 May 1771.

17. Ibid., fol. 20.

18. For an introduction to forms of capitalism in Old Regime France, see Taylor, "Types of Capitalism in Eighteenth-Century France."

19. According to Marcel Marion, the Châtelet contained a total of 1,550 offices "qui conféraient la noblesse personelle après dix ans de service, la noblesse transmissible après quarante (ou après vingt si les officiers décédaient revêtus de leurs offices)" (see Marion, *Dictionnaire des Institutions de la France*, 88–90).

20. This description of Old Regime legal culture is based on Bell, *Lawyers and Citizens*, 21–40.

21. AB 12395, fol. 18, interrogation of La Rivoire by Mutel, Bastille, 2 May 1771.

22. Bell, *Lawyers and Citizens*, 31, 153–55; Maza, "Le tribunal de la nation"; idem, *Private Lives and Public Affairs*.

23. AB 12395, fol. 82, undated letter from La Rivoire, "Memoire to be consulted with the agreement of Monsieur the Lieutenant General of Police."

24. AB 12395, fol. 48, La Rivoire to Sartine, Bastille, 16 May 1771.

25. AB 12395, fol. 21, interrogation of La Rivoire by Mutel, Bastille, 2 May 1771.

26. For an analysis of the *Causes célèbres*, see Lüsebrink, *Kriminalität und Literatur*.

27. On the case of Martin Guerre, see Davis, *Return of Martin Guerre*.

28. AB 12395, fol. 69, testimony of the *maîtres écrivains*.

29. AB 12395, fol. 82, undated letter from La Rivoire, "Mémoire to be consulted with the agreement of Monsieur the Lieutenant General of Police."

30. AB 12395, f. 22, letter from La Rivoire, 3 May 1771.

31. AB 12395, fol. 80, La Rivoire to Sartine, 20 May 1771.

32. AB 12395, fol. 82, undated letter from La Rivoire, "Mémoire to be consulted with the agreement of Monsieur the Lieutenant General of Police."

33. AB 12395, fol. 31, undated letter, Louis Etienne de La Rivoire to Sartine.

34. AB 12395, fol. 32, letter from La Rivoire to M. Gobron, 8 May 1771.

35. AB 12395, fol. 47, La Rivoire to Sartine, 16 May 1771.

36. AB 12395, fol. 169, unsigned letter "To the King of Unhappy France," late March 1770.

37. AB 12395, fol. 31, Louis Etienne de La Rivoire to Sartine, 8 May 1771.

38. AB 12395, fol. 87, letter from Louis Etienne de La Rivoire, 25 May 1771.

39. AB 12395, fol. 110, undated letter, La Rivoire to "Monseigneur le Chancelier et garde des Sceaux."

40. AB 12395, fol. 93, La Rivoire to Sartine, 10 June 1771.

41. AB 12395, fols. 114–15, La Rivoire to Sartine, 13 August 1771.

42. AB 12395, fol. 118, La Rivoire to Sartine, 2 September 1771.

43. AB 12395, fol. 121, La Rivoire to Sartine, 5 September 1771.

44. Ibid.

45. AB 12395, fol. 123, letter from La Rivoire, 7 September 1771.

46. AB 12395, fol. 130, La Rivoire to Sartine, 12 September 1771.

47. Habermas, *Structural Transformation of the Public Sphere;* Koselleck, *Critique and Crisis.* Dena Goodman has analyzed the two arguments in relation to one another in her incisive article "Public Sphere and Private Life."

48. AB 12395, fols. 134–35, La Rivoire to Sartine, 14 September 1771.

49. AB 12395, fols. 130–31, La Rivoire to Sartine, 12 September 1771.

50. AB 12395, fol. 52, "La Queue du Chat."

51. Joan Landes discusses the charges leveled against the court and the nobility in *Women and the Public Sphere.* Littré defines *mollesse* as a temperamental "défaut de résistance" (lack of resistance). Supplemental definitions include: (1) "manque de vigueur et de fermété dans le caractère, dans la conduite" (lack of vigor and firmness in character and conduct); and (2) "delicatesse d'une vie effeminé, moeurs effeminés" (delicacy associated with an effeminate lifestyle, effeminate manners) (*Dictionnaire de la langue française,* 1873 ed., s.v. "mollesse").

52. Robert Darnton discusses the symbolics of cats in the early modern psyche in "The Great Cat Massacre," in his book by the same name.

53. AB 12395, fol. 53, unsigned letter, late November 1770.

54. AB 12395, fol. 66, unsigned and undated letter.

55. Ibid. The term *muets* was a reference to the servants of the ancient Ottoman sultans who were charged with carrying out summary executions and who could only express themselves through sign language. For the definition of *muet,* see *Trésor de la langue française,* 1985 ed., s.v. "muet."

56. See Montesquieu's description of monarchy in *Spirit of the Laws,* vol. 1, bks. 2–4; and Keohane, *Philosophy and the State in France,* 376–415. On judicial Jansenism, see Van Kley, *Religious Origins of the French Revolution,* 203–18, 249–90.

57. AB 12395, fol. 63, unsigned, undated letter "To the King Himself."

58. Ibid.

59. Ibid.

60. AB 12395, fol. 190, unsigned, undated *mémoire* "To the King if there is One or There is not One Left."

61. On sacred kingship, see Bloch, *The Royal Touch;* and Kantorowicz, *The King's Two Bodies.* For the coronation ceremony, see *Le sacre des rois.* For a discussion of the role of family values in eighteenth-century French political culture, see Maza, "Luxury, Morality, and Social Change."

62. AB 12395, fol. 164, undated, unsigned letter.

63. AB 12395, fol. 195, unsigned, undated letter "To the King and all his trouble-makers and adherents." On judicial Jansenism, see Van Kley, *Religious Origins of the French Revolution*, 204–14.

64. AB 12395, fol. 161, unsigned, unfinished letter "To the King Himself."

65. Baker, "Public Opinion As Political Invention," 167–99.

66. AB 12395, fol. 169, unsigned letter "To the King of Unhappy France," late March 1770.

67. Ibid.

68. Ibid., fol. 170.

69. AB 12395, fol. 172, unsigned letter, 15 May 1770.

70. AB 12395, fol. 195, unsigned, undated letter "To the King and all his trouble-makers and adherents."

71. Steven Kaplan has done extensive research on these problems (see *Famine Plot Persuasion*). For a discussion of contemporary attitudes toward the *gens de finance,* Guy Chaussinand-Nogaret's compact study *Gens de finance* is helpful.

72. AB 12395, fol. 167, unsigned letter "To the King in His Councils," 10 November 1770.

73. AB 12395, fol. 171, unsigned letter, 15 May 1770.

74. Ibid., fol. 172.

75. This line of reasoning is strongly reminiscent of d'Argenson's concept of how the kingdom should be administered on a local level by magistrates, with the king serving as an overseer (see Keohane, *Philosophy and the State in France,* 384–85. On *patriote* resistance to Maupeou's reforms, see Echeverria, *Maupeou Revolution,* 36–123; Egret, *Louis XV et l'opposition parlementaire;* and Doyle, "Parlements of France").

76. Gail Bossenga, "Taxes," in Furet and Ozouf, *Critical Dictionary of the French Revolution,* 582–89.

77. AB 12395, fol. 195, unsigned, undated letter "To the King and all his trouble-makers and adherents."

78. Keith Baker discusses the reliance on a language of classic republicanism in his essay "A Classical Republican in Eighteenth-Century Bordeaux: Guillaume-Joseph Saige," in *Inventing the French Revolution,* 133–39. See also Echeverria, *Maupeou Revolution;* and Egret, *Louis XV et l'opposition parlementaire.*

79. For a discussion of the pamphlet literature circulating during the Maupeou crisis, see Bell, *Lawyers and Citizens,* 138–63; Hudson, "In Defense of Reform"; Van Kley, *Religious Origins of the French Revolution,* 254–74; and idem, "The Religious Origins of the Patriot and Ministerial Parties in Pre-Revolutionary France."

80. AB 12395, fol. 204, unsigned, undated letter "To the King Himself."

81. AB 12395, fol. 164, unsigned, undated letter.

82. AB 12395, fol. 175, unsigned, undated letter "To the King Himself."

83. For the ceremony of the *sacre*, see Jackson, *Vive le roi!* and Vignerie, "Les serments du sacre des rois de France à l'epoque moderne et plus spécialement le 'serment du royaume,'" in *Le sacre des rois*, 205–17; and Bayard, *Sacres et couronnements royaux.*

84. AB 12395, fol. 161, unfinished letter "To the King Himself."

85. AB 12395, fol. 187, unsigned, undated letter "To the King."

86. Van Kley, *Religious Origins of the French Revolution*, 254–62.

87. AB 12395, fol. 178, unsigned, undated letter "To the King in his Council."

88. Ibid.

89. AB 12395, fol. 164, undated letter "To the King Himself."

90. Ibid.

91. AB 12395, fol. 199, letter "To the King Himself."

92. AB 12395, fol. 190, unsigned, undated letter "To the King if there is One."

93. AB 12395, fol. 199, unsigned, undated letter "To the King."

94. AB 12395, fol. 177, letter "To the King."

95. Ibid.

96. AB 12395, fol. 174, unsigned letter "To the King Himself."

97. Ibid.

98. AB 12395, fol. 186, unsigned, undated letter "To the King."

99. AB 12395, fol. 82. Undated letter by La Rivoire, "Mémoire to be consulted with the agreement of Monsieur the Lieutenant General of Police."

Conclusion

1. AB 11979, fol. 73, interrogation of Jacques Roy by Commissioner François Simon Chastelus, Bastille, 8 January 1757.

2. Ibid.

3. Ibid., fol. 73.

4. This phrase is taken from Baker "Public Opinion As Political Invention," 178–85. The concept of unity in French political culture is central to Michel Winock's argument in *Parlez-moi de la France.*

5. Hunt, *Family Romance of the French Revolution.*

6. Winock, *Parlez-moi de la France*, 65, 123.

7. On the presidency under the Fifth Republic, see Revel, *L'absolutisme inefficace.* In 1989 a panel of writers debated the topic of constitutional reform, in particular the functions of the executive branch, in a forum organized by *Le Débat* (see Duhamel et al., "Sur la monarchie présidentielle").

8. Two books that offer a critical assessment of the efforts to commemorate the bicentennial are Hobsbawm, *Echoes of the Marseillaise;* and Kaplan, *Farewell, Revolution.*

9. *Le Nouvel Observateur,* January 1993.

10. Alan Riding, "It's a Little Late, but Still, Bouquets for Louis XVI," *New York Times,* 22 January 1993.

11. Winock, *Parlez-moi de la France,* 107.

12. Ibid., 124.

13. Bercé, *Le roi caché.*

14. See above, n. 7, as well as Jeambar et al., "Mitterand"; and Winock, *Parlez-moi de la France,* 107–33.

15. To cite one example of this language: "Le train de vie présidentiel même a d'ailleurs atteint les sommets d'un luxe souvent indécent, où la satisfaction néronienne des caprices personnels de l'homme va très au-délà du faste qu'implique naturellement la fonction de chef d'Etat, à condition qu'il ne soit pas étendu à la vie privée" (The style of presidential life itself, moreover, has attained often indecent summits of luxury, where the Neronian satisfaction of the personal whims of the man far exceeds the ostentatious display naturally associated with the function of the head of state, on the condition that it not be extended to the realm of personal life) (Revel, *L'absolutisme inefficace,* 99). For an analysis of the attacks leveled against Marie-Antoinette in the prerevolutionary pamphlet literature, see Hunt, "The Many Bodies of Marie-Antoinette"; and Revel, "Marie-Antoinette in Her Fictions," 111–29.

16. Craig R. Whitney, "La Ministre? Over the Immortals' Dead Bodies," *New York Times,* 1 July 1998.

BIBLIOGRAPHY

· ❧ ·

Notes on the
Bibliography

The research for this book draws on three collections of police archives. Research in police archives fosters a taste for detective work. The desired information is generally available, but it takes effort, instinct, and a bit of luck to locate it. By focusing on a specific type of crime, *mauvais discours,* within a fixed period of time, 1744–74, I managed to surmount some of these obstacles.

The Bibliothèque Nationale's Collection Joly de Fleury comprises twenty-five hundred volumes of primarily administrative and judicial records. The collection is indexed in A. Molinier's *Inventaire sommaire de la Collection Joly de Fleury.* I consulted those volumes that contain reports of individuals arrested for *mauvais discours* during and after the Damiens affair. They include a significant amount of internal correspondence between Parisian authorities and provincial subordinates concerning procedures for arrest and instructions for investigations. They also include official transcriptions of criminal interrogations and depositions.

The most extensive phase of research concentrated on the Archives de la Bastille, located in the Bibliothèque de l'Arsenal in Paris. These police reports are arranged in cartons chronologically and alphabetically. An invaluable resource for this collection is the tenth volume of François Ravaisson's catalog of the Bibliothèque de l'Arsenal. Ravaisson provides an inventory of the Archives de la Bastille, which allows one to identify cases by subject matter, name, or date fairly rapidly. In addition, Ravaisson includes a brief description of particularly important cases.

Finally, there are Series X and Series Y, located at the Archives Nationales. The X series contains the records of the Parlement of Paris, the highest court in the kingdom. This is where one finds trial proceedings and criminal sentences. The Y series contains documents generated by the various officers attached to the Châtelet, the principal royal jurisdiction in Paris. It includes the papers of the Paris police commissioners. The Y series, which has never been cataloged, is arranged by jurisdictional divisions and chronology. I used a technique of selective sampling, surveying blocks of criminal reports for *mauvais discours* at five moments in the reign of Louis XV. The five moments correspond to the dates of the cases discussed in chapters 2–6.

In the bibliography that follows I indicate the range of documents consulted in the different collections. Specific references in the notes provide source information for the cases discussed. In several instances documents for a single case were scattered among different collections.

Primary Sources

LIBRARIES AND ARCHIVES

Bibliothèque Nationale

Anonymes: pamphlets concerning the ceremonies
  celebrating the king's recovery in 1744.
Collection Delamare. MSS 21722, 21750.
Collection De Vinck. Vol. 1, Ancien Régime.
Collection Hennin. Vols. 97–119.
Collection Joly De Fleury. Vols. 2068–79.
Manuscrits Français. MSS 7667, 10983, 12253.

Bibliothèque de l'Arsenal

Archives de la Bastille. Cartons 10155–70,
  10315, 10319, 11563–12444.
Manuscrits. MS 6104.

Bibliothèque Historique de la Ville de Paris

Papiers Marville. MSS 719–21.

Archives Nationales

Series X:
registers and trial records of the Parlement of Paris.
X2A.
X2B.

Series Y

Papers of the Paris police commissioners, 10719–17623.
Records of the Grand Criminel for the years 1744–74, 10103–351.

Archives de la Préfecture de Police de Paris

Series AA. Cartons 4–8. Records of prisoners detained in 1660–1756.

JOURNALS AND OTHER
PUBLISHED MATERIALS

Barbier, Edmond-Jean François. *Chronique de la régence et du règne de Louis XV.* 8 vols. Paris, 1866.

Bonafon, Mlle de. *Tanastès.* [Rouen], 1745.

D'Argenson, René Voyer. *Mémoires et journal inédit du Marquis D'Argenson.* 5 vols. Paris, 1857–58.

————

Secondary Sources

Abbiateci, André, François Billacois, Yvonne Bongert, Nicole Castan, Yves Castan, and Porphyre Petrovitch. *Crimes et criminalité en France, XVIIe–XVIIIe siècles.* Cahiers des Annales, no. 33. Paris, 1971.

Andrews, Richard Mowery. *The System of Criminal Justice.* Vol. 1 of *Law, Magistracy, and Crime in Old Regime Paris, 1735–1789.* Cambridge, 1994.

Antoine, Michel. *Louis XV.* Paris, 1989.

Apostilides, Jean-Marie. *Le prince sacrifié: Théâtre et politique au temps de Louis XIV.* Paris, 1985.

————. *Le roi-machine: Spectacle et politique au temps de Louis XIV.* Paris, 1981.

Baker, Keith. *Inventing the French Revolution.* Cambridge, 1991.

————, ed. *The Political Culture of the Old Regime.* Vol. 1 of *The French Revolution and the Creation of Modern Political Culture.* Oxford, 1987.

Bayard, Jean Pierre. *Sacres et couronnements royaux.* Paris, 1984.

Beauroy, Jacques, Marc Bertand, and Edward T. Gargan, eds. *The Wolf and the Lamb: Popular Culture in France.* Saratoga, N.Y., 1976.

Bée, Michel. "Le spectacle de l'exécution dans la France de l'Ancien Régime." *Annales: Economies, sociétés, civilisations* 38 (July–August 1983): 843–63.

Bell, David A. *Lawyers and Citizens: The Making of a Political Elite in Old Regime France.* Oxford, 1994.

————. "The 'Public Sphere,' the State, and the World of Law in Eighteenth-Century France." *French Historical Studies* 17 (fall 1992): 912–34.

Benabou, Erica-Marie. *La prostitution et la police des moeurs au XVIIIe siècle.* Paris, 1987.

Bercé, Yves Marie. *Le roi caché.* Paris, 1990.

Bertaud, Jean Paul. *The Army of the French Revolution.* Trans. R. R. Palmer. Princeton, N.J., 1988.

Bien, David. *The Calas Affair.* Princeton, N.J., 1960.

Bloch, Marc. *The Royal Touch: Sacred Monarchy and Scrofula in England and France.* Trans. J. E. Anderson. London, 1973.

Bluche, François. *Les magistrats du Parlement de Paris.* Paris, 1986.

Boislisle, Arthur-Michel de, ed. *Lettres de M. de Marville, lieutenant-général de police au ministre Maurepas, 1742–1747.* 3 vols. Paris, 1896–1905.

Bosher, John. *French Finances, 1770–1795: From Business to Bureaucracy.* Cambridge, 1970.

Boureau, Alain. *Le simple corps du roi: L'impossible sacralité des souverains français, XVe–XVIIIe siècle.* Paris, 1988.

Boutier, Jean, Michel Cassan, and Nicole LeMaître. *Croyances, pouvoirs et société des Limousins aux Français.* Triegnac, 1988.

Boutry, Maurice. *De la cour de Versailles aux Bernardines de Moulins, 1745–1759.* Moulins, 1898.

Boutry, Philippe, and Jacques Nassif. *Martin l'archange.* Paris, 1985.

Boxer, Marilyn, and Jean H. Quartaert, eds. *Connecting Spheres: Women in the Western World, 1500 to the Present.* Oxford, 1987.

Brennan, Thomas. *Public Drinking and Popular Culture in Eighteenth-Century Paris.* Princeton, N.J., 1988.

Browning, Reed. *The War of the Austrian Succession.* New York, 1993.

Bryant, Lawrence. *The King and the City in the Parisian Royal Entry Ceremony.* Geneva, 1986.

Burgière, André. "Histoire d'une histoire: La naissance des Annales." *Annales: Economies, sociétés, civilisations* 34 (November–December 1979): 1344–59.

Cerruti, Simone. *La ville et les métiers: Naissance d'un langage corporatif: Turin, XVIIe–XVIIIe siècle.* Paris, 1990.

Chartier, Roger. *Cultural History: Between Practices and Representations.* Trans. Lydia G. Cochrane. Ithaca, N.Y., 1988.

———. *The Cultural Origins of the French Revolution.* Trans. Lydia G. Cochrane. Durham, N.C., 1991.

———. *The Cultural Uses of Print in Early Modern France.* Trans. Lydia G. Cochrane. Princeton, N.J., 1987.

———. *On the Edge of the Cliff: History, Language, and Practices.* Trans. Lydia G. Cochrane. Baltimore, Md., 1997.

———, ed. *The Passions of the Renaissance.* Trans. Arthur Goldhammer. Vol. 3 of *A History of Private Life,* ed. Philippe Ariés and Georges Duby. Cambridge, Mass., 1989.

———. *Pratiques de la lecture.* Paris, 1985.

Chartier, Roger, and Henri Jean Martin, eds. *Le livre triomphant, 1660–1789*. Vol. 2 of *Histoire de l'édition française*. Paris, 1984.

Chassaigne, Marc de. *La lieutenance générale de police de Paris*. 1906. Reprint. Geneva, 1975.

Chaussinand-Nogaret, Guy. *The French Nobility in the Eighteenth Century*. Trans. William Doyle. Cambridge, 1985.

———. *Gens de finance au XVIIIe siècle*. Paris, 1972.

Church, William F. *Richelieu and Reason of State*. Princeton, N.J., 1972.

Clark, Anna. "Queen Caroline and the Sexual Politics of Popular Culture in London, 1820." *Representations* 31 (summer 1990): 47–68.

Cobb, Richard. *The Police and the People*. Oxford, 1970.

Cobban, Alfred. *Old Regime and Revolution, 1715–1799*. Vol. 1 of *A History of Modern France*. New York, 1984.

Colley, Linda. "The Apotheosis of George III: Loyalty, Royalty, and the British Nation, 1760–1820." *Past and Present*, no. 102 (1984): 94–129.

———. *Britons: Forging the Nation*. New Haven, Conn., 1993.

Corvisier, André. *Armies and Societies in Europe, 1494–1789*. Trans. Abigail T. Siddall. Bloomington, Ind., 1979.

———. "Hiérarchie militaire et hiérarchie sociale à la veille de la Revolution." *Revue Internationale d'Histoire Militaire* 30 (1970): 77–91.

Cunningham, Hugh. "The Language of Patriotism, 1750–1914." *History Workshop* 12 (1981): 8–33.

Darnton, Robert. *The Corpus of Clandestine Literature*. Cambridge, Mass., 1991.

———. *The Forbidden Bestsellers of Pre-Revolutionary France*. New York, 1995.

———. *The Great Cat Massacre and Other Aspects of French Cultural History*. New York, 1984.

———. *The Literary Underground of the Old Regime*. Cambridge, Mass., 1982.

Davis, Natalie Zemon. *Fiction in the Archives: Pardon Tales and Their Tellers in Sixteenth-Century France*. Stanford, Calif., 1987.

———. *The Return of Martin Guerre*. Cambridge, 1983.

———. *Society and Culture in Early Modern France*. Stanford, Calif., 1975.

———. "Towards Mixtures and Margins." *American Historical Review* 97 (December 1992): 1409–16.

Dejean, Joan. *Tender Geographies: Women and the Origins of the Novel in France*. New York, 1991.

Delumeau, Jean. *L'aveu et le pardon: La difficulté de la confession, XIIIe–XVIIIe siècle*. Paris, 1990.

Doyle, William. "The Parlements of France and the Breakdown of the Old Regime, 1771–1788." *French Historical Studies* 6 (fall 1970): 415–58.

Dufort de Cheverny, Jean Nicolas. *Mémoires de Dufort de Cheverny: La cour de Louis XV.* Ed. Jean-Pierre Guicciardi. Paris, 1990.

Duhamel, Olivier, Maurice Duverger, Jacques Juillard, Philippe Raynaud, Bertrand Renouvin, Dominique Rousseau, Alain Touraine, Simone Veil, and Jean-François Revel. "Sur la monarchie présidentielle." *Le Débat,* no. 55 (1989): 22–47.

Duncan, Carol. "Fallen Fathers: Images of Authority in Pre–Revolutionary French Art." *Art History* 4 (1981): 186–202.

Dupieux, Paul. "L'agitation parisienne et les prisonniers de la Bastille en 1771–1772." *Bulletin de l'histoire de Paris et de l'Ile-de-France* 58 (1931): 45–57.

Durand, Yves, ed. *Hommage à Roland Mousnier: Clientèles et fidelités en Europe à l'epoque moderne.* Paris, 1981.

Echeverria, Durand. *The Maupeou Revolution: A Study in the History of Libertarianism in France, 1770–1774.* Baton Rouge, La., 1985.

———. "The Pre-Revolutionary Influence of Rousseau's 'Contrat Social.'" *Journal of the History of Ideas* 33 (1972): 543–60.

Egret, Jean. *Louis XV et l'opposition parlementaire, 1715–1774.* Paris, 1970.

———. "Le procès des Jesuites devant les Parlements de France, 1761–1770." *Revue Historique* 204 (1950): 1–27.

Ekstein, Nina. "Appropriation and Gender: The Case of Catherine Bernard and Bernard de Fontenelle." *Eighteenth-Century Studies* 30 (fall 1996): 59–80.

Fairchilds, Cissie. *Domestic Enemies: Servants and Their Masters in Old Regime France.* Baltimore, 1984.

Farge, Arlette. *Les fatigues de la guerre: XVIIIe siècle, Watteau.* Paris, 1996.

———. *Fragile Lives: Violence, Power, and Solidarity in Eighteenth-Century Paris.* Trans. Carol Shelton. Cambridge, Mass., 1993.

———. *Le goût de l'archive.* Paris, 1989.

———. "La mort du roi et l'imaginaire collectif, affaire Thorin (visions et crédulité), 1758." In *Le Père: Métaphore paternelle et fonctions du père: L'interdit, la filiation, la transmission,* preface by Marc Augé, 325–37. Paris, 1979.

———. *Subversive Words.* Trans. Rosemary Morris. University Park, Pa., 1995.

———. *Vivre dans la rue à Paris au XVIIIe siècle.* Paris, 1979.

———. *Le vol d'aliments à Paris au XVIIIe siècle.* Paris, 1974.

Farge, Arlette, and Michel Foucault. *Le désordre des familles: Lettres de cachet des Archives de la Bastille au XVIIIe siècle.* Paris, 1982.

Farge, Arlette, and Jacques Revel. *The Logic of a Crowd: Child Abductions in Paris in 1750*. Trans. Claudia Mieville. Cambridge, 1991.

Farge, Arlette, and André Zysberg. "Les théâtres de la violence à Paris au XVIIIe siècle." *Annales: Economies, sociétés, civilisations* 34 (September–October 1979): 984–1015.

Flandrin, Jean Louis. *Families in Former Times: Kinship, Household, and Sexuality*. Trans. Richard Southern. Cambridge, 1979.

Fogel, Michèle. *Les cérémonies de l'information dans la France du XVIe au milieu du XVIIIe siècle*. Paris, 1989.

Forrest, Alan. *The Soldiers of the French Revolution*. Durham, N.C., 1990.

Foucault, Michel. *Discipline and Punish: The Birth of the Prison*. Trans. Alan Sheridan. 1978; reprint, New York, 1995.

Funck-Brentano, Frantz. *La Bastille et ses secrets*. Paris, 1979.

Furet, François. *Interpreting the French Revolution*. Trans. Elborg Forster. Cambridge, 1981.

Furet, François, and Mona Ozouf. *A Critical Dictionary of the French Revolution*. Trans. Arthur Goldhammer. Cambridge, Mass., 1989.

———. "Fallait-il tuer Louis XVI?" *Le Nouvel Observateur*, 14 January 1993, 4–11.

Garrioch, David. *Neighborhood and Community in Paris, 1740–1790*. New York, 1986.

———. "Parish Politics, Jansenism, and the Paris Middle Classes in the Eighteenth Century." *French History* 8 (December 1994): 403–19.

———. "The Police of Paris As Enlightened Social Reformers." *Eighteenth-Century Life* 16 (February 1992): 43–59.

Garrioch, David, and Michael Sonenscher. "Compagnonnages, Confraternities, and Associations of Journeymen in Eighteenth-Century Paris." *European History Quarterly* 16 (January 1980): 25–45.

Gates, Henry Louis, Jr. "The End of Loyalty." *New Yorker*, 9 March 1998, 34–44.

Gaxotte, Pierre. *Louis XV and His Times*. Trans. J. Lewis May. Philadelphia, 1934.

Giesey, Ralph. "Modèles de pouvoir dans les rites royaux français." *Annales: Economies, sociétés, civilisations* 41 (May–June 1986): 579–99.

———. *The Royal Funeral Ceremony in Renaissance France*. Geneva, 1960.

Giesey, Ralph, Lanny Haldy, and James Millhorn. "Cardin Le Bret and Lese Majesty." *Law and History Review* 4 (spring 1986): 23–54.

Ginzburg, Carlo. *The Cheese and the Worms: The Cosmos of a Sixteenth-Century Miller*. Trans. John Tedeschi and Anne Tedeschi. Baltimore, 1980.

————. *Clues, Myths, and the Historical Method.* Trans. John Tedeschi and Anne C. Tedeschi. Baltimore, 1989.

Goodman, Dena. *Criticism in Action: Enlightenment Experiments in Political Writing.* Ithaca, N.Y., 1989.

————. "Public Sphere and Private Life: Toward a Synthesis of Current Historiographical Approaches to the Old Regime." *History and Theory* 31 (1992): 1–20.

————. *The Republic of Letters: A Cultural History of the Enlightenment.* Ithaca, N.Y., 1994.

Gordon, Daniel. "Philosophy, Sociology, and Gender in the Enlightenment Conception of Public Opinion." *French Historical Studies* 17 (fall 1992): 882–911.

Graham, Lisa Jane. "Crimes of Opinion: Policing the Public in Eighteenth-Century Paris." In *Visions and Revisions of Eighteenth-Century France,* ed. Christine Adams, Jack Censer, and Lisa Jane Graham, 79–104. University Park, Pa., 1997.

Grosrichard, Alain. *Structure du sérail: La fiction du despotisme asiatique dans l'Occident classique.* Paris, 1979.

Guery, Alain. "Les finances de la monarchie française sous l'Ancien Regime." *Annales: Economies, sociétés, civilisations* 33 (March–April 1978): 216–39.

Guicciardi, Jean-Pierre. "Between the Licit and the Illicit: The Sexuality of the King." Trans. Michael Murray. In *'Tis Nature's Fault: Unauthorized Sexuality during the Enlightenment,* ed. Robert Parks Maccubin, 88–97. Cambridge, 1987.

Habermas, Jürgen. *The Structural Transformation of the Public Sphere: An Inquiry into a Category of Bourgeois Society.* Trans. Thomas Burger and Frederick Lawrence. Cambridge, Mass., 1989.

Halevi, Ran. *Les loges maçonniques dans la France de l'Ancien Régime.* Paris, 1984.

Hammond, Paul. "The King's Two Bodies: Representations of Charles II." In *Culture, Politics, and Society in Britain, 1660–1800,* ed. Jeremy Black and Jeremy Gregory, 13–48. Manchester, 1991.

Hanley, Sarah. *The Lit de Justice of the Kings of France: Constitutional Ideology in Legend, Ritual, and Discourse.* Princeton, N.J., 1983.

————. "Engendering the State: Family Formation and State Building in Early Modern France." *French Historical Studies* 16 (spring 1989): 4–27.

Herman, Arthur L., Jr. "The Language of Fidelity in Early Modern France." *Journal of Modern History* 67 (March 1995): 1–24.

Hobsbawm, Eric. *Echoes of the Marseillaise: Two Centuries Look Back on the French Revolution.* New Brunswick, N.J., 1990.

Hudson, David. "In Defense of Reform: French Government Propaganda during the Maupeou Crisis." *French Historical Studies* 8 (spring 1973): 51–76.

————. "The Parlementary Crisis of 1763 in France and Its Consequences." *Canadian Journal of History* 7, no. 2 (1972): 97–117.

Hufton, Olwen. *The Poor in Eighteenth-Century France, 1750–1789*. Oxford, 1974.

Hunt, Lynn. *The Family Romance of the French Revolution*. Berkeley, 1992.

————. "French History in the Last Twenty Years: The Rise and Fall of the Annales Paradigm." *Journal of Contemporary History* 21 (1986): 209–24.

————. *Politics, Culture, and Class in the French Revolution*. Berkeley, 1984.

————, ed. *Eroticism and the Body Politic*. Baltimore, 1991.

Jackson, Richard. *Vive le Roi! A History of the French Coronation from Charles V to Charles X*. Chapel Hill, N.C., 1984.

Jacob, Margaret C. *Living the Enlightenment: Freemasonry and Politics in Eighteenth-Century Europe*. Oxford, 1991.

Jeambar, Denis, Patrick Coquidé, Marie-Thérèse Guichard, Danièle Molho, and Catherine Pégard. "Mitterand: Le roi et sa cour." *Le Point*, no. 844 (27 November 1988): 70–79.

Jeorger, Muriel. "La structure hospitalière de la France sous l'Ancien Régime." *Annales: Economies, sociétés, civilisations* 32 (September–October 1977): 1025–51.

Kaiser, Thomas E. "Madame de Pompadour and the Theaters of Power." *French Historical Studies* 19 (fall 1996): 1036–69.

Kantorowicz, Ernst. *The King's Two Bodies: A Study in Medieval Political Theology*. Princeton, N.J., 1957.

Kaplan, Steven Lawrence. *Bread, Politics, and Political Economy in the Reign of Louis XV*. 2 vols. The Hague, 1976.

————. *The Famine Plot Persuasion in Eighteenth-Century France*. Transactions of the American Philosophical Society, 72. Philadelphia, 1982.

————. *Farewell, Revolution: Disputed Legacies: France, 1789/1989*. Ithaca, N.Y., 1995.

————. "Notes sur les commissaires de police à Paris au XVIIIe siècle." *Revue d'Histoire Moderne et Contemporaine* 28 (1981): 669–86.

————. "Réflexions sur la police du monde du travail, 1700–1815." *Revue Historique* 261 (1979): 17–77.

————. "Religion, Subsistence, and Social Control: The Uses of Saint Geneviève." *Eighteenth-Century Studies* 13 (winter 1979–80): 142–68.

————, ed. *La Bagarre: Galieni's Lost Parody*. The Hague, 1979.

————. *Understanding Popular Culture: Europe from the Middle Ages to the Nineteenth Century*. New York, 1984.

Kaplow, Jeffrey. *The Names of Kings*. New York, 1972.

Kaufmann, Joanne Soames. "The Critique of Criminal Justice in Late Eighteenth-Century France: A Study of the Changing Social Ethics of Crime and Punishment." Ph.D. diss., Harvard University, 1976.

Kelly, George Armstrong. *Mortal Politics.* Waterloo, Ont., 1986.

Keohane, Nannerl O. *Philosophy and the State in France: The Renaissance to the Enlightenment.* Princeton, N.J., 1980.

Kettering, Sharon. "The Household Service of Early Modern French Noblewomen." *French Historical Studies* 20 (winter 1997): 55–85.

Kleinman, Ruth. "Social Dynamics at the French Court: The Household of Anne of Austria." *French Historical Studies* 16 (spring 1990): 517–35.

Koselleck, Reinhart. *Critique and Crisis: Enlightenment and the Pathogenesis of Modern Society.* Cambridge, Mass 1988.

Kreiser, B. R. *Miracles, Convulsionaries, and Ecclesiastical Politics in Eighteenth-Century Paris.* Princeton, N.J., 1978.

La Bruyère, Jean de. *Characters.* Trans. Jean Stewart. Baltimore, 1970.

Landes, Joan. *Women and the Public Sphere in the Age of the French Revolution.* Ithaca, N.Y., 1988.

Laqueur, Walter. "The Queen Caroline Affair: Politics As Art in the Reign of George IV." *Journal of Modern History* 54 (September 1982): 421.

La Vopa, Anthony J. "Conceiving a Public: Ideas and Society in Eighteenth-Century France." *Journal of Modern History* 64 (March 1992): 79–116.

Lebigre, Arlette. *La justice du roi: La vie judiciaire dans l'ancienne France.* Paris, 1988.

LeJeune, Philipe. *On Autobiography.* Ed. Paul John Eakin. Trans. Katherine M. Leary. Minneapolis, 1988.

Levi, Giovanni. *Inheriting Power: The Story of an Exorcist.* Trans. Lydia G. Cochrane. Chicago, 1988.

———. *Le pouvoir au village: La carrière d'un exorciste dans Le Piémont du XVIIe siècle.* Paris, 1989.

Lucas, Colin. "The Theory and Practice of Denunciation in the French Revolution." *Journal of Modern History* 68 (December 1996): 768–85.

Lüsebrink, Hans-Jurgen. *Kriminalität und Literatur in Frankreich des 18. Jahrhunderts.* Munich, 1983.

Maire, Catherine Laurence. *Les convulsionnaires de Saint-Médard.* Paris, 1985.

Mansel, Philip. *The Court of France: 1789–1830.* Cambridge, 1988.

Marion, Marcel. *Dictionnaire des institutions de la France au XVIIe et XVIIIe siècles.* 1923. Reprint. Paris, 1993.

———. *Histoire financière de la France depuis 1715.* Paris, 1914.

Martin, Henri-Jean. *The French Book: Religion, Absolutism, and Readership, 1585–1785.* Trans. Paul Saenger and Nadine Saenger. Baltimore, 1996.

May, Georges. *Le dilemme du roman au XVIIIe siècle.* Paris, 1963.

Maza, Sara. "Luxury, Morality, and Social Change: Why There Was No Middle-Class Consciousness in Prerevolutionary France." *Journal of Modern History* 69 (June 1997): 199–229.

———. *Private Lives and Public Affairs: The Causes Célèbres of Pre-Revolutionary France.* Berkeley, 1993.

———. *Servants and Masters in Eighteenth-Century France: The Uses of Loyalty.* Princeton, N.J., 1983.

———. "Le tribunal de la nation: Les mémoires judiciaires et l'opinion publique à la fin de l'Ancien Regime." *Annales: Economies, sociétés, civilisations* 42 (January–February 1987): 73–90.

———. "Women, the Bourgeoisie, and the Public Sphere: Response to Daniel Gordon and David Bell." *French Historical Studies* 17 (fall 1992): 935–50.

Ménétra, Jacque-Louis. *Journal of My Life.* Trans. Arthur Goldhammer. New York, 1986.

Merrick, Jeffrey. *The Desacralization of the French Monarchy in the Eighteenth Century.* Baton Rouge, La., 1990.

———. "Fathers and Kings: Patriarchalism and Absolutism in Eighteenth-Century French Politics." *Studies on Voltaire and the Eighteenth Century* 308 (1993): 281–303.

———. "Sexual Politics and Public Order in Late Eighteenth-Century France: The *Mémoires Secrets* and the *Correspondance secrète*." *Journal of the History of Sexuality* 1 (1990): 68–84.

Metayer, Christine. "De l'école au palais de justice: L'itinéraire singulier des maîtres écrivains de Paris (XVIe–XVIIIe siècle)." *Annales: Economies, sociétés, civilisations* 45 (September–October 1990): 1217–39.

Minois, Georges. *Censure et culture sous l'Ancien Regime.* Paris, 1995.

Molinier, A. *Inventaire sommaire de la Collection Joly de Fleury.* Paris, 1881.

Montesquieu. *Persian Letters.* Trans. C. J. Betts. Baltimore, 1973.

———. *The Spirit of the Laws.* Trans. Thomas Nugent. 2 vols. New York, 1949.

Mousnier, Roland. "Les concepts d' 'ordres,' d' 'états,' de 'fidélité' et de 'monarchie absolue' en France de la fin du XVe siècle à la fin du XVIIIe." *Revue Historique* 502 (April–June 1972): 289–312.

———. *The Institutions of France under the Absolute Monarchy, 1598–1789.* Trans. Brian Pearce. 2 vols. Chicago, 1979.

Norberg, Kathryn, and Sarah E. Melzer, eds. *From the Royal to the Republican Body:*

Incorporating the Political in Seventeenth- and Eighteenth-Century France. Berkeley, 1998.

Ozouf, Mona. *Festivals and the French Revolution.* Trans. Alan Sheridan. Cambridge, Mass., 1988.

———. "Le concept de l'opinion publique du XVIIIe siècle." In *L'homme régénéré,* 21–53. Paris, 1989.

Piasenza, Paolo. "Juges, lieutenants de police et bourgeois à Paris aux XVIIe et XVIIIe siècles." *Annales: Economies, sociétés, civilisations* 45 (September–October 1990): 1189–1217.

Quétel, Claude. *De par le Roy: Essai sur les lettres de cachet.* Paris, 1981.

———. *Escape from the Bastille: The Life and Legend of Latude.* Trans. Christopher Sharp. New York, 1990.

Ranum, Orest. "Lèse-Majesté Divine: Transgressing Boundaries by Thought and Action in Mid-Seventeenth-Century France." In *Proceedings of the Ninth Annual Meeting of the Western Society for French History,* 68–80. Lawrenceville, Kans., 1982.

Ravaisson, François. *Les Archives de la Bastille.* Vol. 10 of *Catalogue des manuscrits de la Bibliothèque de l'Arsenal.* Paris, 1892.

Rétat, Pierre. *L'attentat de Damiens: Discours sur l'événement au XVIIIème siècle.* Lyon, 1979.

Revel, Jacques. "Histoire et sciences sociales: Les paradigmes des Annales." *Annales: Economies, sociétés, civilisations* 34 (November–December 1979): 1344–76.

———. "Marie-Antoinette in Her Fictions: The Staging of Hatred." In *Fictions of the French Revolution,* ed. Bernadette Fort, 111–29. Evanston, Ill., 1991.

———, ed. *L'espace français.* Paris, 1989.

———. *Jeux d'échelle: La micro-analyse à l'expérience.* Paris, 1996.

Revel, Jean-François. *L'absolutisme inefficace ou contre le présidentialisme à la française.* Paris, 1993.

Richet, Denis. "Autour des origines idéologiques lointaines de la Révolution Française: Elites et despotisme." *Annales: Economies, sociétés, civilisations* 24 (January–February 1969): 1–23.

Riley, James C. *The Seven Years War and the Old Regime in France.* Princeton, N.J., 1986.

Rogister, John. *Louis XV and the Parlement of Paris, 1737–1755.* Cambridge, 1995

Rombouts, Stephen. "Art As Propaganda in Eighteenth-Century France: The Paradox of Edme Bouchardon's Louis XV." *Eighteenth-Century Studies* 27 (winter 1993): 255–82.

Sabean, David. *Power in the Blood.* Cambridge, 1984.

Le sacre des rois: Actes du Colloque International d'Histoire sur les Sacres et Couronnements Royaux. Reims, 1975.

Schwarz, Robert M. *Policing the Poor in Eighteenth-Century France.* Chapel Hill, N.C., 1988.

Smith, Jay M. "'Our Sovereign's Gaze': Kings, Nobles, and State Formation in Seventeenth-Century France." *French Historical Studies* 18 (fall 1993): 396–415.

Smithers, James R. "The St. Bartholomew's Day Massacre and Images of Kingship in France, 1572–1574." *Sixteenth Century Journal* 22 (spring 1991): 27–46.

Solmon, Jean François. *La Cour de France.* Paris, 1987.

Soman, Alfred. "Press, Pulpit, and Censorship in France before Richelieu." *Proceedings of the American Philosophical Society* 120 (December 1976): 439–63.

———. "Les procès de sorcellerie au Parlement de Paris (1565–1640)." *Annales: Economies, sociétés, civilisations* 32 (July–August 1977): 790–814.

Starkey, David. "Representations through Intimacy." In *Symbols and Sentiments: Cross-Cultural Studies in Symbolism,* ed. Ioan Lewis, 187–224. London, 1977.

Strayer, Bryan. "*Lettres de Cachet* and Social Control in the *Ancien Régime,* 1659–1789." Ph.D. diss., University of Iowa, 1987.

Swann, Julian. *Politics and the Parlement of Paris under Louis XV, 1754–1774.* Cambridge, 1995.

Taylor, George. "Types of Capitalism in Eighteenth-Century France." *English Historical Review* 79 (July 1964): 478–97.

Tocqueville, Alexis de. *The Old Regime and the French Revolution.* Trans. Stuart Gilbert. New York, 1955.

Traer, James F. *Marriage and the Family in Eighteenth-Century France.* Ithaca, N.Y., 1980.

Van Kley, Dale. "The Church, State, and the Ideological Origins of the French Revolution: The Debate over the General Assembly of the Gallican Clergy in 1765." *Journal of Modern History* 51 (December 1979): 629–66.

———. *The Damiens Affair and the Unraveling of the Old Regime, 1750–1770.* Princeton, N.J., 1984.

———. *The Jansenists and the Expulsion of the Jesuits from France, 1757–1765.* New Haven, Conn., 1975.

———. *The Religious Origins of the French Revolution: From Calvin to the Civil Constitution, 1560–1791.* New Haven, Conn., 1996.

———. "The Religious Origins of the Patriot and Ministerial Parties in Pre-Revolutionary France: Controversy over the Chancellor's Constitutional *Coup,* 1771–1775." *Réflexions Historiques* 18 (summer 1992): 17–63.

Velde, François R., and David R. Weir. "The Financial Market and Government

Debt Policy in France, 1746–1793." *Journal of Economic History* 52 (March 1992): 1–39.

Venturi, Franco. "Oriental Despotism." *Journal of the History of Ideas* 24 (1963): 133–42.

Vidal, D. *Miracles et convulsions jansénistes au XVIIIe siècle.* Paris, 1987.

Vignerie, Jean de. "Le roi et le public: L'exemple du Louis XV." *Revue Historique* 563 (July–September): 23–34.

Voltaire. *Histoire du Parlement.* Vol. 16 of *Oeuvres complètes.* Paris, 1878.

Weil, Françoise. *L'interdiction du roman et la librairie, 1728–1750.* Paris, 1986.

Weil, Rachel. "The Crown Has Fallen to the Distaff: Gender and Politics in the Age of Catherine de Medici." *Critical Matrix* 1 (1985): 1–38.

Williams, Alan. *The Police of Paris, 1718–1789.* Baton Rouge, La., 1979.

Winock, Michel. *Parlez-moi de la France.* Paris, 1997.

Woodbridge, John. *Revolt in Prerevolutionary France: The Prince of Conti's Conspiracy against Louis XV, 1755–1757.* Baltimore, 1994.

Zysberg, André. "La société des galériens au milieu du XVIIIe siècle." *Annales: Economies, sociétés, civilisations* 30 (January–February 1975): 43–65.

INDEX

· ❧ ·

absolution, 50

absolutism, 22, 23, 203–4, 255, 277 n. 31; Bonafon on, 80, 85–87; constitutional resistance to, 142; development of, 4–5, 25, 124; emerging public sphere and, 58; fidelity and, 125, 184–85; La Rivoire on, 245–46; paternalism and, 160; and unity, 258. *See also* authority, royal

Aguesseau, Henry-François d', 69

Aiguillon, Emmanuel-Armand de Richelieu, duc d', 216, 220; La Rivoire's political critique of, 235

Aix-la-Chapelle, Treaty of, 60, 96, 98–99

Allègre, Antoine, 15, 96–98, 179, 183, 214, 261; confession of, 112–13; conspiracy plot of, 104–10, 114–19; criminality of, 121; escape of, 110, 111 fig. 5; incarceration of, 135–38; plea-bargaining of, 122–25; police dossier on, 131–35; on royal gaze, 124

Allègre, Joseph, 108, 280 n. 2

Andrews, Richard, 46

Annales, 3–4, 7, 269 n. 5

anticlericalism, 100, 147, 155, 175, 257

Archives de la Bastille, 10–11

Archives Nationales, 11

Argenson, René-Louis de Voyer de Palmy, marquis d', 96, 234, 236, 278–79 n. 60, 296 n. 75; and Allègre's conspiracy plot, 104–10; Allègre's letters to, 121–22; dismissal of, 143; on public opinion of Louis XV, 63–64

Auger, M., 195–96

Austria, 60, 144. *See also* War of Austrian Succession

authority: abuse of, 97, 213–14; male, 84–85; paternal, 160; presidential, 265–66; spiritual and temporal, 202

authority, royal, 9, 139, 160, 212; Allègre on, 124–25, 133–35; basis of, 245–46; Bonafon on, 85–86; and government, 202–3, 215; grace of, 53; La Rivoire on, 240–44, 253–54; police and, 25; public opinion and, 2, 8, 54; role of royal mistresses in, 57–59; Tavernier on, 164

Averdy, François de l', 217

Baker, Keith, 5, 9, 103, 104, 240, 289 n. 98